# EXPLORATIONS IN
# NATURAL RESOURCE ECONOMICS

# Contributors

*Partha Dasgupta*, London School of Economics

*Shantayanan Devarajan*, Harvard University

*Anthony C. Fisher*, University of California, Berkeley

*A. Myrick Freeman III*, Bowdoin College

*DeVerle Harris*, University of Arizona

*Geoffrey Heal*, University of Essex

*Morton I. Kamien*, Northwestern University

*Raymond J. Kopp*, Resources for the Future

*John V. Krutilla*, Resources for the Future

*Lawrence J. Lau*, Stanford University

*Nancy L. Schwartz*, Northwestern University

*Brian J. Skinner*, Yale University

*V. Kerry Smith*, University of North Carolina
   at Chapel Hill

# EXPLORATIONS IN
# NATURAL RESOURCE ECONOMICS

*V. Kerry Smith* and
*John V. Krutilla*, editors

**Published for Resources for the Future, Inc.**
By The Johns Hopkins University Press
Baltimore and London

Published for Resources for the Future
By The Johns Hopkins University Press, Baltimore, Maryland 21218

**Library of Congress Cataloging in Publication Data**
Main entry under title:

Explorations in natural resource economics.

Includes index.
Contents: Toward reformulating the role of natural resources in economic models/V. Kerry Smith and John V. Krutilla—The role of common property resources in optimal planning models with exhaustible resources/Morton I. Kamien and Nancy L. Schwartz—The use of common property resources/Geoffrey Heal—[etc.]
1. Economics—Mathematical models—Addresses, essays, lectures. 2. Natural resources—Economic aspects—Mathematical models—Addresses, essays, lectures. I. Smith, V. Kerry (Vincent Kerry) 1945- . II. Krutilla, John V. III. Resources for the Future.
HB135.E95          333.7   81-47621
ISBN 0-8018-2713-2   AACR2

# Contents

*Preface* xi

PART I   INTRODUCTION AND BACKGROUND   1

**1   Toward Reformulating the Role of Natural Resources in Economic Models**   V. Kerry Smith and John V. Krutilla   3

*The Role of Natural Resources in Economic Models*   4
*The Allocation of Environmental Common Property Resources*   17
*Evaluating Natural Resource Availability*   29

PART II   MODELING THE ROLE OF NATURAL RESOURCES IN ECONOMIC GROWTH   45

**2   The Role of Common Property Resources in Optimal Planning Models with Exhaustible Resources**   Morton I. Kamien and Nancy L. Schwartz   47

*The Literature*   48
*Our Proposal*   56
*Summary*   64
*Appendix*   66

**3   The Use of Common Property Resources**   Geoffrey Heal   72

*Static Analysis*   73
*Dynamic Analysis*   85
*Summary and Research Suggestions*   103

vii

PART III   EVALUATING THE SOCIAL COSTS OF DEGRAD-
ING ENVIRONMENTAL RESOURCES   107

**4   *Environmental Management Under Uncertainty***
Partha Dasgupta   109

*The Problem*   109
*Social Cost–Benefit Analysis Under Uncertainty*   112
*Incentive Schemes for Environmental Management: The General
    Problem*   117
*The Free-Rider Problem in Environmental Improvement*   119
*Taxation vs. Regulations under Uncertainty*   122
*Appendix*   134

**5   *The Health Implications of Residuals Discharges: A Methodological
Overview***   A. Myrick Freeman III   140

*Measuring Health Effects*   141
*Valuing Health Effects*   156
*Conclusions*   162


PART IV   MEASURING THE ROLE OF NATURAL
RESOURCES IN PRODUCTION PROCESSES   165

**6   *The Measurement of Raw Material Inputs***   Lawrence J. Lau   167

*Introduction*   167
*What Is a Material?*   170
*Classification of Material Inputs*   173
*Aggregation by End-Use Sectors*   174
*Aggregation Across End-Use Sectors*   190
*Raw Material Inputs at the Economy Level*   196
*Conclusions*   199

**7   *The Perceived Role of Materials in Neoclassical Models of Production
Technology***   Raymond J. Kopp and V. Kerry Smith   201

*Methods of Analysis*   205
*Experimental Design and Estimation*   216
*Neoclassical Models Applied to the Benchmark Samples*   221
*Implications of Aggregation for Perceived Substitution: The Unconstrained
    Solutions*   229
*Constraints on Residuals Discharges and Perceived Substitution*   223
*Summary and Implications*   237

## PART V  GEOLOGICAL AND ECONOMIC MODELING OF RESOURCE AVAILABILITY  245

**8   The Assessment of Long-Term Supplies of Minerals** ₁
DeVerle P. Harris and Brian J. Skinner   247

*Introducion*   247
*Geological Concepts: The Way Materials Occur and Are Used*   254
*Properties of Mineral Deposits*   266
*Exploration for Mineral Deposits*   274
*Appraisal of Resources*   284
*Modeling and Informational Issues with Regard to Resource*
  *Adequacy and Long-Term Mineral Supply*   305
*Summary*   322

**9   Measures of Natural Resource Scarcity Under Uncertainty**
Shantayanan Devarajan and Anthony C. Fisher   327

*Measures of Scarcity*   328
*Rent, Discovery Cost, and Uncertainty*   330
*Exploration and Extraction Under Uncertainty*   332
*Concluding Remarks*   343

*Index*   347

# Preface

This volume reports the results of a multidisciplinary effort to explore the limits of conventional economic models that describe the role of natural and environmental resources in economic activities. Prompted by the conflicts between the fairly optimistic views held by many economists concerning the prospects for compatibility between resource availability, population, and economic growth, and the more pessimistic perceptions of these same issues held by a substantial number of earth and life scientists, we attempted to consider the fundamental underpinnings of each position and the possibilities for research to begin resolving some of the differences.

Our joint interest in this area began within the natural environments program at Resources for the Future during the early 1970s. The Ford Foundation provided early support for a forum on the adequacy of natural resources, which led to our first attempt (*Scarcity and Growth Reconsidered*) to expose some of the areas of conflict in conventional views of natural resource adequacy. The current effort has focused on understanding the reasons for the differences in these views. In addition, the project attempted to suggest areas where economic models that included natural and environmental resources should be changed to reflect more accurately physical phenomena that may constrain economic activity. The project was supported and, indeed, encouraged by the Directorate of Applied Research of the National Science Foundation. Lynn Preston, the project officer at NSF, was a great help in these efforts.

We were able to attract an outstanding advisory committee to work with us in the identification and explicit development of the critical research issues involved in judging the appropriate treatment of natural resources in economic models. The members of the committee not only had a significant role in identifying the research areas, but in several cases helped in their development. The final product has most certainly been improved in all respects by their generous participation. Members of the committee were: Kenneth J. Arrow, Stanford University; Lawrence Bogorad, Harvard University; Geoffrey Heal, University of Essex; Tjalling Koopmans, Yale University; Joshua Lederberg, Rockefeller University; William A. Nierenberg, Scripps Institute of Oceanography; Nathan Rosenberg, Stanford University; Brian J. Skinner, Yale University; Walter O. Spofford, Resources for the Future; and Robert M. White, Universities Corporation for Atmospheric Research.

In addition to the advisory committee, we had the support of a number of outstanding scholars who lead research efforts associated with our project. The papers in this volume summarize their findings. Each author gave a substantial amount of time to the venture. In addition to preparing the papers, they participated in seminars at RFF and in two working meetings where the full set of research activities was discussed. At our final meeting, we were fortunate to have equally outstanding scholars discuss and evaluate the efforts of our authors. The papers in this volume reflect their generous contributions. Since the papers were all revised to take account of their comments, we have not included formal discussions of each paper. We would like to express our appreciation and the collective thanks of our authors to: Robert U. Ayres, Carnegie-Mellon University; Ernst R. Berndt, Massachusetts Institute of Technology; Preston Cloud, University of California at Santa Barbara; Ralph C. d'Arge, University of Wyoming; W. Erwin Diewert, University of British Columbia; William Hogan, Harvard University; John R. Moroney, Texas A & M University; Roger Noll, California Institute of Technology; William D. Schulze, University of Wyoming; and Joseph E. Stiglitz, Princeton University. Special mention should also be given to William Schulze, who reviewed the entire manuscript prior to publication.

The perceptive insight and tireless attention to clarity of exposition brought to this volume by Ruth Haas of the RFF editorial staff have greatly enhanced the end product. We know all authors share our sincere thanks to her for her contributions. We also know how much our burden was eased by the initiative she took in many instances to improve the volume.

Finally, throughout the research effort we have been assisted by our secretaries, who not only typed many manuscripts but also assisted in arranging all of the logistical details for the meetings and seminars, and made other administrative arrangements that make the difference between success and failure in projects such as this one. Our sincere thanks go to several individuals who worked at these tasks during the project, including Ann Cotterill, Cindy Dwyer, Pat Parker, Virginia Reid, and Diana Tasciotti.

We would also like to express our appreciation to our colleagues at RFF when this work was undertaken, especially Raymond Kopp, who contributed to several aspects of the project. Needless to say, we alone accept responsibility for any remaining shortcomings with the volume.

December 1981                                          *V. Kerry Smith*
                                                       Chapel Hill, N.C.

                                                       *John V. Krutilla*
                                                       Washington, D.C.

# PART I
# INTRODUCTION AND BACKGROUND

# 1

## Toward Reformulating the Role of Natural Resources in Economic Models

### V. Kerry Smith and John V. Krutilla

Public concern with the importance of natural resources in economic activity has been sporadic in the United States over the past quarter century. Today, however, one can hardly dismiss as inconsequential the issues associated with the role of natural resources in economic growth and the maintenance of economic well-being. The dramatic changes in the world price of petroleum and an apparently increasing reliance on foreign sources for many important raw materials have heightened interest in the development of a U.S. resource policy.

In an earlier volume, *Scarcity and Growth Reconsidered* (Smith, 1979), the availability and importance of natural resources were examined by prominent economists, geologists, and engineers.[1] The individual, and diverse, perceptions of these issues ranged from suggestions that finite natural resources ultimately limit all human activities, to the view that progressive technological change, increased availability of lower grade resources, and the prospects for substituting produced or renewable inputs for nonrenewable natural resources would eliminate resource limitations as significant constraints on growth.[2]

In many respects this divergence of opinion reflects different perceptions of the nature of the physical environment and the supply of natural resources.

This work was supported by the Directorate of Applied Research of the National Science Foundation. Thanks are due Shantajan Devarajan, Morton Kamien, and Raymond Kopp for helpful comments on an earlier draft of this paper.
[1] A comparison of the essays by Stiglitz (1979), Daly (1979), and Georgescu-Roegen (1979) provides such an illustration.
[2] See Barnett and Morse (1963, pages 243–245) for further discussion of this viewpoint.

3

It also stems from differences in each discipline's approach to the role of natural resources in production and consumption activities. This volume is a coordinated effort to identify the kinds of research required to narrow the range of differences in both defining these problems and dealing with them.

This introduction is intended as an overview of the research papers that follow. We consider how the definition and treatment of natural resources affects the modeling of economic activities and pay special attention to production processes and to the measurement of the characteristics of these activities. Conventional economic analyses of natural resources have largely treated them as synonymous with raw materials inputs to production. Thus economic modeling has focused on the intertemporal implications of exhaustibility. Indeed, it is only in the most recent literature (see Fisher, 1979, and Pindyck, 1978, as examples) that one finds the modeling structures common in the analysis of renewable resources, such as fisheries or forests, used to great advantage in explaining the incentives for exploratory activity. When the concept of natural resources is broadened to include all the original endowments of the earth, the analysis has to be expanded to include the processes which allocate resources that cannot be exchanged on organized markets; for example, air and water. More specifically, one must inquire if it is possible to use existing institutions or to structure new ones that will reveal the information necessary for efficient allocation of nonmarketable natural resources. Finally, in the last section of this chapter we discuss the relationship between geological sciences and economics in defining the methodology for measuring the long-term availability of minerals and for modeling the processes through which these minerals are discovered and utilized.

## 1. The Role of Natural Resources in Economic Models

In evaluating the prospects for maintaining economic well-being, virtually all the recent work that uses an economic growth framework has concluded that the role of exhaustible resources in production is extremely important to each model's characterization of an optimal plan. It is desirable, therefore, to identify the fundamental elements in these models and to consider how they can be broadened to take into account those open-access resources which do not exchange on private markets but which nevertheless affect each model's description. Research has focused on this problem in three broad categories: modeling, measurement, and estimation.

The first of these, modeling, relates to the analytical treatment of natural resources and its implications for the characterization of optimal allocation plans. In chapter 2, Kamien and Schwartz identify six broad classes of economic models, and in so doing they suggest that the work which accommodates an expanded definition of natural resources is quite limited. The models are all optimal planning frameworks that attempt to show how a centralized decision framework with a given objective function would allocate resources intertemporally. The problem's intertemporal dimension arises from one or more of three sources: (1) accumulation of a stock of reproducible capital that can contribute in each period to productive activities; (2) reduction of a fixed stock of some natural endowment (i.e., an exhaustible resource) as production and consumption activities proceed over time; and (3) accumulation of a stock of pollutants or increased environmental degradation that occurs as a production and consumption by-product and that can impair future production or reduce the utility of any given consumption bundle.

Kamien and Schwartz classify these models according to the variables of central interest. Three models are chosen because they focus on only a single variable—reproducible capital, an exhaustible natural resource, or pollution. In each case, the definition of the variable provides the single intertemporal linkage in resource allocations. For example, in a model concentrating on allocation decisions involving reproducible capital, the allocation of output between consumption and investment determines the rate of increase in the capital stocks and the capacity for future output. This capacity for future production links the maximum utility that can be derived from output consumed in the future with current allocation decisions.

Other models simultaneously incorporate two of these three variables. The recent literature examining the effects of exhaustible natural resources on economic welfare contains models of this type. Here one finds that two opposing factors influence economic welfare—a reduction in available stocks of a natural resource and the accumulation of capital. It is not surprising then that the size of the elasticity of substitution between the two has such significance for the role the model implicitly assigns to the natural resource. The elasticity provides a gauge of whether capital can compensate for the depletion of the resource.

The last class of models, and the one least well developed in the literature, includes all three intertemporal effects—accumulation of capital, pollution, and the depletion of the conventionally perceived natural resources. In chapter 2, Kamien and Schwartz describe in general terms the kind of model that would be needed to take into account a broader definition of natural resources. In addition, they consider a special case of this model, which is analytically tractable, in order to begin identifying the essential elements in modeling the role of natural resources. Basically, their structure begins with the capital–natural resource framework and includes an accumulating stock of pollution by relating it directly to the extraction process (i.e., the stock of pollution is some function of the cumulative extraction of the natural resource). Pollution is assumed to impair the economy's ability to produce output (which can be either consumption or investment). It scales down output, as in equation (1):

$$Q* = Q/g(p) \tag{1}$$

where $Q*$ is actual output
  $Q$ is potential output (in absence of pollution)
  $p$ is stock of pollution
  $g(p) \geq 1$ for all $p$

It is therefore similar in many respects to the amendments proposed earlier by Fisher (1979) in considering the usefulness of a Hotelling model for understanding the properties of scarcity indexes. However, in Fisher's case the stock variable was incorporated into the model to reflect the increased costs of extracting lower grade deposits.

The Kamien–Schwartz model is deliberately simplified to expose the structural elements that lead to tractable solutions. Utility is assumed to be described with a specific functional form ($U = \ln C$) and production with a Cobb–Douglas function. They find an interesting and surprising result in this setting—the functional forms of the temporal paths of the optimal output, consumption, and capital stocks are independent of the form of the pollution function $g(\quad)$. Of course, the levels depend on the pollution function as well as on the initial conditions. While their finding is described as "path independent" with respect to the form of the $g(\quad)$ function, it is important to recognize that the introduction of this pollution term does have a significant effect on optimal plans. More specifically, the adjustment factor $g*(\bar{s}) - g*(0)$ can be considered a reflection of the net increase in the exhaustible resource that would be required if pollution were at its *maximum level* for the whole planning horizon, over what it would be if pollution were at its minimum level. When considered in these terms, the Kamien–Schwartz model suggests that the form of $g(\quad)$ is not important because the optimal plan adjusts output, consumption, and capital levels *as if* pollution were at its highest value for the full planning horizon. Therefore, their model may not illustrate a case in which these externalities have the smallest impact, but rather the most substantial. Of course, this result should be regarded as special and directly related to their assumptions. As such, when it is compared with some indirectly related earlier literature, it is possible to highlight the modeling directions necessary before one can begin to understand fully the implications of broadening the natural resource definition to include common (or open-access) as well as private property resources.

First, it should be recognized that in such dynamic optimization models, the number of channels through which past resource allocations introduce constraints on the future allocation decisions is quite important to the solution of the model. In these models, such effects can be transmitted over time only through the accumulation or depletion of stocks. The flow variables are assumed to be either fully dissipated or contributing in some way to the status of the stock variables. Kamien and Schwartz select a simple way of reducing a two-stock variable model so it appears to have only one. The rate of increase in the pollution measure is equal to the rate of depletion of the natural resource. Thus, their model differentiates the respective roles of the remaining stock of the natural resource and the accumulated stock of pollution according to their individual influences on production and consumption activities. The rate of change in pollution has no direct role in the model. It is simply a by-product of the rate of resource depletion. When one considers the contribution of the flow variable that is designated by the rate of use of the natural resource, three impacts can be identified: (1) the stock of the natural resource available for future use is reduced by the amount consumed in each period (i.e., there is no regeneration, as in the case of a renewable resource); (2) the level of use of the natural resource contributes to the production of consumable output in the period; and (3) the stock of pollution is increased according to the level of use of the natural resource. They assume that there is no inherent assimilative capacity in the natural environment.

In order to explore further the implications of the Kamien and Schwartz assumptions in simplifying the nature of the intertemporal links between resource allocations, it is necessary to understand the effects of alternative specifications of the role of stock variables in similar types of optimal planning models. Three examples highlight the importance of the Kamien–Schwartz specifications. They relate to redefining the utility function to include stock variables.

The first of these models, by Kurz (1968), examines the effects of a specification which implies that wealth (as well as current consumption) contributes to utility. The second considers a type of stock variable intended to reflect the effects of habit, learning, or intertemporal dependence in preferences. This analysis, first developed by Ryder and Heal (1973), has been expanded by Heal to consider the specific relationship to common property resources (see chapter 3). The last model, by Cropper (1976), evaluates the effects of uncertainty on optimal plans by relating the probability of a catastrophic event to the stock of accumulated pollution. Thus, treatment of this form of uncertainty in an expected-value framework is equivalent to the specific introduction of a pollution stock variable in society's utility function. While the motivations for these earlier efforts differ greatly, the mechanisms selected for analysis and indeed, their results, are quite comparable. That is, they each serve to illustrate the importance of the intertemporal channels of influence (i.e., the state or stock variables) in characterizing optimal solutions.

For example, the Kurz (1968) analysis found that there may be many steady-state solutions satisfying the optimality conditions. Cropper and Heal (in chapter 3) identify the prospects for multiple solutions, and Heal also describes the conditions under which cyclic behavior might be shown. Finally, these studies indicate how important the initial conditions are for the optimal profiles of the relevant choice variables.

The Kamien and Schwartz analysis in chapter 2, while somewhat less clear-cut on these observations, offers results that are consistent with this last conclusion because the levels of output, consumption, and capital stock depend on the initial conditions. The general result is unusual, as Heal documents (chapter 3). One does not often find that the asymptotic behavior of a dynamic system is sensitive to the system's initial conditions. However, we should recognize that these conclusions are not new. Indeed, the literature on neo-classical growth models extended the qualifications identified through Kurz's (1968) analysis to more complex formulations of the problems associated with optimal economic growth. Basically, this work related to the difficulties associated with solutions to a two-sector model. Britto's (1973) survey of contributions to the theoretical models of economic growth clearly identifies the importance and unsettling nature of the conclusions that emerged from this work. In summing up the prospects for defining simple policy directives based on these growth models that would be independent of the features of the assumed utility functions, Britto (1973, page 1359) observes that:

> Recent work in this area has shattered the hope that such recommendations can be justified, even theoretically. M. Kurz looked at optimal paths when wealth is included (together with consumption) in the utility function and discovered that there might be several steady-state paths satisfying the optimality conditions. It has since been established that multiple efficient steady states can arise with other assumptions as well: e.g., the uniqueness of the steady state satisfying the optimality conditions cannot be demonstrated in two-sector models with joint production of the two goods (the consumption and the investment good), even if the utility functional contains only per capita consumption. In such cases there arises the possibility that the turnpike for the economy depends on either the initial capital stock (the boundary conditions) or the length or the horizon. . . . Curiously enough the presence of a positive discount rate appears to be a necessary condition for multiple turnpikes—why this is so remains at the moment an unsettled question.

To our knowledge, research since Britto's overview has not provided an adequate reason for the effects that seem to be associated with specifying a model with a positive discount rate. Moreover, the relevance of these admonitions in the literature on economic growth models has not been adequately appreciated in more recent work on the role of natural resources in economic activities. This absence of a clear pattern of "learning" from our past work is especially unsettling once it is recognized that the formal analytical structures involved are quite similar. Kamien's and Schwartz's taxonomic classification (see chapter 2) highlights these similarities. One explanation for failing to profit from earlier work is the preconception of the analyst. The accumulation of stocks of pollutants has not, until recently, been regarded as an important problem (see Pearce, 1976, and Smith, 1977, for some related discussion). Alternatively, it may also be a result of the complex analytical issues raised by earlier work.

Further insight into the relative lack of attention given to these analytical issues can be found in Burmeister's and Dobell's text (1970) on economic growth. In commenting on the Kurz (1968) work, as well as other related findings, they summarize the results and their interpretation as follows (pp. 411–412):

> It has been observed that in some models a stationary solution . . . to the Euler–Lagrange equations need not be unique, a circumstance which raises questions about consumption turnpike theorems asserting characteristic features of optimal paths. However, these results have generally been derived with a criterion function in which not only consumption flows, but also state variables such as wealth or capital stocks enter. When perfect foresight and perfect certainty are assumed, it may be argued that such models are inappropriate in that they "double count" the benefits of additional stocks—presumably in a riskless world of perfect capital markets, increments to wealth or capital stock at a point in time increase welfare only to the extent that they contribute to future consumption of the utility of future bequests, the value of which is already measured in the criterion function . . . .

Of course, their conclusion is a misleading guide for our problems. The process of consumption may give rise to by-products that affect the ability of society to consume goods in the future. The accumulating stock of pollution is one such by-product. This phenomenon can be modeled in a variety of ways; Cropper's (1976) characterization of the problem as increasing the likelihood of catastrophic effects arising from the pollution stock is an extreme example. Another is the presence of irreversibilities in investment decisions that affect society's welfare, as discussed formally by Fisher, Krutilla, and Cicchetti (1972), and in more detail by Krutilla and Fisher (1975). Neither of these cases exhibits the inconsistency identified by Burmeister and Dobell (1970) as a reason for questioning the relevance of these formulations.

Indeed, the presence of a stock variable in the utility function, together with the potential for multiple stock variables within the planning problem, are among the important issues in modeling the role of environmental resources in economic activities. Before turning to a summary of specific features deserving further attention, it may be useful to inquire whether multiple solutions and cyclic behavior can arise only through the introduction of these stock effects in the utility function. In fact, it appears that there are other cases that can be related to these. For example, Liviatan and Samuelson (1969) have shown that the problem of multiple turnpikes can arise from the specification of the production possibilities for the economy. If a two-sector framework with joint production is postulated, then, here again, the same features of nonuniqueness can arise.

Do these findings contradict the sufficiency conditions for an optimal program? Not necessarily. As a consequence, they lead to rather serious problems as to how one should interpret the prescriptions developed for the optimal programs. Moreover, the Liviatan–Samuelson example can be seen to be quite consistent with those arising from direct specification of the presence of stock variables in the utility function. For example, suppose production can be represented with the transformation function given in equation (2).

$$C = F(I, K) \tag{2}$$

where  $C$  is consumption
       $I$  is investment
       $K$  is capital stock

The implication of this formulation is that $C$ and $I$ are produced jointly with the services of capital stock. If the utility function is assumed to be a function of $C$ only, it is apparent that in this case joint production has the effect of introducing a stock variable into a redefined utility function. For example, equation (3) defines general utility function.

$$U = U(C) \tag{3}$$

Substitution for $C$ in equation (3) yields an equivalent problem with the stock effect in the objective function, as in equation (4).

$$U = U[F\ (I,K)] \tag{4}$$

How should the prospects for multiple solutions be interpreted? One important dimension we have observed is that, potentially, both initial and terminal conditions can be important to optimal profiles. Or, as Heal observes in chapter 3, it may not be possible to set out conditions for optimal resource plans that are independent of the boundary constraints specific to each problem. Of course, for sufficiently long time horizons, it is reasonable to expect that it will be possible to define optimal long-horizon (or limiting) plans that are independent of terminal conditions, but *not* invariant with respect to the initial conditions. Nonetheless, this raises the question of how useful such results are for policy purposes.[3] The limiting properties of these resource allocation profiles are not likely to have much relevance for many policy problems associated with actual allocation decisions involving natural and environmental resources.

To summarize, the analysis in chapter 2 has indirectly exposed the significance of features of optimal planning models that the earlier growth literature dismissed as inconsistent with rational behavior. More specifically,

---

[3] We are grateful to Tjalling Koopmans for calling this point to our attention and for his discussions of the difficulties associated with interpreting the results from optimal planning models for practical policy making.

the presence of one or more of three of them in an optimal planning model seems to give rise to multiple optimal solutions and a dependence of optimal plans on boundary conditions. These features include: (1) multiple independent state (or "stock") variables; (2) inclusion of a state variable in the objective function for the planning model; and (3) specification of the planner's supply options in terms of certain types of joint production. Thus, it is necessary to consider both a broader range of modeling specifications and, as Heal illustrates, the economic implications of alternative definitions of a common property resource.

As attempts are made to develop these planning models with increasingly complex specifications, objective functions, processes by which goods are produced, and functions governing accumulation of durable goods within the model, it should be recognized that analytical solutions may not be feasible. Moreover, linearization of these systems for convenience may lead to conclusions that are misleading since they require such a specialized or "local" analysis of the system that any policy implications derived would be unwarranted for precisely those situations that the models were intended to consider in the first place—the long-range issues providing broad characterizations of the types of problems facing an economy. Therefore, it seems reasonable to suggest that, in some cases, analyses of models with these attributes may require the use of simulation methods to enhance understanding of the information that is available with more conventional analytical treatments.

More generally, these problems suggest a fundamental difficulty with optimal planning models. The traditional methods for characterizing optimal solutions are incomplete. They tend to reflect only the long-term or asymptotic features of the solutions and to ignore the characteristics of the immediate dimensions of the optimal plan. In practice, it may well be that the most useful interpretation of the results derived from such models is that the best that can be expected for actual behavior (whether in a centralized or a decentralized economy) is allocation patterns that might resemble a sequence of the initial steps in such plans. In that case, a more complete understanding of the immediate features of optimal plans is essential in order to judge their role for policy under actual conditions.[4]

Several authors have emphasized the sensitivity of the results of these models to the assumptions made about substitution between reproducible capital and exhaustible natural resources in an aggregate production function.[5] Indeed, Dasgupta and Heal's recent book (1979, page 206) readily acknowledges this property, noting that:

> The main analytical novelty that exhaustible resources present in the analysis of growth possibilities open to an economy is that one has to be particularly conscious about the properties of production functions at the "corners." The banality

---

[4] We are grateful to Kenneth Arrow for calling this point to our attention.
[5] See Cummings and Schulze (1977), and Smith and Krutilla (1979).

of this observation is matched only by the problems this poses in obtaining empirical estimates . . . the assumption that the elasticity of substitution is independent of the capital/resource ratio may be a treacherous one to make. Past experience may not be a good guide for judging substitution possibilities for large values of K/R [capital to natural resources].

It has also been observed that the highly aggregative nature of these models requires that the natural resource measure reflect its use in many diverse sectors. As a consequence, it is necessary to question whether, in a comparative static framework, it is possible to derive a consistent aggregate measure of natural resources, even if its scope is limited to the conventional perception of natural resources as raw materials inputs. Equally important, can such a measure of materials inputs be used consistently in representing the aggregate technology? Lau, in chapter 6, addresses these issues by considering the conditions for a consistent aggregate using both direct and indirect aggregation practices.

The direct method does not utilize information on behavior in the construction of the aggregation. It relies on assumed knowledge of the broad characteristics of the production technology to permit the definition of a relationship between the prices of all types of materials and their attributes. Such a relation implies that the estimation of a function, designated the resource conversion function, would permit the analyst to reduce all materials to a common accounting scheme based on each material's contribution to the production activity under study. It is the necessary element for aggregation. Lau's analysis proceeds from the simplest context in which these issues might arise, to progressively more difficult aggregations considered in a sequential manner, using direct and indirect aggregation practices.

The indirect procedure develops the necessary resource conversion function using duality theory. Simply stated, if it can be assumed that firms' or individuals' behavior can be described in terms of an optimizing model and that we know what their objectives are, then these objectives can be used to help sort out the meaning of materials acquisition decisions and to derive the conversion functions necessary for aggregation. For example, if cost minimization is assumed, then this information can be used in the neoclassical cost function to estimate the appropriate conversion function for aggregation in terms of the material's characteristics.

Lau reviews several important cases, including the following: (1) the production technology is assumed to exhibit a factor augmentation form in materials; (2) the conversion functions for raw materials are assumed to be dependent on other inputs; (3) the production activities are specified as joint and the materials' conversion function is assumed to be independent of at least one of them (but not of all products); (4) all preceding analyses are extended to aggregation over production units (either process or plants, depending upon how one defines the micro unit of analysis); and, finally, (5) all preceding analyses are extended to aggregation over end-use sectors.

By detailing the assumptions and information necessary to estimate the appropriate conversion functions for consistent aggregation, Lau has introduced a wide range of new research relating to both theoretical and empirical issues. Considering only the assumptions he utilized in his analysis of aggregations to the end use level, it seems clear that previous work (notably Spencer, 1973, and Radcliffe, 1976, for raw materials, and many others too numerous to detail for energy) has used as the aggregate a particular individual physical attribute such as heat content (Btu for energy), rather than developing the aggregate to reflect all of the materials' characteristics, as would be the case in Lau's resource conversion function. Lau has suggested that these earlier practices implicitly assume perfect substitution among the materials being aggregated. Specifically, Lau observes in chapter 6 that:

> A constant conversion ratio between different kinds of raw materials inputs is valid *if and only if* the production function has the factor augmentation form in the inputs. This also implies that the different inputs are perfect substitutes. If heat values are used as weights to aggregate different fuels, it is implicitly assumed that there is perfect substitution among the fuels in production. If iron content is used as a weight to aggregate different iron ores, it also implies perfect substitution among iron ores.

There are at least three questions which emerge from his analysis of the lowest level of aggregation. First, is it feasible to estimate the resource conversion functions he has defined to reflect the contributions of materials in production activities at the micro level? There is an interesting relationship between the models he has developed and the earlier literature. His simplest model specifies the attributes of materials as entering the production technology in a factor augmentation format. Such specifications are quite similar to the engineering-economic studies of the production technology. One notable example is the demand for capital for steam-generating electric plants (see Cowing, 1974; Ohta, 1975; and Stewart, 1979, as examples). Of course, these specifications also have direct parallels to the literature dealing with hedonic models for analysis of consumers' preferences. However, to our knowledge, such models have not been applied in the case of materials.[6]

Two of the strongest assumptions necessary for this model to function properly are (1) a requirement that the markets for materials completely adjust so that prices can reflect the desirability of alternative configurations of attributes in each type of material; and (2) the assumption of a perfectly elastic supply of materials. Whether actual conditions approximate these requirements reasonably closely is an empirical issue that needs to be investigated. If they do not, further theoretical work will be necessary, paralleling that discussed by Rosen (1974) and Freeman (1979), involving hedonic models for consumer preferences.

---

[6] There have been two related discussions of these issues. Berndt (1978) has considered the nature of an appropriate aggregate for energy, and Ayres (1978) has discussed in some detail the implications of alternative classification schemes for materials.

The second issue arising from Lau's simple model concerns the assumption that the characteristics of materials and other factor inputs are independent. When this assumption is relaxed, the conversion functions for constructing a consistent materials aggregate at the micro level must reflect the levels of other inputs (in the direct aggregation case) or of the factor prices (given cost minimization in the indirect case). Here the aggregation results derived by using the hedonic function implied by the direct method (i.e., by a derivation of the resource conversion relationships that is based on the production function) will be different from those implied by a cost function derivation of the appropriate conversion functions. Thus, a selection between these two must be made on the basis of which offers the most accurate representation of the role of materials inputs.

One basis for such a selection would be in terms of the implied contributions of materials. In the cost function approach to the derivation of the conversion function, materials are assumed to be used in the technology in a manner that resembles prior processing to form "standardized" raw materials inputs. This distinction is not implicit in the production function characterization.

A second possible distinction relates to which offers the "best" approximation of the conversion function. Under this view, we are approximating the conversion function that would be implied by an unknown production relationship and must select the best procedure for doing so. Research similar to that of Denny and Fuss (1977), Blackorby and Russell (1976), and Lau (1979), in another context, will be necessary to understand the conditions under which each approach offers the best results. Of course, one might suggest that there is no specific functional relationship between the attributes of materials and their roles for production activities. There may be a set of distinct unit processes or elemental tasks that identify how each type of material might be used to serve the objectives specified. Here the process density across the attributes of materials would determine the accuracy of the assumption of a true resource conversion function. If the assumption of a functional relationship is not a reasonable starting point, then it may be necessary to conduct analyses paralleling those of Ayres (1978) and Kopp and Smith (chapter 7) at the empirical level, and of Marsden, Pingry, and Whinston (1974) at the theoretical level, to determine the degree of error introduced in using a conversion function for the aggregation of materials inputs.

The last question which arises with respect to Lau's analysis of aggregation across plants (or processes) within an end-use category is whether the use of procedures necessary for consistent aggregation is important to our objectives. The answer would seem to be yes for several reasons. First, evaluations of the importance of materials inputs for the production technology in theoretical models are based on the assumption that there is a single materials input. While Lau does offer a new and appealing method for defining specific materials in terms of their attribute "clusters," in practice it is probably fair to suggest that production activities will involve more than one materials input. Moreover, these inputs are generally not used in fixed proportions (Kopp–Smith provide one illustration of this point in chapter 7).

Lau also suggests that aggregating materials inputs to the level considered feasible in analyses of the role of natural resources in aggregate planning models probably would not be possible in a consistent manner. This portion of his analysis also suggests that the measurement of the prospects for substitution between materials and other inputs at the end-use level may need to identify more specifically the relationship between the attributes of materials and other inputs, such as capital and labor. Unfortunately, past analyses of production activities and input substitution have, as a rule, shown little recognition of these problems.[7] The one notable exception is models of steam electric generation technology in which analyses have reflected the character of the capital equipment and the fuel type (see Cowing and Smith, 1978, for a review). Further support for this perspective can be found in a matrix of materials substitution and their relationship to the attributes of those materials as suggested by Ayres (in private correspondence) and reproduced here as table 1.1. Ayres' suggested taxonomy leads to a distinction between the features of materials, together with their uses in the production activities, that is consistent with Lau's interaction model for materials characteristics and other inputs.

Lau's theoretical analysis of the conditions for deriving a consistent materials aggregate, taken together with the empirical research in this area, suggests two additional directions for further research. The first of these compares the implications of the measurement practices for materials types used in these studies with the methods recommended by Lau. The best of the past measures (which is also likely to be inadequate on theoretical grounds) considers aggregate materials as a Tornqvist approximation to Divisia quantity indexes of intermediate goods purchased by establishments (see Berndt and Wood, 1975). Since this practice is not necessarily consistent with those developed by Lau, one might question whether the differences are important to the perceived characteristics of the technology. Kopp and Smith address a closely related issue in chapter 7. They examine the implications of materials aggregation within a cost function framework, using data from engineering, process analysis models of three different iron and steel technologies. Their analysis strongly supports concern about the importance of these aggregation issues.

Indeed, while the Kopp–Smith results indicate that the neoclassical models, comparable to those postulated by Lau, do a reasonably good job of describing

---

[7] The general issues associated with the physical constraints on production imposed by materials have been discussed by Ayres (1978) in his recent book.

**Table 1.1.**   Use Categories of Minerals

| | Conventional factor inputs | | | Embodied materials — Metals | | | | | Embodied materials — Nonmetals | | | | | | Nonembodied — Miscellaneous | | | | | |
|---|---|---|---|---|---|---|---|---|---|---|---|---|---|---|---|---|---|---|---|---|
| | 1 | 2 | 3 | 4 | 5 | 6 | 7 | 8 | 9 | 10 | 11 | 12 | 13 | 14 | 15 | 16 | 17 | 18 | 19 | |
| **Conventional factor input** | | | | | | | | | | | | | | | | | | | | |
| 1. Labor | | | | | | | | | | | | | | | | | | | | |
| 2. Capital equipment | s | | | | | | | | | | | | | | | | | | | |
| 3. Fuel energy or | | c | | | | | | | | | | | | | | | | | | |
| electricity | s | s | | | | | | | | | | | | | | | | | | |
| **Embodied materials** | | | | | | | | | | | | | | | | | | | | |
| **Metals** | | | | | | | | | | | | | | | | | | | | |
| 4. Structural | | | | | | | | | | | | | | | | | | | | F |
| 5. Protective "skin" | | | | | c | | | | | | | | | | | | | | | F |
| 6. Electrical/electronic | | | | | | | | | | | | | | | | | | | | F |
| 7. Alloying/coating | | | | c | c | | | | | | | | | | | | | | | F |
| 8. Other | | | | | | | | | | | | | | | | | | | | F |
| **Nonmetals** | | | | | | | | | | | | | | | | | | | | |
| 9. Structural | | | | s | c | c | | | | | | | | | | | | | | F |
| 10. Protective "skin" | | | | c | s | | | | | c | | | | | | | | | | F |
| 11. Transparent "skin" | | | | c | s | | | | | c | s | | | | | | | | | F |
| 12. Other dielectric | | | | | | | | c | | | | | | | | | | | | F |
| 13. Coatings and pigments | | | | c | c | | | | | c | c | | | | | | | | | F |
| 14. Chemical reactant | | | | | | | | | | | | | | | | | | | | F |
| **Nonembodied materials** | | | | | | | | | | | | | | | | | | | | |
| **Physical actant** | | | | | | | | | | | | | | | | | | | | |
| 15. Surfactant | s | s | | | | | | | | | | | | | | | | | | |
| 16. Lubricant | | c | | | | | | | | | | | | | | | | | | |
| 17. Solvent/modifier | s | s | | | | | | | | | | | | | | | | | | |
| 18. Refrigerant working fluid | c | | | | | | | | | | | | | | | | | | | |
| 19. Other | | | | | | | | | | | | | | | | | | | | |

Note: Complementary relationships in production are indicated by c; and s designates substitution relationships in production, F is fixed in relation to output.

the respective underlying engineering technologies, the performance of the model deteriorates with all of the conventional aggregation schemes for constructing a price index for alternative materials aggregates. That is, the Kopp–Smith analysis seeks to use neoclassical cost functions (and therefore factor input prices) to measure the features of the underlying technology by relying on duality theory (as Lau's indirect aggregation procedures do). Their results indicate that the effect of aggregation varies with the features of the underlying technology (as given by the plant type, such as the basic oxygen, open-hearth, or electric arc furnaces). This finding suggests that further research should examine Lau's interaction model of the relationship between the materials' attributes and other inputs (notably capital).

Finally, the Kopp–Smith results also confirm the importance of the need to consider joint production patterns in developing the conversion functions. The substitution relationships between inputs seemed to be affected at both the disaggregated and the aggregated levels by constraints on the discharge of by-product residuals (pollutants) that are not reflected in the models used to estimate these substitution possibilities.

The second general area of research emerging from Lau's consideration of the most aggregated materials indexes is work such as that of Fisher (1971) and, later, that of Fisher, Solow, and Kearl (1977) who analyze the consequences, for the measured characteristics, of the technology of the simultaneous presence of two forms of aggregation—the aggregation of these inputs (even if improper) and the aggregation of micro units. While the Kopp–Smith findings reported here did not address this issue directly, their related analysis (1980) suggests that such appraisals should not be confined to smooth neoclassical functions only. The need to treat production functions as approximations of the underlying engineering activities is also an important dimension of the research.

## 2. The Allocation of Environmental Common Property Resources

The preceding section considered the implications of common property environmental resources in optimal planning models in cases in which the planning authority is assumed to have full knowledge of the consequences of all possible use patterns. The production and utility functions specified in the planning problem are assumed to represent information sufficient to fully determine the marginal costs and benefits associated with any resource utilization profile. Transforming concepts developed in the model into operational counterparts and designing public policies to influence the allocation of both private and common property resources is difficult. It is clear that information of this type generally is not available. It is also unlikely to be revealed for public goods in the same manner as it is for private goods, that is, directly through market transactions. Therefore, one must recognize that information on the importance of these resources to economic agents using their services is incomplete. This deficiency exists regardless of whether the problem is considered as one of central planning, or decentralized market allocation with selective public involvement. Accordingly, research must be directed to understanding the ways in which information such as that furnished by ideal comprehensive markets might be obtained.

In order to organize the discussion of the methods for gauging the relative valuations of public goods in this volume, the material is divided into two broad categories. Within each category we will discuss the relevant contributions of the papers and attempt to relate them to the existing literature.

The two broad categories are designated as the *technical* and *economic* approaches to evaluating the demands for public goods in order to identify the predominant focus of each approach; the categories are not necessarily mutually exclusive. The technical approach largely involves the derivation of functional representations of technical relationships, such as air pollution and physical damage to structures or impairment to human health. By contrast, the economic approaches use individual behavior in the allocation of resources to infer the valuation of the resources.

The technical approaches are discussed in terms of one of the most important types of such analyses—modeling the relationship between air pollution and human health. While there are a wide variety of other technical analyses relevant to environmental policy making, these will not be treated here. The problems involved in each can be viewed as parallel to those discussed by Freeman in his overview and critique of the mortality–air pollution studies (see chapter 5).

The economic approaches are further subclassified in order to accommodate the various approaches to inferring individual valuations for nonmarketed public goods (in this case, the services of environmental common property resources). Each of these categories uses some additional information to sort out the individual's valuations for nonmarketed goods (or services) based on his choices for marketed goods. To summarize, briefly, they are each based on using different types of constraints in conjunction with a behavioral model to decompose (or induce a decomposition) an individual's responses. The three types of constraints involved may be designated as behavioral, technical, and institutional.

## The Technical Approach—Mortality-Air Pollution Models

To illustrate the technical approach to deriving information on the value of the services of environmental common property resources, we have selected one of the most popular and controversial areas—mortality–air pollution models. Freeman, in chapter 5, considers the elements in the mechanisms that would give rise to a measurable human health response to certain patterns of residual discharges and how they might be perceived within statistical models. Thus, he identifies the strategic details of the underlying mechanisms that are implicitly maintained when measured statistical associations between human mortality and pollution are used as indicators of causal relationships.

Freeman's analysis begins with the observation that the mechanisms which would make these models consistent reflections of a causal relation have three elements. First, residual discharges lead to a certain level and pattern of exposure for a given human population. The factors influencing this association are both physical and economic. For example, physical and chemical conditions determine both the possible chemical transformations of substances once they are in the environment, as well as their concentration and duration. Moreover, individual behavior, as reflected in choice of residence, jobs, recreation, and health care also influences exposure at the individual level. Conscious actions can be undertaken to avoid exposure (Zeckhauser and Fisher, 1976, described them as forms of averting behavior). These might range from migration to avoid the possible health hazards of environmental conditions, to investments in air conditioning or filtering equipment.

The second element of these models is also partly a physical one, in that different patterns of realized exposure can yield quite diverse physiological changes among individuals. This may be caused by the level and duration of the exposures or genetic and physical differences in individuals, or all of these things. Moreover, biological models for evaluating the likelihood of health effects are still rather primitive. The process by which exposure to pollutants leads to health effects is acknowledged to be a probabilistic one. Unfortunately, there is little agreement on the character of the mechanism giving rise to the possible health-related events or their respective probabilities. For example, models which attempt to explain the relationship between potential carcinogens and the incidence of cancer range from those based on a "single hit" framework, in which the level of exposure or degree of irritation is not particularly important to the health effect, to models in which the degree of irritation is the crucial determinant. It would be a difficult task to integrate such information into the specification of statistical models, and it is one to which we will return later.

The third element of Freeman's framework relates to how the health effects of exposure patterns are reflected in measures of human health levels. These measures can, in principle, take a number of forms, depending on the subtleties of the health impacts. However, most attention has focused on two health effects—patterns of mortality and of morbidity, with the former variables being the most frequently used for statistical analysis.

There are a number of reasons for this greater emphasis on mortality data, the most important being that they are more readily available. Nevertheless, it is reasonable to expect that morbidity effects of pollution are also important. They are, however, difficult to define and measure consistently. Indeed, Freeman identifies problems with both measures. Mortality is usually the death rate for a given population, and the linkages described above are reflected in that population's characteristics. Thus, one would expect that the ability to accurately measure the health impact of a particular pollutant will depend upon the ability to control the factors that influence how it may affect the population involved.

The use of mortality rate as an indicator of health represents a rather crude method both for identifying health effects and for measuring the influence of individual circumstances on them. Accordingly, analysts have attempted to account for other influences on death for specific population groups. In order to gauge the success of this scaling of impact, one must consider the degree of heterogeneity in the groups for which the rates are constructed. For example, it is possible to control for some factors, such as age, race, and sex, with appropriate adjustment of the mortality rates. However, there are many factors that cannot be controlled, such as genetic endowment, specific features of an individual's health status, eating and exercise patterns, and the like. Of course, regression analyses have attempted to control for some of these factors by including measures of the general characteristics of the population group in the set of explanatory variables. As a rule, however, these are measures of the central tendency and do not reflect the full distribution of each of these factors across the relevant population group.

The problems associated with interpreting such models are akin to aggregation problems for the economic models identified earlier in this chapter. For example, assume that the relationship between the probability of death and a set of determining factors for each individual can be specified. Even if one assumes that each individual receives exactly the same exposure profile, the distribution of the other factors influencing health across the population considered in aggregate and the consistency of the functional relationships across individuals will determine whether there exists a single aggregate model that is expressed in terms of measures of central tendency. Indeed, the problems here parallel some of the previous comments made with respect to aggregating production functions. (See also Green, 1964, for an introductory discussion.)

Of course, the important question is whether using an approximate relationship as representative of the impacts for the "average" individual does great mischief. This question has many dimensions. First, is it possible to determine whether pollution of various types affects human health? That is, will the aggregation problems conceal actual associations or induce false ones? Second, can these estimated relationships be used to accurately measure the health impacts? This distinction is important because one might well find that the statistical models permit a decision on whether such an association exists without permitting an accurate measure of the nature of the impact. Unfortunately, past research has not considered this dichotomy, and it seems a useful one to consider.

Freeman's analysis also considers the extent to which economic behavior influences the statistical models relating air pollution to mortality rates. Indeed, his comparison of the Lave–Seskin (1977) work with the more recent analyses of Crocker et al. (1979) suggests that a direct accounting for the potential effects of economic behavior can substantively affect the estimated relationships. Clearly, the work of Crocker and his associates is simply a beginning. Further research is needed that recognizes the potential for simultaneity in measures that determine health expenditures and act as indicators of health status. Moreover, as Freeman has suggested, such expenditures are one of a number of responses available to the individual, and these other responses affect the reliability of the exposure measures.

Migration patterns affect the actual exposure history of a given population. Statistical studies implicitly assume that the technically measured levels of pollution during the year in which the mortality rates are calculated and, perhaps, for those years in the immediate past, are credible proxy measures of the exposure pattern for the population involved. Of course, as the latency period preceding the observed health effect increases, this assumption becomes increasingly tenuous. This feature is one that is more problematic for the population in the United States, where migration is frequent, than in some other areas of the world. This suggests that international comparative studies may be important for confirming the findings of U.S. analyses.

Freeman also suggests constructing exposure measures based on both the actual levels of pollution and a general migration model capable of predicting the past movement of populations in each geographic area. On the matter of a latency period, Freeman proposes using longitudinal studies, based perhaps on existing panel surveys with supplementary health information, rather than relying on amending the cross-sectional studies to include lagged measures of the exposure variables.

Turning to the questions associated with measuring other health effects, Freeman carefully identifies several important differences. He observes that:

> Measures of morbidity must take into account the fact that unlike mortality, morbidity is not an event, but a process involving time. Cases observed during a period may fall into any of four categories: (1) onset before the period and termination by either recovery or death during the period; (2) onset before the period and termination after the period; (3) onset during the period and termination during the period; and (4) onset during the period and termination after the period.

Measures reflecting items 3 and 4 are more relevant to measuring causal associations between exposure to pollution and changes in health status, while all four will be equally important to measures of the social costs of any changes in health status. This is because duration is an important element in calculations of the economic costs of health impairments. Given the very limited number of studies of the determinants of morbidity, it is clear that additional research in this area is needed. However, developing this research will be difficult, given the data limitations. It may be possible to use mortality data for specific causes of death as an indicator of the associated morbidity. Thus, it is an interesting and potentially important research issue to determine whether age, sex, and death-specific mortality rates can be used to reflect morbidity in evaluating some aspects of the economic costs of pollution-related health effects.

Further technical issues can be raised with respect to the statistical methodologies that have been used in these studies. The study by Crocker and his associates (1979) emphasizes the importance of reflecting the simultaneity that may be present in measuring the health status and the health care expenditures of a given population. Failure to account for this simultaneity can lead to biased estimates of the parameters of the mortality–pollution models. Since the empiricial findings of the study by Crocker et al. (1979) are quite different from those of Lave and Seskin (1977), one might conclude that this effect is important. While this conclusion may well be valid, it is also important to place the issue in perspective.

More specifically, estimates of mortality–pollution relationships with the available data bases have a number of limitations. It can be quite misleading to single out the issue of simultaneity and attach great significance to it. In order to provide some appreciation of the difficulties involved, we must consider the assumptions underlying classical statistical methods and the theory associated with inference based on them. This methodology maintains that the analyst is given a model *a priori* the exact features of which are completely specified before an evaluation of the model with a given data set. It is especially important to recognize the full dimensions of these assumptions. The exact functional relationships—that is, linear, semilog, log-linear, or whatever—are known in advance, as are the explanatory variables in that model. If these variables cannot be measured exactly, a specific set of features is assumed for the types of errors introduced with the measures that are used.

With this information, the analyst then utilizes a given data set to estimate the parameters of the model and to test hypotheses about the parameters. One or more samples are used in this process. However, it is important to recognize that this process relies on the fact that the model's specification is given. In short, the character of the model is assumed to be completely independent of the sample used for estimation and testing.

As one moves from textbook discussions of the estimation of models to actual empirical analyses, it is clear that this is not the way most such analyses proceed. This is especially true in the nonexperimental sciences, where in order to test their models analysts must rely on data collected to serve other objectives. Thus, they cannot fully control the process that generates the information.

In practice, model specification and estimation are part of what might be designated an analysis strategy. That is, the investigator often considers a wide array of model specifications, including varying functional forms, different sets of explanatory variables, and subsampling practices in the process of arriving at a final model. Among the essential ingredients in the analysis strategy are the formal method for analyzing the sample information at each stage and the decision rules used to move through the alternatives hypothesized as relevant to the choice set, to the final model. Theil (1961) proposed a similar position nearly twenty years ago in commenting on the econometric methodology. He observed (pages 206–207) that:

> Economic theory can give some indications as to the variables that are possibly relevant; it may even give some vague indications as to curvature and as to the numerical magnitude of some coefficients . . . but it rarely gives any indication about the probability properties of disturbances. The obvious result is that, if a "maintained" hypothesis gives unsatisfactory results, it is not maintained but rejected, and replaced by another "maintained" hypothesis, etc. It is hardly reasonable to say that this kind of experimentation is incorrect, even if it affects the superstructure built on such "maintained" hypotheses. It is especially unreasonable to reject such an experimental approach, because . . . the statistical theory which forbids the rejection of a "maintained" hypothesis is not fully satisfactory either in view of the difficulty of its application. *What is incorrect, however, is to act as if the final hypothesis presented is the first one, whereas in fact it is the result of much experimentation. Since every econometric analysis is an essay in persuasion—just as is true for any other branch of science—the line of thought leading to the finally accepted result must be expounded* [emphasis added].

From this position, Theil (1961) observed that the difficulty with experimenting with different hypotheses is that it must be recognized that greater accuracy is attributed to the estimates than should be. At the time of Theil's study, there was no clear body of research on how to explicitly reflect this overstatement.

Within the past few years, however, there has been great interest in this area, producing a growing literature on the implications of pretesting and specification search procedures for the properties of the estimates (see Judge, Bock, and Yancey, 1974; Wallace, 1972, 1977; and Leamer, 1978, as examples). This literature is relevant for statistical analyses of mortality relationships. In simple terms, the arguments developed more recently suggest that these analysis strategies involve mechanisms for incorporating prior restrictions on the model into the estimation process. While they do this sequentially, for expositional purposes they can be described by using a simple example which involves considering the effects of imposing exact constraints on the estimation of a model with regression analysis. Prior restrictions, whether correct or not (in terms of the "true" model), will always improve the precision with which the parameters of any model are estimated. However, if they are incorrect, this improvement comes at a cost—the estimate is biased. That is, the explicit use of prior information can induce two changes in the probability distributions for the estimated parameters. Increased precision is synonymous with a reduction in the spread (or variance) of the distribution, while increased bias means that the central tendency (or the location parameters of this probability distribution) may be displaced from the true value.

Every time an analyst adopts an analysis strategy, an implicit tradeoff is made between bias and variance. How does this issue specifically relate to the mortality–pollution models? The relation is direct. These models are replete with compromises, approximations, proxy variables, and the like. Each has implications for the precision and bias in the resulting estimates. The questions of simultaneity raised by Crocker and his coauthors (1979) are but one set of these and may not be the most important. Indeed, in the literature that evaluates the consequences of ignoring simultaneity in estimating linear simultaneous equation models, the results of sampling studies (see Smith, 1973; Sasser, 1970; and Mosbaek and Wold, 1970) clearly indicate that a choice of methods that ignore it, compared with those that adjust for simultaneity, comes down to a tradeoff between bias (caused by the simultaneity that is not accounted for in this case) and precision—with the magnitude of the bias often being a function of the degree of jointness in the determination process.

Before closing our discussion of Freeman's analysis of mortality–air pollution studies, it is important to consider the valuation process for these health effects once they have been estimated. His discussion focuses on the problems of evaluating the marginal damages associated with predicted health effects. Here, he proposes that increased attention be given to indirect approaches for evaluating the economic damages associated with an increased probability of death, using, wherever possible, wage rate and occupational risk models rather than direct-questioning methods. Greater attention, however, must be given to the morbidity period that might precede death in these cases, to the latency period and the individual's perception of the risk, and to the individual's knowledge of the alternatives.

### Economic Approaches to Deriving Values for Environmental Common Property Resources

At the outset we suggested a broad similarity between three ways in which economic analysis has been used to obtain information on the environmental consequences of alternative resource use patterns. At a conceptual level, all involve a link between the services provided by environmental common property resources and some privately observable action or transaction. However, the mechanism which gives rise to this linkage is quite different for the three cases and, in fact, involves very different types of assumptions.

Before describing each, it is important to recognize that they can be used to reveal either the marginal costs or the marginal benefits of assuring the services of environmental resources. While most of the examples used to illustrate these approaches relate to revealing marginal valuations, there is no reason for limiting their scope. The first two ways (i.e., *behavioral* and *technical* restrictions) of using economic analyses of the behavioral responses to particular constraints often are designated indirect methods of eliciting marginal valuations or marginal costs. These methods suggest that the transactions taking place on the markets for certain private goods are also capable of revealing the demand for environmental services, despite the fact that these services are not themselves the direct objective of the exchanges. Two different types of assumptions regarding the constraints or influences on behavior have been used to assure that market transactions for private goods reveal demand for environmental services. The first of these, introduced formally by Mäler (1974), assumes that an individual's preference structure is such that there is a direct association between the nonmarketed service and some private good. This association is termed weak complementarity. It refers to a special kind of jointness in the utility formation process. In these cases, the marginal value of an increment in the services of the environmental resource is zero when the individual is not consuming some positive level of the associated good.

This approach would be used to reveal an individual's demand for cream if it could be assumed that his preference structure was such that the marginal valuation of cream would be zero unless he was consuming some amount of coffee. In this case, cream plays a role similar to that we ascribe to the nonmarketed environmental service, and coffee is the private good. Assuming that an individual maximizes utility (or welfare) subject to a budget constraint and that the nature of his demand for this linked private good at all prices (including the one for which the quantity demanded is zero) can be observed, then this restriction on the nature of taste (designated as behavioral) is sufficient to allow privately observable actions to reveal the demand for the nonmarketed good. While this methodology was developed for public goods in general, it also can be directly applied to this case.

Mäler (1974), however, suggests that the approach is subject to important qualifying restrictions. He observes (page 189):

> The knowledge of the demand functions together with condition (34) [equation stating that if the demand for a private good is zero, then the demand for some environmental service will also be zero] has thus made it possible to derive the expenditure function, not only as a function of market prices, but also as a function of the supply of environmental service. This approach is based on some implicit assumptions that may restrict its applicability. . . . In order to estimate the expenditure functions, however, we must have information on the [private] demand functions, not only for a small range of prices, but for all prices above the present price and our approach will be very sensitive to the specification of the demand functions.

In a more recent paper which expands on the Mäler result, Bradford and Hildebrant (1977, pages 113–114) summarize the general principle, observing that, "If one regards the value of all public goods as contingent upon the availability of *some* private goods (if there is no butter there is no demand for guns), the result says that *all* information required for efficient public good provision is embedded in private good demand functions."

The linkage between the nonmarketed public good and the private good is assumed to be present in the nature of preferences or, equivalently, in a specified set of household production functions that are not necessarily objectively measured distinct from preferences (see Hori, 1975, and Smith, 1979, for further discussion).

The second type of restriction on behavior maintains that the linkage between the public and private goods is technically derived. For example, the level of air quality in a region is of immediate concern to those who live in that region. Or at a more micro level, air quality is associated with a particular site. These site-specific linkages are quite important for a number of public goods. Indeed, the original motivation for Tiebout's (1956) analysis of the demand for local public goods was that we might infer from individuals' site selections (i.e., their choice of residential location) the demands for these local public goods. This basic idea can be extended (and has been in some cases) to evaluations of the marginal valuations of air, water, and noise pollution abatement (Freeman, 1979) and to valuing the impacts of climatic changes and the like. In each case there is no market for the public good or service, but it is transferred *jointly* in the transactions involving sites (or other private good acquisitions). Unfortunately, some of the literature on weak complementarity has confused the two kinds of restrictions. Mäler (1974) seems susceptible to this confusion in his examples when he uses Stevens's (1966) work as an illustration of weak complementarity. Stevens's work is based on the fact that in order to be concerned over the direct consequences of an improvement in water quality at a recreational site, one must use the site. Thus, the services of the recreational site are jointly supplied with a level of water quality, and in evaluating the benefits from water quality improvements, he argues that individuals' site selection decisions can be used. The logic is quite analogous to the Tiebout model and, more generally, to the hedonic literature.

While there is no direct market for air or water quality, there is one for sites which have different levels of clean air or water. Thus, in purchasing a site an individual is assured provision of the nonmarketed service as an "attribute" of the site. This technical linkage is, as we have noted, the basis of using the hedonic method together with property values to measure the marginal benefits of improved air or water quality (this is discussed extensively in Freeman's 1979 book). In contrast to the behavioral restriction, this form of linkage can be objectively observed. One can measure what levels of air or water quality will be present at a site. Thus, it is not necessary to assume that preferences are structured in a particular way, as in the case of the weak complementarity approach. However, it is necessary to know the relationship between objective measures of the services of environmental common property resources at a particular site and the individual's perception of them. In order for this indirect method to reveal the nature of the individual's marginal valuation, it is important to know how he forms his perception or processes the information at his disposal.

While the economic literature has not developed counterparts to these concepts to measure the marginal costs of meeting certain levels of pollution abatement and thereby to increase the availability of the environmental resource service for other purposes, the parallels are direct. If there is some association between a privately marketed input or output inherent in the technology that is akin to weak complementarity or technical association in its features (such as the sulfur content of fuel), and the firm's responses over a range of constraints on these activities can be observed, then it should be possible to measure the marginal costs with similar indirect methods. Lau's chapter also illustrates related concepts in his aggregation of materials in the presence of joint production. However, it should also be recognized that economists probably have considered these issues to be less important because they are technical activities and therefore are often assumed to be directly observable. Thus, the revelation problem is assumed to be absent.

The third type of restriction used with economic methods to evaluate the marginal benefits (or costs) of the services of environmental resources consists of what we shall designate institutional constraints on individuals' behavioral responses. These approaches are most often found when efforts are made to solicit directly an individual's willingness to pay for the services of the resource. However, in this case, the individual is told his response will influence a tax or payment in a rather special way. This information provides an institutionally based constraint on the response and therefore uses incentives conventionally held to be problematic in direct questioning (see Bohm, 1972; Cicchetti and Smith, 1976; and Brookshire, Ives, and Schulze, 1976, as examples). Dasgupta (chapter 4) addresses aspects of these approaches. While there are a variety of incentive schemes that have been discussed in the recent literature in this area (see Ferejohn, Forsythe, and Noll, 1979, for an interesting discussion of some desirable features of these schemes), there is one general dimension they all have in common. Each represents an *institutionally* induced linkage between a private transaction (i.e., the tax payment an individual must make) and an individual's revealed marginal valuation of some public good. That is, these systems confront the individual with a taxing system that links his required payment to his revelations in such a way that only a forthright response is appropriate. Each scheme is distinguished according to the assumptions maintained concerning any other individuals involved in the provision (or allocation) of the public good, the individual's perception of the behavior of these other parties, and the relationship between the costs of providing the services and the sum of the tax payments.

Dasgupta (chapter 4) considers a modified Groves–Ledyard (1977) process to assure an efficient allocation of resources among consumers, given the requirement of a balanced budget. He uses game theory to analyze the character of the outcomes with a Nash equilibrium concept. Once a solution is found, there is no incentive for an individual to change the outcome by distorting his revealed preference. Nonetheless, each individual's optimal strategy is dependent upon that solution and, therefore, on others' preferences. A stronger solution concept would be a situation in which each person has a dominant strategy or a response which is best regardless of what others do. In some cases, as Dasgupta points out in his treatment of regulation in the presence of an information gap, truth-telling is a dominant strategy, but balancing the regulator's budget is not assured. This application is related to the firm's revelation of the cleanup costs associated with pollution regulation.

The difficulty with demand-revealing processes (or, alternatively, with methods for institutionally linking an individual's revelation of his marginal valuation of a public good to a private transaction in a way that induces an honest response) is that under actual conditions individuals may not perceive the full dimensions of the incentive scheme. That is, as in the case of the technical links between public and private goods, the transactions on the private markets will only reveal the marginal valuation of the public good if the quantity of that public good is accurately perceived. These approaches require that the individual understand the scheme and consciously take it into account in his choices.

As a result of these considerations, Dasgupta acknowledges that there may be greater prospects for demand-revealing processes with firms than with individuals. Thus, an important research issue with these incentive mechanisms concerns how they are perceived in actual practice.

A more general set of research questions emerges from the overall classification we have proposed for the economic methods. When one considers the behavioral and institutional restrictions, it is indeed reasonable to ask which is a better research strategy—to attempt to determine whether consumer preferences exhibit the properties required (as described by Mäler and Bradford and Hildebrandt), or to consider the prospects for individuals fully perceiving institutionally defined constraints with these incentive mechanisms? Where are these approaches best suited individually? That is, does one need demand-revealing mechanisms based on institutional constraints, or are the behavioral and technical constraints relevant in most cases? These issues are, of course, related to how well the markets for the relevant private goods work. This is an empirical question, the answer to which will likely be specific to the problem. Unfortunately, past work has not considered these methods under this general organizing principle, so that research is often not defined in these terms.

## 3. Evaluating Natural Resource Availability

The appraisal of natural resource availability involves both economic and physical science considerations. Harris and Skinner (chapter 8) summarize the importance of these two dimensions of resource availability by quoting Zimmerman's (1964) "Resources are not, they become." Unfortunately, most economic analyses of resource availability have tended to oversimplify the role of physical constraints on resource availability. Geological concepts, for example, are very important in evaluating the availability of extractive raw materials. To provide a flavor of this, in what follows we focus on mineral resources. Even so, it is fair to say that it is not easy to evaluate mineral resource availability. Recent theoretical and empirical contributions to the subject (see Brown and Field, 1979; Barnett, 1979; and Fisher, 1979) attest to the difficulty of doing so.

In order to analyze the problems associated with evaluating the availability of an extractive resource, one must first consider the different perceptions that economists and geologists have of the physical availability of extractive resources. The economist's perspective usually takes one of two forms. In one of these, nonrenewable resources are treated as exhaustible. This form is most often associated with analyses developed from Hotelling's (1931) evaluation of the behavior of the firm or from more recent analyses of optimal intertemporal extraction profiles. The second view, which has largely been associated with the empirical analysis and interpretations of Barnett and Morse (1963), holds that there is a distinct relationship between each grade of an extractive resource and the quantity available in that grade, where grade is a measure of the quality of the resource. For minerals, economists would likely consider grade as equivalent to the percentage of the rock that is pure mineral in a given deposit. More specifically, this view holds that as the demands for raw materials require utilization of lower grades, one will always find greater quantities available. Unfortunately, the economist is often not clear as to precisely what is implict in this assumption. The interpretation of it is certainly open to question. For example, does it mean that there are a greater number of equivalently sized deposits at these lower grades? Does it imply simply that there are more deposits and provide no judgment as to their respective sizes? Or, are the deposits simply larger? From a geophysical perspective these different interpretations may be quite important, but economic models have often ignored them.[8] We shall argue that the treatment of physical availability in economic models may not be correct.

While both of the views discussed above are represented in economic models, it is fair to suggest that most economists, if polled, would subscribe to the view that as firms are forced to mine lower grade deposits, there will be larger volumes of the mineral ore available in them. That is, there seems to be an inherent faith that extractible raw materials, possessing the appropriate characteristics, will be available indefinitely to meet continuously increasing production requirements. This view holds that either the resources will be available or the technology will adjust to accommodate what is available. Indeed, Peterson and Fisher (1977), after a comprehensive review of most of the early and current literature, conclude (page 711) that:

> Looking at the extractive sector more specifically, two major conclusions emerge from theory and evidence. First, extractive resources are probably allocated by competitive markets about as well as other resources, subject to the usual variety of imperfections. *Second, though stocks are obviously being run down in a physical sense, technical change, economies of scale, and product and factor substitution have largely prevented erosion of the resource base of the economy. On the contrary, it appears that extractive commodities have become less scarce, in terms of the sacrifices required to obtain them, over the past hundred years or so* [emphasis added].

Thus, while economic models have considered the implications of resource exhaustibility as a potential absolute limit on economic activities, they usually do so to serve one of two objectives. One is to provide the formal mechanisms needed to evaluate the properties of particular institutions, such as the market, for allocating a fixed resource among individual users at an instant in time and over time. The other objective that such models serve is to provide the potential for characterizing the "worst case," thereby offering an upper bound for the adverse consequences of exhausting the sources of raw materials. These models have been reviewed by Kamien and Schwartz in chapter 2.

Economic analyses developed to consider the impacts of the special features of exhaustible resources that would affect an efficient allocation or the ability to maintain constant or increasing levels of per capita consumption in the presence of a finite resource base are important exercises. However, if we consider the geologists' approach to estimating resource availability, questions arise as to whether the economists' characterization of these problems is correct. More specifically, Harris and Skinner (chapter 8) argue that the definitions of materials must reflect their geochemical features for three important reasons: (1) the chemical features of substances affect their physical occurrence in nature since deposits are the result of chemical processes; (2) the geochemical properties also influence the costs of mining, concentration, and smelting; and finally, (3) the chemical characteristics are very likely to be important to the materials' end uses.

Their arguments imply that a reformulation of economic models to more accurately reflect the characteristics of the constraints imposed by the

---

[8] Vickrey (1967) indirectly took note of these issues by calling attention to the contribution of transportation costs to the prices of resources.

physical availability of materials is clearly called for. However, before discussing the nature of this research, we first review in simple terms some of the explanations for the formation of different substances in the earth's crust and then consider their relationship to an appropriate vocabulary and to how the physical availability of natural resources might be incorporated into economic models.

In the formation of crystal structures, positively charged ions—cations—within a specific size range can substitute for each other without changing the geometry of the structure.[9] Harris and Skinner indicate that if the difference in the radii of such substituting cations is within 15 percent, then complete substitution is generally possible. Of course, temperature and pressure conditions affect this process. It is also possible to have coupled substitutions within a given crystal structure so long as there are similar ionic radii and the same total charge. Thus, the prospects for a mineral deposit with particular features depend upon whether the opportunities for these substitutions are present (of course, the fine details of the chemistry are more involved than this simplified discussion suggests). Moreover, this rule suggests that a distinction in these substances ought to be made on the basis of crystal structures and, indeed, this is what Harris and Skinner propose. They call for distinguishing *minerals* as solid crystalline chemical elements or chemical compounds; *mineraloids* as amorphous substances resembling minerals, but lacking both the crystal structure and the specific composition; and *rocks* as natural aggregations of one or more of the minerals or mineraloids.

To understand the physical occurrence of these substances, it is necessary to consider the general chemical principles underlying the formation of minerals and mineraloids. This requires that one understand the relationship between the chemistry of silicate minerals; oxide minerals; carbonates of calcium, magnesium, and iron; sulfides of iron; and sulfates of calcium, together with the geological processes that might contribute to the chemistry of mineral formation. When the primary processes leading to the formation of rocks are considered, it is possible to understand why large local enrichments and the associated formation of minerals are so rare.[10]

The features of the geochemical process giving rise to mineral deposits have important implications for both the physical features of the deposits and the number and size of each type of deposit. As a result, they will also have implications for economic models of the exploration process. Many earlier efforts have followed the logic used by Devarajan and Fisher (chapter 9) in analyzing the activities associated with resource exploration. Exploratory output, or additions to reserves, are seen as related to the effort devoted to exploration.

[9] A cation is normally defined as an ion that moves or would move toward a cathode, and thus it is usually a positive ion.

[10] Harris and Skinner define the major rock-forming processes as weathering and sedimentation, melting and fractional crystallization, and mineral regrowth by heat and pressure.

The Harris–Skinner analysis suggests that this conception must be expanded. It would add substantial complexity to Pindyck's (1977) recent analysis of exploration. Pindyck's model specifies additions to the stock of reserves of a given substance (the exhaustible resource in his terms) as a function of both the exploratory effort and cumulative reserve additions. This latter variable reflects his interpretation of the geological availability of new discoveries. That is, they become more difficult to obtain as the amount of the resource that has been discovered increases. The geochemistry of most minerals suggests that this simple formulation is but the beginning. The exploration function in his model must be amended to reflect the attributes of the substances of interest and their effects on the types of additions to the reserves. His formulation also assumes that these additions are all of homogeneous quality in terms of the further stages of processing. Harris and Skinner's analysis (chapter 8), however, offers some evidence to suggest that this assumption may be unrealistic. Thus, it would seem that if the effects of the physical occurrence of nonrenewable natural resources are to be appropriately reflected in economic models, they will require a respecification of the exploration production function. There are several important dimensions of such a respecification.

First, explicit account must be taken of the attributes of the mineral and their relationship to its occurrence in nature. This modification implies that both the production function for additions to reserves and the assumed probability structure in the Devarajan–Fisher model of exploration under uncertainty may be related to these attributes. Second, the features of each newly discovered deposit–including size, variation in ore quality, and depth—must be incorporated into the model and, for the uncertainty case, into the probability structure. The Pindyck model implicitly assumes that a difficult aggregation problem has been resolved. That is, it assumes that the mechanism by which these features influence the construction of a homogeneous measure of the quantity of the resouce is known, and is implicit in the relationship specified between the exploration production function and the cumulative sum of the aggregate of discoveries in terms of this homogeneous measure. This problem is akin to Lau's resource conversion function discussed in chapter 6.

Ideally, one would like to know how these various attributes are evaluated by firms. There are certainly parallels between the hedonic functions described by Lau and the Harris–Skinner discussion of the problems in isolating a grade-tonnage relationship by using data derived from firms' behavioral responses to the attributes.

The second area in which the physical attributes of both the substance and its deposits are likely to affect economic models of resource availability is in the extraction process. Here, past efforts by Fisher (1979) and by Devarajan and Fisher (chapter 9) introduce a stock effect to reflect such an influence.

That is, they assume that as the cumulative amount of the resource extracted increases, the remaining sources are of lower quality and this lower quality causes extraction costs to rise. Their specification implicitly accepts the view that the impediments to realizing a supply of any substance that is of constant quality arise only in the extraction process, as the cumulative amount of the resource used increases (or equivalently, in the case of a finite stock, as the amount that is left declines). Once again, this type of model is consistent with the observations of Harris and Skinner, but needs enrichment; moreover, the detail may be quite important. Indeed, in his earlier work, Fisher did consider the impact of including cumulative past discoveries in the exploration production function. With such amendments we see that the rent will be equated to marginal discovery costs minus a term reflecting the shadow price of a unit added to the stock of discovered resources. The sign of this price will reflect the influence of cumulative discoveries on the exploration production function. Thus, from a theoretical perspective, even a simple amendment can be important. Without additional geological information, it is not clear how this fairly straightforward amendment will affect the extraction profile and relationship between rent and marginal discovery costs.

The Harris–Skinner example of copper suggests that when extraction, concentration, and smelting are considered, there may not be a smoothly increasing cost function as the character and quality of the available deposits of a mineral change. While their analysis is in terms of energy requirements for each stage, unit costs may also be a discontinuous function (i.e., in steps) of the physical characteristics of the deposits.

Economic models have often ignored these details, so that there have been no attempts to incorporate these effects into economic models of the extractive industries. Indeed, the available data are quite limited. For example, see Moroney and Trapani (1978) for an econometric analysis of these processing activities for selected industries. Nonetheless, the evidence that is available from process analysis models such as those of Russell (1973), Russell and Vaughan (1976), Thompson and coauthors (1977), and others support the Harris–Skinner observations for the refining processes with all the raw materials that have been studied.

Assuming that their description offers a credible representation of the status of mineral extraction and refining processes (for a subset of our important minerals), then it implies that the impacts of the availability of resources on economic activity at the aggregate level, or on firm behavior at the micro level, may well be much greater than previously expected. Moreover, the efficiency properties established for markets will depend to a significant degree on how well the steps in costs can be anticipated.

The final avenue for impact relates to the end-use implications of these same mineral characteristics. Harris and Skinner propose four schemes for classifying materials: (1) those used for their yield of metals; (2) those used for their chemical and fertilizer properties; (3) those used for their special or aggregate physical properties; and (4) those used for their energy content. While they note that there is only "a rough and inexact correspondence" between their four use categories and geological classifications, the important aspect of their analysis is establishing the potential for a relationship between the attributes of materials that will affect their physical occurrence in nature; the ability to extract, concentrate, and refine them; and the ability to accomplish particular end objectives.

This final association on the demand or end-use side of the analysis was recognized in the early literature by Scott (1962) who observed (page 91) that:

> Demand for minerals is derived from demand for certain final goods and services. Therefore, certain properties must be obtainable from raw materials from which such services and types of final goods are produced. *Man's hunt for minerals must properly be viewed as a hunt for economical sources of these properties* (*strength, colour, porosity, conductivity, magnetism, texture, size, durability, elasticity, flavour and so on*) [emphasis added].

However, the effects of specific properties of minerals on their availability were not recognized. Indeed, it is possible that the classification should be more detailed with respect to the attributes of materials. Ayres has suggested the further distinctions between embodied and nonembodied uses of materials shown in table 1.1. Further, Ayres's own work (1978) has suggested that the physical attributes of materials influence the availability of substitutes that can serve particular end uses.

To summarize the discussion thus far, we have argued that geochemistry imposes important constraints on economic models. The attributes of materials influence their physical occurrence, extraction, concentration, and refining. Thus, the supply schedule of attributes must reflect these relationships. The relevance of this observation can be seen directly once it is recognized that in Lau's analysis the supply schedule for a given material was assumed to be perfectly elastic. These observations imply that this elasticity assumption may need to be modified. Therefore, economic analyses of the type described by Lau will need to address specifically the issues raised in Rosen's (1974) analysis of hedonic modeling. That is, the supply functions for attributes may be upward sloping (and potentially discontinuous). Thus, in interpreting the implications of the relationship between the price of a material and its attributes, one faces a problem that is conceptually similar to the classic identification problem in econometric analysis of demand and supply functions. However, in this case the attributes of materials do not exchange directly. Rather, they are a part of the goods being exchanged. Rosen (1974) discussed some of these problems in his paper on hedonic techniques. One difficulty in applying conventional theory to this case relates to whether certain geochemical properties are always present together. In the literature of the hedonic model, can they be "repackaged"? If not, this constraint may cause problems in interpreting the results of private transactions when the geo-chemistry of mineral formation induces jointness in supply, but the charac-teristics involved are not jointly required in end uses (see Muelbauer, 1974; and Fisher and Shell, 1972, for discussion). Indeed, this interpretation of the Harris–Skinner arguments provides further support for their questioning of the grade-tonnage relationships.

The research questions that emerge from linking the Pindyck paper and the Harris–Skinner, Devarajan–Fisher, and Lau chapters are both theoretical and empirical. The long time spans involved in developing mineral resources may reduce the instantaneous interaction between supply and demand functions that is implied within a hedonic framework. The hedonic models developed for consumer behavior, for example, are exclusively static models. The dynamic features of the problems associated with nonrenewable resources cannot be ignored. The required amendments to theory are difficult, and we cannot expect that results developed in a comparative static framework will be upheld (an example in another context is found in Berndt, Fuss, and Waverman, 1977). Equally important, a substantial amount of empirical analysis is required to gauge the effects of each substance's geochemical properties on each of the three stages of its delivery to an end use. These considerations may not be important for all materials. Since the analysis of the supply of nonrenewable resources in these terms has been extremely limited, there is little on which to base a judgment of the empirical significance of this aspect of the Harris–Skinner results.

One further issue should be noted that is not identified in the Harris–Skinner analysis, although it is completely consistent with their framework and analysis, since it relates to the general issues in our research effort. The research associated with modeling the relationship between production ac-tivities and generation of residuals also can be related to the physical char-acteristics of the materials used (as well as to the engineering features of the production activities (see pages 209–211 for a more detailed discussion). Indeed, Bower's (1975) review of RFF's experience with residuals manage-ment models for industrial application strongly supports this conclusion, as do other recent econometric analyses (see Kopp, 1978, as an example). Furthermore, the Smith–Vaughan analyses (1980) suggest that the com-plexity of these process analyses is related, in part, to the detail provided for the materials inputs to production, and the complexity of the model in turn affects the solutions derived from the production activities.

For the most part our discussion has considered the research of Devarajan and Fisher arising out of its connection with the analysis by Harris and Skinner. The Devarajan–Fisher paper also raises an important set of addi-tional issues. Two specifically deserve comment. First, within the context of a simple theoretical model of firm behavior, how does uncertainty in ex-ploration results affect a firm's decisions on allocating capital between exploration *and* extraction? Second, the authors reconsider a method, first proposed by Fisher (1979), and also by Pindyck (1978), that might be used to measure the scarcity rents of an *in situ* resource. Specifically, they suggest that while these rents would be very difficult to measure, if the firm's objectives are known (and we are willing to make a number of qualifying assumptions), the rent can be measured by using the marginal discovery costs of an additional increment to the firm's reserves. This suggestion seemed quite appealing from both intuitive and empirical perspectives. However, these analyses assumed that the exploration process involved a certain relationship between effort and results. This specification was quite restrictive. It implicitly required an exact relationship between effort and the outputs of exploratory activities.

In chapter 9 Devarajan and Fisher evaluate the correspondence between rent and the marginal cost of finding another unit of a resource for the risk-averse firm. Their findings are somewhat surprising and reinforce the need for greater interaction with the geological sciences. Specifically, they observe that:

> Not surprisingly, we find that uncertainty does affect the behavior of a risk-averse firm that maximizes the expected utility of profits. Surprisingly, perhaps, the direction of effect is ambiguous. Typically, uncertainty leads to a reduction in the level of an activity, such that marginal benefit exceeds marginal cost, with the difference equivalent to a risk premium. We find, instead, that the uncertain firm may explore to a point where expected marginal cost *exceeds* rent, the marginal benefit. *Whether it does so in fact depends on some key parameters in the exploration and extraction production functions, and the two-stage decision process, as well as the strength of the firm's aversion to risk* [second emphasis added].

Thus, their analysis indicates the importance of the physical relationships that have been identified by Harris and Skinner. Furthermore, it also leads to a number of interesting questions about the recent contributions to the literature on the economics of exhaustible resources. First, the complications discussed recently by Brown and Field (1979), and Fisher (1979) in developing measures of natural resource scarcity are compounded by uncertainty. Second, the informational benefits of exploration have not been incorporated in this model and require further attention. That is, exploration efforts that do not lead to discoveries are not valueless. They provide information on where deposits have not been found and, as a consequence, provide evidence that can be used to refine geochemical models of mineral occurrence. If this information is available to other participants in the exploration process, it seems reasonable to expect that it will influence levels of exploration activity. However, it may not be in a firm's interests to share this information. Thus, overall efficiency in resource allocation decisions may require public intervention.

In our review of the research issues associated with the differences between geological and economic conceptions of the physical constraints imposed by extractive natural resources, we have focused largely on models of a firm's behavior. Our discussion applies with equal force to aggregate modeling of the implications of resource exhaustion. However, in this case it reinforces the reservations raised by Lau (chapter 6) regarding the prospects for consistent measurement and modeling of the role of materials in economic activities at an aggregate level (i.e., above the end-use sectors). The prospects of aggregating the supply relationships associated with materials become doubtful given the significance of Harris and Skinner's analysis of the importance of physical attributes in occurrence, extraction, concentration, and refinement costs, and potential role in end uses.

Thus, serious reservations regarding current aggregate modeling practices in evaluating the role of materials can be raised from both the supply side (Harris and Skinner) and the demand side (Lau) of the analysis. We hope that these theoretical results, taken together with the experimental evidence of Kopp and Smith (chapter 7) promote serious theoretical *and* empirical analyses of the role of materials inputs at the micro level. This suggestion implies that, given the rather severe data limitations in such analyses (see Humphrey and Moroney, 1975; Moroney and Toevs, 1977; and Moroney and Trapani, 1978 for some discussion), a serious effort should also be made to develop a more adequate data base for the required research.

## *References*

Ayres, Robert U. 1978. *Resources, Environment and Economics* (New York, Wiley).

Barnett, Harold J. 1979. "Scarcity and Growth Revisited," in V. Kerry Smith, ed., *Scarcity and Growth Reconsidered* (Baltimore, Md., Johns Hopkins University Press for Resources for the Future) pp. 163–197.

———, and Chandler Morse. 1963. *Scarcity and Growth: The Economics of Natural Resource Availability* (Baltimore, Md., Johns Hopkins University Press for Resources for the Future).

Berndt, Ernst R. 1978. "Aggregate Energy, Efficiency, and Productivity Measurement," *Annual Review of Energy* vol. 3, pp. 225–273.

———, M. A. Fuss, and L. Waverman. 1977. *Dynamic Models of the Industrial Demand for Energy*, EPRI, EA 580 Research Project 683-1 (Palo Alto, Calif., Electric Power Research Institute).

———, and D. O. Wood. 1975. "Technology, Prices and the Derived Demand for Energy," *Review of Economics and Statistics* vol. 57, pp. 259–268.

Blackorby, Charles, and R. Robert Russell. 1976. "Functional Structure and the Allen Partial Elasticities of Substitution: An Application of Duality Theory," *Review of Economic Studies* vol. 43 (June) pp. 285–292.

Bohm, Peter. 1972. "Estimating Demand for Public Goods: An Experiment," *European Economic Review* vol. 3 (June) pp. 111–130.

Bower, Blair T. 1975. "Studies in Residuals Management in Industry," in E. S. Mills, ed., *Analysis of Environmental Problems* (New York, National Bureau of Economic Research).

Bradford, David F., and George G. Hildebrandt. 1977. "Observable Preferences for Public Goods," *Journal of Public Economics* vol. 8, pp. 111–131.

Brannon, Gerald M. 1975. "Existing Tax Differentials and Subsidies Relating to the Energy Industries," in G. M. Brannon, ed., *Studies in Energy Tax Policy* (Cambridge, Mass., Ballinger).

Britto, Ronald. 1973. "Some Recent Developments in the Theory of Economic Growth: An Interpretation," *Journal of Economic Literature* vol. 11 (December) pp. 1343–1366.

Brobst, Donald A. 1979. "Fundamental Concepts for the Analysis of Resource Availability," in V. Kerry Smith, ed., *Scarcity and Growth Reconsidered* (Baltimore, Md., Johns Hopkins University Press for Resources for the Future) pp. 106–136.

Brookshire, David S., Berry C. Ives, and William D. Schulze. 1976. "The Valuation of Aesthetic Preferences," *Journal of Environmental Economics and Management* vol. 3 (December) pp. 325–346.

Brown, Gardner M., and Barry Field. 1979. "The Adequacy of Measures for Signaling the Scarcity of Natural Resources," in V. Kerry Smith, ed., *Scarcity and Growth Reconsidered* (Baltimore, Md., Johns Hopkins University Press for Resources for the Future) pp. 218–245.

Burmeister, Edwin, and A. Rodney Dobell. 1970. *Mathematical Theories of Economic Growth* (New York, Macmillan).

Cicchetti, Charles J., and V. Kerry Smith. 1976. *The Costs of Congestion: An Econometric Analysis of Wilderness Recreation* (Cambridge, Mass., Ballinger).

Clark, Colin W. 1976. *Mathematical Bioeconomics* (New York, Wiley).

Clark, E. G. 1971. "Multipart Pricing of Public Goods," *Public Choice* vol. 11 (Fall) pp. 17–33.

Cowing, Thomas G. 1974. "Technical Change and Scale Economies in an Engineering Production Function: The Case of Steam Electric Power," *Journal of Industrial Economics* vol. 23, pp. 135–152.

———, and V. Kerry Smith. 1978. "The Estimation of a Production Technology—A Survey of Econometric Analyses of Steam-Electric Generation," *Land Economics* vol. 54, no. 2 (May).

Crocker, Thomas D., William D. Schulze, Shaul Ben-David, and Allen V. Kneese. 1979. "Experiments in the Economics of Air Pollution Epidemiology," Draft Report (Washington, D.C., Environmental Protection Agency).

Cropper, Maureen L. 1976. "Regulating Activities with Catastrophic Environmental Effects," *Journal of Environmental Economics and Management* vol. 3 (June) pp. 1–15.

Cummings, Ronald, and William D. Schulze. 1977. "Ramsey, Resources, and the Conservation of Mass-Energy," Paper presented at Conference on Natural Resources Pricing, Trail Lake, Wyoming, August.

Daly, Herman E. 1979. "Entrophy, Growth and the Political Economy of Scarcity," in V. Kerry Smith, ed., *Scarcity and Growth Reconsidered* (Baltimore, Md., Johns Hopkins University Press for Resources for the Future) pp. 67–85.

d'Arge, Ralph C., and K. C. Kogiku. 1973. "Economic Growth and the Environment," *Review of Economic Studies* vol. 40 (January) pp. 61–78.

Dasgupta, Partha, and Geoffrey M. Heal. 1979. *Economics of Exhaustible Resources* (Cambridge, England, Cambridge University Press).

Denny, Michael, and Melvin Fuss. 1977. "The Use of Approximation Analysis to Test for Separability and the Existence of Consistent Aggregates," *American Economic Review* vol. 67 (December) pp. 408–418.

Ferejohn, John A., Robert Forsythe, and Roger G. Noll. 1979. "Practical Aspects of the Construction of Decentralized Decisionmaking Systems for Public Goods," in Clifford S. Russell, ed., *Collective Decision Making: Applications from Public Choice Theory* (Baltimore, Md., Johns Hopkins University Press for Resources for the Future) pp. 173–188.

Fisher, Anthony C. 1979. "On Measures of Natural Resource Scarcity," in V. Kerry Smith, ed., *Scarcity and Growth Reconsidered* (Baltimore, Md., Johns Hopkins University Press for Resources for the Future) pp. 249–271.

——, John V. Krutilla, and Charles Cicchetti. 1972. "The Economics of Environmental Preservation: A Theoretical and Empirical Analysis," *American Economic Review* vol. 62, pp. 605–619.

——, and Frederick M. Peterson. 1976. "The Environment in Economics: A Survey," *Journal of Economic Literature* vol. 14 (March) pp. 1–23.

Fisher, Franklin M. 1969. "The Existence of Aggregate Production Functions," *Econometrica* vol. 37, pp. 553–577.

——. 1971. "Aggregate Production Functions and the Explanation of Wages: A Simulation Experiment," *Review of Economics and Statistics* vol. 53, pp. 305–325.

——, and K. Shell. 1972. *The Economic Theory of Price Indices* (New York, Academic Press).

——, Robert M. Solow, and James M. Kearl. 1977. "Aggregate Production Functions: Some CES Experiments," *Review of Economic Studies* vol. 44, pp. 305–320.

Freeman, A. Myrick, III. 1979. *The Benefits of Environmental Improvement* (Baltimore, Md., Johns Hopkins University Press for Resources for the Future).

Georgescu-Roegen, Nicholas. 1975. "Energy and Economic Myths," *Southern Economic Journal* vol. 41, pp. 347–381.

——. 1977. "The Steady State and Ecological Salvation: A Thermodynamic Analysis," *Bioscience* (April) pp. 266–270.

——. 1979. "Comments on Papers by Daly and Stiglitz," in V. Kerry Smith, ed., *Scarcity and Growth Reconsidered* (Baltimore, Md., Johns Hopkins University Press for Resources for the Future) p. 95.

Gilbert, Richard. 1976a. "Optimal Depletion of an Uncertain Stock," Technical Report No. 207 (Palo Alto, Calif., Stanford University Institute of Mathematical Studies and Social Sciences).

——. 1976b. "Search Strategies for Nonrenewable Resource Deposits," Technical Report No. 196 (Palo Alto, Calif., Stanford University Institute of Mathematical Studies and Social Sciences).

Goeller, Harold E., and Alvin M. Weinberg. 1976. "The Age of Substitutability," *Science* vol. 191, pp. 683–689.

Green, H. A. J. 1964. *Aggregation in Economic Analysis: An Introductory Survey* (Princeton, N.J., Princeton University Press).

Groves, Theodore, and John Ledyard. 1977. "Optimal Allocation of Public Goods: A Solution to the 'Free-Rider' Problem," *Econometrica* vol. 44, pp. 783–809.

Heal, Geoffrey. 1975. "Economic Aspects of Natural Resource Depletion," in David

W. Pearce, ed., *The Economics of Natural Resource Depletion* (New York, Wiley) pp. 118–139.

———. 1976. "The Relationship Between Price and Extraction Cost for a Resource with a Backstop Technology," *Bell Journal of Economics* vol. 7, no. 2, pp. 371–378.

———. 1977. "The Long-Run Movement of the Prices of Exhaustible Resources," Paper presented at the International Economic Association Conference on Economic Growth and Resources, Tokyo, Japan, September.

Herfindahl, Orris C. 1974. "Can Increasing Demands on Resources Be Met?" in David B. Brooks, ed., *Economics: Selected Works of Orris C. Herfindahl* (Baltimore, Md., Johns Hopkins University Press for Resources for the Future) pp. 274–277.

Hori, Hajime. 1975. "Revealed Preference for Public Goods," *American Economic Review* vol. 65 (December) pp. 978–991.

Hotelling, Harold. 1931. "The Economics of Exhaustible Resources," *Journal of Political Economy* vol. 39, pp. 137–175.

Houthakker, H. S. 1955–56. "The Pareto Distribution and the Cobb–Douglas Production Function in Activity Analysis," *Review of Economic Studies* vol. 23, pp. 27–31.

Humphrey, David B., and John R. Moroney. 1975. "Substitution Among Capital, Labor and Natural Resource Products in American Manufacturing," *Journal of Political Economy* vol. 83 (February) pp. 57–82.

Johansen, Leif. 1972. *Production Functions* (Amsterdam, North-Holland).

Judge, George C., M. E. Bock, and Thomas A. Yancey. 1974. "Post Data Model Evaluation," *Review of Economics and Statistics* vol. 56 (May).

Kamien, Morton I., and Nancy L. Schwartz. 1976. "The Optimal Resource Capital Ratio and Market Structure," Discussion Paper No. 233 (Evanston, Ill., Center for Mathematical Studies in Economic and Management Science, Northwestern University).

———, and ———. 1977. "A Note of Resource Usage and Market Structure," *Journal of Economic Theory* vol. 15, pp. 394–397.

———, and ———. 1975. "Market Structure and Innovation: A Survey," *Journal of Economic Literature* vol. 13 (March) pp. 1–37.

Kneese, Allen V., and Blair T. Bower. 1968. *Managing Water Quality: Economics, Technology, Institutions* (Baltimore, Md., Johns Hopkins University Press for Resources for the Future).

———, and William D. Schulze. 1977. "Environment, Health and Economics—The Case of Cancer," *American Economic Review* vol. 67, no. 1 (February) pp. 326–332.

Kopp, Raymond J. 1978. "The Impact of Pollution and Pollution Abatement Equipment on Technical Efficiency in the Steam Electric Power Industry" (Ph.D. Dissertation, State University of New York at Binghamton).

———, and V. Kerry Smith. 1980. "Input Substitution, Aggregation, and Engineering Descriptions of Production Activities," *Economic Letters* vol. 8, pp. 289–296.

Krutilla, John V., and Anthony C. Fisher. 1975. *The Economics of Natural Environments: Studies in the Valuation of Commodity and Amenity Resources* (Baltimore, Md., Johns Hopkins University Press for Resources for the Future).

Kurz, Mordechai M. 1968. "Optimal Economic Growth and Wealth Effects," *International Economic Review* vol. 9 (October) pp. 348–357.

Lau, Lawrence J. 1979. "On Exact Index Numbers," *Review of Economics and Statistics* vol. 61 (February) pp. 73–82.

Lave, Lester B., and Eugene P. Seskin. 1977. *Air Pollution and Human Health* (Baltimore, Md., Johns Hopkins University Press for Resources for the Future).

Leamer, Edward E. 1978. *Specification Searches: Ad Hoc Inference with Non-Experimental Data* (New York, Wiley).

Levhari, David. 1968. "A Note on Houthakker's Aggregate Production Function in a Multifirm Industry," *Econometrica* vol. 36, pp. 151–154.

Lewis, Tracey R., S. A. Mathews, and H. Stuart Burness. 1979. "Monopoly and the Rate of Extraction of Exhaustible Resources: Comment," *American Economic Review* vol. 69 (March) pp. 227–230.

Liviatan, Nissan, and Paul A. Samuelson. 1969. "Notes on Turnpikes: Stable and Unstable," *Journal of Economic Theory* vol. 1 (December) pp. 454–457.

Mäler, Karl-Göran. 1974. *Environmental Economics: A Theoretical Inquiry* (Baltimore, Md., Johns Hopkins University Press for Resources for the Future).

Marsden, James, David Pingry, and Andrew Whinston. 1974. "Engineering Foundations of Production Functions," *Journal of Economic Theory* vol. 9, pp. 124–140.

Moroney, John R., and Alden Toevs. 1977. "Factor Costs and Factor Use: An Analysis of Labor, Capital and Natural Resource Inputs," *Southern Economic Journal* vol. 44 (October) pp. 222–239.

———, and John Trapani. 1978. "Options for Conserving and Substituting for Nonfuel, Nonrenewable Resources in the United States" paper (Tulane University).

Morse, Chandler. 1976. "Depletion, Exhaustibility and Conservation," in William A. Vogley, ed., *Economics of the Mineral Industries* (New York, American Institute of Mining, Metallurgical and Petroleum Engineers).

Mosbaek, Ernest J., and Herman Wold. 1970. *Interdependent Systems: Structure and Estimation* (Amsterdam, North-Holland).

Muelbauer, John. 1974. "Household Production Theory, Quality, and the Hedonic Technique," *American Economic Review* vol. 64 (December) pp. 977–994.

Nadiri, M. I. 1970. "Some Approaches to the Theory and Measurement of Total Factor Productivity," *Journal of Economic Literature* vol. 8, pp. 1137–1177.

Nordhaus, William D. 1973. "The Allocation of Energy Resources," *Brookings Papers on Economic Activity* no. 3(a), pp. 529–570.

———. 1977. "Economic Growth and Climate: The Carbon Dioxide Problem," *American Economic Review* vol. 67, pp. 341–346.

———. 1974. "Resources as a Constraint on Growth," *American Economic Review* vol. 64, pp. 22–26.

Ohta, M. 1975. "Production Technologies of U.S. Boiler and Turbogenerator Industries and Hedonic Price Indexes for their Products: A Cost Function Approach," *Journal of Political Economy* vol. 83 (February) pp. 1–26.

Page, R. Talbot. 1977. *Conservation and Economic Efficiency* (Baltimore, Md., Johns Hopkins University Press for Resources for the Future).

Pearce, David W. 1976. "The Limits to Cost-Benefit Analysis as a Guide to Environmental Policy," *Kyklos* vol. 29, pp. 97–112.

Peterson, Frederick M. 1975. "Two Externalities in Petroleum Exploitation," in G. M. Brannon, ed., *Studies in Energy Tax Policy* (Cambridge, Mass., Ballinger).

————, and Anthony C. Fisher. 1977. "The Exploitation of Renewable and Nonrenewable Natural Resources," *Economic Journal* vol. 85, pp. 681–721.

Pindyck, Robert S. 1978. "The Optimal Exploration and Production of Nonrenewable Resources," *Journal of Political Economy* vol. 86, no. 5 (October) pp. 841–862.

Plourde, C. B. 1972. "A Model of Waste Accumulation and Disposal," *Canadian Journal of Economics* vol. 5, pp. 119–125.

Radcliffe, S. Victor. 1976. "World Changes and Chances: Some New Perspectives for Materials," *Science* vol. 191 (February) pp. 700–707.

Rosen, Sherwin. 1974. "Hedonic Prices and Implicit Markets: Production Differentiation in Pure Competition," *Journal of Political Economy* vol. 82 (January/February) pp. 34–55.

Russell, Clifford S. 1973. *Residuals Management in Industry: A Case Study of Petroleum Refining* (Baltimore, Md., Johns Hopkins University Press for Resources for the Future).

————, and William J. Vaughan. 1976. *Steel Production: Processes, Products, and Residuals* (Baltimore, Md., Johns Hopkins University Press for Resources for the Future).

Ryder, Hal E., Jr., and Geoffrey M. Heal. 1973. "Optimum Growth with Intertemporally Dependent Preferences," *Review of Economic Studies* vol. 40, pp. 1–32.

Sasser, W. Earl. 1970. "A Finite-Sample Study of Various Simultaneous Equation Estimators" (Ph.D. Dissertation, Duke University, Durham, N.C.).

Sato, Kauzo. 1975. *Production Functions and Aggregation* (Amsterdam, North-Holland).

Schulze, William D. 1974. "The Optimal Use of Non-Renewable Resources: The Theory of Extraction," *Journal of Environmental Economics and Management* vol. 1, pp. 53–73.

Scott, Anthony. 1962. "The Development of the Extractive Industries," *Canadian Journal of Economics and Political Science* vol. 28, pp. 70–87.

Smith, V. Kerry. 1977. "Cost-Benefit Analysis and Environmental Policy: A Comment," *Kyklos* vol. 30, pp. 310–313.

————. 1973. *Monte Carlo Methods: Their Role for Econometrics* (Lexington, Mass., D.C. Heath).

————. 1979. "Indirect Revelation of the Demand for Public Goods: An Overview and Critique," *Scottish Journal of Political Economy* vol. 26, no. 2 (June) pp. 183–189.

————, ed. 1979. *Scarcity and Growth Reconsidered* (Baltimore, Md., Johns Hopkins University Press for Resources for the Future).

————, and John V. Krutilla. 1979. "Resource and Environmental Constraints to Growth," *American Journal of Agricultural Economics* vol. 61, no. 3 (August) pp. 395–408.

————, and William J. Vaughan. 1980. "The Implications of Model Complexity for Environmental Management," *Journal of Environmental Economics and Management* vol. 7, no. 3 (September) pp. 184–208.

Smith, V. L. 1977. "Control Theory Applied to Natural and Environmental Resources: An Exposition," *Journal of Environmental Economics and Management* vol. 4 (March) pp. 1–24.

Solow, Robert M. 1974a. "The Economics of Resources or the Resources of Economics," *American Economic Review* vol. 64, pp. 1–14.

————. 1974b. "Intergenerational Equity and Exhaustible Resources," in *The Review of Economic Studies*, Symposium on the Economics of Exhaustible Resources, pp. 29–46.

——, and F. Y. Wan. 1976. "Extraction Costs in the Theory of Exhaustible Resources," *Bell Journal of Economics* vol. 7, pp. 359–379.

Spencer, V. E. 1973. "Raw Materials in the United States, 1900–1969," Working Paper no. 35 (Washington, D.C., U.S. Department of Commerce, Bureau of Census).

Stevens, Joe B. 1966. "Recreation Benefits from Water Pollution Control," *Water Resources Research* vol. 2, no. 2, pp. 167–182.

Stewart, John F. 1979. "Plant Size, Plant Factor, and the Shape of the Average Cost Function in Electric Power Generation: A Non-homogeneous Capital Approach," *Bell Journal of Economics* vol. 10, no. 2 (Autumn) pp. 549–565.

Stiglitz, Joseph. 1979. "A Neoclassical Analysis of the Economics of Natural Resources," in V. Kerry Smith, ed., *Scarcity and Growth Reconsidered* (Baltimore, Md., Johns Hopkins University Press for Resources for the Future).

Theil, Henry. 1961. *Economic Forecasts and Policy* (Amsterdam, North-Holland).

Thompson, Russell G., et al. 1977. *The Costs of Electricity* (Houston, Texas, Gulf Publishing Co.).

Tiebout, Charles. 1956. "A Pure Theory of Local Expenditures," *Journal of Political Economy* vol. 64 (October) pp. 416–424.

Vickrey, William. 1967. "Economic Criteria for Optimum Rates of Depletion," in Mason Gaffney, ed., *Extractive Resources and Taxation* (Madison, University of Wisconsin).

Wallace, T. Dudley. 1977. "Pretest Estimation in Regression: A Survey," *American Journal of Agricultural Economics* vol. 59 (August) pp. 431–443.

——. 1972. "Weaker Criteria and Tests for Linear Restrictions in Regression," *Econometrica*, pp. 689–698.

Zeckhauser, Richard, and Anthony C. Fisher. 1976. "Averting Behavior and External Diseconomies" (Department of Economics, University of Maryland).

Zimmerman, E. W. 1964. *Introduction to World Resources* (New York, Harper & Row).

# PART II
# MODELING THE ROLE
# OF NATURAL RESOURCES
# IN ECONOMIC GROWTH

# 2

## The Role of Common Property Resources in Optimal Planning Models with Exhaustible Resources

Morton I. Kamien and Nancy L. Schwartz

According to *The Limits to Growth* (Meadows and coauthors, 1972), the world is destined to end either by starvation, exhaustion, or suffocation, unless a limit is imposed on population growth and industrialization. The first of these sources of doom was recognized at least as far back as Malthus. The second goes back at least as far as Jevons. The third appears to be of a much more recent vintage. The direness of the message, however, is not in the identification of the individual sources of doom, but in the claim that they work in concert. If society escapes one, it runs into another. Some persons have responded to this warning by calling for a halt to economic growth and a transition to a steady-state economy (see, e.g., Daly, 1973), perhaps with direct sunlight as the primary source of energy (Georgescu-Roegen, 1976). Others have responded by reexamining these claims in terms of the neoclassical economic growth framework; the papers by Solow (1974) and Stiglitz (1979) synthesize these responses. A major weakness in these responses has been that they have occurred in a piecemeal fashion.

An optimal aggregative economic planning model that is to give policy makers some guidance must take into account the essentiality and exhaustibility of certain natural resources. These natural resources are both marketed, such as fossil fuels and other extractive resources, and nonmarketed, such as clean air and water and other amenity or environmental resources. Economic theorists have dealt with each of these facets separately. There are prototypical, dynamic economic models of optimal growth, of optimal extractive resource exploitation, and of optimal pollution (the use of an amenity

The authors gratefully acknowledge the suggestions of V. Kerry Smith and other participants in the conference that produced this volume.

resource). Each of these three prototypes has been considerably researched, with a myriad extensions and modifications. More recently, some researchers have combined aspects of two of the three prototypes to achieve a more comprehensive model. As yet, there has been no successful attempt to meld all three components into a single unified treatment. The reason, we believe, is not lack of interest or failure to recognize the desirability of such integration, but rather the technical difficulty of deriving useful insights from models incorporating all three features nontrivially.

This chapter briefly reviews the state of economic theory with respect to these three areas, focusing on the literature that accommodates pairs of features. We outline a program of research that we believe can be fruitfully followed to gain insights on optimal aggregative planning in the presence of both exhaustible extractive resources and common property environmental resources.

## 1. The Literature

### Capital

The prototypical economic growth model stems from the work of Ramsey (1928). In it, the single produced good is divided between current consumption $C$, yielding immediate utility or satisfaction $U(C)$, and investment $K'$ to enlarge the economy's future productive capacity $K$ so as to maximize the present value of the utility stream over the future. Thus,

$$\begin{array}{c} \text{maximize} \\ C \geq 0 \end{array} \int_0^T e^{-rt} U(C) dt \tag{1}$$

$$\text{subject to } K' = f(K) - C - hK, \quad K(0) = K_0, \quad K \geq 0 \tag{2}$$

where $C = C(t)$ and $K = K(t)$ are functions of time to be chosen and $K' = dK/dt$. The production function $f(K)$ gives the rate of output of the produced good from the stock of productive capital $K$. The functions $U$ and $f$ are assumed to be concave and nondecreasing throughout. The discount rate $r$ and the rate of decay (depreciation) $h$ of capital are nonnegative parameters.

Investigations with this model include studying the impact of the choice of horizon $T$, the discount rate $r$, and the depreciation rate $h$. Modifications defy listing here, but include incorporation of an explicit labor force that is a factor of production as well as the consumer and that may grow exogenously or endogenously; differentiated producer goods and final goods; and exogenous and endogenous technical advances. Throughout these analyses, however, the possibility of an exhaustible resource is ignored, implying the tacit supposition that either no nonreproducible resource is in finite supply or that substitution of capital for the nonreproducible resource is unlimited. See, for example, Burmeister and Dobell (1970, chapter 11) or Intriligator (1971, chapter 16) for a summary exposition of the basic work done in extending Ramsey's pioneering model; Britto (1973, section VI), for a brief update; and Shell (1967) for a collection of representative papers.

### Exhaustible Resources

The prototypical model of optimal exhaustible resource extraction is commonly attributed to Hotelling (1931). In its simplest form, a finite stock is to be allocated over time to maximize the present value of the discounted stream of utility received from consuming the resource (or its product). Thus

$$\underset{R \geq 0}{\text{maximize}} \quad \int_0^T e^{-rt} U(R)dt \tag{3}$$

$$\text{subject to } S' = -R, \quad S(0) = S_0, \quad S \geq 0 \tag{4}$$

where $R = R(t)$ is the resource extraction rate, $S = S(t)$ is the remaining stock of the resource, $U(R)$ is the utility obtained from the resource or good manufactured with its aid, and $r$ is the nonnegative discount rate. The horizon $T$ may be given exogenously, or it may be chosen optimally. The effect of market structure on the extraction rate and comparison with the consumer-surplus-maximizing rate are among the major policy questions addressed with this model.

Some of the extensions of this model were made by Hotelling himself, and some have appeared subsequently. The resource may be extracted only at a cost, and this cost may depend upon the amount already withdrawn. According to Hotelling (1931), the utility depends not only on the extraction rate but also on the remaining stock; $U(R)$ is replaced by $U(R,S)$. Equivalently from a mathematical viewpoint, the remaining stock may affect current utility because of some psychic factor, such as a conservation motive (Vousden, 1973; Banks, 1974) or an induced change in taste (Manning, 1978). An exogenous but foreseen shift in the utility function can affect the optimal extraction pattern (Kemp and Long, 1977). The resource may be renewable—fish, forests, and game animals reproduce. Then equation (4) is replaced by $S' = g(S) - R$, where $g(S)$ is the natural growth rate of the resource when the current stock is $S$ (see, for example, Pielou, 1969, and Clark, 1976). There may be multiple grades of the resource, each withdrawn at a cost specific to that grade (see Schulze, 1974). The total available stock may be augmented by exploration at a cost; then one seeks an optimal exploration and extraction policy (see Peterson, 1978; Pindyck, 1978; and Lewis,

1977). There may be uncertainty about the stock on hand (see Kemp, 1976), about the stock available to be found, about future availability and characteristics of substitutes that are as yet undiscovered (Hoel, 1978b). Technical advance may be endogenous or exogenous, gradual or discrete, and may affect the efficiency of the extraction, the productivity of the resource, or the features and availability of a substitute productive factor. See Schulze (1974) and Smith (1977) for expositions of control theory models of natural resource exploitation, and Peterson and Fisher (1977) for a more comprehensive survey of the exploitation of extractive resources.

Pollution

The prototypical aggregative pollution model (Forster 1973a) can be written as

$$\text{maximize} \int_0^T e^{-rt} U(C,P)dt \tag{5}$$

$$\text{subject to } P' = Z(C) - bP, \quad P(0) = P_0 \tag{6}$$

where $P = P(t)$ is the stock of pollution and $C = C(t)$ is the consumption rate. Utility varies directly with the rate of consumption and inversely with the level of pollution. The function $Z(C)$ is the rate of addition to pollution when consumption is at rate $C$. The nonnegative parameter $b$ is the rate of decay of the pollution stock caused by the self-cleansing ability of the environment. In this formulation, the function $Z(C)$ is a summary statement and permits the pollution to be associated with the implicit production process or with consumption. Pollution abatement may be implicit in the function, as $Z(C) = g(C) - f(Q - C)$ may be the difference between the pollution generated $g(C)$ by consuming $C$ and the pollution abated $f(Q - C)$ by diverting $Q - C$ of the output $Q$ from consumption to pollution control.

Extensions of the basic formulation have incorporated an explicit labor force, whose efforts may be divided among production of the consumption good, pollution control, and recycling of the waste (pollution) into a productive factor or into a harmless residue (see Plourde, 1972, and Lusky, 1976). Pollution $P$ may enter the objective smoothly (typical case) or abruptly, with no real disutility experienced until the pollution level reaches a particular, perhaps unknown, critical level (Cropper, 1976). The effect of pollution decaying according to a generalized function has also been explored (Forster, 1975). See Fisher and Peterson, 1976, for a survey of the treatment of the environment in economics.

### Capital and Exhaustible Resources

During the 1970's, work began on melding the optimal growth model with the exhaustible resource model. A representative version is

$$\text{maximize} \quad \int_0^T e^{-rt} U(C)dt \tag{7}$$

$$\text{subject to } X' = R, \quad X(0) = X_0, \quad X \le S_0 \tag{8}$$

$$K' = F(K,R) - C, \quad K(0) = K_0, \quad K \ge 0 \tag{9}$$

Nonnegative paths of consumption $C = C(t)$ and resource extraction $R = R(t)$ are to be chosen to maximize the present value of the stream of utilities from consumption. Both a produced factor, capital $K = K(t)$, and the extractive resource are used in producing the single output, $F(K,R)$. The output is divided between current consumption and investment in the capital good. The capital good may depreciate, in which case equation (9) would be modified on the right by a term $-hK$, as in the previous capital model. A labor force, perhaps one that is growing, may also be included, and technical advance can be incorporated.

Anderson (1972) analyzed a model in which there are three productive factors: capital, labor, and an extractive resource. Capital and labor are substitutes, in the usual neoclassical fashion, but the rate of resource depletion is proportional to the rate of output. This proportion decreases through time because of exogenous technical advance that permits more efficient use of the exhaustible resource. Anderson concluded that the inclusion of the exhaustible resource in the optimal growth model results in a tendency to postpone capital accumulation and to use capital less intensively because of the need to conserve on the complementary use of the depletable resource.

Mäler's second paradigm (1974, chapter 3) involves two resource deposits that are exploited with the aid of capital. Final output is produced with capital and uses the extractive resource in a quantity proportional to output, as in Anderson's model. Mäler finds that, in the absence of discounting, the best deposit will be used first if the economy is growing, but it will be saved for later (when capital rents are larger) in case the initial endowment of capital is so large that the economy is optimally contracting. If future utilities are discounted, then for the case of an expanding economy the conclusion is reinforced, but it becomes ambiguous for a contracting economy.

The 1974 symposium issue of the *Review of Economic Studies* contains a number of papers addressing optimal growth models with exhaustible resources. Dasgupta and Heal (1974) start from a framework as given in equations (7) through (9) and show that consumption may optimally rise for a time, but will eventually peak and fall. The resource extraction rate tends to fall throughout. The elasticity of substitution between capital and the resource in production plays an important role in the long-run behavior. Dasgupta and Heal also allow a discrete exogenous technical advance at an uncertain future time that releases the constraint imposed by the resource. If capital and resource stocks become worthless upon the advent of new technology, then the uncertainty over the timing of the technological change is formally equivalent to an appropriate increase in the discount rate.

Solow (1974) explored the largest sustainable level of consumption in a model in which the productive factors are capital, labor, and an exhaustible resource, and in which there is steady exogenous technical progress. The population may grow. Stiglitz's model is similar but the objective is of the usual form [equation (7)]. In these cases, it is shown that sufficiently rapid exogenous technical progress can offset the limitations of the exhaustible resource.

Ingham and Simmons (1975) explored a model with no discounting and a growing population. They concur with earlier writers that the elasticity of factor substitution is an important parameter in determining the nature of the solution path. They report solution patterns similar to those of Dasgupta and Heal and Solow for the case of a Cobb–Douglas production function, despite the different objectives assumed in the three papers.

Koopmans (1973) has combined the models by making the objective an additive function of both consumption and the resource extraction rate, subject to equations (2) and (4). He shows that the shadow price of the resource grows approximately exponentially (at rate $r$) relative to that of the consumption good.

Several integrative models and surveys of the relevant literature were produced in 1977 (Ayres, 1977; Blank, Anderson, and d'Arge, 1977). Cummings and Schulze (1977) worked with a model as given in equations (7)–(9), modified to reflect a materials balance requirement that the resource usage rate be an upper bound on the output rate at any time. Then the solution has two phases. During the first, the materials balance constraint is not tight, and the solution involves the familiar increasing use of capital as resource usage declines. However, the materials balance constraint imposes an upper bound on $K/R;$ once it is reached, capital and the resource cease to be substitutes and are complementary, reminiscent of Anderson (1972) and Mäler (1974).

The impact of extraction costs has been explored by several researchers. Solow and Wan (1976) modified Solow's (1974) earlier model by supposing that the producible output is needed to extract the resource and that there is more than one grade of the resource (measured by differences in the cost of extracting a single unit). The most striking finding was that the numerical examples suggest a relative insensitivity of the maintainable consumption level (the objective) to the size of the resource endowment.

Heal (1976) also assumes that the resource extraction consumes some of the produced output. However he supposes a backstop technology that provides an upper bound to the unit cost of extraction. The optimal solution in the absence of a backstop technology shows the implicit price of the resource differing from the marginal extraction cost by an exponentially growing amount. This deviation is attributable to the limited and decreasing remaining supply. In Heal's model, in contrast, the difference between implicit price and marginal extraction cost falls toward zero as use of the backstop becomes more imminent. The supply is unbounded (due to the backstop) and the deviation is attributable to the fact that present extraction, by depleting a lower cost deposit, raises the future extraction costs.

Hanson (1978) has explored the sensitivity of results to the assumed extraction technology in another way. Suppose there are two homogeneous exhaustible resources with different extraction costs. Then, as has been shown by others, the lower cost resource is typically depleted first and the higher cost resource is used thereafter. However, Hanson shows that if the alternative resources are not perfect substitutes, so that the final production function is strictly concave, there will be a transition period during which both resources are employed.

Finally, productive factors may be diverted into research and development for a substitute that replaces the irreplenishable resources (Kamien and Schwartz, 1978a; Davison, 1978; Dasgupta, Heal, and Majumdar, 1976). Davison's model differs from the others in the research and development function, so input is a stock rather than a flow. He finds that capital for R&D and consumption both decrease over time, while the other authors found that R&D effort and consumption might rise over some initial period before ultimately falling (if the new technology is not yet forthcoming).


Exhaustible Resources and Pollution

The work combining both the extractive resource and environmental resources is diverse in its modeling details. d'Arge and Kogiku (1973) permit the objective to increase with consumption and the remaining resource stock and decrease with the waste density in the environment. The objective function may also depend on the time at which the exhaustible resource is depleted (the endogenous horizon). Output is produced by the extractive resource. Waste accumulates from production (related to the resource extraction rate) and from consumption. D'Arge and Kogiku find that the extractive resource rate and hence consumption will eventually rise. High consumption rates are postponed until they are needed to compensate for the increasing disutility imposed by the rising waste density. D'Arge and Kogiku extended their model to include capital for recycling.

Lusky (1975) offered a model in which labor and the extractive resource are productive factors. The objective depends on the resource extraction rate, the resource stock, and leisure, that is, labor available but not used for extraction or recycling. A fraction of the resource extracted and consumed is waste that can be recycled, via labor, to be used again. Interest was focused on tax-subsidy schemes by which the socially optimal solution could be realized by a decentralized economy. In a special case it is shown that the fraction of waste that is recycled varies inversely with the remaining stock, with no recycling if the remaining stock is sufficiently large.

Beckmann (1975) discussed a model in which utility depends on consumption of goods and on the levels of certain environmental quality variables. Exhaustible resources and produced goods are inputs. The outputs can be consumed or used as factors of production. The quality variables are modified by the productive activities and also by the use of factors for quality modification. All the production functions are of the Cobb–Douglas form, with exogenous technical progress. Beckmann finds that a sufficiently large rate of technical progress can prevent the decline in the rate of output, offsetting the limitations of the irreplenishable resource.

Forster (1977) explored three models using pollution and an exhaustible resource. In the first, the exhaustible resource is the sole productive factor. It yields consumption and a pollution flow (nonaccumulating). Forster finds that if the horizon is short, the environmental considerations prevail, but if the horizon is long, the environment is ignored and the usual resource extraction rule is followed.

In the second model, pollution can accumulate and it can be abated by applying some of the extractive resource to that end. Forster finds that resources should not be used for pollution abatement; rather the extraction rate (for consumption) should be limited to reduce pollution in the early period. The optimal extraction rate rises over time. Finally, Forster admits a renewable source of the sole productive factor, to augment that obtained by extraction. The flow of resource therefrom is proportional to the plant size, which is set at the beginning of the planning period. Forster finds that this alternative lowers the rate of use of the depletable resource and thereby extends the planning horizon within which the environment is a relevant planning consideration.

Schulze (1974) presented a model in which the extractive resource is enjoyed but some fraction of it becomes waste. The waste can be recovered at a cost and recycled for consumption. Schulze also finds that if the time horizon is sufficiently distant, the extraction rate will eventually increase. Hoel's (1978a) model is similar, except that there is no limit on the amount of material available for recycling; thus the recycling activity can also be interpreted as production via a backstop technology. Analyses were undertaken under alternative suppositions about the disutility of residuals, assimilative ability of the environment, and other parameters. Hoel found that extraction takes place first, at a decreasing rate, followed by recycling at a constant or decreasing rate.


Capital and Pollution

Economic growth models with environmental considerations have received relatively little attention. Keeler, Spence, and Zeckhauser (1971) offer a half dozen models, suggest different modeling possibilities, and recommend future relaxation of assumptions. In the first model, utility depends on consumption and the pollution stock. The sole productive factor is capital, which is divided among consumption, pollution control, and capital accumulation. They find that the solution can tend to a steady state. Other models involve labor as the productive factor or pollution having disutility as it is produced, or both.

Forster (1973b) developed a simple model in which pollution is a flow accompanying production of the final good. Pollution can be reduced by applying the final good to pollution control. Capital is the single productive factor. Thus the final good is to be optimally divided among current consumption, pollution abatement, and investment. Forster is able to compare the steady-state solution of this model with that of the corresponding model in which pollution is ignored; he finds the steady-state capital and consumption levels are both lower when pollution is taken into account.

In Gruver's (1976) model, pollution is a flow that accompanies production but can be reduced through application of pollution control capital. Capital is also used for production of the final good, which can be consumed or invested. Thus the decision variables are the fraction of current output allocated to consumption, the division of the capital investment between production and pollution abatement, and the division of current output between consumption and investment. In the absence of discounting and with simple separable functional forms, Gruver finds that capital will be devoted solely to production during the early period, with investment to reduce pollution following later. He believes these tendencies are robust with respect to more general functional forms and in the presence of discounting.

Finally, in this volume Heal in chapter 3 has reinterpreted a model of Ryder and Heal (1973) so that pollution enters the prototypical capital growth model. The pollution stock grows with consumption and is subject to natural decay. It is an argument in the utility function along with consumption. The standard capital equation completes the model [see equation (2)]. The introduction of pollution into the standard capital model qualitatively affects the solution. The steady state no longer need be unique, so the state approached may depend on the initial conditions. Further, the optimal path may involve cycles rather than a monotone path.

Capital, Exhaustible Resources, and Pollution

There has been just one notable attempt to develop a model of aggregative economic planning that incorporates irreplenishable factors of production, environmental quality, and reproducible capital, namely, that given as Mäler's fourth paradigm (1974, chapter 3). As in his second paradigm discussed earlier, production employs capital according to a concave function and also the extractive resource in fixed proportion, reflecting the materials balance viewpoint. The produced output can be consumed, invested in productive capital, or invested in capital for recycling waste into productive raw material. Environmental quality is a stock $Y$ whose value ranges between zero (bad) and 1 (excellent), and whose time rate of change is given by

$$Y' = a(1 - Y) - bz \tag{10}$$

where $a$ and $b$ are given parameters and $z$ represents the net discharge of residuals into the environment. (This differential equation was derived to describe the concentration of pollutants in a lake. It incorporates consideration of the pollutant discharges to the lake and the water outflow from the lake. It may be suitable for a wide array of applications.) The parameter $a$ reflects the self-purification ability of the environment. While Mäler's model is attractive, it is sufficiently complex that it is amenable to little more than a statement of the necessary conditions obeyed by an optimal solution.

The dearth of satisfactory models dealing with all three components may be due to the analytical difficulty of learning something from a model with more than one state variable. We propose a formulation that we believe will be amenable to analysis. Not only will this permit conclusions to be drawn about economic planning that take these considerations into account, but it will also be a vehicle for studying the sensitivity to modifications in parameters and other assumptions of the formulation. The current literature is not particularly amenable to widespread parametric analysis because some of the essential features are missing from each model, and because the modeling is so diverse. Slight variations invite comparisons; gross differences support the conviction that the assumptions affect the conclusions.

## 2. Our Proposal

We present a general characterization of the problem, and then discuss the solution of a specific case. Finally, we will indicate generalizations that may be amenable to analysis. The problem will be posed from the standpoint of a social planner seeking to maximize the present value of the utility stream to a society composed of a fixed number of identical individuals.

Let $C(t)$ be the aggregative consumption rate at time $t$; $K(t)$ the stock of productive capital at time $t$; $R(t)$ the natural resource extraction rate at time

$t$; $P(t)$ the stock of pollution at time $t$; and $X(t)$ the cumulative extraction by time $t$.

Then, suppressing the argument $t$, the problem is to

$$\underset{C \geq 0, R \geq 0}{\text{maximize}} \int_0^\infty e^{-rt} U(C,P)dt \tag{11}$$

subject to

$$X' = R, \quad X(0) = 0, \quad X \leq S \tag{12}$$

$$K' = F(K,R,P,X) - C - hK, \quad K(0) = K_0, \quad K > 0 \tag{13}$$

$$P' = G(K,R,P,X,C) - bP, \quad P(0) = P_0 \tag{14}$$

Utility $U$ at any time is an increasing function of the consumption rate and a nonincreasing function of the stock of pollution. Equation (12) assures that cumulative extraction never exceeds the initial endowment $S$ of the resource.

In equation (13), $F$ denotes the production function for the single produced good of fixed quality. Output increases with either productive factor (capital or extractive resource) and may decrease with the stock of pollution or cumulative resource extraction. The first two arguments are familiar. The adverse effect of pollution may be attributable to the use of environmental factors, such as air or water. To the extent that pollution degrades these environmental inputs, more capital or extractive resource may be needed to offset this effect (perhaps by cleaning the environmental factor so it is fit for use). Cumulative extraction may enter the production function if increasing amounts of factors are required for extraction as the most accessible deposits are depleted, or if successively lower grades of the resource are less productive.

Equation (13) indicates that the current output can be divided among current consumption $C$, restitution of the depreciating capital stock $hK$ (where $h$ is the given nonnegative depreciation rate), or stock augmentation $K'$. The capital stock is given initially and may not become negative. This formulation permits capital to be consumed.

Equation (14) governs the pollution stock. Pollution may increase as a by-product of extraction, production, consumption, or capital depreciation. It may be reduced by applying factors to pollution control or cleansing. All this can be taken into account in a general way by letting the pollution augmentation function $G$ depend on all the other variables. The natural absorptive and self-cleansing capacity of the environment is taken into account by letting the pollution stock decay at a constant proportionate rate $b$.

In case there is some absolute limit $\overline{P}$ on the total stock of pollution that can be tolerated, $P$ can be bounded above: $P \leq \overline{P}$. It seems preferable that the limit be implicit in the specification of the utility function $U$ [as $V(C,P)$

$\rightarrow -\infty$ as $P \rightarrow P_1$] or of the production function [as $F(K,R,P,X) \rightarrow 0$ as $P \rightarrow P_2$]. The former indicates that as pollution approaches a certain level, no amount of the consumption good could compensate for the disutility imposed by the pollution. The second reflects the assumption that if pollution were to approach a certain level, production would become impossible despite however much of the productive factors might be applied.

The model outlined in equations (11) through (14) of this section, while quite general in certain respects, omits several important features that we believe to be necessary in a complete study. First, the model omits renewable resources. Second, no provision has been made for recycling pollution into productive factors. Third, technical advance should be incorporated; productive factors might be applied to develop a producible substitute for the exhaustible resource, to develop an alternative technology that makes more efficient use of the limited amount of extractive factor, or reduces the polluting nature of current economic activities. The fourth is uncertainty. There may be uncertainty about the total stock of extractive resource available. Further, the research and development activity mentioned may be subject to uncertainty both with regard to the amount of research effort (i.e., factor employment) required to produce a technical advance and also with regard to the specifics of the advance achieved (scope, magnitude, implications). The fifth is decentralization. What type of market structure will reliably generate and implement the optimal solution that would be computed by a social planner? How should the market be supplemented to assure the desired result? The sixth is an explicit labor force and population growth. One question in this regard is the limit to population growth that is imposed by the extractive and absorptive resources. We believe that all these features must be taken into account, but have omitted them from the preliminary work on this project (although we have addressed some of them in earlier works).

To illustrate the mode of analysis and the nature of results to be anticipated, we now specialize equations (11)-(14). First, we assume that the environment has no self-cleansing ability, so that pollution does not decay naturally ($b = 0$). Second, pollution is associated with the extractive resource only and grows in direct proportion with the rate of use. Consequently, we may take $P \equiv X$ and hence $G \equiv R$. Third, we assume the harmful effects of pollution are felt directly only in the productive sector. That is, pollution does not enter into the utility function. Indirectly, the effect of pollution is ubiquitous because it reduces the yield of output of fixed quality from the productive factors.

Further, we assume the specific form of utility function

$$U(C) = \ln C \tag{15}$$

This is a commonly employed increasing concave function. Fourth, we assume the capital stock does not depreciate, so $h = 0$. Fifth, we assume the production function takes the form

$$Q \equiv F(K,R,X) = AK^{1-a}R^a/g(X) \tag{16}$$

where $0 < a < 1$ and $g > 0$, $g' \geq 0$. The numerator is the common, constant returns, Cobb–Douglas form, where $A$ and $a$, the output elasticity of the extractive resource, are given constants. The factor $g(X)$ allows output from given factor inputs $K$, $R$ to decline as the stock of pollution grows. An advantage of this specification is that the special case of no deleterious effects from pollution is obtained by letting $g(X) \equiv 1$. In this way, we will be able to consider the benchmark case $g(X) \equiv 1$, along with the general case of increasing $g$. Since $g$ is a nondecreasing function, we may assume either

$$\lim_{X \to \overline{X}} g(X) = \infty \text{ for some } \overline{X} < S \tag{17}$$

or

$$g(X) < \infty \text{ for all } X \leq S \tag{18}$$

In case equation (17) holds, production becomes impossible as the pollution stock (that is, cumulative extraction) approaches the level $\overline{X}$. In equation (18), production is possible for all levels of pollution that are attainable. In either case, we can let $\overline{S}$ denote the least upper bound on $X$:

$$\overline{S} = \begin{cases} \overline{X}, \text{ if equation (17) holds} \\ S, \text{ if equation (18) holds} \end{cases} \tag{19}$$

With all these specializations, equations (11) to (14) become

$$\underset{C \geq 0, R \geq 0}{\text{maximize}} \int_0^\infty e^{-rt} \ln C \, dt \tag{20}$$

subject to

$$X' = R, \quad X(0) = 0, \quad X \leq \overline{S} \tag{21}$$

$$K' = AK^{1-a}R^a/g(X) - C, \quad K(0) = K_0 > 0, \quad K \geq 0 \tag{22}$$

Necessary conditions for solution of this optimal control problem are developed in the appendix to this chapter. The solution is characterized below; appendix equation numbers are listed for reference to the relevant development there. Some notation is introduced to facilitate compact statement of results.

Define the function $f(t;k)$ by

$$f(t;k) = k^{(a-1)/a} \int_t^\infty e^{-rs}(k + as)^{-1} ds, \quad t \geq 0, \quad k > 0 \tag{23}$$

While a closed-form analytical expression for $f$ is not available, it is readily shown that $0 < f(t;k) < e^{-rt}/r(k + at)k^{(1-a)/a}$. Using equation (23), we then define the function $f^*(k)$ by

$$f^*(k) \equiv k^{1/a}f(0;k)/\int_0^\infty f(t;k)dt \qquad (24)$$

Further, define $g^*(X)$ by

$$g^*(X) = \int g^{-1/a}(X)dX \qquad (25)$$

For example, if $g(X) = 1$, then $g^*(X) = X$. If $g(X) = (1 + X)^{an}$, then $g^*(X) = (1 + X)^{1-n}/(1 - n)$. Next, let the value of the parameter $k$ be given implicitly by equation (26) [see also equation (A.29)]:

$$f^*(k) = K_0 A^{-1/a}/[g^*(\overline{S}) - g^*(0)] \qquad (26)$$

and then $C_0$, the optimal initial consumption rate, will be

$$C_0 = K_0/k^{1/a} f(0;k) \qquad (27)$$

[see also equation (A.22)]. In equation (28) [see also equation (A.19)], we obtain the optimal consumption plan

$$C(t) = C_0 e^{-rt}(1 + at/k)^{(1-a)/a} \qquad (28)$$

the optimal capital plan [see also equation (A.21)],

$$K(t) = C_0 f(t;k)(k + at)^{1/a} \qquad (29)$$

and the optimal production rate [see also equation (A.23)],

$$Q(t) = C_0 f(t;k)(k + at)^{(1-a)/a} \qquad (30)$$

Note that the optimal capital/output ratio grows linearly at rate $a$, the output elasticity of the extractive resource:

$$K(t)/Q(t) = k + at \qquad (31)$$

It is now apparent that the ubiquitous constant $k$ [whose value is specified in equation (26)] is in fact the optimal initial capital/output ratio.

Cumulative extraction $X(t)$ is given implicitly by

$$g^*[X(t)] = g^*(0) + C_0 A^{-1/a} \int_0^t f(s;k)ds \qquad (32)$$

[see also equation (A.26)]. Current extraction is then

$$R(t) = C_0 f(t;k) \{g[X(t)]/A\}^{1/a} \qquad (33)$$

[see also equation (A.24)]. The shadow price of the resource is

$$-\lambda_1(t) = ae^{rt}\{k^{1-a}A/g[X(t)]\}^{1/a}/C_0 \qquad (34)$$

[see also equation (A.32)], while the shadow price of capital is

$$\lambda_2(t) = e^{rt} (1 + at/k)^{(a-1)/a}/C_0 \qquad (35)$$

[see also equation (A.18)].

Consumption, capital, and output are single-peaked functions of time, and all tend to zero as $t$ grows without bound. This is caused by the essentiality and exhaustibility of the extractive resource. Nonetheless, the capital to output ratio grows linearly. This result seems not to have been noticed before. The ratio of consumption to capital tends to grow in the limit at the discount rate $r$, in agreement with the earlier finding of Dasgupta and Heal [1974, equation (1.27)]. And the consumption to output ratio ultimately grows without bound as $t$ does; in the distant future, both consumption and output tend to zero, but the latter includes not only the meager current output but also disinvested capital stock. This asymptotic behavior is independent of the initial endowment $K_0$, $\overline{S}$. On the other hand, the values of $C(t)$, $K(t)$, and $Q(t)$ all depend on the initial endowment (directly and through the parameter $k$, which depends on them).

While the solution paths of all the variables could be studied profitably at greater length, our current concern is with the impact of environmental degradation on the solution. In particular, the environmental resource enters the model through the function $g(X)$. The special case that $g(X) = 1$ is the usual situation of no environmental influence and is the benchmark. Reviewing the paths of output [equation (30)], consumption [equation (28)], and capital [equation (29)], one is struck by the apparent absence of $g(X)$. In fact, the total impact of $g(X)$ is felt through the determination of the optimal initial capital/output ratio $k$ [equation (26)]. The functions $Q(t)$, $C(t)$, and $K(t)$ each in turn depend upon $k$.

Thus, for the particular formulation we have chosen, the entire influence of the specification of environmental impact function $g(X)$ on the optimal paths of $Q$, $C$, and $K$ is fully reflected in a single parameter $k$. Indeed, what matters about the function $g(X)$ is not its particular shape, but rather the number $g^*(\overline{S}) - g^*(0)$. For any given resource stock $S$, there is an infinity of nondecreasing differentiable degradation functions $g$ that yield the same value of $g^*(\overline{S}) - g^*(0)$, hence the same value of $k$, and, therefore, the same solution paths for $Q(t)$, $C(t)$ and $K(t)$. This can be called an "independence of path" property. Of course, the particular optimal extraction path $R$ does depend on $g$ [see equation (33)].

An obvious measure of the cost of environmental degradation $g$ is the difference in the discounted value of the utility stream [equation (20)] available with the benchmark $g \equiv 1$ and that available with the given degradation function $g$. However, certain alternative measures are suggested by our results. For any given function $g$, one can compute the cost in terms of the increment to the productive efficiency parameter $A$ or to the initial endowments $K_0$ or $S$ required to generate the same paths of output, consumption, and capital as would the benchmark. Thus it is possible to find the increment to $A$ or to $K_0$ or to $S$ that is required to just offset the adverse environmental impact of pollution, resulting in the identical paths of $Q(t)$, $C(t)$, and $K(t)$ that would be achieved with the given efficiency $A$ and endowments $K_0$ and $S$ in the absence of adverse environmental impact.

In particular, we find that the incremental efficiency $\Delta A$ that just compensates for the environmental degradation function $g$ is $\Delta A/A = \{S/[g^*(\overline{S}) - g^*(0)]\}^a - 1$. Alternatively, the compensating incremental capital $\Delta K$ is $\Delta K/K = [g^*(\overline{S}) - g^*(0)]/S - 1$. Or, the incremental resource endowment that would compensate for the environmental degradation satisfies $g^*(\overline{S} + \Delta S) = g^*(0) + S$, provided that $\overline{S} = S$ and, indeed, that $g(S + \Delta S) < \infty$. Otherwise, there is no way of compensating for environmental degradation through an incremental natural resource endowment. That is, if $\overline{S} < S$, then incremental resource endowment is useless because no more than $\overline{S}$ can be productively employed [review equations (17), (18), and (19)]. Finally, we can give a composite, namely, the combinations of changes in the initial conditions that would compensate for pollution. These changes satisfy $(1 + \Delta K/K)(1 + \Delta A/A)^{-1/a} = [g^*(\overline{S} + \Delta S) - g^*(0)]/S$. In sum, we have three (or four) alternative measures of the cost of environmental degradation, in addition to the usual measure in terms of forgone utility.

A related question is what initial conditions would be required to achieve any predetermined level of aggregate utility. Alternatively, one may ask for the set of initial conditions that would lead to a predetermined level of optimal initial consumption $C_0$, since that number summarizes the levels of consumption, capital, and output to be achieved throughout the planning horizon [see equations (28), (29), and (30)]. To any chosen level $C_0$, a corresponding value of $k$ is determined in equation (27). Then equation (26) implicitly indicates the combinations of initial conditions $A$, $K_0$ and $S$ supporting that value of $k$ and hence the corresponding value of $C_0$. Our efforts at drawing out these relationships explicitly (rather than implicitly) have not been fruitful.

Generalizations of equations (20), (21), and (22) that should be considered fall into three broad groups. We suggest several to be tried using the analytic outline provided in the appendix to this chapter.

First, allow the environment to have some self-cleansing ability by letting the pollution function [equation (14)] be $P' = R - bP$ and replace $X$ in equation (22) by $P$. In this way, the pollution decays naturally at some positive proportionate rate $b$. This modified model reduces to the case already studied in the limiting situation of $b \rightarrow 0$.

Second, because of the use of fixed (but implicit) factors such as land or labor, there may well be decreasing returns to scale in the use of capital and extractive resource. This can be accommodated by replacing equation (22) by $K' = AK^n R^a/g(P) - C$, where the parameters $A$, $n$, and $a$ are all positive but $n + a$ is no longer restricted to be equal to one.

Third, the utility function in equation (15) is a special case of a wider class, $U(C) = C^v, v < 1$. The case already considered is attained in the limiting case of $v \to 0$.

Fourth, the capital stock may decay at a constant proportionate rate $h$: $K' = AK^nR^a/g(P) - C - hK$.

Fifth, a finite time horizon might be imposed, to eliminate any impact of asymptotic behavior on the solution. We have considered the special case $T \to \infty$.

In sum, we believe the model

$$\begin{array}{c} \text{maximize} \\ C \geq 0, R \geq 0 \end{array} \int_0^T e^{-rt} C^v dt$$

subject to

$$X' = R, \quad X(0) = 0, \quad X \leq S$$

$$K' = AK^nR^a/g(P) - C - hK, \quad K(0) = K_0, \quad K \geq 0$$

$$P' = R - bP$$

may be amenable to analysis along the lines already followed for the special case [equations (20) through (22)]. However, we have not yet checked this conjecture. A second set of generalizations may be less readily accommodated, but warrant study.

Sixth, pollution may adversely affect utility as well as productivity. Common ways of modeling this are to let $P$ enter $U$ either additively $U(C,P) = U_1(C) - U_2(P)$, or multiplicatively $U(C,P) = U_1(C)U_2(P)$. The latter seems more "realistic," although the former can be found in the literature, doubtless because of its greater amenability to analysis. We propose the latter form and suggest trying $U(C,P) = C^v/u(P)$.

We have been unable to develop any model containing pollution as a nontrivial argument of the utility function that yields an "independence of path" characterization of the solution. In case pollution itself affects utility, it appears that the optimal solution will be of a different functional form than in corresponding models without such a feature. Indeed, the formulation of equation (22) may be very special; that is, the class of models for which the impact of environmental considerations can be fully summarized in a single parameter may be very narrow indeed. This conclusion is based not only on our own work but also on that of others.

Several papers demonstrate that having another argument in the utility function affects the nature of the optimal solution. Kurz (1968) modified the prototypical capital growth model by inserting the capital stock into the utility function as a second argument. He found that, rather than being assured of a single steady-state level of consumption and capital toward which the optimal path tends (as is the case for the prototype model), there could be several such steady states. The particular levels approached would then depend upon the initial conditions.

Ryder and Heal (1973) have modified the prototypical capital model by inserting an exponentially weighted average of past consumption into the utility function. They also found the nature of the solution affected, particularly if there is satiation of utility.

Cropper (1976) suggests that a different effect occurs if pollution is added to the utility function. She has modified the prototypical pollution model by assuming that the utility will be realized only if a catastrophe has not yet occurred; the probability of catastrophe is a nondecreasing function of the pollution stock. This new consideration changed the solution from being one with a unique steady state to one with the possibility of multiple steady states, or none. When the pollution stock is inserted in the utility function of that model, it assures at least one steady state.

Seventh, thus far we have assumed that the pollution grows in direct proportion to the use of the extractive resource. There are alternative sources of pollution. It may be directly related to consumption or production, or both. The impact of these alternative suppositions should be explored.

Last, and more important, it seems desirable to introduce provisions for pollution control. The stock of pollution can be reduced by diverting resources to that end.

The generalizations proposed to this point will result in analysis of the model shown in equations (11) through (14), with most of the effects included, but with some specialization of functional forms. A third tier of generalizations includes provision for uncertainties, for research and development, and for consideration of market structures that can realize the optimal solutions. We will not elaborate on these features here, but instead refer the reader to our earlier works in which it is shown how these essential features can be accommodated.

## 3. Summary

We have reviewed the three-pronged theoretical base for work on the role of common property resources in optimal planning models with exhaustible resources. We then began work on the first unified model incorporating all three features—capital, common property environmental resources, and exhaustible resources. Finally, we used our experience to propose a research program and to indicate concretely how such a program might be fruitfully developed.

To generalize broadly from the literature, in models of economic growth, consumption, the capital stock, and utility all grow toward steady-state levels. Models with pollution also involve growing consumption, but utility need not improve through time because the greater consumption merely offsets the disutility of growing pollution. In models with exhaustible resources, the pattern is still different, with consumption and utility both declining toward zero. Of course, this summary overgeneralizes and omits myriad variations on the basic prototypes. It is apparent that a composite model will involve these countervailing forces, but no single pattern is suggested by a study of the extant disparate models of the various components.

Our preliminary model incorporates rudiments of the three key features. It is highly specialized. The utility function depends only on the consumption of a single good of uniform quality. Pollution increases directly with exhaustible resource extraction and is controlled only through selection of the extraction rate. Environmental degradation increases the amounts of resources required to produce the single output of uniform quality at any given rate. Further, we assume simple and convenient functional forms. A special case of our model in which pollution is absent has been studied by Dasgupta and Heal (1974).

Incorporating pollution into the model through the production function (raising the amount of resources needed for a given output rate) is both plausible and tractable. We have characterized the optimal solution, showing that the functional form of the optimal consumption path noted by Dasgupta and Heal is preserved, although its level is reduced by the necessity to use more resources to offset environmental degradation. In particular, the consumption path is single-peaked with respect to time and tends to zero as time increases without bound. The level of the path depends both on the initial endowments and the environmental degradation function. Since explicit solutions have been obtained, further quantitative comparisons may be possible via numerical analysis.

We then proposed a line of work to incorporate numerous important features into our rudimentary framework. We have asked far more questions than we have answered. They are not novel, but rather reflect the questions of the day. On the other hand, we have suggested an approach that may be fruitful. Perhaps the question in which the greatest interest lies is the effect of incorporating the pollution stock into the utility function, to reflect adverse effects upon health, risk of death, and aesthetics. We believe it is likely that the functional form of the optimal consumption path will be affected. Other important features to be taken into account are provisions for self-cleansing of the environment and for more general functional forms, for alternative sources of pollution, for research and development and technical advances, for uncertainties, and for market structures or institutional arrangements that can support optimal solution paths in a decentralized fashion.

# Appendix

To solve the problem shown in equations (20) through (22) in the text it is convenient to define

$$y \equiv R/K \tag{A.1}$$

Then the problem can be written as

$$\text{maximize} \int_0^\infty e^{-rt} \ln C \, dt \tag{A.2}$$

subject to

$$X' = Ky, \quad X(0) = 0, \quad X \le \overline{S} \tag{A.3}$$

$$K' = AKy^a/g(X) - C, \quad K(0) = K_0 > 0 \quad K \ge 0 \tag{A.4}$$

Let $\lambda_1$ and $\lambda_2$ be the current value multipliers associated with equations (A.3) and (A.4) respectively. Then the current value Hamiltonian is $H = \ln C + \lambda_1 Ky + \lambda_2[AKy^a/g(X) - C]$.

An optimal solution satisfies not only equations (A.3)–(A.4), but also

$$H_C = 1/C - \lambda_2 \le 0 \quad CH_C = 0 \tag{A.5}$$

$$H_y = \lambda_1 K + a\lambda_2 AKy^{a-1}/g(X) \le 0 \qquad yH_y = 0 \tag{A.6}$$

$$\lambda_1' = r\lambda_1 + \lambda_2 AKy^a g'(X)/g^2(X) \tag{A.7}$$

$$\lambda_2' = r\lambda_2 - \lambda_1 y - \lambda_2 Ay^a/g(X) \tag{A.8}$$

$$\lim_{t \to \infty} e^{-rt} \lambda_1 \ge 0 \; \lim_{t \to \infty} e^{-rt} \lambda_1(\overline{S} - X) = 0 \tag{A.9}$$

$$\lim_{t \to \infty} e^{-rt} \lambda_2 \ge 0 \; \lim_{t \to \infty} e^{-rt} \lambda_2 K = 0 \tag{A.10}$$

If there is an optimal solution, both $C > 0$ and $y > 0$ throughout [see equations (A.5) and (A.6)]. From equation (A.5), $\lambda_2 > 0$ and then, from equation (A.6), $\lambda_1 < 0$. The marginal valuation of the exhaustible resource is $-\lambda_1$, while the marginal valuation of capital is $\lambda_2$.

It follows, then, from equation (A.6) that

$$-\lambda_1 = a\lambda_2 Ay^{a-1}/g(X) \tag{A.11}$$

Differentiating equation (A.11) totally gives

$$\lambda_1'/\lambda_1 = \lambda_2'/\lambda_2 - (1 - a)y'/y - g'(X)X'/g(X) \tag{A.12}$$

Use equation (A.11) to eliminate $\lambda_2$ from equation (A.7) and rearrange the result to give expression for $\lambda_1'/\lambda_1$; similarly, use equation (A.11) to eliminate

$\lambda_1$ from equation (A.8), and rearrange the result to give expression for $\lambda_2'/\lambda_2$. Substitute these expressions for $\lambda_1'/\lambda_1$ and $\lambda_2'/\lambda_2$ into equation (A.12) and collect terms, yielding

$$X'g'(X)/g(X) - ay'/y = aAy^a/g(X) \tag{A.13}$$

Define

$$Z = g(X)/Ay^a \tag{A.14}$$

Then equation (A.13) is just $Z'/Z = a/Z$, or, equivalently,

$$Z' = a \tag{A.15}$$

Integrating,

$$Z(t) = k + at \tag{A.16}$$

where $k$ is a constant to be determined.

Using equations (A.11), (A.14), and (A.16), we can write equation (A.8) as

$$\lambda_2'/\lambda_2 = r - (1 - a)/(k + at) \tag{A.17}$$

Integrating, we obtain

$$\lambda_2(t) = e^{rt}(1 + at/k)^{(a-1)/a}/C_0 \tag{A.18}$$

Using equation (A.18) in equation (A.5) gives also

$$C(t) = C_0 e^{-rt}(1 + at/k)^{(1-a)/a} \tag{A.19}$$

Next, substitute from equations (A.14), (A.16), and (A.19) into (A.4) to get the differential equation to be solved for $K$. Using the integrating factor $(k + at)^{-1/a}$, we find that

$$K(k + at)^{-1/a} = C_0 k^{(a-1)/a} \int_t^\infty e^{-rs}(k + as)^{-1}\, ds$$

under the supposition that the left side tends to zero as $t \to \infty$. Now define

$$f(t;k) \equiv k^{(a-1)/a} \int_t^\infty e^{-rs}(k + as)^{-1}ds \tag{A.20}$$

so that

$$K(t) = (k + at)^{1/a} C_0 f(t;k) \tag{A.21}$$

In particular, $K(0) = K_0 = k^{1/a} C_0 f(0;k)$ so that the constant $C_0$ can be written as

$$C_0 = K_0/k^{1/a} f(0;k) \tag{A.22}$$

Output $Q$ can be written as $Q = AKy^a/g(X) = K/Z$. Substituting from equations (A.16) and (A.21) gives

$$Q(t) = C_0 f(t;k)(k + at)^{(1-a)/a} \tag{A.23}$$

Definition (A.14) may be rearranged to express $y$ in terms of $Z$. Substitute that expression for $y$ and equation (A.21) for $K$ into equation (A.3) to yield

$$X' = C_0 f(t;k)[g(X)/A]^{1/a} \tag{A.24}$$

which is a separable differential equation

$$g^{-1/a}(X)dX = C_0 A^{-1/a} f(t;k)dt.$$

Defining

$$g^*(X) \equiv \int g^{-1/a}(X)dX \tag{A.25}$$

its solution can be written as

$$g^*[X(t)] = g^*(0) + C_0 A^{-1/a} \int_0^t f(s;k)ds \tag{A.26}$$

Equation (A.26) implicitly specifies $X(t)$. Furthermore,

$$g^*(\overline{S}) = g^*(0) + C_0 A^{-1/a} \int_0^\infty f(s;k)ds \tag{A.27}$$

Therefore,

$$C_0 = A^{1/a}[g^*(\overline{S}) - g^*(0)] \Big/ \int_0^\infty f(s;k)ds \tag{A.28}$$

Equating the two expressions for $C_0$ in equations (A.22) and (A.28), and rearranging them, gives us

$$f^*(k) = K_0 A^{-1/a}/[g^*(\overline{S}) - g^*(0)] \tag{A.29}$$

where we have let the function $f^*$ be defined by

$$f^*(k) \equiv k^{1/a} f(0;k) \Big/ \int_0^\infty f(t;k)dt \tag{A.30}$$

Equation (A.29) implicitly specifies the constant $k$ in terms of given parameters $K_0, A, a, r, \overline{S}$.

To find $y$, put equation (A.16) into equation (A.14) and solve:

$$y(t) = \{g[X(t)]/A(k + at)\}^{1/a} \tag{A.31}$$

Finally, to find $\lambda_1$, substitute for $\lambda_2$ from equation (A.18), $y$ from equation (A.31), and $X$ from equation (A.26) into equation (A.11) to get

$$-\lambda_1(t) = ae^{rt}\{k^{1-a}A/g[X(t)]\}^{1/a}/C_0 \tag{A.32}$$

# References

Anderson, Kent P. 1972. "Optimal Growth when the Stock of Resources is Finite and Depletable," *Journal of Economic Theory* vol. 4, pp. 256–267.

Ayres, Robert. 1977. "Models of Entropy," Paper presented at the Conference on Natural Resource Prices, Trail Lake, Wyoming, August.

Banks, F. E. 1974. "A Note on Some Theoretical Issues of Resource Depletion," *Journal of Economic Theory* vol. 9, pp. 238–243.

Beckmann, Martin J. 1975. "The Limits to Growth in a Neoclassical World," *American Economic Review* vol. 65, pp. 695–699.

Blank, Fred, Curtis Anderson, and Ralph d'Arge. 1977. "A Taxonomic Analysis of Natural Resource Models," Paper presented at the Conference on Natural Resource Prices, Trail Lake, Wyoming, August.

Britto, Ronald. 1973. "Some Recent Developments in the Theory of Economic Growth: An Interpretation," *Journal of Economic Literature* vol. 11, pp. 1343–1366.

Burmeister, Edwin, and A. Rodney Dobell. 1970. *Mathematical Theories of Economic Growth* (New York, Macmillan).

Clark, Colin W. 1976. *Mathematical Bioeconomics: The Optimal Management of Renewable Resources* (New York, John Wiley).

Cropper, M. L. 1976. "Regulating Activities with Catastrophic Environmental Effects," *Journal of Environmental Economics and Management* vol. 3, pp. 1–15.

Cummings, Ronald G., and William D. Schulze. 1977. "Ramsey, Resources, and the Conservation of Mass-Energy," Paper presented at the Conference on Natural Resource Prices, Trail Lake, Wyoming, August.

Daly, Herman E., ed. 1973. *Toward a Steady-State Economy* (San Francisco, Calif., Freeman) chapter 7.

D'Arge, Ralph C., and K. C. Kogiku. 1973. "Economic Growth and the Environment," *The Review of Economic Studies* vol. 40, pp. 61–77.

Dasgupta, Partha, and Geoffrey M. Heal. 1974. "The Optimal Depletion of Exhaustible Resources," *The Review of Economic Studies*, Symposium on the Economics of Exhaustible Resources, pp. 3–28.

——, ——, and M. Majumdar. 1976. "Resource Depletion and Development," Cornell University Department of Economics Discussion Paper No. 109.

Davison, R. 1978. "Optimal Depletion of an Exhaustible Resource with Research and Development towards an Alternative Technology," *Review of Economic Studies* vol. 45, pp. 355–367.

Fisher, Anthony C., and Frederick M. Peterson. 1976. "The Environment in Economics: A Survey," *The Journal of Economic Literature* vol. 14, pp. 1–33.

Forster, B. A. 1973a. "Optimal Consumption Planning in a Polluted Environment," *Economic Record* vol. 49, pp. 534–545.

——. 1973b. "Optimal Capital Accumulation in a Polluted Environment," *Southern Economic Journal* vol. 39, pp. 544–547.

——. 1975. "Optimal Pollution Control with a Nonconstant Exponential Rate of Decay," *Journal of Environmental Economics and Management* vol. 2, pp. 1–6.

——. 1977. "Optimal Energy Use in a Polluted Environment," Paper presented at the Conference on Natural Resource Prices, Trail Lake, Wyoming, August.

Georgescu-Roegen, Nicholas. 1976. *Energy and Economic Myths: Institutional and Analytical Essays* (New York, Pergamon) chapter 1.

Gruver, G. 1976. "Optimal Investment in Pollution Control Capital in a Neoclassical Growth Context," *Journal of Environmental Economics and Management* vol. 3, pp. 165–177.

Hanson, Donald A. 1978. "Efficient Transitions from a Resource to a Substitute Technology in an Economic Growth Context," *Journal of Economic Theory* vol. 17, pp. 99–113.

Heal, Geoffrey. 1976. "The Relationship Between Price and Extraction Cost for a Resource with a Backstop Technology," *Bell Journal of Economics* vol. 7, pp. 371–378.

Hoel, Michael. 1978a. "Resource Extraction and Recycling with Environmental Costs," *Journal of Environmental Economics and Management* vol. 5, pp. 220–235.

———. 1978b. "Resource Extraction When a Future Substitute Has an Uncertain Cost," *The Review of Economic Studies* vol. 45, pp. 637–644.

Hotelling, Harold. 1931. "The Economics of Exhaustible Resources," *Journal of Political Economy* vol. 39, pp. 137–175.

Ingham, A., and P. Simmons. 1975. "Natural Resources and Growing Population," *The Review of Economic Studies* vol. 17, pp. 191–206.

Intriligator, Michael D. 1971. *Mathematical Optimization and Economic Theory* (Englewood Cliffs, N.J., Prentice-Hall).

Kamien, Morton I., and Nancy L. Schwartz. 1978a. "Optimal Exhaustible Resource Depletion with Endogenous Technical Change," *The Review of Economic Studies* vol. 45, pp. 179–196.

———, and ———. 1978b. *Technical Change Inclinations of a Resource Monopolist*, in G. Horwich and J. P. Quirk eds., *Essays in Contemporary Fields of Economics* (West Lafayette, Ind., Purdue University Press, 1981) pp. 41–53.

———, and ———. 1977a. "A Note on Resource Usage and Market Structure," *Journal of Economic Theory* vol. 15, pp. 394–397.

———, and ———. 1977b. "Disaggregated Intertemporal Models with an Exhaustible Resource and Technical Advance," *Journal of Environmental Economics and Management* vol. 4, pp. 271–288.

Keeler, Emmett, Michael Spence, and Richard Zeckhauser. 1971. "The Optimal Control of Pollution," *Journal of Economic Theory* vol. 4, pp. 19–34.

Kemp, Murray C. 1976. "How to Eat a Cake of Unknown Size," in M. C. Kemp, ed., *Three Topics in the Theory of International Trade* (New York, American Elsevier) chapter 23.

———, and N. V. Long. 1977. "Optimal Control Problems with Integrands Discontinuous with Respect to Time," *The Economic Record* vol. 53, no. 141 (September) pp. 405–420.

Koopmans, Tjalling C. 1973. "Some Observations on Optimal Economic Growth and Exhaustible Resources," in C. Bos, H. Linnemaan, and P. de Wolff, eds., *Economic Structure and Development: Essays in Honor of Jan Tinbergen* (New York, North-Holland) pp. 239–255.

Kurz, Mordecai. 1968. "Optimal Economic Growth and Wealth Effects," *International Economic Review* vol. 9, pp. 348–357.

Lewis, Tracy R. 1977. "Attitudes Toward Risk and the Optimal Exploration of an Exhaustible Resource," *Journal of Environmental Economics and Management* vol. 4, pp. 111–119

Lusky, Rafael. 1975. "Optimal Taxation Policies for Conservation and Recycling," *Journal of Economic Theory* vol. 11, pp. 315–328.

―――. 1976. "A Model of Recycling and Pollution Control," *Canadian Journal of Economics* vol. 9, pp. 91–101.

Mäler, Karl-Göran. 1974. *Environmental Economics: A Theoretical Inquiry* (Baltimore, Md., Johns Hopkins University Press for Resources for the Future).

Manning, R. 1978. "Resource Use with Demand Interdependent over Time," *The Economic Record* vol. 54, pp. 72–77.

Meadows, Dennis, Donnella H. Meadows, Jørgen Randers, and William H. Behrens III. 1972. *The Limits to Growth* (New York, Universe Books).

Peterson, Frederick M. 1978. "A Model of Mining and Exploring for Exhaustible Resources," *Journal of Environmental Economics and Management* vol. 5, pp. 236–251.

―――, and Anthony C. Fisher. 1977. "The Exploitation of Extractive Resources: A Survey," *The Economic Journal* vol. 87, pp. 681–721.

Pielou, E. C. 1969. *An Introduction to Mathematical Ecology* (New York, Wiley-Interscience).

Pindyck, Robert S. 1978. "The Optimal Exploration and Production of Nonrenewable Resources," *Journal of Political Economy* vol. 86, pp. 841–861.

Plourde, C. G. 1972. "A Model of Waste Accumulation and Disposal," *Canadian Journal of Economics* vol. 5, pp. 119–125.

Ramsey, Frank P. 1928. "A Mathematical Theory of Saving," *Economic Journal* as reprinted in K. J. Arrow and T. Scitovsky, eds. (1969). *Readings in Welfare Economics* (Homewood, Ill., Richard D. Irwin).

Ryder, Harl E., Jr., and Geoffrey M. Heal. 1973. "Optimum Growth with Intertemporally Dependent Preferences," *The Review of Economic Studies* vol. 40, pp. 1–31.

Schulze, William D. 1974. "The Optimal Use of Non-Renewable Resources: The Theory of Extraction," *Journal of Environmental Economics and Management* vol. 1, pp. 53–73.

Shell, Karl, ed. 1967. *Essays on the Theory of Optimal Economic Growth* (Cambridge, Mass., M.I.T. Press).

Smith, Vernon L. 1977. "Control Theory Applied to Natural and Environmental Resources: An Exposition," *Journal of Environmental Economics and Management* vol. 4, no. 1, pp. 1–24.

Solow, Robert M. 1974. "Intergenerational Equity and Exhaustible Resources," *The Review of Economic Studies* Symposium volume, pp. 29–45.

―――, and Frederic Y. Wan. 1976. "Extraction Costs in the Theory of Exhaustible Resources," *Bell Journal of Economics* vol. 7, pp. 359–370.

Stiglitz, Joseph E. 1974. "Growth with Exhaustible Natural Resources: Efficient and Optimal Growth Paths," *The Review of Economic Studies* Symposium volume, pp. 123–137.

―――. 1979. "A Neoclassical Analysis of the Economics of Natural Resources," in V. Kerry Smith, ed., *Scarcity and Growth Reconsidered* (Baltimore, Md., Johns Hopkins University Press for Resources for the Future).

Vousden, Neil. 1973. "Basic Theoretical Issues of Resource Depletion," *Journal of Economic Theory* vol. 6, no. 2 (April) pp. 126–143.

# 3

## The Use of Common Property Resources

### Geoffrey Heal

This chapter reviews some of the economic issues associated with the use of free access or common property goods such as the air, the oceans, fisheries, etc. Clearly, this is in principle a vast area and beyond the scope of a single review, so that our choices are very selective. We focus mainly on two types of material: (1) issues out of which policy recommendations emerge naturally, and (2) areas where it seems to us that the state of received theory is weak. Material of the first type is covered in section 1, in which we review the classic static, deterministic common property problem or "problem of the commons," and analyze various institutional changes that have been suggested as possible ways of resolving this problem.

Discussion of the dynamic aspects of the problem, which is undertaken in section 2, brings us up against limitations in the information available about the long-run macrodynamics of many common property resources. The cases of fisheries and forests have of course been well documented, and our analysis rests very much on the former of these. We would like to be able to apply it also to the dynamics of bodies of polluted air and water, but there is little literature on which one can base analytical formulations of these processes. We have therefore made some rather tentative applications of our analysis to these cases, but feel that there is a strong case for collaborative work between economists and environmental scientists in producing a more definitive treatment of these issues. In any event, it seems to us that the results that emerge from the dynamic analysis are sufficiently surprising to merit further study.

## 1. Static Analysis

The Classic Common Property Problem

This section presents the basic analysis of the use of free-access goods in a static context. The main result to emerge—that in a well-defined sense such goods are likely to be overused—is not of course new. We hope, however, that we have a formulation which is clear and tractable, and which enables us to synthesize earlier contributions and clarify a number of points.

We are concerned with a free-access good which is used to an extent $x_i$ by each of $N$ given firms, $i = 1, 2, \ldots, N$. One could think of $x_i$ as the number of cows farmer $i$ grazes on a common, or the number of hours boat $i$ works in a particular fishing ground. The total benefit $B$ derived from the good is supposed to depend upon the *sum* of the $x_i$ according to

$$B(x) = F(x) + E(x) \tag{1}$$

where $x = \sum_{i=1}^{N} x_i$

Here $F(0) = 0$, $F' \leq 0$, $F'' < 0$, and $E' \leq 0$. $F(x)$ represents the output produced from the free-access resource—the total weight gain of the cows in the case of a common, or the weight of fish caught for a fishery. We assume diminishing returns to this productive activity, which is clearly a very reasonable assumption when increasing input levels are being applied to a constant resource base. $E(x)$ represents the environmental or amenity benefit derived from the common property resource, and we assume this to be nonincreasing in the level of economic exploitation of the resource. We are, in other words, assuming that there is competition between industrial (in the broadest sense) and recreational uses of common property: again, this seems the appropriate assumption.

We assume that the cost to a firm of using the facility to an extent of unity (i.e., $x_i = 1$) is $P$ (so that average and marginal costs are equal and constant). The output is also assumed to be the numeraire with a given price determined, for example, by competition from substitutes; suppose that firms' profit $\pi_i$ is given by

$$\pi_i = \frac{x_i F(x)}{x} - P x_i \tag{2}$$

This equation embodies the assumption that if a firm contributes a fraction $x_i/x$ of the total inputs to using a facility, it receives a proportion $x_i/x$ of the value of output $F(x)$ produced from it. Thus if a boat contributes 10 percent to the fishing effort put into a ground, it catches 10 percent of the total fish caught: firms may therefore differ in their scale of operation, but not in their efficiency.

In the special case when all derivatives of $F(\ )$ other than the first are zero, equation (2) of course gives

$$\pi_i = x_i \, (F' - P)$$

and the firms have a set of linear and independent production processes. More generally, let $x_{-i} = \Sigma_{j \neq i} \, x_j$, so that

$$\pi_i = \frac{x_i \, F(x_{-i} + x_i)}{x_{-i} + x_i} - Px_i \tag{3}$$

If all firms have the same technology and profit function, as we have already assumed, it is reasonable to expect all to operate at the same scale at equilibrium: let this scale be $\hat{x}$. Of course, it remains to define what an equilibrium is in the present context. There are a number of possible candidates, but we shall consider a noncooperative Nash equilibrium. A noncooperative equilibrium concept seems appropriate because the problem with which we are concerned is known to arise from a lack of cooperation and coordination between firms. Given that firms are symmetrically placed, Nash's seems the relevant noncooperative concept.

In a Nash solution, each firm chooses $x_i$ to maximize $\pi_i$, given the activities of others as summarized by $x_{-i}$. Using equation (3), it is routine to show that the Nash equilibrium usage levels $\hat{x}$ satisfy

$$\frac{F(N\hat{x})}{N\hat{x}} - \frac{1}{N} \left[ \frac{F(N\hat{x})}{N\hat{x}} - F'(N\hat{x}) \right] = P \tag{4}$$

and one can confirm that this equation has a positive solution in $\hat{x}$ provided that the very obvious condition

$$F'(0) > P$$

is satisfied. The first term in (4) is the average product of the inputs, and the second, the difference between their average and marginal products. Clearly, the second term goes to zero as $N$ goes to infinity, so that for very large $N$ one has the following approximate characterization of a Nash equilibrium:

$$\frac{F(N\hat{x})}{N\hat{x}} = P \tag{5}$$

In words, average productivity is equated to marginal cost. Equation (5) is of course widely known. For small $N$ and sharply curved functions $F(x)$, the bracketed expression in (4) could be quite significant. Indeed, in the case when $N = 1$ and the use of the resource is monopolized, (4) reduces to

$$F'(N\hat{x}) = P \tag{6}$$

the equation of marginal cost and value of marginal product. In general (4) can be written as

$$\frac{F(N\hat{x})}{N\hat{x}} \frac{N-1}{N} + \frac{1}{N} F'(N\hat{x}) = P$$

so that a weighted mean of average and marginal products is being equated to marginal cost, the weight shifting toward the average product as the numbers increase. As for strictly concave $F(\ )$ the average product exceeds the marginal for any value of $N\hat{x}$, this implies of course that the Nash equilibrium usage level increases from the level given by (6) to the level given by (5) as $N$ increases.

Having pinpointed the competitive level of use of a common property resource, we turn briefly to a description of the socially optimal use level. If there are $N$ symmetrically placed firms each operating at the same scale, then it will be optimal from the point of view of maximizing the surplus of benefits over costs if this common scale is chosen to:

maximize $F(Nx) - PNx + E(Nx)$

which of course requires $x$ to be set at the level $x^*$, which satisfies

$$F'(Nx^*) + E'(Nx^*) = P \tag{7}$$

As $F'$ is the marginal benefit, and $P - E'$ the marginal cost of extra usage, this has an obvious interpretation. If we consider the case when $E' = 0$, then (7) and (6) are identical, that is, for $N = 1$, $x^* = \hat{x}$. Of course, from the earlier results it is also clear that for $N > 1$, $x^* < \hat{x}$. In general, then, the competitive use level exceeds the optimal one by an amount which increases with the number of firms, being zero when this is one and tending to an upper limit as the number of firms becomes infinite. This conclusion has been reached on the assumption that $E'(Nx) = 0$: it is clearly reinforced if $E'(Nx) \leq 0$.

We have now given a statement of the classic version of the problem of the commons. We have used a very particular and rather tractable formulation of this problem, and before moving on to consider possible policy responses, it seems appropriate to consider the robustness of our conclusions with respect to variations. As we have formulated it here, the problem involves an activity in which output is a function of total inputs, and each firm receives a share of that output equal to the function of total inputs that it supplies. This is a very specific formulation which has the merit, as noted, of yielding neat solutions. At the other extreme would be a statement that a common property resource exists whenever a firm's outputs are affected by other firm's activities. This would in effect amount to defining such a resource as a carrier of externalities—very much the approach taken by Dorfman (1974). Such a formulation would simply yield the standard analysis of externalities, with none of the structure normally associated with the common property problem.

If $y_i$ is firm $i$'s output, we would have

$$y_i = F_i(x_i, x_{-i}) \text{ and}$$

$$\pi_i = F_i(x_i, x_{-i}) - Px_i$$

so that profit maximization leads to $\partial F_i/\partial x_i = P$, whereas social efficiency would require

$$\sum_j \partial F_j/\partial x_i = P$$

so that outputs associated with negative externalities would be overproduced.

An intermediate approach, which retains some of the structure and conclusions of the usual formulation, while allowing for a more general technology, is the following. If $\mathbf{x} = (x_1, x_2, \ldots, x_n)$ is the vector of inputs, then total output is given by $F(\mathbf{x})$ so that we are distinguishing between the inputs of the various firms. It will be assumed that the output ($y_i$) received by a particular firm is a certain share $s_i$ of the total output, where $s_i$ is a function of $r_i$, firm $i$'s input relative to that of the other firms:

$$y_i = s_i(r_i)F(\mathbf{x}), \quad r_i = \frac{x_i}{\sum\limits_j x_j}$$

where both $s_i$ and $F$ are assumed to be concave. In this case a Nash equilibrium can be characterized as follows:

$$\frac{\partial F(\mathbf{x})}{\partial x_i} s_i + \frac{F(\mathbf{x}) \sum\limits_{j \neq i} x_i}{\sum\limits_j x_j \sum\limits_j x_j} \frac{ds_i(r_i)}{dr_i} = P$$

This is clearly a generalization of the earlier result that a weighted mean of average and marginal products should be equated to marginal cost: if the equilibrium is symmetric, with $x_i = x_j$ for all $i$ and $j$, then $\sum_{j \neq i} x_j/\sum_j x_j$ is just $(N-1)/N$, and if $s_i = x_i/\sum_j x_j$ then $s_i = 1/N$ and $ds_i/dr_i = 1$. So, as before, we have the result that the resource is overexploited by an amount that varies from zero if there is only one firm ($s_i = 1$, $ds_i/dr_i = 0$), to an amount given by the equation of average product times $ds_i/dr_i$, to price as the number of firms rises without bound. Within the kind of generalization considered here, then, the essence of the simpler case remains valid.

Before moving on to consider possible remedies to the problem of the commons, there are a number of points that we feel merit particular emphasis.

1. Although the equilibrium situation involves overuse of the resource, it does not involve unlimited overuse—as seems to be suggested, for example, by Hardin's analysis (1968). The extent of overuse depends on the curvature

of the function $F(Nx)$: if this is a constant gaussian curvature function of the form $F(Nx) = A(Nx)^a$, then if $X(6)$ is the total input level satisfying equation (6) (and so is the optimal input level for $E' = 0$), and $X(5)$ is the total input level satisfying equation (5) (and so is the upper bound on the competitive input level), it is easily shown that

$$\frac{X(5)}{X(6)} = a^{1/(a-1)}$$

and the extent to which the maximum competitive input level exceeds the optimal one depends on the curvature of $F$.

2. The solution concept upon which our analysis is based is Nash's non-cooperative equilibrium. The problem does not appear to fit naturally into the prisoner's dilemma framework, in spite of assertions to this effect in the literature. In particular, it is not true without further assumptions that overfishing is a dominant strategy, as would be required for the prisoner's dilemma framework.

3. We have analyzed here the nature and causes of the overexploitation only in a static context. It may be the case that there is a critical minimum level of the resource such that once its amount falls below this level, it then necessarily declines to zero. This is alleged to be the case with certain animal and fish resources, and if true would imply that the long-run implications of overexploitation might be very dramatic if it were to force the population below this critical level. This is an important issue to which we shall return in section 2.

4. There are further reasons, presented by Henry (1974), for supposing that the long-run impact of overuse may be greater than the analysis in this section suggests. These work through the impact of overuse on future resource allocation decisions. The point is most easily made with the kind of example that Henry used, involving patterns of land use. Suppose that of a certain total amount of land initially completely unused, an amount $G$ is made available for grazing on a free-access basis, and so, by our earlier arguments, will be overgrazed. Suppose further that the total output $O$ from this grazed land depends on the area $G$ and the amount $C$ of complementary inputs: $O = O(C,G)$. This production function $O$ shows diminishing returns both to scale and proportions. If the amount of land $G$ is available on a free-access basis, the amount of complementary inputs $C$ applied will of course exceed the efficient quantity, so that the input/land ratio $C/G$ will be "too high." Under the stipulated assumptions about $O(C,G)$, this will raise the marginal product of land $\partial O/\partial G$ above the value it would assume at an efficient allocation. Now the important point is that this marginal productivity provides a natural measure of the benefits of bringing more land into cultivation. If a project involving the use of more land for grazing is considered by the techniques of

marginal cost-benefit analysis, then marginal productivity is an obvious benefit measure. Free-access use patterns will result in its being biased upward, so that in the long run one may not only find that commercialized land is too intensively used: there may also be too much under commercial use because commercial usage causes the usual signals about resource allocation patterns to be biased.

### Institutional Reforms

The problem we have analyzed is of course one of externalities: the extent of one firm's use of a common property resource affects the production possibilities of others. There are thus important interactions between firms which are external to the market system as it exists in this framework. A natural response to such a description of the problem is to attempt to extend the scope of the market in such a way as to incorporate these interactions. The easiest way of doing this is to imagine that each firm has a separate production function $F_i(\ )$ (though of course the $F_i$ are all identical), and to think of firm $j$ as providing inputs to all production processes, not merely its own. Thus if $x_{ji}$ is $j$'s input to $i$'s production process, and $y_i$ is $i$'s output,

$$y_i = \frac{x_{ii} F_i \left(\sum_j x_{ji}\right)}{\sum_j x_{ji}} = \frac{x_i F\left(\sum_j x_j\right)}{\sum_j x_j} \tag{8}$$

Equation (8) formalizes the fact that $i$'s output depends upon a service (or disservice) $x_{ji}$ provided by $j$ to $i$. In order to try and resolve the inefficiency in the usual way, we need to ensure that there is a price on, and a market for, this service. One would then hope that the price would adjust to equilibrate supply and demand, and in so doing would in the usual manner convey sufficient information to all parties to ensure the efficient coordination of these interactions.

There are unfortunately two major difficulties with this "back-to-the-market" approach. The first is that the markets concerned are likely to be extremely thin, and hence far from competitive. For example, in the market for $x_{ji}$, firm $j$'s input to firm $i$'s production, there is only one seller ($j$) and one buyer ($i$). It is bilateral monopoly, rather than competition, that is the order of the day. One could rely on a cooperative solution to this problem being efficient, but there is no presumption about the efficiency of noncooperative solutions.

A second and perhaps more severe problem, noted by Starrett (1972), concerns the nature of the dependence of $i$'s output $y_i$ on the input $x_{ji}$. $F$ is of course assumed to be a well-behaved production function, but $y_i$ depends on $x_{ji}$, not only through its appearance as an argument of $F$, but also through

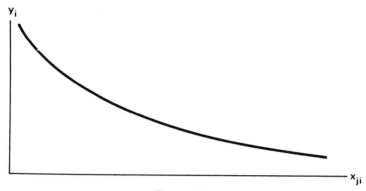

**Figure 3.1.**

its appearance in the denominator in (8). If $F_i$ is strictly concave, then a graph of $y_i$ against $x_{ji}$, everything else remaining constant, is as shown in figure 3.1. The crucial point about this is that the feasible set, the set of points on or below the production frontier, is nonconvex. In other words, once we recognize that the $x_{ji}$, for $j = 1, 2, \ldots, N$, are all inputs to firm $i$, then firm $i$'s production possibility set is seen to be nonconvex. And as the usual theorems about the existence of a competitive equilibrium depend upon the assumption of convex production possibility sets, we are unable to assert that markets in interactions $x_{ji}$ will have a competitive equilibrium even if they are not thin in the sense discussed above.

In view of this, it is natural to inquire if there are mechanisms other than the competitive one which could be used to reach an efficient outcome in the presence of nonconvexities. The natural candidates are regulatory mechanisms that involve pricing at marginal cost. In general these are incompatible with profit maximization or even breaking even, though recent work by Brown and Heal (1980) shows that, if an efficient allocation can be reached by marginal cost pricing, then it can be reached by a system of marginal cost pricing supplemented by two-part tariffs, which may be chosen to ensure that the sums collected via the fixed parts cover any losses from pricing at marginal cost. However, another paper by the same authors (Brown and Heal, 1979) also indicates that in many cases one cannot reach an efficient allocation by marginal cost pricing in the presence of increasing returns. The possibility of achieving efficiency in the face of nonconvexities depends on many factors, including the distribution of income.

The "back-to-the-market system," then, is unappealing. An alternative approach lies via the reform of legal rather than economic institutions, in the introduction of a system of property rights in the free-access good. In effect, establishing property rights in free-access goods transforms them from a common property resource to a normal private property good which is immune from the particular problems analyzed here. At a formal level, the point can be seen most easily by examining equations (6) and (7) and noting that when $E' = 0$ and $N = 1$, $x^* = \hat{x}$. What this shows is that if one neglects the environmental benefits $E$ from the resource, then if the right to use the resource is vested in a single firm, which thus acquires a monopoly of the resource, there will be no overexploitation. If establishing a monopoly seems unattractive on other grounds, it may be possible to divide up the common property resource between a number of firms, giving each an exclusive right to use a certain fraction, but leaving them to compete in input and output markets. This is what normally happens in the enclosure of common grazing lands.

The establishment of property rights is clearly an appealing way of tackling the problem: it is intellectually simple, and in many situations (as with grazing lands) would presumably be easy to administer. It may lead to significant changes in social structure—enclosure movements in agrarian societies have usually had this effect—and this may be held against it. It should also be emphasized that there are many common property resources—fugacious resources—for which the establishment of property rights is well-nigh impossible. The difficulties in defining and maintaining private property rights in air, water, fish, wildlife, and large mobile bodies of oil are all well documented.

There is a further possible shortcoming with this approach, which has recently been noted by Arrow (1978). The proposition that the establishment of property rights will "internalize" an externality and lead to an efficient allocation is often premised on the so-called "Coase theorem" (1960). In essence this is an argument which claims that, given a suitable legal framework, free bargaining between the parties to an externality can be guaranteed to lead to an efficient outcome. The point is that inefficiency implies that all parties could be made better off simultaneously, and it is argued that as a consequence rational bargainers would never agree to an inefficient outcome. However, Arrow observes that if the bargainers are groups rather than individuals, this argument is far from persuasive: the outcome will depend very much on the internal structure of the groups and the incentives they provide to their members to accurately reveal information about the true costs and benefits to them of various proposals.

Formally, the "Coase theorem" holds only if the groups devise internal structures that solve the "free rider" or "incentive compatibility" problem. The reason for this is that the provision of a higher level of a common property resource, such as clean water or air, amounts to the provision of a greater quantity of a public good. Any environmental good or common property resource is a public good to those who use it—it has long been realized that many externalities are carried by public goods. So attempting to ascertain a group's preferences for the level of an externality amounts to attempting to obtain information about their preferences for a public good. The problems that arise in this case are well known, and are discussed at length in Partha Dasgupta's chapter in this volume.

We have now discussed possible institutional reforms—extending the scope of the market and changing the legal environment—which if successful would ensure that the modified system would achieve efficiency without government intervention. The prospects here seem less than promising: we have noted that these reforms would encounter the problems posed by nonconvexities and by public goods—two rather intractable types of problems. So we turn now to reviewing possible regulatory measures. The options here are threefold: quotas, licenses, and taxes. Clearly, there is little that needs to be said about quotas: an efficient outcome could be achieved in principle by just instructing each firm that its use of inputs to the common property resource should not exceed $x^*$.

A licensing scheme consists of the government issuing a fixed number $\overline{X}$ of licenses for the total level of input that can be applied to the resource and allowing a market for these licenses to develop among firms. If $N$ is large, it is plausible that the market for these licenses is more or less competitive. Let us suppose that this is so. Denote by $\overline{p}$ the competitive price of a license when $\overline{X}$ is the total number of licenses issued. It follows that each firm now faces a price $p + \overline{p}$ per unit input. What is done with the government revenue generated by the issuance of these licenses is a distributional question that we do not go into at this stage. For our actual example, we might wish to consider the firms jointly issuing the total number of licenses $\overline{X}$, allowing a competitive market to develop for them, and then dividing the resulting revenue equally among themselves. We now construct the market equilibrium. If the $i$th firm were to assume that each of the other firms will introduce inputs to a level $\overline{x}$, its profit will be defined by

$$\frac{x_i F[(N-1)\overline{x} + x_i]}{(N-1)\overline{x} + x_i} - (p + \overline{p})x_i$$

Consequently $x_i$ would be chosen so as to satisfy the condition

$$\frac{(N-1)\overline{x}F[(N-1)\overline{x} + x_i]}{[(N-1)\overline{x} + x_i]^2} + \frac{x_i F'[(N-1)\overline{x} + x_i]}{(N-1)\overline{x} + x_i} = p + \overline{p} \tag{9}$$

If condition (9) is to lead to an equilibrium, one must have $x_i = \overline{x}$, given that firms are identical. It follows that (9) reduces to

$$\frac{(N-1)\overline{x}F(N\overline{x})}{(N\overline{x})^2} + \frac{F'(N\overline{x})}{N} = p + \overline{p} \tag{10}$$

where $N\overline{x} = \overline{X}$, the number of licenses issued. But presumably the government issues precisely $X^*$ ($=Nx^*$) licenses, since it is concerned with sustaining the

Pareto efficient allocation. Recall equation (7) and set $E' = 0$. It follows that (10) reduces to

$$\frac{(N-1)x^*F(Nx^*)}{(Nx^*)^2} + \frac{F'(Nx^*)}{N} = F'(Nx^*) + p^*$$

and consequently

$$p^* = \frac{(N-1)}{N}\left[\frac{F(Nx^*)}{Nx^*} - F'(Nx)\right] > 0 \tag{11}$$

where $p^*$ denotes the equilibrium price of a license when $X^*$ licenses are issued in all. It follows that if $X^*$ is the total number of licenses issued by the government (regulatory agency), the equilibrium price $p^*$ of a license will be given by (11) and, faced with this price, each firm will find it most profitable to introduce precisely $x^*$ units of input if it is supposed that the other firms will purchase $(N-1)x^*$ licenses in all. In other words, the government's problem consists solely in the choice of the total number of licenses it issues.

An alternative regulatory device, often called the *pure tax scheme*, is in some sense a mirror image of the pure licensing scheme. The idea is that the government (regulatory agency) imposes a tax per unit of input introduced by each firm. As in the case of the pure licensing scheme, we are not concerned at this stage with what is done with the tax revenue. As before, we might like to suppose that the firms impose an *ad valorem* tax on themselves and divide the resulting revenue equally among themselves. If this is so, and if we can show that there exists a tax equilibrium that is efficient in the sense that each firm finds it most profitable to limit itself to $x^*$ boats, when it assumes that each of the other firms will limit itself to $x^*$ boats, then the pure tax scheme and the pure licensing scheme envisaged earlier would be identical.

Denote by $t$ the *ad valorem* tax imposed on each unit of input. If the $i$th firm were to assume that each of the other firms will introduce $\bar{x}$, its profit will be defined by

$$\frac{x_iF[(N-1)\bar{x} + x_i]}{(N-1)\bar{x} + x_i} - (p+t)x_i$$

Consequently $x_i$ would be chosen so as to satisfy the condition

$$\frac{(N-1)\bar{x}F[(N-1)\bar{x} + x_i]}{[(N-1)\bar{x} + x_i]^2} + \frac{x_iF'[(N-1)\bar{x} + x_i]}{(N-1)\bar{x} + x_i} = p+t$$

If this is to lead to an equilibrium, one must have $x_i = \bar{x}$, given that firms are identical. It follows that

$$\frac{(N-1)\bar{x}F(N\bar{x})}{(N\bar{x})^2} + \frac{F'(N\bar{x})}{N} = p+t \tag{12}$$

But we want to choose $t$ so as to ensure that $x_i = x^*$ is a possible equilibrium value. In other words, if each firm supposes that each of the others will introduce $x^*$ inputs, then $\bar{x}$ would be its profit-maximizing input level. Toward this set $t$ at $t^*$, where

$$t^* = \frac{(N-1)}{N}\left[\frac{F(Nx^*)}{Nx^*} - F'(Nx^*)\right] \tag{13}$$

Using (13) in the right-hand side of (12) and setting $\bar{x} = x^*$, one obtains the condition $F'(Nx^*) = p$, which is precisely what is desired. Comparing equations (11) and (13), one notes that $p^* = t^*$ and therefore that at the optimum for our problem, the competitive price of the licenses is equal to the tax per vessel that the government selects. This might suggest that the pure licensing scheme and the pure tax scheme are identical. For the present problem, the results obtained by the two schemes are the same. Nevertheless, the schemes are different in spirit. We have noted that in the pure licensing scheme the government dictates the number of licenses permitted (i.e., the total number of vessels allowed) and the price system developed for this fixed number of licenses allocates these licenses among the $N$ firms. In the pure tax scheme, the government does not dictate directly the total level of inputs allowed. Profit-maximizing firms decide on how many inputs to introduce as a response to the license fee established by the government.

Having now reviewed five alternative approaches to the "problem of the commons," it might be convenient to summarize briefly the conclusions we have reached. There are two possible institutional reforms—extending the scope of markets and extending the scope of property rights. Given that one can have markets only in goods in which there are well-defined property rights, the relationship between these approaches is obvious. We have seen that neither of these is an ideal solution: problems with the introduction of markets are the "thinness" of these markets and the probable nonconvexities in the production sets of the individual firms once the activities of other firms are recognized as inputs into these. The problems with the introduction of property rights are primarily those of feasibility: in addition, there may be problems stemming from the internal structures of groups which are party to any bargaining that arises as a result of the newly defined rights.

These shortcomings suggest that from now on attention should be focused on the three regulatory approaches—quotas, licenses, and taxes. This is done in the following sections.

## Policy Implementation Under Certainty

Suppose that it has been decided that the optimal total level of input applied to a common property resource should be $x^*$. How this has been decided is not our concern here, though we must emphasize that a choice of $x^*$ can be based only on information which will in general be extremely difficult to obtain. This issue is discussed at some length in Dasgupta's chapter in this volume, where it is shown that if firms are aware of the reason why information is being sought from them, it will usually be in their interests to misrepresent it. Accurate information can be elicited only under very special circumstances, though under a rather larger class of circumstances it may be possible to devise procedures for eliciting satisfactory proxies for accurate information. Such procedures are referred to as indirect revelation mechanisms.

For the moment we neglect this, suppose $x^*$ to be known, and ask what sort of regulations can best ensure that the actual level of use equals this chosen level. In particular, we are interested in the relative merits of quotas, taxes, and licenses. The arguments here are standard, and are clearly presented in the literature—see for example, Kneese (1977), Baumol and Oates (1975), and Dales (1968). Here we rehearse them only briefly.

Let us consider quotas first. An obvious drawback is that if firms differ in their level of efficiency in using the resource (a circumstance we have ruled out so far, but one which is obviously realistic), then the quotas must vary from firm to firm, with larger quotas going to more efficient firms. This requires the computation of as many different quotas as there are firms (as opposed to just one tax rate if taxes are used) and also requires that the regulatory agency have detailed information about the production possibilities of the firms. If this detailed information is not available and a uniform quota is imposed (or if a uniform quota is imposed in the interests of equity), the result will invariably be inefficiency, with the marginal productivity of the inputs applied to the resource varying from firm to firm.

With a uniform tax on the use of the resource, on the other hand, one can be certain that such inputs as are used are allocated efficiently among the firms. The problem here is that the total level of inputs applied is a function of the tax rate, and again only if very detailed information about production possibilities is available can the tax rate be chosen so that inputs $x^*$ are applied. If this information is not available, then inputs will be efficiently allocated among firms, but the desired level of use may be exceeded. Thus the consequences of inadequate information are rather different under quota and tax schemes: under the former one can guarantee the correct level of inputs, but cannot ensure that they are applied efficiently, whereas under the latter one can guarantee the efficient use of whatever inputs are chosen, but cannot guarantee that the total is correct.

The licensing scheme has none of these disadvantages. It is clear that by setting the number of licenses available, the regulatory authority can fix the level of inputs applied at any chosen level. Further, because firms are free to choose their activity levels in the light of input costs consisting of prices and license fees which are uniform across firms, the inputs used will also be allocated efficiently among firms. A system of marketable licenses is therefore preferable to either quotas or taxes as a way of ensuring a given level of use of a common property resource. It requires less informational input, and so runs less risk of error, either in leading to inefficiency or in missing the target use level.

## 2. Dynamic Analysis

### Dynamics of Common Property Resources with Free Access

At various points in the discussion of the static aspects of the use of common property resources, we noted that the long-run impact of certain measures might be of more concern than their immediate impact. The classic case is a fishery. The short-run effect of overexploitation is inefficiency and waste: the long-run effect may be extinction. There is a natural growth process with which economic exploitation interferes, and the eventual fortunes of the fishery depend upon this interaction. In this section and the subsequent one, we analyze this interaction under various behavioral assumptions. In particular, this section is concerned with the case involving free access to the common property, with new users being attracted if profits are positive, and existing users leaving if the reverse is true. We present our analysis primarily in terms of the dynamics of fisheries, because this is the most widely studied and well-documented common property resource, and has dynamic characteristics that seem likely to be similar to those of a number of other important resources. At various points in our analysis we comment on the extent to which the models used appear to be applicable to other resources.

We now present the basic model of the dynamics of a fishery. Denote its population size at time $t$ by $Z_t$. Let $\theta$ represent a short interval of time. The population size, $Z_{t+\theta}$, will generally depend on a whole host of factors. One supposes, quite naturally, that it will depend on $Z_t$ and on the length of the interval $\theta$. It will depend on a variety of other factors as well, such as the age structure at $t$, the availability and quality of its means of sustenance, the impact of nonhuman predators, and its own biological characteristics. We denote these other factors generically by $\lambda$ which may, in turn, depend on $t$ as well. Symbolically we express by $G$ a function defined over all the factors we have enumerated and express the demographic progress of the species as

$$Z_{t+\theta} = G(Z_t, \lambda, \theta) \tag{14}$$

A simple form of $G$ that has been much studied is the case where $\lambda$ is regarded as constant and where $G$ can be expressed as

$$G = Z_t + H(Z_t)\theta,$$

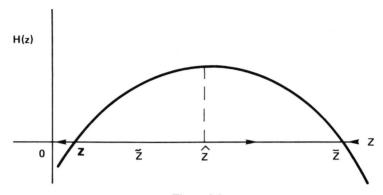

**Figure 3.2.**

and, consequently, that

$$Z_{t+\theta} - Z_t = H(Z_t)\theta \tag{15}$$

It is therefore being supposed in (15) that at any given value of $Z_t$ the increment in the population size during the short interval $(t, t + \theta)$ is simply proportional to $\theta$.

Most often it will prove convenient to regard time as a continuous variable. In this case, divide both sides of equation (15) by $\theta$ and, taking the limit as $\theta \rightarrow 0$, obtain the ecological balance between this species and its natural environment as

$$\dot{Z}_t = H(Z_t), \text{ with } Z_t \geq 0 \tag{16}$$

Certain special forms of $H$ may now be mentioned.

1. When $H(Z) = 0$ the species is assumed to have a constant population size. It is undoubtedly best exemplified by exhaustible resources such as fossil fuels and minerals, though using the term "species" to characterize such resources is no doubt somewhat odd.
2. The case where $H(Z) = \lambda Z$ ($\lambda > 0$) is presumably appropriate for "small" enough population sizes, for it would seem plausible that at levels of $Z$ at which there is an abundance of the means of sustenance, the exponential growth curve is a reasonable first approximation.
3. An appealing set of considerations for many animal, bird, and fish populations is captured by the functional form of $H$ shown in figure 3.2.

Since we shall make use of this functional form, it will prove useful to characterize this formally. $H''(Z) < 0$ for all $Z \geq 0$. Furthermore, there are two values, $\overline{Z}$ and $\mathbf{Z}$ (with $\overline{Z} > \mathbf{Z} > 0$) at which $H(\mathbf{Z}) = H(\overline{Z}) = 0$. Consequently, there is a unique $\hat{Z}$ at which $H'(\hat{Z}) = 0$.

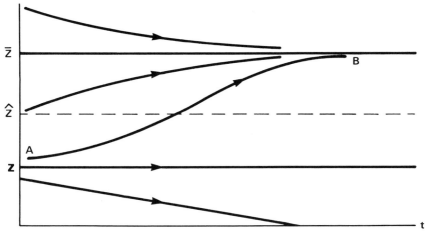

**Figure 3.3.**

It follows immediately from equation (16) that $\dot{Z}_t = 0$ if either $Z_t = \mathbf{Z}$ or $Z_t = \overline{Z}$. These are the two stationary points of (16). Of these, $\mathbf{Z}$ is unstable, while $\overline{Z}$ is stable. The intuitive idea is as follows. For very small population sizes, the chance that the species will become extinct is rather large since mating encounters are low, given the thinness of the population. Since we are considering deterministic models, the idea is caught sharply by specifying a threshold value of $Z$ (here $\mathbf{Z}$), such that if the species population size ever gets below $\mathbf{Z}$, it will eventually become extinct. The biotic potential for various land animals is "low." For such species $\mathbf{Z}$ would be "large." Unlike these, various species of fish have a "high" biotic potential. For them $\mathbf{Z}$ would be "low"; and indeed for all practical purposes it may be convenient to regard $\mathbf{Z} = 0$ for them.

In the demographic interval $(\mathbf{Z}, \hat{Z})$, conditions for the species are really favorable. The population increment $H(Z)$ is increasing in the range [i.e., $H'(Z) > 0$] because there is ample food for its sustenance. But the rate of increase is decreasing [i.e., $H''(Z) < 0$] because of the constancy of the food supply. In the range $(\hat{Z}, \overline{Z})$ the constant food supply has really begun to have effect. While $H(Z)$ is still positive, it is declining at an increasing rate [i.e., $H''(Z) < 0$] so that each marginal increase in the population size imposes an accelerating pressure on the reduction in population increment. For $Z > \overline{Z}$, the population size relative to the constant food supply is too large and the net reproduction rate is negative.

All this is, of course, very stylized. In essence we are supposing that the species inhabits a stable environment. The general form of the integral of equation (16), and thus the time profile of the population size of the species, is simple to determine and it is represented in figure 3.3. The population profile $Z_t$ depends critically on the initial population size $Z_0$. If $\mathbf{Z} > 0$ and $Z_0 < \mathbf{Z}$, the species is doomed, for one has $\lim(t \to \infty) Z_t = 0$. But even if $\mathbf{Z} < Z_0 < \overline{Z}$, there are two broad cases. If $\mathbf{Z} < Z_0 < \hat{Z}$, the population curve assumes the well-known S-shaped curve AB, where the point of inflexion is that value of $t$ at which $Z_t = \hat{Z}$. If $\hat{Z} < Z_0 < \overline{Z}$, the population curve has no point of inflexion. The critical thing to notice, however, is that if $Z_0 > \mathbf{Z}$, the $\lim(t \to \infty) Z_t = \overline{Z}$. Thus there is a ceiling to the population size that is imposed by the constant environment, in the sense that the size cannot remain indefinitely above $\overline{Z}$ by a fixed positive amount. One would regard $\overline{Z}$ as the largest sustainable population size.

Unquestionably the most famous special form of this general class of bell-shaped curves, $H(Z)$, is the case where $H$ is quadratic in $Z$, that is, where

$$H(Z) = -\alpha + \beta Z - \gamma Z^2$$
with $\alpha \geq 0$; $\beta, \gamma > 0$ and $\beta^2 > 4\alpha\gamma$ \hfill (17)

A yet more special case is where $\alpha = 0$ and, thereore, $\mathbf{Z} = 0$. Equation (17) then reduces to

$$\dot{Z} = \beta Z - \gamma Z^2 \tag{18}$$

This is simple to integrate explicitly, yielding as its solution

$$Z_t = \frac{\beta Z_0}{Z_0 + (\beta - \gamma Z_0)e^{-\beta t}} \tag{19}$$

Equation (19) denotes the classic logistic curve.

We now turn to a discussion of a concept of great importance for an understanding of the economics of a common property resource, the own rate of return on that resource. Recall the discrete time formulation (14) of the growth equation. If $Z_t$ is the population size at $t$, we know that the size at $t + \theta$ will be $Z_t + H(Z_t)\theta$. Suppose instead that at $t$ the size is not $Z_t$ but $Z_t + \Delta Z_t$, where $\Delta Z_t$ is a small positive number. The question is: What will be the size of the population at $t + \theta$?

Let us denote it by $Z_{t+\theta} + \Delta Z_{t+\theta}$. Figure 3.4 depicts the situation where a stock of size $Z_t$ gives rise to an *addition* to the stock of $OA$ over the next time period $\theta$, and a stock of size $Z_t + \Delta Z_t$ gives an addition of size $OB$. An increase in the stock by $\Delta Z_t$ therefore leads to an increase in the addition to the stock by $AB$. Since by assumption $\Delta Z_t$ is small, $AB/\Delta Z_t$ is approximately equal to $H'(Z_t)$. In other words,

$$\frac{\Delta Z_{t+\theta}}{\Delta Z_t} - 1 \simeq H'(Z_t)\theta \tag{20}$$

But equation (20) expresses the fact that $H'(Z_t)$ is the per period percentage change in the population size in the period $(t, t + \theta)$ if the population size at

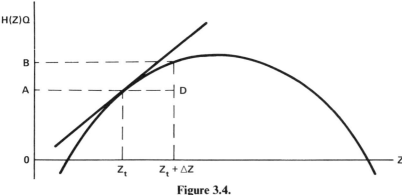

**Figure 3.4.**

$t$ were to be increased from $Z_t$ to $Z_t + \Delta Z_t$. It is this latter that is referred to as the *own rate of return* on the species at the population size $Z_t$. It is worth emphasizing that by definition the own rate of return is the *marginal* rate of return on the species. This is to be distinguished from the average rate of return, which is obviously $H(Z)/Z$. Indeed, such a model of population growth bears a striking resemblance to the more familiar models of capital accumulation. The importance of the own rate of return becomes clear when we introduce into its natural environment a second species, the human population, which preys on this one. In the remainder of this section we explore the implications of such interactions when the population growth function $H$ satisfies the equation described earlier.

Denote by $Y_t$ ($\geq 0$) the total rate of catch at $t$. It follows that the growth equation (16) then reads as

$$\dot{Z}_t = H(Z_t) - Y_t \tag{21}$$

Questions of economic interest arise when $Y_t$ can be controlled. If $\mathbf{Z} > 0$ and if past exploitations had gone on at such massive scales that $Z_0 < \mathbf{Z}$, there is not much to say. Since $Y_t \geq 0$, the species is doomed in any case. But plainly various possibilities are open if $Z_0 > \mathbf{Z}$. Notice that if $\mathbf{Z} < Z_0 < \overline{Z}$, then one can always choose $Y_t = H(Z_0)$ for all $t \geq 0$ so that $Z_t = Z_0$ for all $t \geq 0$. This would be the policy of creaming off precisely the net addition to the population at every instant so as to keep the population size constant over time. One naturally calls such a course of action a *stationary policy*. Notice that among the stationary policies the maximum rate of catch is attained when $Z = \hat{Z}$, so that $Y = H(\hat{Z})$. This maximum sustainable yield is analogous to the Golden Rule in the literature on capital accumulation. Notice as well that if $Z_0 > \mathbf{Z}$ then provided one is willing to wait long enough, the population size can reach any prescribed level so long as it is no greater than $\overline{Z}$. If $\mathbf{Z} < Z_0 < \overline{Z}$, and if $\tilde{Z}$ (where $Z_0 < \tilde{Z} < \overline{Z}$) is the target population size one is aiming for, then the policy that would enable the population size to attain this target in the shortest possible time would consist of setting $Y_t = 0$ until $Z_t$ attains the level $\tilde{Z}$. One would call such a course of action the *time-minimizing policy* for attaining $\tilde{Z}$.

We have now presented the basic framework within which the analysis in this section and the next is conducted. The paradigm we are working with is that of the fishery, though the model obviously is relevant to any biological population. Less immediately clear is its relevance to other common property resources. There is, as we have already mentioned, little in the way of firm evidence on this issue: most thorough studies of the dynamics of nonbiological common property resources have been conducted at a very micro level and do not readily yield information that can be integrated into the sort of framework used here.

Some of the world modelers have attempted to formalize the interactions between pollution and the environment (Forrester, 1971; Meadows et al., 1972). These attempts have been widely criticized (Cole et al., 1973; Freeman and Jahoda, 1978), and from the two sides of this argument one can assemble the following general picture for the case of pollution of environmental common properties such as the atmosphere and bodies of water. These have the capacity to absorb many types of pollutants up to a certain level without significantly worsening their cleanliness. Increases in pollutant inputs above this level reduce their purity, but if the flow of pollutants is stopped, the body of air or water is gradually returned to a state of cleanliness by diffusion and chemical and biological processes. In certain cases, however, particularly with bodies of water, the self-cleansing properties may be destroyed if the level of pollution exceeds an upper threshhold: they atrophy.

Figure 3.5 incorporates these general features into the framework already used. $Z$, the variable on the horizontal axis, now denotes cleanliness or purity: low $Z$ implies a high level of pollution. The curve $H(Z)$ now shows the rate at which the resource is cleaned as a function of its current state of cleanliness. The fact that very high levels of pollution (low levels of cleanliness) lead to atrophy implies that for cleanliness levels below some lower bound $\mathbf{Z}$, the rate of cleansing becomes negative. Hence the left-hand end of the $H(Z)$ curve is negative, as for population growth models. It seems reasonable that as $Z$ rises above $\mathbf{Z}$, the rate of cleansing is increasing over at least some range of $Z$; that is, the more effectively cleansing processes work, the less polluted the environment. What happens to $H(Z)$ for high values of $Z$ is less clear: it could be that it continues to rise as $Z$ approaches the zero pollution level (the case of $A\,B$), or that very low concentrations of pollutant are removed only very slowly (the case $A\,C$). The former seems more in accord with the earlier observation that low-level pollution is often absorbed with very little impact.

In either event, it is clear that we can construct a body of analysis very similar to that for fisheries. Figure 3.6 is the analog of 3.3, showing the time

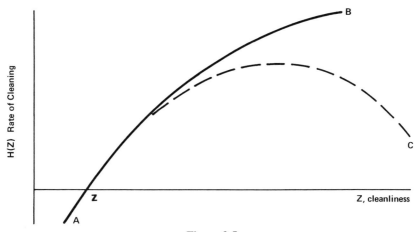

**Figure 3.5.**

paths of $Z$. If the $H(Z)$ curve has no turning point, paths converging to the upper limit will do so at an increasing rate: otherwise they will show a point of inflection, as in figure 3.3. However, it must be emphasized that this analysis is tentative: there is clearly a need for collaboration between economists and environmental scientists in investigating and modeling the dynamics of exploited common property resources.

Now that we have formalized the dynamics of a common property resource, we can investigate the impact of human use. In what follows we shall in the main analyze a fishery with free entry, with occasional comments on the way the model would need to be adapted to other cases.

Consider an economic environment in which the catch is valued in the market at a price $q$, which is independent of time and independent of the size of the catch. It may be simplest to think of there being many schools of such species, differing only in their location, and that we are analyzing the con-

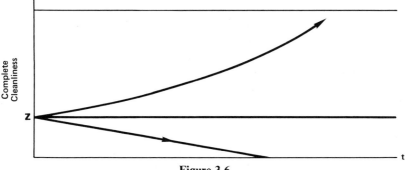

**Figure 3.6.**

sequence of free entry into a given catchment area. Alternatively, it may be supposed that while there are only a few catchment areas, the value of the catch is derived from its immediate product (say oil, if whale is the species in question), which has perfect substitutes in the market. Similarly, we assume that $q$ is constant over time. As earlier, let $X$ denote the total number of units of the variable input. Let $y$ denote the size of the output per unit input, and let $Y$ denote the total output. We take it that

$$y = f(Z,X), \text{ where } f_Z \geq 0 \text{ and } f_X \leq 0$$

$$Y = Xf(Z,X) \cong F(Z,X) \text{ where } F_X > 0, F_{XX} \leq 0 \qquad (22)$$

$$F_{ZX} \geq 0, F(Z,0) = 0, \text{ and } F(0,X) = 0$$

Notice that equation (22) does not rule out the possibility that $F$ is increasing returns to scale in $Z$ and $X$. Moreover, the only significant feature in which the production function $F$, as caught in equation (22), differs from the technology of section 1 is the explicit introduction of the total stock in (22). Since the problem was posed in the context of a single period in section 1, this population size, $Z$, was merely an implicit parameter in the production function there. But in our analysis here $Z$ may well vary over time, and if the stock size affects the ease with which the output can be obtained, it needs to be introduced in the production function. One supposes that generally a larger stock makes the output easier to obtain. This explains why one would wish to suppose $f_Z \geq 0$. If $F_X < 0$, there is crowding among inputs as well. This was a central assumption in our discussion of the commons' problem in section 1. In fact, for the single-period problem analyzed there, crowding was precisely the source of the inefficiency of the market equilibrium. For certain activities, however, crowding may well be a negligible problem for relevant input sizes. This may be so in the case of hunting for a species in the Great Plains, or indeed for the use of the water and the atmosphere for waste disposal. In such instances $f_X = 0$. The other assumptions regarding $F$ are, of course, self-explanatory.

For simplicity we take it that firms enter or depart, depending on what is instantaneously the profitable thing to do. To simplify yet further, we identify each unit input with a different firm. Consequently, the aim is to study the adjustment of the total number of units of input in the catchment area as a response to instantaneous profit. Denote by $p$ the rental price of a single unit of input. Assume that $p$ is constant. It follows that net profit, $\pi_t$, accruing to each input (and hence each firm) is $qf(Z_t, X_t) - p$. Imagine then that the adjustment mechanism can be expressed as

$$\dot{X}_t = \mu\pi_t = \mu[qf(Z_t,X_t) - p], \text{ where } \mu > 0$$

In other words, it is being supposed that the rate of change of the total number of inputs is simply proportional to $\pi_t$. It follows that the adjustment is adaptive, for the tendency is for $X$ to increase so as to wipe out $\pi_t$ if it is positive and to decrease so as to raise $\pi_t$ to zero if it is negative. But the adjustment does not necessarily occur instantaneously. $\mu$ would be regarded as the speed of adjustment.

Recall now that equation (21) can be expressed as

$$\dot{Z}_t = H(Z_t) - F(Z_t, X_t) \tag{23}$$

The preceding equations are a pair of nonlinear differential equations in $X$ and $Z$ and the question arises as to the behavior of their solutions over time. In fact, the solutions can be described qualitatively without much difficulty. For our purposes here we simplify a good deal further to provide the flavor of the kind of problems that can arise with the minimum of technical considerations. The quickest route to a simplification of the pair of equations is to consider the special case where $\mu = \infty$ and the adjustment is instantaneous. It transpires that this special case is not misleading, in that *qualitatively* most of the features of interest that emerge when $\mu$ is assumed finite emerge as well when $\mu$ is assumed infinite.

Since the adjustment is assumed to be instantaneous (i.e., $\mu = \infty$), one has $\pi_t = 0$ for all $t$. It follows, then, that

$$qf(Z_t, X_t) = p \tag{24}$$

The ecological system is now described by equations (23) and (24). Let us then eliminate $X_t$ between these two equations and thereby reduce the system to a single first-order differential equation in $Z$. In order to achieve this elimination most easily, assume further that the catch function (22) is of the form

$$F(Z,X) = Z^a X^b, \quad 0 < a,b < 1 \tag{25}$$

Using (24) and (25), it follows that $qZ_t^a X_t^{b-1} = p$. So $X_t = (q/p)^{1/(1-b)} Z_t^{a/(1-b)}$ and therefore $Z_t^a X_t^b = (q/p)^{b/(1-b)} Z_t^{a/(1-b)}$. But $f = F/X$.

Therefore equation (23) becomes

$$\dot{Z}_t = H(Z_t) - \left(\frac{q}{p}\right)^{b(1-b)} Z_t^{a(1-b)} \tag{26}$$

The problem has been reduced to analyzing the single first-order differential equation (26).

Figures 3.7 and 3.8 describe the two broad cases that arise. In figure 3.7 it is assumed that $q/p$ is sufficiently "small" compared with the other parameters of the system so that in fact there are two stationary points of equation (26) (i.e., points at which $Z = 0$). They are denoted by $Z_e$ and $Z^e$, the intersections of the curves $H(Z)$ and $(q/p)^{b/(1-b)} Z^{a/(1-b)}$. The solution path of $Z$ depends on $Z_0$, its initial value. The natural initial value to contemplate is $\overline{Z}$, the long-run stock size in the natural environment, that is, prior

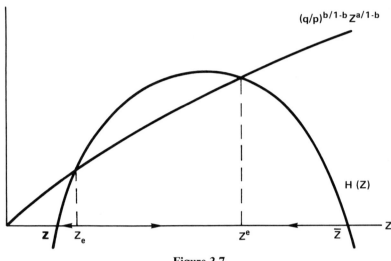

**Figure 3.7.**

to encroachment by the human population. In this event the stock size tends in the long run to $Z^e$, as one can confirm from figure 3.7. The species certainly survives under this adjustment mechanism with the given parameter values: indeed, the species survives so long as $Z_0 \geq Z_e$.

But now consider figure 3.8, where $q/p$ is assumed sufficiently "large" compared to the other parameters of the system, so that there is no stationary value of $Z$. The problem is that the curves $H(Z)$ and $(q/p)^{b/(1-b)}Z^{a/(1-b)}$ simply do not intersect. In this event the solution $Z_t$ of equation (26) declines monotonically and in *finite* time attains the value zero irrespective of what its initial value is.

It is interesting to see why the price ratio, $q/p$, matters with regard to the existence of a positive equilibrium point of equation (26). If $q/p$ is "small," then the industry's profit is nil at a "low" value of $X$ [see equation (24)]. It follows that the total catch $F$ is "low," and the species survives indefinitely. If $q/p$ is "large," then the industry's profit is nil only at a "large" value of $X$. It follows that the size of the total catch, $F$, is "high." Consequently the species is simply not allowed to regenerate itself. Notice as well that for "large" $q/p$, so long as the instability of the system—that is, the impending extinction of the species—is detected before $Z_t$ attains the value **Z**, regulatory measures can be contemplated to allow the species to survive. But once $Z_t < $ **Z**, the species is doomed. No subsequent regulations can rescue it from extinction. Why, then, do firms not see the impending extinction of the species? It is possible that firms know nothing of the growth function $H$. Indeed, if $H$ is not known with much accuracy, there is no way to tell that $Z_t < $ **Z**. So long as $Z_t > 0$, the species is still in existence. So long as **Z** $> 0$, there is no natural signal from the species to suggest that it is doomed.

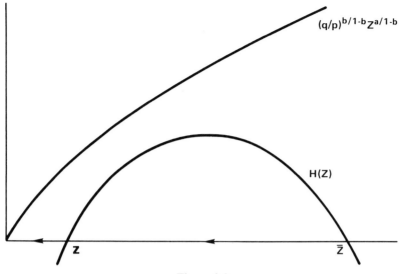

$(q/p)^{b/1-b}Z^{a/1-b}$

$H(Z)$

$Z$     $\bar{Z}$

**Figure 3.8.**

It is clear that although the foregoing relates primarily to the exploitation of biological resources, a similar analysis could be conducted for environmental goods. Suppose these are used to dispose of waste, with $X$ the level of inputs complementary to waste disposal, and $y$ the amount of waste disposed of per unit of this input. Equation (22) then has a natural reinterpretation, with the productivity of the input $X$ being greater the cleaner the relevant environment. The price $p$ of a unit of input $X$ has the same interpretation as before, but one has to regard the value of output $q$ as being the costs saved by disposing of wastes into the environment—as opposed, say, to using purification techniques. In this case the assumption of constant $q$ independent of $y$ becomes less tenable than before, though still a first approximation worth investigating. The interpretation of our equation for $\dot{X}$ using (22) is now that the rate at which firms expand or contract their processes for discharging wastes into the environment depends on the extent of cost savings $\pi$ obtained from doing this, and the rest of the analysis follows as before. It is perhaps worth remarking that if, as is often alleged, the costs of purification are high relative to the costs of discharging untreated wastes, then this implies that $q/p$ is "large" and consequently the case depicted in figure 3.8 is the more likely.

### Profit-Maximizing Use of a Common Property Resource

Our discussion of the static aspects of common property problems made it clear that the extent of overexploitation depended on market structure. This section illustrates a similar point in the dynamic context by analyzing the outcome of a use pattern designed to maximize the present value of the profits that can be extracted from a self-renewing resource. We shall show that overexploitation is less likely under these conditions than under conditions of free access, so that it is not necessarily profit maximization *per se*, but the absence of property rights or equivalent institutions that is likely to lead to overuse.

To obtain some idea of the problem, let us consider the simple case where the species can be caught, or the environment used, costlessly. In other words, no resources are required as inputs. As before, denote the industry's total output at $t$ by $Y_t$. Let $r$ denote the competitive market interest rate, assumed positive and constant, and assume furthermore that it is also the rate that is regarded as being appropriate for discounting purposes. Since in this simple case gross revenue at each instant measures net profit at that instant, we can express the present value of the industry's flow of profits as

$$\int_0^\infty e^{-rt} q Y_t dt \qquad (27)$$

It follows that the industry's policy should be to choose a feasible time profile of $Y_t$ that would maximize (27). But a feasible time profile of $Y_t$ is simply a nonnegative schedule that satisfies the population growth equation (21). Now recall figure 3.4. Denote by $\tilde{Z}$ the solution of the equation $H'(Z) = r$. This is the stock size at which the own rate of return on the resource equals the competitive market rate of interest. Since $r > 0$, it follows that $\overline{Z} < \hat{Z}$. To have an interesting problem, we shall wish to suppose as well that $\mathbf{Z} < \tilde{Z}$. This last assumption, quite apart from being realistic for many cases, is the interesting one analytically since otherwise in terms of pure profits the stock is not worth preserving.

Denote by $Z_0$ the stock size at $t = 0$, the date at which the industry's entire future policy is being contemplated. Assume that $\mathbf{Z} < Z_0 < \tilde{Z}$. Plainly, $H'(Z_0) > H'(\tilde{Z}) = r$. Consider now an interval $(0,\theta)$ of sufficiently small duration. The question is whether $Y$ should be chosen positive during this interval. The answer is "no," since given that $q$ is constant, setting $Y = 0$ during $(0,\theta)$ and creaming off from a larger stock in the future would enable the industry to earn a higher return $[H'(Z_0)\theta]$ than $r\theta$. This implies that the industry's present value of profits would be higher. This argument continues to hold so long as $Z_t < \tilde{Z}$. It follows that there is an initial period during which the industry ought to set $Y_t = 0$. Meanwhile the stock size grows. With $Y_t = 0$, the stock size will reach $\tilde{Z}$ in finite time. Should the industry allow the population size to grow beyond $\tilde{Z}$? No, since at a higher stock level the own rate of return falls below $r$ and an exactly reverse argument would be called into play. At $Z$, we have $H'(Z) = r$. At the margin the industry will be indifferent between holding the stock of the resource as an asset, or holding the

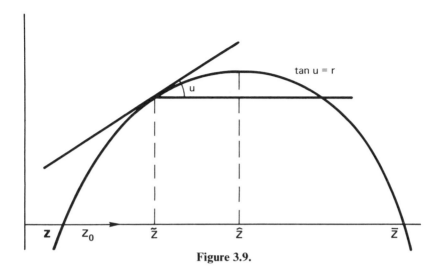

**Figure 3.9.**

numeraire asset earning $r$. It follows that from the instant when $Z_t = \tilde{Z}$ the industry ought, in the interest of profits, to allow the stock size to stay put at $\tilde{Z}$ and simply cream off the net addition to the stock. It ought to set $Y_t = H(\tilde{Z})$ from this instant onward.

To sum up: If $Z < Z_0 < \tilde{Z}$, and if the resource can be used costlessly, then the industry's present value of profits is maximized by setting $Y_t = 0$ until $Z_t = \tilde{Z}$. That is, the industry's policy should be to aim at a target stock $\tilde{Z}$ [where $H'(\tilde{Z}) = r$] and to achieve this target via the time-minimizing policy. The optimal policy subsequent to achieving the target is to pursue the stationary program. Since $r > 0$, it is also the case that the rate of use $H(\tilde{Z})$ along the stationary program is less than the rate along the Golden Rule $H(\hat{Z})$. That is, the optimal long-run rate of use is less than the maximum sustainable rate (see figure 3.9).

It should be noted that this result, namely that the optimal policy is stationary and is reached by the time-minimizing path, depends upon the assumption that the population growth function $H(z)$ is concave. More generally, if for example, this function has a convex and then a concave segment, it is possible that the profit-maximizing policy involves extinction. This is discussed in Clark (1971).

This result, which will cause no surprise to the economist, is instructive for at least three reasons. It implies (1) that the goal of intertemporal profit maximization is not necessarily inconsistent with the conservationist's aims; (2) that a total temporary ban on the exploitation of a seriously depleted stock could be advocated not merely by a conservationist, but by a hard-headed profit maximizer as well; and (3) that there is no sanctity about the maximum sustainable rate of catch as a long-run policy.

The first two points are particularly telling given that we have analyzed the problem solely in terms of what would loosely be called the "economic value" of the resource. It has been valued only in terms of the potential profit it will yield. The essential point is that because of its assumed self-renewing properties (via population growth or self-cleansing), the resource is an asset capable of yielding a positive rate of return because the increase in the stock makes future use more effective and less costly. It is therefore appropriate to manage the resource in such a way that the return it yields is comparable with returns available elsewhere in the economy, and we have seen that in many cases this will mean preserving and indeed improving the resource stock. Whether such an outcome is likely, as opposed to desirable, will depend on ownership of, or rights of access to, the resource. We saw in the last section that if access is free, so that there is no ownership of the resource, the outcome will involve overexploitation relative to the profit-maximizing solution. The solution of this section could only be operated by a monopoly owner of the resource or by the dynamic analogs of the regulatory policies discussed in section 1.

### Optimal Growth and the Emission of Pollutants

For the final section of our analysis of the dynamics of common property resoures, we look at a simple aggregative model of optimal pollution management. Though the model is simple, its analysis turns out to be complex and we shall only outline the detailed technical arguments here. What is important is that the conclusions that emerge appear to differ qualitatively from those reached by earlier analysis.[1]

It is assumed that the process of consumption gives rise to pollution, at a rate which increases with the level of consumption. Consumption, therefore, augments the stock of pollution. However, because of the absorptive and regenerative capacities of the natural environment, referred to in the previous section, the stock of pollution will decrease if no further additions are made to it. The rate of change of the stock of pollutants is therefore determined by the balance of two forces, the rate at which consumption augments this stock, and the rate at which the regenerative powers of the environment decrease it. We assume these to depend on how great the existing stock is, and formalize the process as follows. If $c$ is the level of consumption and $s$ the stock of pollution,

$$\dot{S} = g\,(c,s)$$

In particular we consider at length the special case

---

[1] Keeler, Spence, and Zeckhauser (1972) analyze a model which has similarities with this one, and which leads to some of the same conclusions.

$$\dot{S} = \rho\,(c - s)   \rho > 0, \text{ constant} \tag{28}$$

In equation (28), consumption augments pollution stocks at a rate directly proportional to the level of consumption, whereas in the absence of consumption, pollution stocks decay exponentially at a rate of $\rho$.

We suppose that the satisfaction derived from a consumption level $c$ depends both on $c$ and on the pollution stock $s$, via a function $U(c,s)$, with $\partial u/\partial c$ positive and $\partial u/\partial s$ negative. The idea here is that pollution, by lowering the level of environmental quality, reduces the enjoyment associated with any given level of material consumption.

The utility function $U(c,s)$ and the pollution growth function (28) are now embedded in a conventional neoclassical growth model where a production process uses labor and capital to produce a single output, which may be either consumed or invested. Within this framework, we inquire into the division of output between consumption and investment (the latter determining the rate of growth of the system) which maximizes the discounted value of the utility of consumption over an unbounded horizon. In other words, we are seeking to characterize the optimal investment and growth paths in a simple aggregative growth model, given that consumption generates pollution which then interferes with the satisfaction from consumption, and given that the environment has a capacity to absorb and degrade pollutants.

The problem of characterizing the optimal growth and investment paths in a simple aggregative model without any explicit formulation of pollution outputs and environmental absorptive capacity is a familiar one. Our purpose therefore is to see what difference it makes to the outcome to include these factors. Anticipating matters a little, the answer is that it makes a considerable difference. In particular, in the usual model without the effects of concern here, it is well known (see Heal, 1973) that the paths of consumption and capital per head must be chosen so as to converge monotonically over time to constant values which are independent of the initial conditions. In the present model, however,

1. If there are stationary values to which consumption and capital per head asymptote, these will not be independent of initial conditions. History matters.
2. Convergence to stationary values need not be monotone, but may involve cyclical behavior of the variables.
3. The variables may in fact asymptote to stable limit cycles, rather than to stationary values.

The feature of this model which leads to the qualitative differences from the conventional solution path is the inclusion in the utility function of a stock variable which is dependent upon the entire past history of the economy. A number of authors have investigated models that have this characteristic:

our work is based closely upon Heal and Ryder (1973), though Kurz (1968) has analyzed models which fall into this class. Only Ryder and Heal demonstrate the existence of cyclical solutions.

It is clear, then, that the introduction of pollution generation, of pollution as an argument of the preference function, and of the absorptive capacity of environmental resources does make a difference to the qualitative characteristics of an optimal growth and investment program. Unfortunately space prevents us from exploring this matter as far as it seems to merit here, but in the remainder of this section we set out a formal model which substantiates the points made earlier.

The problem with which we are concerned can be stated as:

$$\text{maximize} \int_0^\infty U(c,s)e^{-rt}\, dt$$

subject to

$$\dot{k} = f(k) - \lambda k - c$$
$$0 \leq c \leq f(k)$$
$$\dot{s} = \rho\,(c - s)$$

and $s$, $k$ given at $t = 0$ \hfill (29)

Here $c$, $s$, and $k$ are the levels of consumption (a flow), pollution, and capital (stocks) per capita. All are understood to be functions of time. $f(k)$ is the output per head obtained from capital per head of $k$, $\lambda$ is the rate of population growth and $r \geq 0$ is a discount rate. The problem is clearly an extension of the usual neoclassical optimal growth problem: formally it is an optimal control problem with two state variables (the stocks $k$ and $s$) and one control variable, $c$. It is also important to note that its mathematical structure is identical to that of the problem analyzed by Heal and Ryder (1973), although the interpretation is rather different. We therefore draw on the results of that paper, without giving proofs here.

We use the following assumptions:

(A1)    $U_c(c,s) = \partial u/\partial c > 0$

(A2)    $U_s(c,s) = \partial u/\partial s \leq 0$

(A3)    $U_{cc}(c,s) < 0,\ U_{cc}(c,s)\, U_{ss}(c,s) - \{U_{cs}(c,s)\}^2 \geq 0$

The payoff is therefore concave in $c$ and $s$, and strictly concave in $c$.

(A5)    $f(k) > 0, f'(k) > 0, f''(k) < 0$

        for all $k > 0$, and $\lim_{k \to 0} f(k) = 0$,  $\lim_{k \to \infty} f(k) = \infty$

(A6)    $\lim_{k \to 0} f'(k) = \infty$,  $\lim_{k \to \infty} f(k) = 0$

(A5) and (A6) are standard assumptions on production functions, implying

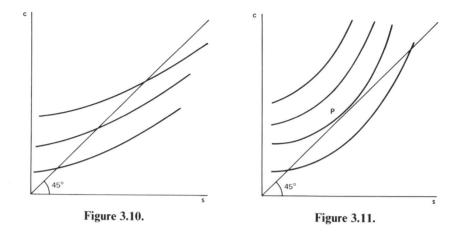

Figure 3.10.                                    Figure 3.11.

constant returns to scale, diminishing returns to proportions and certain regularity conditions at corners.

The solution to problem (29) is very sensitive to the specification of the utility function $U(c,s)$. Two possibilities are given in figures 3.10 and 3.11, which show the contours of $U$ in the $c - s$ plane. Both diagrams show the contours of functions $U(c,s)$ which are increasing in $c$ and decreasing in $s$. The crucial difference is in their behavior along the 45° line. This line is important because from (28) it is clear that if consumption is kept constant at a level say $\bar{c}$, then the pollution stock will also tend to a constant value equal to $\bar{c}$. [There is clearly a dimensionality problem in an equation such as $\bar{c} = \bar{s}$, or even in the term $c - s$ in (28): we should imagine $s$ being multiplied by a constant which performs the necessary conversion, the units of $s$ being chosen so that the numerical value of this constant is unity.] It follows that in a stationary solution, $c$ and $s$ are equal and the system lies on the 45° line in figures 3.10 and 3.11. In the former, $U$ is monotonically increasing along this line, whereas in the latter it reaches satiation at the point of tangency $P$ and declines thereafter. In behavioral terms we are distinguishing the following two cases:

1. An increase in a constant consumption level and its associated equilibrium pollution level always raises welfare. Formally, $U_c(c,c) + U_s(c,c) > 0$. This is figure 3.10,
2. An increase in a constant consumption level and its associated equilibrium pollution level may reduce welfare. Now we may have $U_c(c,c) + U_s(c,c) < 0$: this is figure 3.11.

Either case seems possible: intuitively, the issue is whether in a long-run equilibrium situation the gain in well-being from a rise in consumption is or is not outweighed by the decline in well-being from the associated decline in

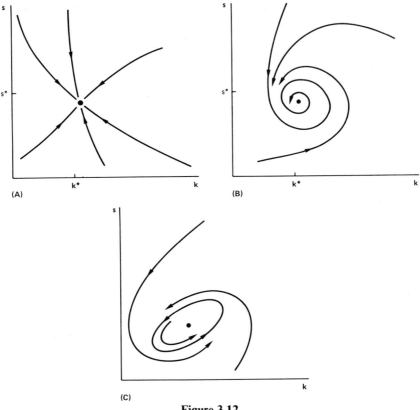

**Figure 3.12.**

environmental benefits. This is a matter on which there is clearly room for disagreement, with a number of particularly vocal contributions arguing in favor of case (1) and figure 3.11 (Mishan, 1977; Meadows, et al., 1972).

Let us now move to a formal statement of the results. It is shown by Heal and Ryder that in case (1) (figure 3.10) there are three possible outcomes.

1a.  There are unique stationary values $s^*$ and $k^*$ of $s$ and $k$ to which any solution to (29) asymptotes. The pair $(s^*,k^*)$ form a stable node in the $s - k$ plane so that the approach is essentially monotonic.

1b.  There may be unique stationary values as in (1a), but these form a stable focus so that the approach is via damped oscillations.

1c.  By using the Hopf bifurcation theorem, one can also show (Benhabib, 1978) that there may be a stable limit cycle to which any solution to (29) will tend. These outcomes are shown in figure 3.12.

Which of these outcomes occurs depends in a rather complex way on the parameters $r$ and $\rho$ and on the function $U(\ )$. Roughly speaking, however, the cyclical cases are more likely to occur, as $\rho$ increases. [For details, see

Ryder and Heal (1973).[2]] The existence of cyclical paths is unexpected and merits discussion. What seems to happen along these is that a high level of industrial output, leading to high levels of pollution, is followed by a period of lower output. The pollution stock falls (rapidly because $\rho$ is large) and once this has happened, output again rises, leading to a period of high consumption with a low level of pollution in the environment until pollutant stocks catch up. One could perhaps describe this as a policy of intermittent reductions in industrial output designed to reduce the burden on the environment and give its self-regenerative powers time to degrade and diffuse the accumulated load of wastes.

In case (2), corresponding to figure 3.11, matters are a good deal more complex. There may now be many pairs $(s_i^*, k_i^*)$ in the $s - k$ plane which provide stationary solutions to the differential equations characterizing a solution to problem (29). Any solution to (29) will approach one of these pairs asymptotically, but which one it will approach will depend on the initial conditions $s(0)$ and $k(0)$. This is an interesting and important conclusion. It is of general interest to economists because in optimal growth models such as those analyzed here, it is unusual to find that the asymptotic behavior of the system is sensitive to initial conditions. (Of course, over any finite interval the behavior does depend on these conditions.)

More specifically, it is of interest because it implies that the industrial-environmental balance (represented by the values of $k$ and $s$) at which a nation or region should aim depends upon the balance from which it starts. The targets at which a heavily industrialized and environmentally despoiled region should aim may be very different from and involve higher pollution levels than those that would be appropriate for a geographically similar region beginning with a better preserved environment. One might find some justification here for the idea of designated *disaster areas*, which has been suggested on occasions. Another important implication would seem to be that the industrial–environmental configuration for which developing countries should plan would not necessarily be appropriate for developed countries even if both had access to similar technologies and were similarly endowed geologically, just because of the differences in initial conditions.

## 3. Summary and Research Suggestions

We have attempted here a partial review of the literature on the use patterns of common property resources, and we have indicated a number of apparently interesting and fruitful extensions of that literature.

---

[2] In the case of cyclical paths, irreversibility of investment may change the nature of the solution. (See, e.g., Fisher, Krutilla and Cicchetti, 1972.)

The essence of "the problem of the commons" is overexploitation, and we have seen in both static and dynamic contexts that the likelihood of this depends upon the institutional and market structure of the economy within which the resource is used. The extent of this overexploitation may be reduced by institutional reform, such as redefinition of property rights or extension of the scope of markets, or by regulatory measures such as taxes, quotas, and licenses. We considered these options in detail in the static case, noting that none is a panacea. Property rights may be hard to define, and the Coase theorem upon which some of their supposed efficacy rests is vulnerable to problems of incentive compatibility. The necessary markets, on the other hand, would be thin, and nonconvexities in the technologies over the extended commodity space might condemn them to perpetual disequilibrium. Regulatory measures also face problems which are largely of an informational type. One cannot regulate without knowing in detail the costs and benefits of different kinds of outcome.

In a dynamic setting, the problems become even more complex. Here our concern was largely to analyze the dynamics of exploited common property resources under two different institutional structures—free access and single ownership. The outcomes were in keeping with what one would expect from the static analysis, though it is quite clear that we need more information about the dynamics of nonbiological common property resources before we can be convinced of the relevance of our models to these cases. It is also possible that some of the problems of eliciting information about the consequences of different policies may be less severe in a dynamic context because of the possibilities for learning provided by repeated observations. Again, we have not had space to pursue this point at length, and it would clearly constitute a major research program. It might well be instructive to pose the regulatory problem as a super-game: in other areas not entirely unrelated, we have evidence that repeated play games are more likely to have efficient solutions than the equivalent one-shot games. (See, for example, Friedman, 1977 and Heal, 1976.)

In our final section we reviewed the problem of optimal management of consumption-linked pollution in an environment with a limited capacity to degrade pollution. The results of that study were unexpected and certainly suggest the need for further analysis of models of this sort. It is of interest to note that Cropper (1976) also finds multiple stationary solutions in a model of growth-environment interactions.

## References

Arrow, Kenneth J. 1969. "Classificatory Notes on the Production and Transmisson of Technological Knowledge," *American Economic Review, Proceedings* vol. 59, pp. 29–35.

————. 1978. "The Property Rights Doctrine and Demand Revelation under Incomplete Information," I.M.S.S.S. Technical Report No. 243, Stanford University.

————, and Anthony C. Fisher. 1974. "Preservation, Uncertainty and Irreversibility," *Quarterly Journal of Economics* vol. 87, pp. 312–319.

Baumol, William J., and W. E. Oates. 1975. *The Theory of Environmental Policy* (Englewood Cliffs, N.J., Prentice-Hall).

Benhabib, J. 1979. "A Note on Optimal Growth and Intertemporally Dependent Preferences," *Economics Letters*.

Brown, D. J., and Geoffrey M. Heal. 1979. "Equity, Efficiency and Increasing Returns," *Review of Economic Studies* vol. 46 (October) pp. 571–586.

————, and ————. 1980. "Marginal Cost Pricing, Two-Part Tariffs and Increasing Returns in a General Equilibrium Model," *Journal of Public Economics* vol. 13 (February) pp. 25–50.

Clark, Colin W. 1971. "Economically Optimal Policies for the Utilization of Biologically Renewable Resources," *Mathematical Biosciences* vol. 12, pp. 245–260.

Coase, R. H. 1960. "The Problem of Social Cost," *Journal of Law and Economics* vol. 3, pp. 1–44.

Cole, H. S. D., et al. 1973. *Thinking about the Future* (London: Chatto and Windus for Sussex University Press).

Cropper, Maureen L. 1976. "Regulating Activities with Catastrophic Environmental Effects," *Journal of Environmental Economics and Management* vol. 3, pp. 1–15.

Dales, J. H. 1968. *Pollution, Property and Prices* (Toronto: University of Toronto Press).

Dasgupta, Partha, and Geoffrey M. Heal. 1979. *Economic Theory and Exhaustible Resources* (Cambridge, England, Cambridge Economic Handbooks).

Dorfman, Robert. 1974. "The Technical Basis for Decision-Making," in E. T. Haefle, ed., *The Governance of Common Property Resources* (Baltimore, Md., Johns Hopkins University Press for Resources for the Future).

Fisher, Anthony C., John Krutilla, and Charles Cicchetti. 1972. "The Economics of Environmental Preservation: A Theoretical and Empirical Analysis," *American Economic Review* vol. 62, pp. 605–619.

Forrester, J. W. 1971. *World Dynamics* (Cambridge, Mass., M.I.T.).

Freeman, Christopher and Marie Jahoda. 1978. *World Futures: The Great Debate* (Oxford, Martin Robertson).

Friedman, James. 1977. *Oligopoly and the Theory of Games* (Amsterdam, North-Holland).

Hardin, Garrett. 1968. "The Tragedy of the Commons," *Science* vol. 162, pp. 1243–1248.

Heal, Geoffrey M. 1973. *The Theory of Economic Planning* (Amsterdam, North-Holland).

————. 1976. "Do Bad Products Drive Out Good?" *Quarterly Journal of Economics* vol. 90, pp. 499–502.

Henry, Claude. 1974. "Option Values in the Economics of Irreplaceable Assets," *Review of Economic Studies*, Symposium on the Economics of Exhaustible Resources, pp. 89–104.

————. 1978. "On Some Reasons Why Space is Wasted," *Ecole Polytechnique*, Paris, France, Discussion Paper.

Keeler, Emmett, Michael Spence, and Richard Zeckhauser. 1972. "The Optimal Control of Pollution," *Journal of Economic Theory* vol. 4, pp. 19–34.

Kurz, Mordechai. 1968. "Optimal Growth with Wealth Effects," *International Economic Review* vol. 9, pp. 348–357.

Meadows, Dennis, Donella H. Meadows, Jørgen Randers, and William Behrens III. 1972. *The Limits to Growth* (New York, Universe Books).

Mishan, Ezra. 1977. *The Economic Growth Debate* (London, Allen & Unwin).

Ryder, H. E., and Geoffrey M. Heal. 1973. "Optimal Growth with Intertemporally Dependent Preferences," *Review of Economic Studies* vol. 40, pp. 1–32.

Starrett, David A. 1972. "Fundamental Non-Convexities in the Theory of Externalities," *Journal of Economic Theory* vol. 4, pp. 180–199.

# PART III
# EVALUATING THE SOCIAL COSTS OF DEGRADING ENVIRONMENTAL RESOURCES

# 4

# Environmental Management
# Under Uncertainty

## Partha Dasgupta

## 1. The Problem

Schemes for protecting the environment are usually devised in the face of uncertainty. More often than not, the effects of emissions of different sorts of environmental pollutants are unknown. This is unavoidable. No doubt in many instances pilot studies can be conducted to determine these effects, but they take time, particularly if the effects are cumulative over time. Meanwhile, decisions have to be made about the appropriate control of pollution (although the decision often may be to introduce no control whatsoever). This uncertainty is one reason why debates on environmental issues are often so acrimonious. Even the experts differ. This is as true for effects of mercury deposits on marine life as it is for the effect of high-altitude supersonic jets on the upper layers of the atmosphere.[1] As new products and new technologies are introduced, new effluents are added to the environment. Even as information is acquired about the effects of existing pollutants new forms whose

This paper is based on chapter 5 of *The Social Management of Environmental Resources*, to be published by the United Nations (forthcoming 1982). I am most grateful to Edward Dommen and Jack Stone of the United Nations Conference on Trade and Development, and to Yusuf Ahmad of the United Nations Environment Programme for encouraging me to write the book. I am also grateful to the participants in the RFF/NSF Conference on "The Implications of Resource and Environmental Constraints on Economic Growth;" to Eric Maskin, with whom I have had extensive discussions on the problem of incentive compatibility; and to Geoffrey Heal for numerous discussions on the economics of natural resources.

[1] Perhaps the most publicized environmental debate has been centered on the safety of nuclear reactors generating electricity. Disagreements about the likelihood of radiation leakage have probably been the sharpest among those who have access to the greatest information.

impact is unknown are created. To make matters worse, the continuing emission of certain pollutants has irrevocable consequences if the environment displays what ecologists call threshold effects.[2]

It is convenient to distinguish at the outset environmental risks that are borne by individuals from those borne by society as a whole. An increase in the emissions from automobiles in a region increases the chance that individuals will suffer from bronchial disorders. But individuals face independent risks, depending on such factors as age and health, and an increase in atmospheric contamination merely increases such risks. In contrast, the possible effects of massive deforestation on the global climate are jointly faced by all. Such risks are perfectly correlated, and the most extreme examples are the ones that generate apocalyptic visions.

Environmental risks that are borne by individuals more or less independently of one another are somewhat easier to handle analytically, for one can appeal directly to the traditional theory of externalities. Moreover, economic theory tells us something about the relation between the ideal price of insurance against such risks and the risks themselves.[3] Consequently, for the most part this chapter discusses those environmental risks that are borne by society as a whole.

Even casual thinking on environmental problems alerts us to the fact that they often involve a small chance of large-scale damage to society as a whole. These are precisely the kinds of problems that decision theory finds awkward. It is easy to cast doubt on the plausibility of the "expected utility" hypothesis in the case of risks that are characterized both by "low" probability and "high" damage, but it cannot be claimed that there is anything as systematic (and at the same time more persuasive) that could replace it. In what follows, therefore, I conduct the discussion from the viewpoint of Bayesian decision makers—recognizing all the while that this framework of thought may well be questioned when it is applied to environmental risks.

It is customary in welfare economics to encourage the government to accept the tastes and beliefs of individuals and then aggregate them in a suitable way. The fundamental theorem of welfare economics is addressed to this kind of political environment. To be sure, it is recognized that it is desirable to make public various expert opinions and so enable individuals to base their beliefs on better information. One would like to suppose that the government is vigorously engaged in initiating such public debates, that is, in the supply of such public goods. At any rate, one supposes at the very least that there is public debate, whether or not the government has been responsible for its initiation. However, it is possible to argue that in many cases (especially where

---

[2] For a discussion of the possible sources of such threshold effects, see for example, Dasgupta and Heal (1979), chapter 5.

[3] See Malinvaud (1972).

public health is at issue) environmental protection is rather like a merit good, and so the case for the government to base its policies on only the most informed opinions ought not to be ruled out.[4]

In what follows I avoid facing this issue by simply supposing that the government (regulator) can construct an (expected) damage function—a function that relates the (expected) social damage to the level of pollutant emission. How such a function is arrived at by the government is also something I shall not elaborate on here. If social damages are assessed on the basis of the citizens' willingness to pay for reducing the level of pollutants, the government is faced with the classical free-rider problem—an issue that has been discussed at length in recent years.[5]

While the social damages caused by pollutants have received considerable attention in the literature, so far as regulatory agencies are concerned, there is usually a good deal of uncertainty over the costs of pollution control programs. Even if cleanup costs are known by individual firms (which have the required expertise), they are unlikely to be known by the regulators. Again, it might be argued that with time the regulatory agency can, by inviting expert opinion, obtain precise information on such costs. But pollution control programs take a while to plan and implement and the investments undertaken in such programs are also largely irrevocable. A good deal of uncertainty on the part of the regulatory authorities will persist. Once this is recognized, it is clear that one is up against a moral problem as well. There will be a strong incentive on the part of priviate firms to overstate cleanup costs, which the regulatory agency will not be able to confirm.

To sum up: environmental discussions need to be conducted with the clear recognition that (1) the emission of pollutants usually has serious external diseconomies; (2) the diseconomics may well be irrevocable; (3) the effect of pollutants on the environment is uncertain; and (4) the moral problem is large, constraining the kinds of regulations that might be envisaged. It is no wonder that environmental problems are formidable.

This chapter discusses some of the problems that arise in prescribing efficient policies for the public management of environmental resources under uncertainty. The next section concentrates on decision rules under environmental uncertainty. The remainder of the chapter is concerned with the harder problem of formulating planning rules when a government is not only faced with environmental uncertainty, but when there also is an information gap between the different agents in the economy. Section 3 poses the problem in a general setting and looks at its general structure. Section 4 illustrates one class of incentive scheme designed to circumvent the classical free-rider problem. Section 5 and the appendix contain a fairly comprehensive account

---

[4] For a discussion of merit goods, see Musgrave (1959).
[5] See, for example, Groves and Ledyard (1977).

of incentive scheme for environmental control when only the firms know the pollution abatement costs. The problem is presented in the context of the debate on the merits of effluent charges versus standards.

## 2. Social Cost–Benefit Analysis Under Uncertainty

### Environmental Research Projects

One way to reduce risks is to spread them by choosing one's actions appropriately. Indeed, a good part of the early literature on the economics of uncertainty was concerned with exploring circumstances in which diversification pays, and with analyzing the related question of how mutual insurance schemes enable a society to achieve this diversification.

A second way to reduce risks is to obtain further information on the uncertain areas. Pilot studies designed to investigate the environmental effects of pollutants and research designed toward discovering cheaper pollution abatement technologies are examples. This is not the place to discuss the strong *a priori* reasons for supposing that a market economy is unlikely to sustain the right amount of expenditure in obtaining such information and directing it along the right routes. This has been analyzed at length by Arrow (1970) and Dasgupta and Stiglitz (1977). Instead, we assume that at least a part of environmental R&D expenditure is carried out by the public sector. What I propose to show in this section is (1) that environmental R&D projects often carry with them an insurance value, so that the social costs of risks associated with such projects are often *negative*, and (2) that a government following Bayesian decision rules should not attempt a complete diversification among R&D strategies, even if they are uncorrelated, but instead would be well advised to specialize in only a few avenues of research.

Suppose society is uncertain about the precise effects of environmental pollution associated with specific economic activities. For example, it may not be known whether polychlorinated biphenyls (PCBs) have a large or small effect on the marine food chain. Since research on this question is under way, only time will tell which is the case. The issue to be decided now is whether to undertake, for example, a research project to discover methods for breaking PCB molecules into harmless constituents. Even if such a project were successful, the realized gross social benefit from it will be high only if it is found that PCB has a large detrimental effect on the marine food chain; not otherwise. This is another way of saying that the social return on such a project is inversely associated with society's social income (i.e., national income corrected for environmental effects). This means that such a project provides society with insurance against adverse environmental effects. In this case, provided the variance of the project is not too great, a risk-averse society would prefer such a project to a sure project with the same expected return that was not environmental. In other words, society would prefer such an uncertain project to a sure project even if its expected social return is slightly less than the return from the sure project—the social cost of risk associated with the project is negative.

The second point worth emphasizing here is best illustrated by the observation that research activity in general is concerned with the acquisition of information. This acquisition requires the expenditure of resources, but not all information is worth this expenditure. Nor in general does the acquisition of information eliminate uncertainty, but this is no reason for not seeking it. Even when uncertainty is not eliminated, the information obtained may alter plans, and therein lies its value. Instead of taking an action in the absence of further information, one may wish to wait until more information is available. Of course, payment has to be made for this information. At the time one pays for the information (e.g., R & D expenditure) one does not know precisely what will be acquired (the outcome of the R & D project). However, one knows in advance that the optimal course of action will be based on the information acquired. The value of a research project is the expected social net benefit to be obtained from it. While I have provided a verbal account, the value of information can be represented in a precise mathematical manner (see, e.g., Marschak and Radner, 1972, and Dasgupta and Heal, 1979).

Suppose we were to represent environmental R & D projects of a certain kind by the degree of refinement in the experiments that define the projects. For example, all projects in the class so defined may be concerned with the effects of PCB in the marine food chain, but they may differ in the precision with which the investigator determines the effects. Suppose we were to denote the degree of precision (and therefore a research project) by $x$ ($\geq 0$); thus a higher value of $x$ denotes a more detailed experiment. We may represent the quantity of information by $x$; therefore, $x = 0$ is the most crude experiment of all—namely, no experiment! Suppose that the marginal social cost of information is positive. Then it can be shown (see Radner and Stiglitz, 1975, and Wilson, 1975) that under fairly weak conditions the net value of information declines in the neighborhood of zero information (see figure 4.1). Thus, if it is worth acquiring information of a certain type (as in figure 4.1), the amount of information ought to be no less than a certain positive level. But this means presumably that the decision maker (here the government) ought to specialize in certain types of research.

The net value of information declines in the neighborhood of no information because first, no conceivable outcome of a completely noninformative experiment can alter the prior probabilities of the decision maker concerning alternative states of nature, and second, the *gross* value of information associated with any research project is computed on the assumption that the decision maker optimizes for each and every possible outcome of the project. It follows from these two observations (and a few technical assumptions) that

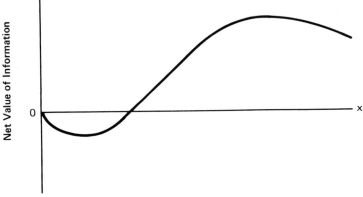

**Figure 4.1.**

the derivative of the *net* value of information at $x = 0$ is exactly equal to the negative of the marginal cost of information at $x = 0$. Since by assumption the marginal cost is positive, the net value of information declines initially.

These arguments suggest the possibility of increasing returns in the value of information (which, incidentally, has nothing to do with possible lumpiness in R&D expenditure). Accordingly, a society ought to channel its R&D expenditure, not minutely into every possible avenue, but substantially into a few.

### Irreversible Investment Under Uncertainty and Option Values

In the preceding section it was noted that one way to reduce risks is to purchase information. It was noted as well that an individual (or government), when choosing a particular research project, does not know the precise outcome of the project, but will delay taking action until the results are available.

This section analyzes a very special case of this, a case provided by the passage of time. We are uncertain about tomorrow's weather at a given location. But tomorrow we shall know. How nice it would be, then, if we could postpone until tomorrow a decision with a value sensitive to tomorrow's weather (e.g., a picnic). This is what one means by keeping options open; the general principle is the principle of flexibility. It is preferable to keep one's plans flexible—that is, to take actions today which are less costly to revise later, when new information is received. One knows that with the passage of time new information will be received—perhaps without cost.

Nowhere has the principle of flexibility been appealed to more than in environmental resources, whether it be mineral exploitation of areas of scenic beauty, cutting down redwood trees, or damming a river for a power project. Each of the actions involved in these examples is irrevocable or, at least, reversible only at a high cost. Since this also means that there is no flexibility in these decisions, concern about such actions in the presence of uncertainty is understandable. In this section we study an example designed to capture this issue (see Henry, 1974, and Arrow and Fisher, 1974). We note that an irrevocable decision forces a risk-neutral decision maker to act in a manner that suggests a form of risk-aversion.

Before presenting the example formally, it is well to point out its salient ingredients. Since we are concerned with the question of flexibility, the example is concerned with the possibility of a *sequence* of decisions over time. To keep matters simple, we suppose that today's decision is irrevocable; that is, today's action cannot be "undone" tomorrow. Finally, we suppose a risk-neutral decision maker. Since such an individual can replace random variables by their expected values without a blush, we shall be able to calculate easily the value to him of keeping his options open.

Imagine two instants $t = 0, 1$. There is a fixed quantity of land of size unity that is entirely untarnished initially. The net benefit of developing a marginal unit of land at $t = 0$ is known with certainty to be $b_0$ (which is assumed to be independent of the amount developed). There are two states of nature $\theta_s (s = 1, 2)$. The state of nature is revealed at $t = 1$. If $\theta_1$ prevails (the probability of this is $\pi$), then the *net* benefit of a unit of developed land is $b_1$ (which is assumed to be independent of the amount developed). If $\theta_2$ prevails (the probability of this is, by definition, $1 - \pi$), the *net* benefit of a unit of developed land is $b_2$ (also assumed to be independent of the amount developed). In other words, the uncertainty pertains to future benefits from land development. We shall take it that when at $t = 1$ the state of nature is revealed, there is a further choice about how much land to develop at $t = 1$. Thus, decisions have to be made at both instants. Let $D_0$ denote the amount of land that is chosen to be developed at $t = 0$. And let $D_1$ and $D_2$ denote the size of developed land at $t = 1$ under the two states of nature $\theta_1$ and $\theta_2$. Then, expected net benefit can be repesented as

$$b_0 D_0 + \pi b_1 D_1 + (1 - \pi) b_2 D_2 \tag{1}$$

(We suppose, for simplicity, a zero discount rate.) Notice that since expected net benefit is linear in $D_0$, $D_1$, and $D_2$, we are hypothesizing risk neutrality. For an interesting problem, assume $b_1 < 0$, $b_2 > 0$ and $\pi b_1 + (1 - \pi) b_2 > 0$. Thus in state $\theta_1$, net benefit from land development is *negative*, but the expected net benefit from land development at $t = 1$ is positive.

Let us first assume that land can be *un*developed costlessly; that is, the decision at $t = 0$ is a revocable one. In this case the aim would be to maximize (1) by choosing $D_0$, $D_1$, and $D_2$, subject to the constraint $0 \leq D_0, D_1, D_2 \leq 1$. The optimal policy is clear enough. One chooses $D_1 = 0$ and $D_2 = 1$. The optimal value of $D_0$ depends on the value of $b_0$. If $b_0 < 0$, then one should set $D_0 = 0$. Likewise, if $b_0 > 0$, then one should set $D_0 = 1$. If $b_0 = 0$, then there is no unique optimal choice for $D_0$. But the central point is that the optimal decision at $t = 0$ depends solely on the sign of $b_0$.

Now suppose we pretend that the net benefit from land development at $t = 1$ is known with certainty to be $\pi b_1 + (1 - \pi)b_2$. For vividness one might like to suppose that a commitment is made at $t = 0$ regarding the quantity of land to be developed at $t = 1$ irrespective of what the state of nature is. The problem then is to choose $D_0$ and $\tilde{D}$ (with $0 \leq D_0, \tilde{D} \leq 1$), with a view to maximizing

$$b_0 D_0 + [\pi b_1 + (1 - \pi)b_2]\tilde{D} \tag{2}$$

Plainly $\tilde{D} = 1$ since $\pi b_1 + (1 - \pi)b_2 > 0$ by assumption. But the optimal initial level of land development depends solely on the sign of $b_0$. No bias results in current decision as a result of replacing the random variable by its expected value in the objective function.

Suppose now that land development is irrevocable. If we continue to pretend that the net benefit from land development at $t = 1$ is known with certainty to be $\pi b_1 + (1 - \pi)b_2$, then the problem consists in maximizing (2) by choosing $D_0$ and $\tilde{D}$ subject to the constraint $0 \leq D_0 \leq \tilde{D} \leq 1$. Given that by assumption $\pi b_1 + (1 - \pi)b_2 > 0$, one has $\tilde{D} = 1$ at the optimum, and the optimal initial level of land development depends once again on the sign of $b_0$. Thus the irrevocability of the act of developing makes no difference to the outcome. But the original problem consisted in choosing $D_0$, $D_1$, and $D_2$ with a view to maximizing (1). With the assumption of irrevocability, the constraint is $0 \leq D_0 \leq D_1, D_2 \leq 1$. Let us compute the true optimum policy. If $D_0$ is the initial amount of land developed, then given that land development is irrevocable, we shall wish to set $D_1 = D_0$, since further development will certainly not be desired if $\theta_1$ is the state of nature. Plainly, one will also desire to set $D_2 = 1$. Consequently (1) reduces to the form,

$$(b_0 + \pi b_1)D_0 + (1 - \pi)b_2 \tag{3}$$

and the planning problem is to maximize (3) by choosing $D_0$ subject to the constraint $0 \leq D_0 \leq 1$. It is clear that the condition for positive initial development is stiffer, it being the case that $b_0 + \pi b_1 \geq 0$. In other words, if $0 < b_0 < -\pi b_1$, then one should ideally set $D_0 = 0$ even though in the preceding analysis such a circumstance would dictate setting $D_0 = 1$.

We conclude that if investment is judged irrevocable, there may well be a tendency toward *over*investment currently if the random future benefit is replaced by its expected value. That is to say, replacing random variables by their expected values is an incorrect move even for the risk-neutral decision maker if current decisions are irrevocable. For the example at hand, the decision maker will require a rate of current benefits of at least the value $-\pi b_1 (> 0)$ in order to foreclose his options.

## 3. Incentive Schemes for Environmental Management: The General Problem

The preceding section was concerned with certain types of "games" against nature which appear to be relevant in the context of environmental management. This and the following subsections study environmental management problems that a regulator (government) faces when there is an information gap between the decision maker and those affected by his (or her) actions. This information gap could, for example, be between the regulator and the firms engaged in environmental pollution. Firms typically will know more about their own cleanup costs than will the regulator, and may balk at providing correct information if it is not in their interest to do so. Information gaps presumably also exist between the regulator and citizens who are affected by pollutants. In fact, it seems plausible that this latter information gap is in general more difficult to close. While it is possible at least in principle for a regulator to discover firms' cleanup costs (e.g., by hiring independent experts), determining the extent of a citizen's disaffection for pollutants is an entirely different matter. Indeed, it is the potential impossibility of closing this latter information gap by getting different individuals to truthfully reveal their preferences that has been referred to as the "free-rider" problem in the theory of public goods.

The problem of devising appropriate incentive schemes in the face of information gaps has been a major concern of economists during the past few years and it is probably too early to attempt a rounded view of the findings. It will nevertheless be helpful here to pose the problem in a rather general setting so as to see precisely what issues are at stake before presenting some specific incentive schemes that are relevant for environmental management.

Consider a society composed of $N(i = 1, \ldots, N)$ individuals and one in which the planning problem is to choose element(s) from a set of feasible social alternatives, which we call $A$. One would suppose that in general the set $A$ is itself not known to the planner, since the set of feasible alternatives may depend on the preferences of individuals which, by assumption, are not known fully by the planner. For our purposes there is no harm in supposing that it is fixed and given, and we shall suppose this to be the case. Assume next that each individual $i$ possesses a characteristic, $\theta_i$, which specifies his preference ordering, $R_i(\theta_i)$ on $A$. Assume further that society's ethical attitudes about collective choices are embodied in what we shall call a social choice rule (SCR), $f$, which is formally a correspondence that selects, for each possible configuration $\theta [= (\theta_1, \ldots, \theta_i, \ldots, \theta_N)]$ of individual preferences and other relevant characteristics, a set $f(\theta)$ of feasible social alternatives; that is $f(\theta) \subseteq A$.

One interprets $f(\theta)$ as the set of welfare optima. For example, if society equates Pareto efficiency with social welfare, its SCR would be the Pareto rule, which selects all Pareto-efficient social alternatives. If the true value of $\theta_i$ were known for each and every $i$ by the planner, the problem of selecting an alternative in $f(\theta)$ [$f(\theta)$ may, of course, be a singleton set] would be trivial because $f(\theta)$ would itself be known. The problem of incentives arises precisely because in general the planner does not know the true value of $\theta$. He may, of course, attempt to learn $\theta$ simply by asking members of society to reveal it. In general, however, if individuals realize how the revealed information is to be used, they will have an incentive to misrepresent. In other words, they will view themselves as participating in a mechanism (or what is called a game form) where the outcome is a social alternative which is welfare optimal with respect to the announced strategies. An equilibrium of this game form may or may not entail truthful revelations of $\theta$. However, the mechanism just described is only one of many available to the planner. The planner is, in general, free to select any conceivable set of strategy spaces for players and any rule for assigning outcomes to strategy configurations. Naturally, he hopes to devise a mechanism (for some appropriate solution concept) whose equilibria are welfare optimal with respect to the individuals' true preferences. A mechanism with this property is said to implement the social choice rule. The planner who is able to devise a mechanism which implements the given SCR will by definition have developed an incentive scheme which in equilibrium enables social optima to be sustained.

To put things more formally, suppose the planner does not know the true value of $\theta_i$ for individual $i$ except that it is a member of a given set of possible characteristics, say $X_i$. Thus, the planner knows only that $\theta \in \Pi_{i=1}^{N} X_i$. By definition, the social choice rule $f$ specifies, for each $\theta \in \Pi_{i=1}^{N} X_i$ a nonempty social choice set $f(\theta) \subseteq A$. Were the true value of $\theta$ known to the planner in advance, he would merely have selected a member of $f(\theta)$ and that would be the end of the matter. But by assumption he does not. So we may imagine that the planner endows each individual $i$ with a set of strategies $S_i$, and urges $i$ to choose a member $s_i \in S_i$ and to inform him of the choice. The planner also announces publicly, before this game is played, that if the announced vector of strategies is $\mathbf{s}$ [$= (s_i, \ldots, s_i, \ldots, s_N)$] with $\mathbf{s} \in \Pi_{i=1}^{N} S_i$, then the social alternative to be chosen will be from the set $g(\mathbf{s}) \subseteq A$. The publicly announced mapping

$$g: \prod_{i=1}^{N} S_i \rightarrow A$$

is, therefore, the mechanism, and in participating in such a mechanism the citizens are engaged in a "game."

It is clear, of course, that for a given solution concept and for each $\theta \in \Pi_{i=1}^{N} X_i$, the mechanism $g$ has a set of possible equilibria. Each equilibrium consists of a vector of strategies $\mathbf{s}^* \in \Pi_{i=1}^{N} S_i$. The set of such equilibria, $Eg(\theta)$, depends on the individuals' true characteristics, $\theta$ [of course $Eg(\theta)$ may be empty]. The set of equilibrium outcomes of the mechanism is $g[Eg(\theta)] =$

$\{g(s^*)|s^* \epsilon\, Eg(\theta)\}$. Formally, the mechanism $g$ is said to implement the social choice rule $f$ if for every $\theta \,\epsilon\, \Pi_{i=1}^{N} X_i$ we have $Eg(\theta)$ nonempty and $g[Eg(\theta)] \subseteq f(\theta)$.

It will have been noted that in the foregoing framework we have not specified the nature of the strategy sets $S_i$ that the planner may wish to invite the individuals to choose from. In general they may be anything (e.g., a set of numbers) and may not have any obvious economic significance. However, one strand of the literature has concentrated on what we shall call direct mechanisms in which $S_i = X_i$ for all $i$. In *direct* mechanisms, therefore, individuals are asked to announce their preference. The appeal of a direct mechanism is that it invites one to explore the possibility of discovering implementable mechanisms in which truthfulness is an equilibrium outcome. We explore this possibility in a problem in environmental pollution. Unfortunately, the class of cases that have implementable mechanisms with truthfulness as the equilibrium outcome is very narrow (see Dasgupta, Hammond, and Maskin, 1979) and it is for this reason that most writers recently have explored implementable indirect mechanisms (see, e.g., Groves and Ledyard, 1977; Maskin, 1977; and Dasgupta, Hammond and Maskin, 1979).

The following section presents an example of an environmental problem in which the social choice rule can be implemented by an indirect mechanism (formulated by Groves and Ledyard, 1977) in which the solution concept being appealed to is Nash's equilibrium concept. The subsequent section reviews a much-discussed environmental problem presented by Weitzman (1974) (note the possible weakness in the Weitzman prescription) and then goes on to discuss the possibility that the full optimum can be implemented by a direct mechanism in which truthfulness is a *dominant* strategy.

## 4. The Free-Rider Problem in Environmental Improvement

The example that follows is based on Groves and Ledyard (1977). It is presented with a view to illustrating the appeal of indirect mechanisms which, as mentioned earlier, are probably what planners in general will have to rely on. We suppose a polluted atmosphere and take it that the government wishes to undertake a cleanup operation. There is no uncertainty about the cost of cleanup, but the planner does not know the citizens' preferences for a cleaner atmosphere. To simplify, suppose there are two goods, "income" and "clean atmosphere," the latter being denoted by the quantity $G$ ($G = 0$ is the current level). Cleanup technology exhibits constant unit costs which without loss of generality we set at unity.

There are three individuals ($i = 1, 2, 3$) and the government knows that their utility functions are linear with income. The government knows that each prefers more $G$ to less (other things being the same) but does not know their precise utility functions. Thus suppose the utility function of $i$ is

$$V_i(G, I_i, \theta_i) = U(G, \theta_i) + I_i \tag{4}$$

where $I_i$ is $i$'s income and $\theta_i$ is a parameter which $i$ knows, but which the planner does not. *The planner's problem is to supply the optimum level of G and so tax the individuals as to balance the government's budget.*

It may appear plausible that for this example the social choice rule (i.e., allocations satisfying the classic Samuelson rule for the supply of public goods) cannot be implemented by a direct mechanism in which truthfulness is a Nash strategy for all individuals. This is in fact the case (see Dasgupta, Hammond, and Maskin, 1979). Indeed, it was the early recognition that if the tax burden on $i$ were to be based solely on the announced value of $\theta_i$, individuals would not reveal their true $\theta$'s, which led to the recognition of what is called the free-rider problem. One therefore searches for indirect mechanisms.

Suppose then that the planner asks each individual to choose a real number and to inform the planner of the choice. The planner announces publicly that if $m_i$ is $i$'s chosen number, then $i$ will be asked to pay tax of the amount

$$T_i(m_i, m_j, m_k) = m_i^2 + 2m_j m_k \ (i \neq j \neq k) \tag{5}$$

It it is further announced by the planner that the sum of the tax proceeds will be spent to supply the public good. Given our assumption about the technology of cleanup, the government can in fact announce that if $m_i$, $m_2$, and $m_3$ are the announced triplet of numbers, the supply of the public good will amount to

$$G = T_1 + T_2 + T_3 = (m_1 + m_2 + m_3)^2 \tag{6}$$

The individuals, therefore, are informed of the mechanism which the planner proposes to use in supplying $G$.

We now suppose noncooperative behavior on the part of the three individuals and look for a Nash equilibrium outcome for this mechanism. Consider $i = 1$. Suppose $I_i$ is an individual's initial income. His problem is to choose $m_i$ (given $m_2$ and $m_3$) so as to

$$\text{maximize } U(G, \theta,) + I_1 - m_1^2 - 2m_2 m_3 \tag{7}$$

Since he knows the mechanism being used by the planner, he knows that (6) will hold. Thus his optimum $m_1$ will satisfy the condition

$$2(m_1 + m_2 + m_3) \, \partial u / \partial G = 2m_1, \tag{8}$$

and likewise for $i = 2,3$. Thus a Nash equilibrium triplet of strategies, $m_i^*$, $m_2^*$, $m_3^*$ will satisfy the condition

$$\sum_{i=1}^{3} \partial u(G_1 \theta_i) / \partial G = 1 \tag{9}$$

which is, of course, the Samuelson rule for the efficient supply of the public good for the example at hand.

Notice that the mechanism just described is an indirect one (individuals are not asked to announce the $\theta$'s), but the planner in fact does not need to know the true $\theta$'s in order to supply the public good optimally. If the planner is confident that a Nash equilibrium outcome is likely, he can, by imposing the foregoing mechanism, ensure the optimum supply of the public good without knowing individual preferences.

Notice as well that the incentive scheme implied in the mechanism described above has the tax burden on individual $i$ depending not merely on $i$'s strategy ($m_i$) but also on the remaining citizens' strategies [$m_j$, $m_k$; see (5)]. It is this latter dependence which is crucial to such schemes, for there is no way by which $i$ can avoid being taxed should the others choose positive numbers [see equation (5)]

The foregoing example is that of an indirect mechanism implementing an SCR. The solution concept we appealed to is the Nash equilibrium. If one feels uneasy with this concept, one may wish to insist on finding mechanisms that implement the given SCR by dominant strategies on the part of individuals. Indeed, the early negative results in this area by Gibbard (1973) and Satterthwaite (1975) were on the nonexistence of mechanisms that would implement SCR's in general if dominant strategies were required for implementation. A dominant strategy equilibrium is of course a Nash equilibrium but has the attractive feature that no individual needs to know the strategies of others in choosing his own optimal strategy since it is independent of the chosen strategies of others.

Now it may be thought that if dominant strategy mechanisms are what ought to be sought, the planner, if he has any hope of locating one, must search for indirect mechanisms. In fact, it can be shown that this is not so (see Dasgupta, Hammond, and Maskin, 1979, theorem 3.1). Roughly speaking, what can be shown is that if there exists a dominant strategy indirect mechanism which implements an SCR, there also exists a direct mechanism which implements this SCR and in which truth telling is a dominant strategy for all individuals.

In fact, some of the earliest examples of direct mechanisms ensuring the optimum supply of a public good in simple environments had truth-telling as a dominant strategy (see Clarke, 1971; Groves and Loeb, 1975; and Green and Laffont, 1977). However, a major defect in the mechanisms studied in these papers was that, unlike the one just analyzed, the planner is not able to ensure that his budget is balanced. The following section discusses the question of appropriate incentive schemes when there is an information gap between the government (regulator) and polluting firms; eventually I wish to consider direct mechanisms. It will be noted that the government will be unable to ensure that its budget is balanced. The technical arguments will be spelled out in the appendix.

## 5. Taxation vs. Regulations Under Uncertainty

An Informal Argument

It is intuitively evident that the effects of optimum taxation and optimum regulation are unlikely to be the same when the planner faces uncertainty about matters that are relevant to the problem at hand. In what follows I use a simple formulation to see what the relevant effects are and how they need to be assessed. In particular I argue that if the resource in question displays threshold effects, then the optimal form of "taxation" is more like a pure regulation than a pure tax;[6] that is, the regulator ought to impose optimal effluent standards, and not optimal effluent charges.

These points can be discussed most tellingly in the context of environmental pollution. To begin with, note that environmental effects of pollution usually take time to make their presence felt. Therefore, the uncertainty about the extent of social damage resulting from pollution will not be resolved until some time in the future.[7] The policy chosen today then must be independent of the resolution of this uncertainty.

For example, suppose we are considering a policy to restrict the discharge of PCB by industries into the seas. To date we are still uncertain about the capacity of zooplanktons to absorb this effluent without undue damage. It is possible that this knowledge will be gained in the future, but today's decision about how much PCB ought to be discharged must be independent of this knowledge.

In fact the planner is usually uncertain as well about the cost of pollution control, that is, cleanup costs. It requires specialized knowledge. Moreover, cleanup programs take time to implement, and firms may not know today precisely what the costs will be. Furthermore, even if firms know their true cleanup costs, the regulator may not, and may not be able to elicit the truth from firms unless it is in their interest to tell the truth. Thus, today's decision on the amount of pollution permitted must be independent of the resolution of this uncertainty as well.

It is now clear why regulations (i.e., effluent standards) and taxes (i.e., effluent charges) are not identical in their effects.[8] Recall that in the pure

---

[6] By a "pure tax" we mean a marginal tax rate that is constant and independent of the state of nature. In what follows we do not consider state-contingent tax rates. One suspects that for administrative reasons they are rarely used. For a thorough discussion of state-contingent prices and the institutions that allow such prices to be mimicked, see Arrow (1971).

[7] It is hardly surprising then that the effects of pollutants begin to be understood only after the pollutants have been deposited for some time. This is seen in the case of DDT, or in the more recent findings of biologists on the effects of PCB on marine life.

[8] In chapter 3 of Dasgupta and Heal (1979) it was demonstrated that, provided the social benefit and cost functions have the right shape, regulations and taxation have identical effects in the absence of uncertainty—provided they are chosen optimally, of course.

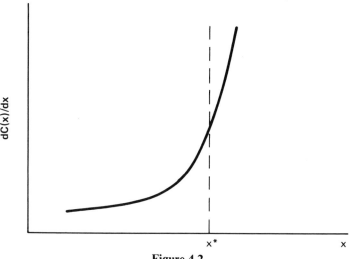

**Figure 4.2.**

regulation scheme the planner selects the total quantity of pollution to be emitted. Firms are prohibited from polluting in excess of this. In the pure tax scheme, the planner imposes a constant tax rate for marginal units of pollution and individual firms then decide how much to pollute. Thus, for any given realization of the social damage function (e.g., realization of the true threshold level of the resource being damaged by the pollutant) taxes encourage too little cleanup if the costs of cleanup are in fact higher than expected and they encourage too much cleanup if they are lower. The problem is reversed for the regulation scheme. Since the total quantity of pollution is decided by the planner in advance, it will be too little if cleanup costs are lower than expected and too much if they are higher.

Given that they are different in their impact, it is important to ask which is superior. As one would expect, the answers depend on the curvatures of the benefit and cost functions, and presently this will be confirmed by an example. But first it will be useful to obtain an intuitive feel for the proposition that it may well be desirable to rely on quantity restrictions rather than effluent charges (i.e., taxes) when the resource displays threshold effects.

Let $x$ denote the total emission of a particular pollutant and let $C(x)$ be the social loss, in the sense of environmental damage caused by this emission. For the moment we are supposing that this loss function is known with certainty. Now suppose that the marginal loss function $[dC(x)/dx]$ takes the shape described in figure 4.2. Such a form seems plausible for a number of environmental problems, where $x^*$ denotes the threshold level of pollution. That is, within a small neighborhood of $x^*$, marginal social damage due to the pollutant increases dramatically.

Now suppose that firms' cleanup costs as a function of the quantity of pollution are unknown by the planner and are therefore functions of random variables as well. Regulation (i.e., the issue of a fixed quantity of licenses to pollute) seems the better of the two schemes because the planner can ensure that the total level of pollution will be less than $x*$—the level at which disaster strikes. Since cleanup cost functions are unknown to the planner, the only way to ensure against firms polluting beyond the level $x*$ via a pollution tax is to set a "high" tax rate. However, a "high" tax rate may be undesirable if there is a good chance that cleanup costs are lower than expected, because in such circumstances the amount of cleanup will exceed the amount desirable. There will be too little pollution!

The argument is reinforced if it is known that there is a threshold level, $x*$, but if the actual level is not known—only that it is within a range. Again, the planner will wish to ensure against the possibility of disaster and guarantee that the level of pollution does not go much beyond the bottom value of the range. Once again, regulations can guarantee this, but pure taxes cannot, unless they are set at prohibitively high levels.

Regulations and pure taxes are polar types of plan instruments. They are extreme cases of a tax rate, which is a function of the quantity of pollution emitted. A pure tax is a special case because the marginal rate is independent of the quantity discharged. A regulation is a zero tax rate up to the quota and an infinite tax rate for amounts in excess of the quota. We note that in the face of uncertainty the optimal tax scheme is one for which the tax rate is a function of the quantity of pollutants discharged and that in general it is neither of the two limiting forms just discussed. Nevertheless, for administrative reasons the planner may be forced to consider only the two limiting forms, and indeed, much of the debate on the appropriate form of intervention in economic activities involving environmental resources has centered on the relative advantages of pure taxation versus regulation.[9] The following section analyzes these issues more formally in the context of a single firm emitting pollutants as a by-product of its production activity and looks briefly at the problem when more than one firm is so engaged. The appendix presents a formal analysis of this problem.

### The Case of a Single Firm

Consider a single firm whose net profit level as a function of the level of pollution it emits $x$ is $\pi(x)$, and that the social damage from $x$ is $C(x)$. Net

---

[9] An interesting combination of these two polar schemes, which is meaningful when more than one firm is engaged in emitting a certain pollutant, is for the government to decide on the total permissible level of pollution and then to issue the firms with a set of transferable licenses which add up to this total. See Dales (1968). We discuss this plan and its variations in section 5.

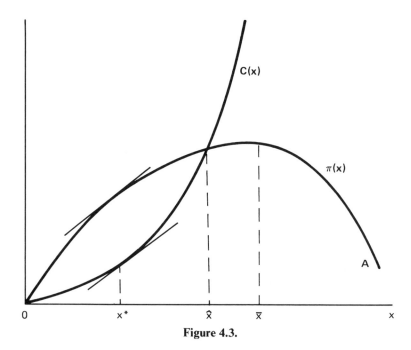

**Figure 4.3.**

social benefit $B(x)$ is assumed to be $\pi(x) - C(x)$ and it is supposed that this is maximized at the pollution level $x^*$ (see figures 4.3 and 4.4). It is clear that the optimum tax rate to impose on the firm is $p^* = C'(x^*)$.

Now suppose the regulator faces uncertainty about both the firm's net profit function, $\pi(x)$ and the environmental damage function, $C(x)$. Regarding the former, it is natural to suppose that the firm knows its technology but that it is the government (regulator) which is uncertain about matters (e.g., cleanup costs). Thus let $\pi(x,\phi)$ denote the net profit accruing to the firm when $x$ is the level of emission and $\phi$ is the random variable reflecting the planner's uncertainty about the firm's technological possibilities. By hypothesis, the firm knows the true value of $\phi$ at the time it chooses $x$. However, we suppose that the planner does not know the true value of $\phi$ when it announces its policy.

Turning now to the social damage function $C$, we take it that the environmental consequences of the given pollutant are uncertain. Thus let $C(x,\theta)$ denote the social value of the damage sustained when $x$ is the level of pollution and $\theta$ is the value of the random variable reflecting the planner's uncertainty.

Suppose that the planner desires to choose that policy which will maximize the *expected* value of net social benefit, that is,

$$E[\pi(x,\phi) - C(x,\theta)] \tag{10}$$

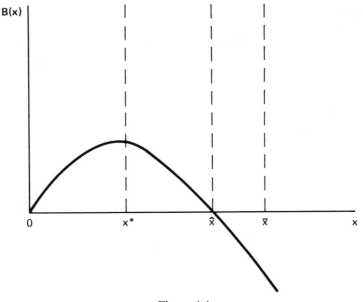

**Figure 4.4.**

where $E$ is the expectation operator.[10] It should be noted that (10) is perfectly consistent with the regulator displaying an aversion toward risk, and we shall see this presently.

It will be supposed that the regulator can monitor the level of pollution $x$ that the firm chooses to emit. For simplicity of exposition, assume that the random variables $\theta$ and $\phi$ are independent of each other. This is reasonable, since $\phi$ reflects uncertainties regarding the firm's technology, and $\theta$ reflects uncertainties regarding the effect of the firm's pollution on the environment. The regulator is interested in maximizing expected net social benefit (10). Moreover, he is aware that the firm, knowing the true value of $\phi$, is interested solely in its net profits.[11] It is then immediately apparent that the optimum policy consists in the planner imposing on the firm a pollution tax schedule $T(x)$ which is of the form:

$$T(x) = E[C(x,\theta)] \pm \text{constant} \tag{11}$$

[10] If $f(\bar{\theta},\bar{\phi})$ is the probability that the two random variables realize the values $\bar{\theta}$ and $\bar{\phi}$, then by definition

$$E[\pi(x,\phi) - C(x,\theta)] = \sum_{\theta} \sum_{\phi} [\pi(x,\phi) - C(x,\theta)] f(\theta,\phi)$$

[11] Thus, the regulator and the firm pursue different goals. It is this feature that distinguishes the problem pursued here from the problem analyzed in the theory of teams. For a thorough discussion of the latter, see Marschak and Radner (1972).

That is, the optimum pollution tax schedule is the expected social damage as a function of the level of pollution $x$ plus or minus a constant.[12] Faced with such a tax schedule $T(x)$, the firm will choose $x$ so as to maximize

$$\pi(x,\phi) - T(x) = \pi(x,\phi) - E[C(x,\theta)] \mp \text{constant} \tag{12}$$

that is, its profit, net of tax payment. Moreover, the regulator knows in advance that the firm will maximize (12).[13]

Notice at once that when the regulator announces the tax schedule (11) he cannot predict precisely what the resulting level of pollution is going to be. This is because by assumption the regulator does not know the true value of $\phi$, and as equation (12) makes clear, the firm's profit-maximizing choice of $x$ depends on $\phi$. Thus the imposition of the optimum tax schedule (11) results in an uncertainty about the amount of pollution that will eventually be emitted, thereby compounding the uncertainty about the final environmental damage. In order to maximize (12) the firm will choose that value of $x$ at which marginal profit (excluding tax payment) equals the marginal tax rate.[14] That is,

$$\partial\pi(x,\phi)/\partial x = E[\partial C(x,\theta)/\partial x] \tag{13}$$

From (13) it is clear that the profit-maximizing $x$, say $\tilde{x}$, is a function of the realized value of $\phi$. That is, $\tilde{x} = \tilde{x}(\phi)$. The regulator by hypothesis does not know the true value of $\phi$, but from (13) he can calculate the response function $\tilde{x}(\phi)$. Note as well that except for the limiting case where $C(x,\theta)$ is of the multiplicative form $xg(\theta)$ [a case we have ruled out because we have supposed $C(x,\theta)$ is strictly convex in $x$], the optimum variable pollution tax $E[C(x,\theta)]$ is not proportional to $x$. It follows that, except for this limiting case, the optimum tax rate on incremental pollution, namely, $dE[C(x,\theta)]/dx$, is not independent of the level of pollution.

The point, however, is that in the presence of uncertainty, the optimal tax schedule, $E[C(x,\theta)]$, except for special cases, is neither a quota, nor a linear tax schedule (i.e., a marginal tax rate that is independent of the level of pollution emitted). We have thus established:

*Proposition 1:* In the presence of uncertainty the social management of environmental pollution is best conducted with the help of tax rates that vary with the quantity of pollutants discharged by a firm. Linear tax schedules

[12] The "constant" in (11), being by definition independent of $x$, is essentially a lump-sum tax or subsidy, depending on its sign. Since by assumption there are no income effects, its magnitude will not affect the outcome. In what follows the reader may wish to ignore it and suppose it to be zero.

[13] Since the expected value of (12) is (10), it is obvious that in maximizing (10) the regulator cannot do better than to impose the schedule (11) on the firm.

[14] We are assuming that (12) is a strictly concave function of $x$ for every value of $\phi$. Moreover, the random variable has been so labeled that, without loss of generality, it is supposed that for each admissible value of $\phi$, there is a unique solution of (13).

and quantity regulations are merely suboptimal limiting forms of such policies.[15]

Let us conduct an exercise with this apparatus. Suppose that $x^*$ is the level of pollution at which expected marginal social profit equals expected marginal social damage (i.e., $x^*$ is the solution of the equation $E[\partial\pi(x,\phi)/\partial x] = E[\partial C(x,\theta)/\partial x]$. Now suppose that environmental uncertainties are small so that the social damage function $C(x,\theta)$ can be approximated around the level $x^*$, in the form

$$C(x,\theta) = a(\theta) + C_1[x - x^* - a_2(\theta)] + C_2[x - x^* - a_3(\theta)]^2 \qquad (14)$$

where $C_1$ and $C_2$ are positive constants, and where, without loss of generality, it is supposed that $a_1(\theta)$, $a_2(\theta)$ and $a_3(\theta)$ are random variables with zero expected values. From equation (14) it is then apparent that

$$E[C(x,\theta)] = C_1(x - x^*) + C_2(x - x^*)^2 + C_2E\{[a_3(\theta)]^2\} \qquad (15)$$

Thus, if the environmental damage function, $C(x,\theta)$, is of the form (14), the optimal pollution tax schedule is of the form (15). This is, of course, neither a linear tax nor a quota. As the third term on the right-hand side of (15) is a constant, we may as well ignore it (see footnote 12). The relevant terms depend on $x$, the first being linear in $x$ and the second being quadratic. Notice now that if $C_2$ is "small," then in the neighborhood of $x^*$ the first term on the right-hand side of (15) dominates the second term, and so

$$E[C(x,\theta)] \simeq C_1(x - x^*) \qquad (16)$$

In this case the optimal tax schedule is approximately linear, with a constant marginal tax rate of $C_1$. On the other hand, if $C_2$ is "large," even a mild departure from $x^*$ results in the firm being taxed heavily, as (15) confirms readily. Confronted with such a schedule, the firm, if $C_2$ is large, will not wish to deviate unduly from the pollution level $x^*$. The effect is then not dissimilar to the case in which the planner imposes a quota level of $x^*$. Thus, if $C_2$ is large, the optimum pollution tax schedule resembles a quantity regulation.

The intuition behind these results ought to be clear enough. If the social damage function is of the form (14), the marginal damage function is

$$\partial C(x,\theta)/\partial x = C_1 + 2C_2[x - x^* - a_2(\theta)] \qquad (17)$$

We already have supposed by way of simplification that the uncertainty is "small." Thus the range of values $a_2(\theta)$ is permitted to take is small. From

---

[15] These two limiting forms were compared and contrasted in a seminal contribution by Weitzman (1974). Notice, however, that for this example, the imposition of $E[C(x,\theta)]$ as the tax schedule is equivalent in its effect to the imposition of the optimum state-contingent pollution tax. Thus, let $\bar{x}(\phi)$ be the solution of (13). Then define $p^*(\phi) = d\pi(x,\phi)/\partial x$, evaluated at $\bar{x}(\phi)$. Then $p^*(\phi)$ is the optimal state-contingent tax, and we are formally back to the model of section 3.

(17) it is apparent that the slope of the marginal damage function (i.e., $\partial^2 C(x,\theta)/\partial x^2$) is equal to $2C_2$. If $C_2$ is large, what (17) tells us is that marginal social damage increases dramatically with increasing pollution in the neighborhood of an uncertain level of pollution, $x^* + a_2(\theta)$. In other words, a large value of $C_2$ in (17) captures the fact that the pollution in question has a threshold effect. However, the threshold level of pollution, $x^* + a_2(\theta)$, is unknown, with an expected value of $x^*$.[16] Therefore, if $C_2$ is large, the polluting firm, faced with a tax schedule of the form (16), will choose not to pollute in excess of $x^*$ and in fact will pollute at a level slightly short of $x^*$ [this last, so as to pick up a small subsidy, is given by the first term of (16)].

One can also see from this example why the planner would go way off the mark in such circumstances if he were to rely on a linear tax schedule (i.e., a constant marginal tax rate). The point is that if the regulator is uncertain about the firm's technology—for example, if he is uncertain about cleanup costs—the only way to ensure that the firm does not pollute beyond $x^*$ is to set a high tax rate. But a high tax rate would be undesirable if cleanup costs turned out to be lower than expected, because in such circumstances the amount of cleanup will exceed the amount desirable. There will be too little pollution! On the other hand, if $C_2$ is small, in the neighborhood of $x^*$ the marginal damage function is approximately constant (equal to $C_1$), as (17) makes clear. However, if marginal social damage is known and constant, it is obviously best to allow the firm full flexibility in finding the optimum level of pollution, since the firm by hypothesis knows the true value of $\phi$ and the regulator, by hypothesis, does not. A constant marginal tax rate (i.e., a linear tax schedule) allows the greatest amount of such flexibility, and so it is not surprising that if $C_2$ is small, the optimal tax schedule resembles a linear schedule. These considerations suggest the following.

*Proposition 2:* To the extent that environmental resources display threshold effects, the optimal tax schedule designed to limit their use resembles regulations governing amount of emission, and if for administrative reasons a choice has to be made solely between the optimum linear tax schedule and the optimum quota, the latter should be chosen.[17]

### The Case of Multiple Firms

Where a single firm is engaged in causing environmental damage, it is a simple matter to compute the form of the optimum tax schedule. In the pre-

[16] Recall that by assumption the expected value of $a_2(\theta)$ is zero.

[17] The second half of the proposition has been discussed by Weitzman (1974). It is important to mention that there are difficult legal problems in certain countries in enforcing regulations. On this, see Kneese and Schultz (1975). We are, quite naturally, ignoring such difficulties here.

ceding section we noted in expression (11) that the regulator ideally should impose a pollution tax schedule which, up to an additive constant, is the expected value of the social damage function. The intuition behind this is rather obvious. For every possible realization of the random variable $\phi$, such a tax schedule, if imposed on the firm, results in the firm's net profit function (12) being identical with the social objective function. In other words, the tax schedule is so designed that the firm's objective (net of tax payment) coincides with society's objective.[18] In such a situation, the firm's profit-maximizing response cannot help but be the response that the regulator would ideally like the firm to make. Matters are more complicated when more than one firm is involved in damaging the environment. The problem is that the damage that any one firm imposes on the environment by marginally increasing its level of pollution discharge now depends, not only on its level of discharge, but also on the levels discharged by others. This interaction, as we shall see, causes difficulties in the computation of the optimum pollution tax schedules, though the analysis is simple enough in general terms.

Suppose then that there are $N$ firms engaged in emitting a specific type of pollutant. Firms are indexed by $i$ or $j$ ($i,j = 1, 2, \ldots, N$). Let $x_i$ be the level emitted by firm $i$ and let us suppose that the net profit function of firm $i$ is $\pi(x_i,\phi_i)$, where $\phi_i$ is a random variable reflecting the regulator's uncertainty about cleanup costs encountered by $i$. As in an earlier section, we shall take it that at the time $i$ chooses $x_i$ it knows the true value of $\phi_i$ but that when the regulator announces its policy the regulator is innocent of the actual value of $\phi_i$. For ease of exposition suppose that the damage suffered by the environment due to pollution depends on the sum of the levels of pollution emitted by each of the firms and a random variable $\theta$. Thus $C = C(\Sigma_{i=1}^{N}x_i,\theta)$. The pollutant is, therefore, a "public bad."[19] Expected net social benefit, we take it, is a direct generalization of expression (10), being the sum of the expected profits minus the expected social damage, that is,

$$B = E\left[\sum_{i=1}^{N} \pi(x_i,\phi)\right] - E\left[C\left(\sum_{i=1}^{N} x_i,\theta\right)\right] \tag{18}$$

and it is this which the regulator is determined to maximize. For the remainder of this section we shall suppose, as before, that $\pi(x_i,\phi)$ is strictly concave in $x_i$ for all $\phi_i$ and that $C(X,\theta)$ is strictly convex in $X$ for all $\theta$, where $X = \Sigma_{i=1}^{N}x_i$ is the total emission of the pollution in question.

Let us begin by analyzing what the full optimum looks like. Suppose then that at the time the firms choose their levels of emission, everyone (i.e., the

---

[18] That is, the imposition of the tax schedule [equation (12)] reduces the problem to a simple example of the general problem raised in the theory of teams (see footnote 11). For a pioneering discussion of incentives in teams, see Groves (1973).

[19] In other words, pollution control is a public good.

$N$ firms and the regulator) knows the realized values of the $N$ random variables $\phi_i$ $(i = 1, \ldots, N)$. Then, clearly, in order that (18) be maximized, firm $i$ $(i = 1, \ldots, N)$ should be made to choose that level of pollution $x^i$ which maximizes[20]

$$\sum \pi(x_i, \phi_i) - E_\theta\left[C\left(\sum_{i=1}^{N} x_i, \theta\right)\right] \tag{19}$$

Suppose, without further ado, that it does.[21] Then firm $i$ should be made to choose that $x_i$ at which

$$\partial\pi(x_i, \phi_i)/\partial x_i = E_\theta[dC(X, \theta)/dX]; \quad i = 1, \ldots, N \tag{20}$$

where $X = \Sigma_{i=1}^{N} x_i$

Equation (20) is $N$ in number, and there are $N$ unknowns $x_i$ to be solved for.[22] The $i$th equation in (20) says that the $i$th firm should pollute up to the level at which its actual marginal profit (left-hand side of 20) equals the expected marginal damage due to aggregate pollution, where the expectation is carried out over the remaining random variable $\theta$. Let $\tilde{x}_i$ $(i = 1, \ldots, N)$ denote the solution of the system of equation (20). It will be noticed that the realized values of the random variables $\phi_i$ $(i = 1, \ldots, N)$ are parameters for this system of equations. Thus $\tilde{x}_i$ depends on the realized values of *all* the $N$ random variables $\phi_j$ $(j = i, \ldots, N)$ and not merely on $\phi_i$. Thus $\tilde{x}_i = \tilde{x}(\phi_1, \ldots, \phi_i, \ldots, \phi_N)$. This is precisely what intuition suggests. For, if it emerges that firm $j$'s cleanup cost at the margin is less than that of firm $i$, the former, in the interest of social welfare, should be forced to pollute less than the latter and the reverse if it emerges that $i$'s cleanup cost at the margin is less than that of $j$. It is therefore clear that the (full) optimum level of emission of firm $i$ is of the form[23] $\tilde{x}_i = \tilde{x}(\phi_1, \ldots, \phi_i, \ldots, \phi_N)$.

The question arises whether the full optimum can be enforced. Two distinct issues are involved here, and we have alluded to them earlier. First, it should be recognized that a knowledge of true cleanup costs involves specialized technical knowledge, and while it is reasonable in many circumstances to

---

[20] $E_\theta$ means that the expectation has been computed only over the random variable $\theta$ since by assumption everyone knows the realized values of $\phi_i$ $(i - 1, \ldots, N)$ at the time $x_i$ is chosen. The remaining uncertainty pertains only to $\theta$.

[21] We can suppose here that firms act in the social interest because by assumption the regulator knows the true values of $\phi_i$ $(i = 1, \ldots, N)$ at the time of effluent emission and therefore we can take it that he can force firms to pollute at the fully optimal levels.

[22] Equation (20) was obtained by differentiating (19) with respect to $x_i$ and setting it equal to zero. Equation (20) is therefore the social benefit-cost rule for locating the fully optimum pollution emissions for the problem at hand.

[23] In the language of statistical decision theory, the set of realizations $(\theta, \phi_1, \ldots, \phi_i, \ldots, \phi_N)$ is a state of the world for the model being discussed. By assumption, decisions are made in the absence of knowledge of the true value of $\theta$. What remains is the set $(\phi_1, \ldots, \phi_i, \ldots, \phi_N)$. Then full optimum is sustained by state contingent pollution levels, $\tilde{x}_i(\phi_1, \ldots, \phi_i, \ldots, \phi_N)$, for $i = 1, \ldots, N$.

assume that firms know their own cleanup costs at the time they make their decisions, it is at least equally reasonable to suppose that the regulator does not. In this event it seems natural to allow the regulator to ask the firms to report their true cleanup costs. But then recall that firms are interested only in their own private profits and not expected social benefits [equation (18)]. If firms know in advance that their answers to the regulator's query will result in the enforcement of the optimum levels of pollution $\tilde{x}_i$, each firm will have a strong incentive to lie. Each firm would like to pretend that its marginal cleanup cost is very high, reasoning that it will be allowed to pollute more than it would be allowed to were the truth known to the regulator. Its reasoning would be correct. Moreover, the regulator would know that this is how firms will reason. Therefore, he will know that the full optimum cannot be reached merely by calculating the functions $\tilde{x}_i$ and asking firms to divulge their private information. If the regulator wants the truth from firms in the environment we are considering, he must provide them with an incentive to tell the truth. The appendix presents incentive schemes that will elicit the truth from firms.

This brings us to the second point, namely, that even if in principle the regulator can elicit the truth from firms, the cost of the transmission of this information from the individual firms to the regulator typically will not be negligible: $\phi_i$ may be a large set of numbers. If such transmission costs are taken into account, it may not be sensible to try and reach what we have called the full optimum, $\tilde{x}_i$. It may be better that the regulator attempt to maximize (18) without asking firms to transmit their private information, but rely instead on information that he can obtain easily.

The appendix analyzes the struture of pollution taxes which will maximize (18) when two-way communication between the regulator and the firms is barred. The remainder of this section looks at some simple regulatory policies that have often been proposed in the literature.

Conceptually, the simplest by far is a direct generalization of effluent standards which was discussed earlier in this section. For the present example it would mean a pollution quota imposed on each firm. Let $x_i^*$ denote the optimum quota for firm $i$. Since the regulator is interested in maximizing (18), $x_i^*$ must be the solution of the equations

$$dE[\pi(x_i,\phi_i)]/dx_i = dE[C(X,\theta)]/dX$$

for $i = 1, \ldots, N$         (21)

where $X = \Sigma_{i=1}^{N} x_i$

or in other words, where expected marginal profit to firm $i$ equals the expected marginal social damage caused by aggregate pollution.[24]

---

[24] The expectations are carried out over all the random variables because, by assumption, the regulator is totally uninformed.

Now, in fact, there is a glaring defect with a scheme of this kind which the reader will have noticed immediately. The point is that social damage, by hypothesis, depends on the aggregate emission of pollution $X$. Therefore if effluent standards are to be used, they ought to be imposed on the industry as a whole and not on each firm separately. It seems plausible that in the interest of expected social welfare it would be better if the regulator could devise a scheme in which firms chose their own levels of emission but were subject to the constraint that total emission must equal the optimum quota for the industry as a whole. The point is, of course, that the regulator ought to encourage firms with low cleanup costs to undertake more cleanup than those having high cleanup costs. But by hypothesis the regulator does not know a firm's actual cleanup costs, and so rule (21) does not allow for this desirable flexibility.

To make the point more clearly, suppose that the random variables $\phi_i$ are independent of one another and suppose furthermore that they are identically distributed. It is then clear from rule (21) that the optimum quota, $x_i^*$, is the same for every firm, say $x^*$. Thus, rule (21) would dictate that total emission be restricted to the level $X^* = Nx^*$, but in fact the true value of $\phi_i$ typically will vary from firm to firm. However, rule (21) tells them in advance to pollute at the same level. It is this lack of flexibility in a firm-specific emission standard scheme which has led authors like Dales (1968) to suggest an improvement, namely, a scheme in which the regulator selects the aggregate allowable level of effluent, which is then auctioned off to the firms in the form of licenses. In our example, the regulator could sell $X^*$ licenses to the firms.[25] If $N$ is large, the resulting "market" price for a license would be akin to a pollution tax. At the resulting market price, say $p^*$, firms with high actual cleanup costs naturally would purchase more licenses than those with low actual cleanup costs. This shifting of the burden of pollution control across firms is, of course, an improvement on firm-specific pollution quotas. It enables the regulator to retain control over the aggregate level of pollution and at the same time allows for a flexibility that firm-specific quotas do not display.

It will have been noticed that in the scheme just outlined the regulator sets the quota on aggregate pollution in advance. At the instant he selects $X^*$ he is uncertain about the fee, $p^*$, which will clear the market for these $X^*$ licenses. At the opposite pole is a scheme in which the regulator announces a license fee or pollution tax (or effluent charge) and firms are allowed to purchase as many licenses as they like at the going fee. In this scheme the regulator does not know in advance the eventual level of pollution. The relative merits of these two schemes depend on much the same considerations that were mentioned in the preceding section. The second part of proposition 2

---

[25] Or alternatively, each firm could be given $x^*$ transferable licenses. In terms of income distribution these two procedures would not be the same.

is relevant here. If the environmental resource in question displays threshold effects, the scheme in which the regulator auctions away the optimal number of licenses is preferable to the imposition of the optimal linear pollution charge.[26]

However, if one recalls proposition 1, one will recognize that it would be better still to allow more flexibility and have the regulator impose suitably chosen firm-specific pollution tax schedules of the form $T_i(x_i)$. For the case of a single firm, locating the optimum pollution tax schedule was an easy enough matter and, as noted in the previous section, such a tax schedule in fact sustains the full optimum. Matters are a good deal more complicated here. Suppose that the $\phi$'s are independent random variables. The point to note is that the imposition of the optimal tax schedules $T_i(X_i)$ will not sustain the full optimum. The reason is easy to see. By assumption firm $i$ knows only the true value of $\phi_i$ and not of $\phi_j (j \neq i)$. Thus, faced with a tax schedule $T_i(x_i)$ and a knowledge of $\phi_i$, firm $i$ will choose $x_i$, which will be insensitive to the realized values of $\phi_j$ ($j \neq i$). However, we have already noted in this section that the full optimum has firm $i$ polluting at the level $\tilde{x}_i$, which is a function of *all* the $\phi_j$'s. Thus firm-specific pollution tax schedules of the form $T_i(x_i)$ cannot be made to sustain the full optimum, but they can be so chosen that in terms of social benefits [equation (18)] such taxes lead to better results than either the pure licensing scheme or the pure pollution tax scheme. A proposition analogous to proposition 1 can be established here. The optimum forms of such tax schedules are studied in the appendix.

# Appendix: Imperfect Information and Optimal Pollution Control

## Introduction

This section addresses the problems raised in section 5 and analyzes the manner in which they may be solved.[27] We take it that there are $N$ polluting

---

[26] A further refinement over the aggregate effluent standard scheme which we have just discussed is one in which the regulator auctions away a fixed number of licenses and at the same time announces that it will pay a fixed subsidy per license purchased by firms in excess of their actual emissions. In this scheme the regulator has to compute two parameters with a view to maximizing (18), namely, the total number of licenses to be issued, and the rate of subsidy. When optimally chosen, this scheme is superior to the two we have already discussed. For details, see Roberts and Spence (1975) and Kwerel (1977).

[27] The sections on one-way and two-way communication are based on Dasgupta, Hammond, and Maskin (1979), which presents results more general than the ones reported here.

firms $(i, j = 1, \ldots, N)$, and that $x_i$ is the level of pollution emitted by firm $i$. As before, we suppose that the private profit function of firm $i$ is $\pi(x_i, \phi_i)$, where $\phi_i$ is a random variable whose realized value is known to $i$, and where $\pi$ is strictly concave in $x_i$ for all admissible values of $\phi_i$. Social damage due to pollution levels $x_i$ $(i = 1, \ldots, N)$ is given by the function $C(X, \theta)$, where $X = \Sigma_{i=1}^{N} x_i$ and where $\theta$ is a random variable. We take it that $C$ is an increasing and strictly convex function of $X$ for every admissible value of $\theta$. Net social welfare is assumed to be given by expression (18), which we rewrite as

$$B = E[\Sigma \pi (x_i, \phi_i)] - E[C(X, \theta)] \tag{A.1}$$

The expression in (A.1) is to be maximized. However, the highest attainable level of (A.1) depends on the class of tax schemes that the regulator can choose from. Given that $\phi_i$ is a variable whose value is known in the first instance only by firm $i$, there are incentive problems in that firms typically would like to claim that their cleanup costs are high at the margin (i.e., that their marginal profitability at high levels of pollution is high). So the question arises whether the regulator can devise tax subsidy schemes which will neutralize such biases in incentives.

The following section presents tax-subsidy schemes which will enable the full optimum to be attained despite this incentive problem. It requires that the regulator receive messages from firms and then use them to construct tax schedules that are imposed on firms. Moreover, firms are informed about how their messages will be translated into tax schedules. We shall suppose that firms do not collude. Our task will be to show that the regulator can so devise tax schemes that (1) firms will report their true profit functions (i.e., the true value of $\phi_i$) and (2) they will choose the fully optimal pollution levels. In section A.3 we suppose that the transmission of messages from firms to the regulator is too costly, so that the regulator is forced to impose tax schedules on firms based only on his knowledge of the probability distribution of the $\phi_i$'s and $\theta$. We show trivially that the full optimum cannot be attained. However, we are able to locate the optimum structure of taxes given this communication constraint.

## Two-way Communication

Imagine that the regulator asks the firms to inform him of their profit functions; that is, firm $i$ is asked to report the true value of $\phi_i$. The regulator informs the firms that their reports (i.e., the reported values of the $N$ parameters $\phi_1, \ldots, \phi_N$) and their pollution emission levels will be used to compute tax schedules $T_i$ which will then be imposed on firms. Moreover, the firms are told in advance of the manner in which the reported values of $\phi_i$ and emission levels $x_i$ will be translated into the $N$ tax schedules, $T_i$. The idea is to construct tax schedules in such a manner that each firm finds it in its economic interest to report the truth irrespective of what other firms do. That is, the tax schedules are so constructed that truth-telling is a dominant strategy for firms. If this can be achieved, then each firm will tell the truth and in fact the full optimum can be attained. The way to construct such tax schedules is simple enough. The idea is to construct tax schemes in such a way that for every possible set of values of the parameters $\phi_1, \ldots, \phi_N$, the net profit for each firm (net of tax payment) coincides with the social objective function (19). We now see how this can be done.

In what follows we suppose firms do not collude. Let $\tilde{x}_i(\phi_1, \ldots, \phi_N)$, $(i = 1, \ldots, N)$, be the full optimum; that is, the solution of equation (20). We want to find tax functions $T_i(x_i, \phi_1, \ldots, \phi_N)$ for $i = 1, \ldots, N$ such that if $\phi_i$ is firm $i$'s actual parameter value, then for any possible announcement $\hat{\phi}_i$ it makes to the regulator, and for any pollution level $x_i$ it chooses, and for any possible announcement $\phi_j$ that firm $j$ $(j \neq i)$ makes,

$$\pi_i[\tilde{x}_i(\phi_1, \ldots, \phi_{i-1}, \hat{\phi}_i, \phi_{i+1}, \ldots, \phi_N), \hat{\phi}_i]$$

$$-T_i[\tilde{x}_i(\phi_1, \ldots, \phi_{i-1}, \hat{\phi}_i, \phi_{i+1}, \ldots, \phi_N), \phi_1, \ldots, \phi_{i-1}, \hat{\phi}_i, \phi_{i+1}, \ldots, \phi_N]$$

$$> \pi_i(x_i, \hat{\phi}_i) - T_i(x_i, \phi_1, \ldots, \phi_{i-1}, \phi_i, \phi_{i-1}, \ldots, \phi_N)$$

for $i = 1, \ldots, N$ $\qquad\qquad$ (A.2)

If (A.2) is satisfied, then each firm will announce its true parameter value and also find it most profitable to pollute at the fully optimal level, $\tilde{x}_i$. A set of tax schedules that satisfies (A.2) is, of course, of the form

$$T_i(x_i, \phi_1, \phi_2, \ldots, \phi_i, \ldots, \phi_N)$$

$$= C\left[\sum_{j \neq i} \tilde{x}_j(\phi_1, \ldots, \phi_N) + x_i\right] - \sum_{j \neq i} \pi[\tilde{x}_j(\phi_1, \ldots, \phi_N), \phi_j]$$

$\pm$ constant $\qquad\qquad$ (A.3)

The point then is this. While the regulator does not know the true values of $\phi_i$ $(i = 1, \ldots, N)$, he can compute the optimal levels of pollution $\tilde{x}_i$ for every possible set of values of $\phi_i$ essentially by solving equation (20). He then asks firms to reveal their $\phi_i$'s and announces that he will impose tax schedules on firms of the form (A.3). Firms will then be allowed to choose their pollution levels and pay taxes according to (A.3). Since (A.2) is satisfied for each $i$ if (A.3) is imposed, each firm will find truth-telling and the optimal level of pollution emission its dominant strategy.

### One-way Communication

It may be felt that the foregoing scheme is unduly cumbersome, requiring as it does the transmission of a great deal of information from firms to the regulator ($\phi_i$ will typically consist of a great many numbers). However, we continue to assume that the regulator can monitor the emission levels costlessly. Much of the literature on environmental control has in fact addressed itself to the problem of designing optimum tax schedules based solely on emission levels. As we recognized in section 5, such tax schemes cannot aspire to achieve the full optimum. I now present optimal tax schedules in those circumstances where the regulator does not receive any information from firms about their private cleanup costs.

We suppose that the $\phi_i$'s are independent random variables whose probability distributions are public knowledge. The regulator's aim is to maximize (A.1) by imposing tax schedules of the form $T_i(x_i)$ on firms.

Let $\bar{x}_i(\phi_i)$, where $i = 1, \ldots, N$, be the solution of the problem of maximizing

$$\pi(x_i, \phi_i) + E\left\{\sum_{j \neq i} \pi[\bar{x}_j(\phi_j), \phi_j]\right\} - E\left\{C\left[\sum_{j \neq i} \bar{x}_j(\phi_j) + x_i, \theta\right]\right\} \qquad \text{(A.4)}$$

A comparison of (A.1) and (A.4) immediately makes it clear that $\bar{x}_i(\phi_i)$ is the socially optimal level of pollution for firm $i$ subject to the informational constraint that firm $i$'s private information (i.e., the true value of $\phi_i$) remains private. Thus $\bar{x}_i(\phi_i)$, $(i = 1, \ldots, N)$ sustains a second-best social optimum. We must now locate tax functions $T_i(x_i)$ for $i = 1, \ldots, N$, such that for $x_i \geq 0$

$$\pi[\bar{x}_i(\phi_i), \phi_i] - T_i[\bar{x}_i(\phi_i)] > \pi(x_i, \phi_i) - T_i(x_i) \qquad \text{(A.5)}$$

for all admissible values of $\phi_i$. If the regulator imposes tax functions which satisfy (A.5) for all $i$, then the second-best solution can be derived. It is now clear that a set of tax schedules which satisfies (A.5) is of the form

$$T_i(x_i) = -E\left\{\sum_{j \neq i} \pi[\bar{x}_j(\phi_j), \phi_j]\right\} + E\left\{C\left[\sum_{j \neq i} \bar{x}_j(\phi_j) + x_i, \theta\right]\right\}$$

$\pm$ constant $\qquad \text{(A.6)}$

The point to note about (A.6) is that while the regulator does not know the true values of the $\phi_i$'s, he can calculate the functions $\bar{x}_i(\phi_i)$ by differentiating (A.4) with respect to $x_i$ and setting it to zero; that is, by solving the $N$ equations

$$\partial\pi(x_i, \phi_i)/\partial x_i = E\left\{dC\left[\sum_{j \neq i} \bar{x}_j(\phi_j) + x_i, \theta\right]/dx_i\right\}$$

where $\bar{x}_j(\phi_j)$, $j = 1, \ldots, N$, is the solution. Therefore the regulator can compute the tax functions (A.6). It is, of course, apparent from (A.6) that in general $dT_i(x_i)/dx_i$ is not a constant. Nor do its effects in general resemble the imposition of a firm-specific quota.

# References

Arrow, Kenneth J. 1970. "Classificatory Notes on the Production and Transmission of Technological Knowledge," *American Economic Review* vol. 59, pp. 29–35.

———. 1971. *Essays in the Theory of Risk-Bearing* (Amsterdam, North-Holland).

———, and Anthony C. Fisher. 1974. "Preservation, Uncertainty and Irreversibility," *Quarterly Journal of Economics* vol. 87, pp. 312–319.

Clarke, Edward H. 1971. "Multi-Part Pricing of Public Goods," *Public Choice* vol. 11, pp. 17–33.

Dales, J. H. 1968. *Pollution, Property and Prices* (Toronto, University of Toronto Press).

Dasgupta, Partha S., and Geoffrey M. Heal. 1979. *Economic Theory and Exhaustible Resources* (Garden City, N.Y., Cambridge Economic Handbooks, James Nisbet).

———, and Joseph E. Stiglitz. 1980. "Industrial Structure and the Nature of Innovative Activity," *Economic Journal* vol. 90, pp. 266–293.

———, Peter J. Hammond, and Eric Maskin. 1979. "The Implementation of Social Choice Rules: Some General Results in Incentive Compatibility," *Review of Economic Studies* vol. 46, pp. 185–216.

———, ———, and ———. 1980. "A Note on Imperfect Information and Optimal Pollution Control," *Review of Economic Studies* vol. 47, pp. 857–860.

Gibbard, Allan. 1973. "Manipulation of Voting Schemes," *Econometrica* vol. 41, pp. 587–602.

Green, Jerry, and Jean J. Laffont. 1977. "Characterization of Satisfactory Mechanisms for the Revelation of Preferences for Public Goods," *Econometrica* vol. 45, pp. 427–438.

Groves,Theodore. 1973. "Incentives in Teams," *Econometrica* vol. 41, pp. 617–631.

———, and John Ledyard. 1977. "Optimal Allocation of Public Goods," *Econometrica* vol. 45, pp. 783–809.

———, and Martin Loeb. 1975. "Incentives and Public Inputs," *Journal of Public Economics* vol. 4, pp. 211–226.

Henry, Claude. 1974. "Option Values in the Economics of Irreplaceable Assets," *Review of Economic Studies*, Symposium on the Economics of Exhaustible Resources, pp. 89–104.

Kneese, Allen, and Charles Schultze. 1975. *Pollution, Prices and Public Policy* (Washington, D.C., Brookings Institution).

Kwerel, Evan. 1977. "To Tell the Truth: Imperfect Information and Optimal Pollution Control," *Review of Economic Studies* vol. 44, pp. 595–601.

Malinvaud, Edward. 1972. *Lectures in Microeconomic Theory* (Amsterdam, North-Holland).

Marschak, Jacob, and Roy Radner. 1972. *An Economic Theory of Teams* (New Haven, Yale University Press).

Maskin, Eric. 1977. "Nash Equilibrium and Welfare Optimality," mimeo Massachusetts Institute of Technology.

Musgrave, Richard. 1959. *The Theory of Public Finance* (New York, McGraw-Hill).

Radner, Roy, and Joseph E. Stiglitz. 1975. "Fundamental Non-Convexities in the Value of Information," mimeo, Stanford University.

Roberts, Marc, and Michael Spence. 1976. "Effluent Charges and Licenses under Uncertainty," *Journal of Public Economics* vol. 5, pp. 193–208.

Satterthwaite, M. A. 1975. "Strategy-Proofness and Arrow's Conditions: Existence and Correspondence Theorems for Voting Social Welfare Functions," *Journal of Economic Theory* vol. 10, pp. 187–216.

Weitzman, Martin L. 1974. "Prices vs. Quantities," *Review of Economic Studies* vol. 41, pp. 50–65.

Wilson, Robert. 1975. "Informational Economies of Scale," *Bell Journal of Economics* (Spring) vol. 6, pp. 184–195.

# 5

## The Health Implications
## of Residuals Discharges:
## A Methodological Overview

### A. Myrick Freeman III

Much of the theoretical and empirical work on depletable resources and re-source scarcity is based on the assumption of perfect markets. This chapter is concerned with one possibly significant type of market failure—the failure to compensate for health effects associated with the use of the environment as a receptacle for residuals from resource extraction, processing, and utilization. Specifically, it is about developing research strategies to identify and quantify the relationships between residuals discharges and their effect on human health, not only to gain a better understanding of the nature and magnitude of these effects, but also to determine how they have changed over time as the economy has adjusted to changing resource availability and use.

The health effects of environmental pollution are an important research area in general, but they can be linked with the particular concerns of this volume in two ways. The first involves the relationship between resource scarcity and economic growth. As Anthony C. Fisher put it, "A measure of a resource's scarcity should have just one essential property: it should summarize the sacrifices direct *and indirect*, made to obtain the unit of resource" (Fisher, 1979). Thus, measures of resource scarcity should include some measure of such external costs as health effects. To the extent that such costs are left out of the calculation, scarcity measures are biased downward.

The author is grateful to Dr. Edward Burger, William V. Hogan, John Krutilla, William Schulze, Eugene Seskin, and V. Kerry Smith for a number of comments and suggestions which were helpful in the preparation of this paper. Also, William Hogan prepared a background paper on the relationships between demographic theory and method and research on health effects. That paper was very useful and portions of this paper are based on his contribution.

Second, where an economy's adjustment to increasing scarcity imposes external costs, such as ill health, some form of governmental intervention may be appropriate on efficiency grounds to correct for market failure. Knowledge of the nature and magnitude of health effects is important for the development of appropriate policies.

These concerns point naturally to two sets of research questions. The first is how to develop more effective research strategies for identifying and measuring the health effects associated with changes in the magnitude and composition of residuals flows. The second set concerns approaches to assigning monetary values to these health effects so that they can be used in measures of scarcity or compared with the costs of control for policy making.

## 1. Measuring Health Effects

Introduction

A major question to be raised at the outset is whether economists can have anything useful to say about the identification and measurement of the health consequences of activities such as residuals discharges. There is a great deal of skepticism on the part of health scientists about the usefulness of the kind of large-scale statistical studies that some economists have conducted. Perhaps the most controversial example of such a study is the work of Lester Lave and Eugene Seskin on the relationship between air pollution and mortality (Lave and Seskin, 1977).[1] The question is whether the economist's analytical tools have anything to offer over and above the research recommendations already made by health scientists. There are three aspects of this question.

First, identifying the causes of ill health and linking changes in health to changes in environmental characteristics seem to be primarily tasks for people trained in health sciences. Not only is there a substantial amount of research being conducted by health scientists in this area, but practitioners in these fields themselves have addressed the question of research strategies. Several reports recommending research strategies have been written by and directed toward this group of researchers.[2] Their major recommendations include the following:

1. Research on the physiological mechanisms involved in carcinogenesis, mutagenesis, and other causes of ill health

---

[1] For one example of the critical reaction of health scientists to this work, see Landau (1978).

[2] See U.S. Department of Health, Education, and Welfare (1970); U.S. Department of Health, Education, and Welfare (1977); and National Academy of Sciences (1977).

2. Better data on environmental levels and human exposures to harmful substances
3. Better data on health, mortality, morbidity, and so on
4. Better statistical techniques for linking exposure to harmful effects

These are sound, useful, and almost obvious recommendations. If this chapter is to make a contribution, it must go beyond these general recommendations to make specific suggestions on uses of data, empirical models that incorporate socioeconomic variables in behavioral relationships, and the possible complementarities between the roles of economists and biomedical researchers.

Parts of this chapter are addressed to two different audiences: epidemiologists with backgrounds in medicine and public health, and economists. Those parts of the chapter dealing with the problems of measuring effects and characterizing exposure may be more useful to economists who are less familiar with the physical and medical aspects of environmental health problems. On the other hand, the discussion of model structure and the possible roles of social and economic behavior in influencing the relationship between environmental exposures and health may be more useful to epidemiologists who are less familiar with behavioral models and simultaneous equations systems.

The second aspect concerns the objectives to be served by large-scale statistical studies.[3] Epidemiologists tend to view statistical studies as playing one of two possible roles in a research strategy. The first is to scan the horizon in an hypothesis-raising fashion; that is, to identify possible relationships which can be the basis for more carefully controlled laboratory and clinical studies. The second is to test under real world conditions hypotheses generated by laboratory and clinical research. My main concern here is with the latter role, because the ultimate objective of economic research in this area is to quantify and value health effects so that measures of value can be incorporated into comprehensive measures of cost and scarcity and into policy evaluations. In carrying out the first role, investigators are concerned primarily with the existence of significant associations, but in carrying out the second, the accuracy (variance and bias) of estimated parameters is of major importance. This has significant ramifications for the ways in which model specification and statistical estimation are carried out. These points will be developed further later.

The third aspect concerns the question of causal inference. It must be acknowledged that the statistical analyses of economists and of classical epidemiologists do not have the power to establish cause-and-effect relationships between environmental pollutants and ill health. As is well known, association

---

[3] I am indebted to Dr. Edward Burger for suggesting the following point.

does not prove causation. Rather, consistent theoretical models and empirical evidence that makes it unlikely the observed associations are due to sampling variation or spurious correlation are what lead to credible causal inferences.[4] A major question to be addressed in this section is the contribution economists can make to the development of evidence regarding possible cause-and-effect relationships.

To see what kinds of contributions economic analysis might be able to make to the problem, it would be helpful to sketch out a model of the process we are concerned with. This model has three elements:

1. Discharges of pollutants lead to human exposure
2. Exposure may produce a variety of individual physiological changes and pathologies
3. These may result in sickness, death, or other more subtle changes in physical function and well-being.

Each of these elements is complicated by a number of factors.

1. There are a variety of pathways that substances can take from their point of origin to the point where they can affect humans. Some substances may be chemically transformed in the environment. There may be temporal and spatial variations in the pattern of ambient concentrations and in exposures. The substance may occur naturally so that the contribution of human activities must be separated from background levels of exposure. Finally, individual behavior influences actual exposure for any given pattern of discharges and ambient concentrations.
2. Biological consequences of exposure may involve changes in absorption, metabolism, storage, and excretion. These functions may be influenced by the pathways of exposure, temporal variations, synergistic, promoter, or antagonistic relationships among substances, genetic and other physical differences among individuals, and differences in behavior. These in turn govern the nature and magnitude of the effective dose to target organs. For any given set of conditions, the physiological and pathological changes associated with a given exposure level may vary according to some predictable stochastic distribution. Finally, it may be some time before any of these changes become manifest.
3. The biological manifestations of a dose may range from transient, self-limited alterations in organ or cell function to pathological changes, with structural or functional impairment. There may be only subtle, difficult-to-observe changes in such things as fertility, emotional state, or rate and extent of mental and physical development in the young.

---

[4] See Lave and Seskin (1977) for a careful discussion of this question in the context of the air pollution–mortality relationship.

Or, the changes may extend to those short- or long-term disabilities and reductions in physical activity that are captured by the usual measures of morbidity. Finally, they may result sooner or later in death.

It is important to note that the ultimate health effects of environmental pollutants may be influenced by social and economic factors and the ways in which they affect individual behavior. For this reason, if the objective of an analysis is to predict a change in health status that would result from changes in residuals discharges and exposure patterns, the traditional methods of health scientists (clinical, basic biomedical, and animal studies) are not adequate. These methods are important in developing hypotheses for testing and for specifying models, but they cannot substitute for an analysis of heterogeneous populations exposed to low levels of substances in a variety of settings, under different conditions, and with varying behaviors.

This also implies that simple cross-section regressions of some measure of health status, for example mortality, against some contemporaneous measures of ambient environmental quality or exposure and other control variables are not adequate, at least if the objective is to measure and predict the magnitude of health effects rather than to simply establish associations. There are several reasons for this:

Ambient concentrations are an imperfect measure of exposure
There may be a lag time before effects are visible, so that contemporaneous measures of ambient concentrations of a pollutant do not measure the relevant exposure
Omitted environmental and behavioral variables may bias estimated coefficients
There may be multicollinearity among independent variables
As reduced-form equations, the regressions may not be representative of the true underlying structure of the system being studied.

Lave and Seskin (1979, page 182) make a similar point when they compare their statistical approach with laboratory experiments and controlled clinical trials.

Laboratory data are inherently incapable of providing estimates of the dose-response relationship of long-term exposure to air pollution in humans. Careful analyses of special groups have more to offer, but randomization is still not possible, and obtaining sample sizes large enough to make accurate estimates can be prohibitively expensive. This is not to say that either type of investigation is useless. The point is that each of the three methods can provide information that is difficult or impossible for the other two to provide. Laboratory experiments provide understanding of the physiological mechanisms and data on acute responses; detailed studies of groups trade off smaller sample size for more careful data on dose and response; general population studies use readily available data to obtain large sample size.

The remainder of this section explores some of the possibilities and problems involved with using regression analysis to explain measures of the health status of populations or groups as a function of a set of variables, including environmental exposures. The unit of observation is the population group and the sample is drawn from the universe of populations so defined.[5] I now discuss some problems in defining and measuring the dependent variable, defining and measuring dose, the inclusion of other variables, and model structure and estimation.

### Defining and Measuring Health Effects

This section discusses three types of measures of health status: those dealing with mortality, those dealing with morbidity, and those reflecting more subtle, nonlethal effects which are not captured by conventional measures of morbidity.

Mortality refers to a well-defined event, death, which for ceremonial and legal reasons almost always is noted and made part of an official record. Thus statistics on mortality are in all likelihood the most accurate of all of the types of measures of health status. The crude mortality rate of a population is the ratio of the total number of deaths from all causes during a period of time to the average number of persons in that population living during that period. This definition of the mortality rate is termed "crude" because it confounds the actual age- and sex-specific mortality rates for subsets of the population with the age and sex distribution of the population as a whole.

The crude mortality rate can also be interpreted as the probability that an individual member of the relevant cohort group will die during a given period. Thus, mortality rates can be translated into life expectancies through the device of the "life table" (a description of the mortality cross section of a stationary population).[6] In attempting to explain the mortality rates of populations, it is useful to distinguish the mortality rates of specific age and

[5] In order to avoid aggregation problems with some of the explanatory variables, it may be desirable to base the analysis on individuals as the unit of observation. However, except for some forms of morbidity, this would pose serious problems in measuring the health status variables. This point will be developed further below.

[6] Life tables are usually constructed from data on many cohorts during some specified time period, usually a year. Because of this, they are referred to as "synthetic" life tables. They represent no actual lifetime mortality patterns, but rather what would happen to a group of persons who lived through their lifetimes subject to the mortality rates that prevail during the period in which the actual mortality measurements were recorded for each of the different age groups. True cohort life tables that are based on the actual cohort's lifetime mortality experience are very rare. They necessarily require a lifetime to record the data and are expensive to construct because of the requirements of keeping track of a large number of people over a long period of time. For further discussion of life tables, see one of the standard references in technical demography, for example Barclay (1958).

sex groups within a population from the effects of differences in the age and sex composition of populations. The crude mortality rate is simply the weighted average of the age, sex, or race-specific rates where the weights are the proportion of the total population in each category. One resolution of the problem is to disaggregate the mortality rate of the population by computing age-, sex-, or race-specific mortality rates for each relevant group and use these rates as dependent variables in separate regressions for each group. The other alternative is to use the age- and sex-specific mortality rates to compute a standardized or adjusted mortality rate for each population. The standardized mortality rate is a weighted average of the age-, sex-; or race-specific mortality rates where the same set of standard weights is utilized for all of the populations in the sample.[7]

If data on cause of death are available, cause-specific mortality rates may also be computed for the population as a whole or for each age, sex, or race grouping. This might be a fruitful approach where the objective is to test hypotheses concerning the mechanisms by which exposures lead to specific pathologies or physiological changes and mortality. However, it appears that many, if not most, potentially harmful substances are capable of causing death through several alternative mechanisms. In these cases, what would be of interest is the impact of the substance on deaths from all causes.[8]

There are several other problems with utilizing cause-specific mortality rates. First, cause of death is itself a complex concept and this complexity is not reflected in the available data. The death registration certificates used in the United States allow the recording physician to list an immediate cause of death. This initial cause may then be attributed to (that is, listed as a consequence of), a second cause; or the second cause may be listed as a contributing complication of the first. This second cause, in turn, may be listed as a consequence of or a concomitant of a third cause. The maximum of three conditions, referred to as causes of death, collectively provide an account of why a person died that is currently acceptable to the medical profession. In nearly all published data, only the primary or immediate cause of death is given. Furthermore, even the immediate cause of death may be inaccurately listed, especially where autopsies and appropriate pathological examinations are not carried out. Finally, where narrowly defined categories of cause of death are under investigation, natural variability in the small sample may prevent meaningful statistical results from being obtained.[9]

Morbidity is defined by the U.S. Public Health Service as "a departure from a state of physical or mental well being, resulting from disease or injury, of which the affected individual is aware." [10] This is an all-encompassing

[7] See, for example, Barclay (1958).

[8] See, for example, Lave and Seskin (1977) who found that suspended particulate and sulfate air pollution were associated with several cause-specific mortality rates.

[9] For further discussion, see Lave and Seskin (1977), pages 67–69.

[10] Cited in Peterson (1975), page 242.

definition. Morbidity can be classified in a variety of ways, for example, according to duration (chronic vs. acute), or by degree of impairment of activity. The National Health Survey uses a variety of concepts to measure the consequences of illness, disease, and disability. "Restricted activity days" are those on which a person is able to undertake some, but not all, normal activities; "bed disability days" are those in which a person is confined to bed, either at home or in an institution; "work lost days" are those on which a person is unable to engage in his ordinary gainful employment (U.S. Department of Health, Education and Welfare, 1964). One difficulty with these measures of morbidity is that they reflect *responses* to ill health rather than the health condition itself. Whether a given clinical manifestation of ill health results in any restrictions on activity, bed disability, or work loss depends upon a number of socioeconomic variables, such as employment and labor-force status, nonlabor sources of income, whether there are other income earners in the household, etc.[11]

Measures of morbidity must take into account the fact that, unlike mortality, morbidity is not an event, but a process involving time. Cases observed during a period may fall into any of four categories: (1) onset before the period and termination by either recovery or death during the period; (2) onset before the period and termination after the period; (3) onset during the period and termination during the period; and (4) onset during the period and termination after the period. The *prevalence rate* encompasses all four categories. It is defined as the total number of cases in the period as a percentage of the average number of persons in the population during the period. The *incidence rate* covers only the third and fourth categories above. It is defined as the number of new cases during the period as a percentage of the average number of persons in the population. Incidence rate data would be more appropriate for investigating causal relationships between changes in exposure or other environmental variables and changes in health status. On the other hand, prevalence rate and measures incorporating data on duration would be more appropriate for analyzing the social costs of morbidity, because the willingness to pay to avoid morbidity is likely to depend on the length as well as the number of cases.

The sparsity of meaningful morbidity data for different populations (for example, for different geographic areas) probably helps to account for the fact that there are relatively few statistical studies on the causes of morbidity, especially in comparison with efforts to explain mortality.[12] Yet it is possible to argue that morbidity may be at least as significant a component of environmentally related ill health as mortality.[13] First, sublethal impairment of function may be the sole, or at least primary, health effect associated with

[11] See, for example, Berkowitz and Johnson (1974) who show how other factors besides health affect disability status as reflected in labor force participation.

[12] See, for example, Lave and Seskin (1977), appendix A.

[13] For some evidence supporting this conjecture, see Crocker and coauthors (1979).

some pollutants. These would go undetected if research attention were devoted solely to mortality. Also, a mobile population and the possibility that medical intervention may either prevent or slow the biological changes leading to death may weaken the link between data on exposure and mortality. While this association may be obscured by such factors, it still may be possible to link the morbidity conditions preceding death to their environmental causes.

Although focusing attention on mortality alone may permit testing for causal relationships, morbidity may be a significant component of the costs of the process leading to death since many environmentally related fatalities are preceded by periods of morbidity. Mortality, because it is easier to measure than morbidity, may be the logical starting point for investigating health effects. It is interesting to determine to what extent mortality data can be used as an indicator of the associated morbidity. Specifically, can mortality rates that are specific for age, sex, and cause of death be accurately related to morbidity conditions for these groups and to the economic costs of ill health?

There is now increasing evidence that chemical contaminants can produce subtle physical or mental changes. They may lead to changes in emotional states or mental capacities. They may impair physical and mental development in infants and children. They may result in lower birth rates.[14] These effects would fall outside the conventional definition of morbidity if the affected individuals were unaware of them. Furthermore, they need not lead to the kinds of behavioral changes that are captured by existing measures of morbidity. These effects may be quite important in human and economic terms, yet it is beyond the capability of the statistical methods being discussed in this chapter to identify and measure these effects, at least given existing types of health status data.

Some, but not all, of the effects described above are related to exposures during the earliest stages of life, that is, fetuses, infants, and young children. Some evidence regarding the existence of these effects might be obtained by careful analysis of data on fertility, and fetal/infant mortality.

Zeckhauser and Shepard (1976) suggested an index of health status which combines the impact of mortality (a means of gauging life expectancy) and morbidity (a means of gauging the quality of one's health), as well as certain assumptions concerning preferences and utility.[15] They called their index Quality Adjusted Life Years (QALY's). Each remaining year of an individual's life expectancy is weighted by a factor reflecting the individual's expected health status during that year. Lower rates would reflect poor health and a lower quality of life. Also, the quality weights *could* be a function of

---

[14] James Allen's studies of primates have shown some of these effects to be associated with polychlorinated biphenyls in mothers' diets. See for example, Barsotti, Marla, and Allen (1976).

[15] See also Raiffa, Schwartz, and Weinstein (1977).

age to reflect the disutility of aging itself. Any increase in morbidity or the probability of dying during any interval would reduce the QALY index. Thus, changes in health status could be measured by changes in the QALY index.

The main difficulty in developing the QALY index lies in finding an appropriate empirical basis for deriving a set of quality weights. At this stage in its development, the QALY index appears to be more useful as a device for organizing information about the consequences of alternative policies for decision makers than as an operational measure of health status for empirical research on the health effects of environmental pollutants.

Measuring Doses

In choosing an appropriate measure of the dose received through exposure, it is important to consider the nature of the physiological mechanism that is hypothesized to be involved in the uptake of the pollutant and the changes it causes. In some physical transformations, the dose rate at the time of testing may be the most appropriate measure, whereas with others a measure of total or accumulated dose may be required.

It is also necessary to determine whether dose or dose rate in a single exposure is sufficient to affect health or whether total exposure or total body burden from all sources should be measured. For example, if the health effect of interest is acute ill health caused by respiratory problems, then it would be appropriate to obtain an indication of dose rate by measuring breathing. Ambient concentrations of the pollutants in question would be a good proxy for dose rates in this case. However, the determination of other effects may require information on total dose rate from all sources—air, water, food, etc. This may be difficult to obtain from available data because the total dose rate is a function of the amounts of the substance in the various media (for example, in drinking water and food) as well as individual behavior (for example, diet).

It is also likely to be difficult to measure cumulative doses for populations, both because of the absence of an historical record, and because of the diverse experiences of individual members. Tissue levels may be the best measure of cumulative dose for substances that accumulate in the body. In fact, they may be better from a biological perspective since they represent the net effect of total dose and detoxification and metabolic processes. However, it may not be practical to obtain data on body burdens for populations.

A major problem for statistical research of this sort arises when a health effect becomes apparent only after a lag or latency period, as in the case of cancer. In such cases, current ambient concentrations or dose rates of pollutants are a poor proxy for past exposures, especially when the latency period may be 20 to 30 years in length.[16] The difficulty of reconstructing accurate exposure histories for populations may be a major barrier to using the statistical method to determine some types of effects.

The discussion to this point has been based implicitly on the assumption that dose or exposure could be measured directly for each individual. But in fact individual measurements are not practical for large sample studies of the sort being discussed here. Ambient levels or concentrations in food or drinking water may be good estimates of individual doses if behavioral differences (for example, diet) among individuals are small, or if concentrations or ambient levels do not vary spatially, but this is not the case for some important air pollutants. In these cases, estimates of the average exposure for the population of a city or Standard Metropolitan Statistical Area must be based on readings taken at only one or a small number of monitoring stations—typically located in areas with lower air quality. If air quality varies across space within the region, the average quality measure is in error, and the error is compounded if individuals move about within the region. If the errors in measurement are random, that is, uncorrelated with the true value, the effect is to bias regression estimates of the coefficient on exposure toward zero. But in the case of urban air pollution, the errors seem likely to be systematic, and in at least one instance could bias regression estimates upward (Freeman, 1979, pp. 26–28).

Air pollution readings are like any other measurement in science in that they are subject to measurement error. The standard errors of the most commonly used analytical techniques are no doubt well understood by analytical chemists. What is probably less well understood is the nature of the errors introduced by careless handling of equipment in the field, and in recording and processing the data. It seems reasonable to assume that these errors are random. They may be small compared with those introduced by spatial variation and individual mobility, but it would be useful to have more information on this.

Another set of problems in constructing accurate measures of dose or exposure arises because of migration among regions or population groups. A health effect observed in an individual in one population may have been caused by an earlier exposure in another area or population. The possibility of migration makes analysis of the health effects of environmental exposures considerably more complicated than it would be otherwise. If migration were a perfectly random process and uncorrelated with differences in environmental quality among regions, the principal effect would be to introduce noise into the system and to make it more difficult to detect systematic relationships

---

[16] Here I am concerned only with the problem of obtaining an appropriate record of exposures. I will discuss lag structures and model specification in a later section.

between environmental exposures and health effects for different populations. However, migration has not been random. There have been systematic flows from the Northeast to the South and West. Further, migration may be influenced by environmental quality differences across regions.[17] Migration is not randomly selective from the population at the source. Thus it will alter the composition of populations at both the origin and the destination in systematic ways. An example is the migration of older people to retirement communities in Florida and the Southwest. The mortality effects of migration-induced changes in the age composition of a population can be controlled for through the use of age-specific mortality rates, but this still leaves a major problem of constructing accurate exposure histories for migrants.

One possible way to resolve this set of problems would be to carry out a large-scale longitudinal study of a large sample of families from different regions. This would enable the construction of more accurate and detailed exposure histories. With sufficiently close monitoring, it would allow the compilation of more complete and meaningful records of health status. Such a study would be expensive and would take a long time to bear fruit.[18] Another possible approach to the problems posed by migration would be to develop a comprehensive model of interurban migration and through simulation use the model to construct a synthetic measure of exposure for each population at some given time.[19]

Modeling may be useful in dealing with some of the other problems of developing adequate exposure measures. For example, an air pollution dispersion model may be used to compute exposures for different groups within the urban area even when accurate pollution monitoring data are not available. Also, it might be possible to model individuals' movements in an urban area (to work, stores, etc.) in order to derive more accurate measures of exposure history as individuals move through a spatially differentiated environment.[20]

The final point to mention is the possibility of interactions among ingested or inhaled substances. Hypotheses about such relationships would be derived from biomedical research and where there is evidence that they exist, statistical studies of populations must be designed to take them into account.

[17] See, for example, Hoch and Drake (1974) and Meyer and Leone (1977) who have found that environmental quality differences across regions help to explain differences in wage rates.

[18] For a description of one such study of the health effects of air pollution now underway, see Speizer, Bishop, and Ferris (1977). Also, it may be possible to use existing longitudinal data sets originally constructed for other purposes. For example, Crocker and coauthors (1979) have used data from Michigan's Survey Research Center to study morbidity.

[19] To the extent that migration is "caused" by environmental factors and migration affects the crude mortality of populations, this introduces an element of simultaneity into the process being analyzed. This point will be discussed in a subsequent section.

[20] See, for example, Harrison and Rubinfeld (1978).

## Other Variables

Previous demographic studies of mortality have found that age, sex, marital status, occupation, education, living conditions, diet, personal health habits, population density, urban versus rural residence, access to medical care, income, and inherited characteristics are among the factors most important in determining the morbidity and mortality of individuals in groups.[21] Any research into the determinants of morbidity and mortality, whether on the basis of individual or aggregate data, should take into account the influence of these variables and the necessity to control for them.

One possible classification of other variables is as follows:

*Physical characteristics:* age, sex, race
*Socioeconomic characteristics:* income, occupation, education, marital status
*Personal characteristics:* smoking, diet, exercise, medical care, genetic characteristics
*Environmental variables:* population density, rural vs. urban, housing, air quality, radiation exposure, drinking water quality, climate, toxic contaminants, food

Some personal characteristics can be controlled for either by including variables to reflect the averages of characteristics (for example, average age, or percentage of nonwhite) in regressions to explain crude mortality rates, or by using age-, sex-, and race-specific mortality rates as dependent variables. However, the latter approach may make it more difficult to control for socioeconomic and personal characteristics, since these data are not likely to be available in a disaggregated form for each of the subgroups for which specific mortality rates are computed.

It may be very difficult to collect meaningful data on some personal characteristics. Cigarette sales or sales tax data have been used in some studies as a proxy for smoking, but this information may not be available for jurisdictions that correspond to the unit of observation. Furthermore, it does not distinguish among the forms of tobacco or differences in individual smoking habits. The data may be distorted by tax evasion efforts. Finally, in all of the cases where the unit of observation is a population, the variables can only reflect averages of the relevant characteristics and may hide significant variations within the relevant population.

It is difficult to overemphasize the importance of controlling for a wide variety of environmental variables. A significant weakness of several large-scale statistical studies on health effects of environmental pollutants is that they have focused on only one class of environmental variables, to the

---

[21] For an extended discussion of the determinants of mortality, see United Nations (1973), chapter V.

exclusion of others. For example, Lave and Seskin (1977) investigated the effects of a variety of air pollutants, but did not include water quality or radiation exposure as controlled variables. Similarly Page, Harris, and Epstein (1976) and Harris, Page, and Reiches (1977) investigated the relationships between drinking water and cancer mortality without including air pollution or dietary variables. Future studies should include as wide a range of environmental variables as possible.

### Model Specification and Estimation

At the beginning of this section, I briefly outlined the major elements of the process we are seeking to investigate with statistical tools. A sequence of events was traced that went from discharges of pollutants, to human exposure, to pathologies and physiological changes, to their manifestation in changes in measures of health status. This way of describing the formalization of the relationship between pollution and human health makes it sound deceptively simple. There are three aspects of model structure and specification which add substantially to the difficulty of designing and carrying out statistical analysis. These are the dynamic characteristics of the process, the functional form of the estimating equation, and the simultaneous equation aspects of the process being modeled. The way in which each of these problems is approached also has implications for the estimation of regression equations and the interpretation of statistical results.

The principal dynamic characteristic of the process is the length of the time interval between the exposure to an environmental pollutant and the development and manifestation of the health effect. For some types of acute effects, for example, lung irritation from air pollution or bacterial contamination of water, the health effect is essentially contemporaneous with exposure. However, many types of health effects result from exposures at an earlier time. For example, cancers may manifest themselves clinically only after latency periods of twenty to thirty years. Econometricians have developed techniques for investigating lag structures, but these techniques may not be readily adaptable to the complexities of the physiological processes involved here.[22] For example, at least for some types of cancer, the length of the latency period varies inversely with the strength of the initial dose of carcinogen. In other cases, the time pattern of the dose may matter. Hypotheses about the nature of the dynamics of the process must come from biomedical research. But another important research task is to develop the appropriate statistical techniques for testing these hypotheses.

---

[22] For an example of an exploration of the lag structure between daily air pollution and mortality levels, see Lave and Seskin (1977), chapter 9.

The second aspect of model specification is the functional form of the estimating equation. Most empirical researchers have used a simple linear form.[23] Again, biomedical research should be the basis for hypotheses about functional form. The appropriate functional form of the dose-response function may be deducible from the hypothesized physiological mechanism involved. For example, the "single hit" hypothesis holds that a single permanent, replicable change in the genetic structure of a cell caused by one molecule of a carcinogen is sufficient to cause cancer. The probability of that cellular event occurring is a linear function of the dose. Thus, with no threshold, the dose-response function is linear.[24] Other hypotheses about cellular mechanisms of carcinogenesis imply different functional forms for the dose-response function.

For other types of health effects, variations in individual characteristics may lead to differences in susceptibility to particular effects. If the degree of susceptibility to a particular chemical agent is distributed normally within a population, then the dose-response function will be nonlinear, and may or may not have a threshold.

The third aspect concerns the structural relationships among variables. Many economic, social, and environmental processes are too complex to be represented adequately by a single equation relating the dependent variable to a set of independent variables. Rather, what may be required is a set of two or more equations in which independent or exogenous variables in some equations are in fact endogenous to the system, that is, appear as dependent variables in other equations. With the exception of Crocker and coauthors (1979), empirical work on the health effects of environmental pollutants has ignored the possibility of simultaneous equation relationships and their effects on statistical estimation. When single equations containing endogenous variables on the right-hand side are lifted out of the simultaneous system and estimated with ordinary least squares, the estimated coefficients may be biased. Where complex processes with simultaneous relationships are involved, the most important of them must be modeled with a set of structural equations reflecting these interrelationships. Then appropriate statistical techniques such as two-stage least squares can be employed. Attention must also be given to the identifiability of the relationships to be estimated.

It is beyond the scope of this chapter to develop a complete model of the processes relating environmental discharges to measures of health effects. In any event, the main features of such a model will depend upon the physiological processes thought to be involved, the type of health effect (death, or some form of ill health), the environmental media through which the

---

[23] Lave and Seskin (1977) investigated a number of alternative functional forms, but found the linear form to give the best results.

[24] For an informative discussion of this and other hypotheses, see Maugh (1978) and National Academy of Sciences (1977), chapter 2.

pollutant is transmitted, the extent to which it is possible to avoid the pollutant, and the nature of the available data, including degree of aggregation.

The following example illustrates the potential for simultaneous relationships in a model of health effects and the potential problems in estimation. First, suppose that some measure of morbidity for a population ($M$) is a function of exposure to an environmental pollutant ($P$), access to medical care ($D$), and other variables. Second, let access to medical care depend upon average income ($Y$). Finally, income itself may depend upon the health status of the population. For example, higher morbidity means more days lost from work and lower earnings. Specifically:

$$M = a_0 + a_1D + a_2P \ldots + u_1 \tag{1}$$

$$D = b_0 + b_1Y + u_2 \tag{2}$$

$$Y = c_0 + c_1M + u_3 \tag{3}$$

where $u_1, u_2$, and $u_3$ are error terms and the coefficients are hypothesized to have the following signs:

$$a_0, a_2, b_1, c_0 > 0$$

$$a_1, c_1, < 0$$

Morbidity, doctors, and income are all endogenous to the system even though they each appear as an independent variable in one structural equation. If (1) were estimated by ordinary least squares, the parameter estimates would be inconsistent. Furthermore, in this specific case, (1) cannot be identified.

Other examples could be constructed in which averting behavior, residential or occupational choices, and migration introduce elements of simultaneity into the model. It is an open question as to which of these relationships are important in terms of affecting the estimation of dose-response functions.

Turning now to estimation, classical statistical inference is based on the assumption that the analyst is given a model *a priori* the exact features of which, including structural relationships, lag structures, and functional form, are completely specified in advance of the statistical evaluation.[25] When the analyst uses a given data set to estimate the parameters of this model and to test hypotheses about them, it is assumed that the model specification is independent of the sample data being used. Clearly, this is not the way empirical work has evolved, particularly since the advent of large-scale computers. In statistical studies of health effects, as well as in other areas, researchers adopt estimation strategies in which they run (often in an unsystematic way) a wide array of alternative specifications, including a variety of different regressors

---

[25] I am indebted to Kerry Smith for assistance and suggestions on this passage.

and functional forms. This procedure can be interpreted as a way of using the sample-based information to revise the character of the model. Thus the model specification is not invariant to the sample information. In effect, the form and composition of regression equations for the estimated model are affected by the information contained in the sample and by that brought to the process from outside the sample (by theory, for example).

Within the past few years there has been great interest in this area and with it a growing literature on the implications of pretesting and specification search procedures for the properties of the estimates.[26] Prior information that is brought to the estimation process independent of the sample itself serves to reduce the variance in point estimates of the model's parameters. It therefore (all else being equal) improves the precision that can be realized in estimating that model. Of course, this is not without a cost. The prior information incorporated in a model specification may be incorrect, and even though it reduces the variance in the point estimates, it does so in this case by increasing the bias in these estimates. Thus these procedures reduce the spread in a distribution at the cost of shifting its central tendency. It is not then clear exactly how one might come out. What is clear, however, is that persons researching health effects should be attentive to the statistical issues raised by pretest estimation of models, or to put it more crudely, by "data mining."

The issue of the tradeoff of bias against variance also arises in the context of the simultaneity problem. Ordinary least-squares estimates of the parameters of a mortality rate model will generally exhibit more precision (i.e., have smaller variance) than the two-stage least-squares estimates, but will be biased. In terms of the mean squared error of the estimates, it is not always clear which is best. The magnitude of the bias is likely to depend on the degree of jointness in the determination process. Whether in a particular case the possible bias is serious enough to justify the use of two-stage least squares is a question which should be investigated.

## 2.  Valuing Health Effects

Although most of the theoretical and empirical literature in this area focuses on mortality, I will discuss both mortality and morbidity and try to identify the most important areas for research. A number of approaches to assigning monetary values to the prevention of mortality and morbidity have been proposed and/or utilized in the literature on the economics of health and safety. These approaches can be broadly categorized as determining values: according to individual preferences (willingness to pay), or according

---

[26] See for example Bock, Yancey, and Judge (1973), and Wallace (1977).

to resource or opportunity cost. A brief discussion and evaluation of these alternative approaches follows. For more extensive discussions, see Schelling (1968), Mishan (1971), Acton (1973), Jones-Lee (1976), and Linnerooth (1979).

The most commonly used approach to the valuation of health effects has been to identify real costs in the form of lost productivity and output and the increase in resources devoted to medical care. When this concept is applied to the valuation of life, it values each life lost at the present value of the expected earnings for that individual had the premature death been avoided. Sickness that results in days of restricted activity is valued on the basis of wage rates. For morbidity and where death is preceded by a significant period of illness, some measure of medical costs would be added.

The productivity component of these measures of cost is based on the assumption that earnings reflect the individual's marginal productivity, and that people are worth what they do. However, this approach does not allow for the probabilistic nature of death and death avoidance in the health and safety areas, or for differing individual attitudes or preferences toward risk and risk avoidance. Also, because of variation in patterns of earnings over the life cycle and differences in labor market experience among individuals, including discrimination, values derived from this approach depend crucially on the age, sex, race, and labor force status of the individuals involved.

Most economists find the willingness-to-pay alternative conceptually more attractive because it is based on individual preferences and behavior. Actually, "willingness to pay" is a misleading term, since this approach would include all measures based on individual preferences, including those based on compensation for increased risk.[27] This approach values increases in longevity or reductions in the probability of death due to accident or illness in a given time period according to what an individual is willing to pay to achieve them.[28]

An individual's willingness to pay for changes in the probability of death can be translated into a more useful figure for policy evaluation, namely, the *value of statistical life* or the *value of statistical death* avoided. Suppose that in a group of 1,000 similar individuals, each would be willing to pay $1,000 for a policy which would reduce the probability of death for individuals in the group by 0.01.[29] This policy is a form of collective good for the individuals

---

[27] In technical terms, both compensating variation and equivalent variation measures of welfare change can be derived for any positive change in health status. The recent theoretical work by Willig (1976) has established the conditions under which income effects will be small enough so that the difference between these two measures can be ignored. These conditions appear to be satisfied for the kinds of problems considered in this section.

[28] This is the compensating variation definition. Alternatively, the equivalent variation measures the sum of money which would be sufficient to induce the individual to forgo the improvement in longevity.

[29] Individuals may have different willingnesses to pay because of differences in age, income, wealth, and so forth. The value of statistical life is still derived from the sum of the different willingness to pay of similarly affected individuals.

involved. The benefit to the group is found by adding across all individuals. Thus, the aggregate willingness to pay would be $1 million, and the expected number of deaths avoided would be 10. The group's aggregate willingness to pay to reduce the number of deaths in the group by one would be $100,000. This is the statistical value of life.

The conceptual basis for determining values of changes in morbidity is the same. For cases of acute morbidity of short duration, it is probably sufficient to determine the willingness to pay to avoid such incidents. For chronic forms of morbidity with longer duration, the probabilistic framework could be used to determine willingness to pay to reduce the probabilities of specified types of morbidity.

In an economy where all medical costs and wages lost due to illness are borne directly by affected individuals, the willingness-to-pay approach would capture all of those components of cost included in the opportunity-cost approach. In addition, it would include the direct disutility of illness. But in a modern economy, a number of social institutions operate to shift some of these costs away from individuals. Medical costs may be subsidized by transfer programs such as Medicaid and Medicare. Medical insurance premiums may not adjust perfectly to changes in individuals' circumstances affecting probability of ill health. Mechanisms such as disability payments, sick leave, and sick pay operate to shift at least part of the cost of lost productivity from the individual to the economy as a whole.

There are several problems in the empirical determination of the values of health effects. First, with respect to mortality, there have been two approaches to the measurement of willingness to pay in the literature. One is to observe market transactions in which individuals actually purchase or sell changes in their risk levels, either explicitly or implicitly. For example, if wage differentials among occupations are related to differences in occupational risk levels, these differences might be interpreted as reflecting, at the margin, the individual's tradeoff between risk/safety and money. Studies of the relationship between price differentials among members of a differentiated class (jobs, or products) and differences in risk levels represent an application of the hedonic price approach to measuring the marginal implicit prices or values of differentiating characteristics.[30] The other approach to measuring willingness to pay is to conduct surveys that ask individuals a series of questions about hypothetical situations involving risk/money tradeoffs. If the questions are designed carefully, and if individuals are truly capable of predicting how they would act if placed in these hypothetical situations, then their answers may reveal the monetary values they attach to reductions in risk.

Efforts to implement these empirical approaches have yielded a wide range of estimates of value. There have been three major studies using wage rates

---

[30] For discussion, see Rosen (1974) and Freeman (1979) chapter 4.

to estimate willingness to pay. Although two of these studies (Thaler and Rosen, 1976, and Smith, 1976) are based on the same wage rate data, they utilize different sets of occupational risk data, thus reaching quite different results. Thaler and Rosen conclude that the statistical value of life lies between $254,000 and $472,000, with the best estimate being $363,000.[31] These figures are in sharp contrast with the results obtained by Robert Smith (1976), whose estimates range between $2.1 million and $4.7 million. In the third study, Viscusi (1978) estimated values for blue-collar workers in the range of $1.7–2.5 million. His paper also includes a careful discussion of the possible explanations for the differences in estimates cited here.

There are similar differences in the results of two efforts to use the survey approach to obtaining values for statistical life. Acton (1973) obtained thirty-six responses from a random sample of residents in the Boston area. The survey instrument contained a number of questions about attitudes and value judgments with respect to efforts to save lives in emergency situations. The question of greatest interest concerned the willingness of the individual to pay for a program of emergency coronary care which would reduce his own probability of death by heart attack. Two different forms of the question implied values for statistical life of $44,000 and $67,000. Jones-Lee (1976) asked a similar small sample of individuals several questions about their willingness to accept higher air fares to travel on lines that had lower probabilities for a fatal crash. The values of statistical life implied by the respondents was about $5.6 million.

Together, these results tend to support the hypothesis that individuals make tradeoffs between safety and other economic goods. However, the results are quite sensitive to the technique and data base utilized to derive the estimate. This suggests that substantially more research is required before reliable estimates of the value of life can be obtained. In view of the well-known problems of bias (strategic bias, instrument bias, starting-point bias, etc.) and accuracy of response where hypothetical situations are involved, I would not recommend major efforts to refine the survey or bidding-game approach to estimating values. I would recommend continued efforts to use wage rate and occupational risk data. It would be helpful to have a data base designed specifically for this type of study—one which would provide more accurate measures of the perceived risks of individual jobs and wages and which would provide for adequate control for other individual characteristics affecting wage rates. Another possibility which should be explored is using other aspects of individual market-related behavior, such as that associated with product safety differences.

One problem which must be taken into account in the empirical estimates of the value of reduced mortality is the possible correlation between the risk

---

[31] All values cited here and in the next paragraph are in 1977 dollars.

of death and the risk of injury, disability, and illness associated with jobs. Assuming adequate information, wage premiums are likely to reflect both the higher risk of death and the higher risk of less serious changes in health status.

A somewhat related question is the potential role of the cause of death in determining the value of reduced mortality. Most of the theoretical models underlying this type of analysis assume that an individual is indifferent as to the cause of death. This seems to run counter to some people's expressed preferences to die by quick means such as airplane crashes or heart attacks rather than as a consequence of lingering diseases such as cancer. We must analytically distinguish between willingness to pay to postpone death by any cause and willingness to pay to avoid prefatal morbidity and the pain, anxiety, and medical costs associated with some forms of death. Estimates of the value of statistical life derived from data on accidental deaths are likely to understate the willingness to pay to avoid the combination of morbidity and mortality associated with environmentally induced cancers.

The latency period or lag between exposure and death creates both theoretical and empirical problems with respect to the measurement of value. When wage rate data are related to the risk of accidental death, they yield an estimate of the willingness to pay now to reduce the probability of death in the present. What is of interest is the willingness to pay now to avoid a present exposure to a substance, thereby decreasing the probability of death during some future interval of time. This latter may be larger or smaller, depending upon the length of the latency period, the pattern of probabilities of dying of other causes now and in the future, and the time pattern of expected income and consumption.[32] Thus, to estimate values properly, the length of the latency period and these other factors must be taken into account explicitly in the empirical model. However, it seems doubtful that this can be done successfully at the empirical level.

One of the basic assumptions of the models on which these empirical studies are based is that individuals have full knowledge of the relative risks of different occupations. In the absence of knowledge of risk differentials, individuals would have no reason to act in such a way as to lead to differences in wage rates across occupations. However, it is the very absence of sound technical information on the effects of environmental and occupational exposures to many chemicals that makes this whole set of issues so perplexing for public policy. If scientists cannot agree on the magnitude and in some cases even the existence of risks associated with exposures to certain substances, there is no reason to expect that individuals will respond accordingly. On the other hand, if acceptable estimates of the value of statistical life can be derived from studies dealing with accidental mortality, it may be possible to use

[32] See Freeman (1979, pages 179–181).

theoretical models to arrive at *reasonable* imputations or adjustments for the intertemporal aspects of environmental exposures and health effects.

Although morbidity may be an important component of the value of improved health status, little empirical work has been done on estimating values or benefits associated with reduced morbidity. There are several problems which must be dealt with if efforts at empirical estimation are to be successful. First, if values are to be based on wage rate differentials or other market information, there must be an adequate data base on the incidence and prevalence of morbidity for the groups or individuals in the sample. Survey questionnaires or bidding games may prove useful since morbidity, at least from the more common causes, is within the range of experience of respondents. Surveys may play a very useful role, especially in cross checking or validating estimates of values derived from other methods. The questions of instrument design, bias, and accuracy inherent in all survey approaches must be dealt with successfully.

Second, empirical studies must deal explicitly with the fact that morbidity as a concept covers a wide variety of health states of different severity and duration. Thus, separate estimates of values for different types of morbidity of specified intensity and duration must be made. Finally, an individual's willingness to pay to avoid a day of a certain type of morbidity may be affected by the social institutions governing the sharing of costs of medical care and lost output (wages). Complete medical insurance may reduce the incremental monetary cost of morbidity borne by the individual to zero. Paid sick leave and other devices for income maintenance may mean that the lost output associated with a restricted activity day is not borne by the individual in the form of lost wages. Thus an individual's willingness to pay to avoid a day of morbidity may understate the social value of preventing that morbidity.

The more subtle health effects described in section 1 pose a particularly severe set of problems for the estimation of values. First and most obvious is the lack of data on the nature and magnitude of these health effects. Even if these effects were fully quantifiable, their estimation would still be difficult because to a substantial extent they lie outside the normal rubric for estimating values of health effects. For example, there may be no increase in medical costs or decrease in life expectancy associated with many of these effects. More important, many of the behavioral changes and defects in physical and mental developmental have the effect of changing individuals in fundamental ways. In such cases it seems particularly inappropriate to employ the assumption of fixed tastes and preferences which is the foundation of the neoclassical theory of welfare economics. For example, if it is known that fetal and infant exposure to a substance will result in a 5-point reduction in the intelligence quotient of the young adult, is it meaningful to ask what that individual would be willing to pay to avoid that change? If research on health effects reveals that this class of problems is significant, then it will be important to turn attention to the ethical and technical problems involved in establishing their economic value.

## 3. Conclusions

As this discussion has shown, there are three areas where economists could make a major contribution to appropriately designed research.

First, it is clear that health effects are the consequence of complex physiological, social, and economic processes. Statistical analyses should be based on equations derived from models which reflect our understanding of these processes as closely as possible. It is necessary to move beyond the statistical search for associations and to base further empirical studies on a sound economic and biomedical foundation.

A second major area for research is morbidity and other subtle but nonfatal health effects. Environmentally induced morbidity may be of major quantitative significance, especially when the morbidity associated with terminal illness is taken into account. The more subtle developmental, behavioral, and reproductive impairments may be of far-reaching importance. However, statistical research on this set of effects will have to await the development of standardized measures and an appropriate data base.

The third major area of interest is well within the economist's traditional territory. It is the estimation of the economic values associated with or attached to changes in health status. Substantial progress has been made at the theoretical and empirical level in developing estimates of the value of reduced mortality. Unfortunately, existing estimates vary widely with the data base and empirical technique used. These differences must be narrowed substantially before these estimates can be taken seriously as objective measures of value in policy discussions. It is also important to develop comparable measures of the value of reduced morbidity, given the likelihood that morbidity effects may be a substantial part of the total health effects associated with environmental pollution.

## References

Acton, Jan P. 1973. *Evaluating Public Programs to Save Lives: The Case of Heart Attacks* (Santa Monica, Calif., Rand Corp.).
Barclay, George W. 1958. *Techniques of Population Analysis* (New York, Wiley).

Barsotti, D. R., Marlar, R. J., and Allen, J. R. 1976. "Reproductive Disfunction in Rhesus Monkeys Exposed to Low Levels of Polychlorinated Biphenyls," *Food and Cosmetic Toxicology* vol. 14.

Berkowitz, Monroe, and William G. Johnson. 1974. "Health and Labor Force Participation," *Journal of Human Resources* (Winter).

Bock, M. E., T. A. Yancey, and G. G. Judge. 1973. "The Statistical Consequences of Preliminary Test Estimators in Regression," *Journal of the American Statistical Association* vol. 68, pp. 109–116.

Crocker, Thomas D., Shaul Ben-David, Allen V. Kneese, and William D. Schulze. 1979. *Methods Development for Assessing Air Pollution Control Benefits* vol. 1, "Experiments in the Economics of Air Pollution Epidemiology" (Washington, D.C., Environmental Protection Agency).

Fisher, Anthony C. 1979. "On Measures of Natural Resource Scarcity," in V. Kerry Smith, ed., *Scarcity and Growth Reconsidered* (Baltimore, Md., Johns Hopkins University Press for Resources for the Future).

Freeman, A. Myrick, III. 1979. *The Benefits of Environmental Improvement: Theory and Practice* (Baltimore, Md., Johns Hopkins University Press for Resources for the Future).

Harris, Robert H., R. Talbot Page, and Nancy A. Reiches. 1977. "Carcinogenic Hazards of Organic Chemicals in Drinking Water," *Origins of Human Cancer* (Cold Spring Harbor, N.Y., Cold Spring Harbor Laboratory).

Harrison, David, and Daniel Rubinfeld. 1978. "The Distribution of Benefits from Improvements in Air Quality," *Journal of Environmental Economics and Management* vol. 5, no. 4, pp. 313–332.

Hoch, Irving, and Judith Drake. 1974. "Wages, Climate, and the Quality of Life," *Journal of Environmental Economics and Management* vol. 1, pp. 268–295.

Jones-Lee, Michael W. 1976. *The Value of Life: An Economic Analysis* (Chicago, University of Chicago Press).

Landau, Emanuel. 1978. "The Danger in Statistics," *The Nation's Health* (March).

Lave, Lester B., and Eugene P. Seskin. 1977. *Air Pollution and Human Health* (Baltimore, Md., Johns Hopkins University Press for Resources for the Future).

———, and ———. 1979. "Epidemiology, Causality, and Public Policy," *American Scientist* vol. 67, no. 2 (March-April) pp. 178–186.

Linnerooth, Joanne. 1979. "The Value of Human Life: A Review of the Models," *Economic Inquiry* vol. 17, no. 1 (January) pp. 52–74.

Maugh, Thomas H. 1978. "Chemical Carcinogens: How Dangerous Are Low Doses?" *Science* vol. 202 (October 6) pp. 37–41.

Meyer, John R., and Robert A. Leone. 1977. "The Urban Disamenity Revisited," in Lowdon Wingo and Alan Evans, eds., *Public Economics and the Quality of Life* (Baltimore, Md., Johns Hopkins University Press for Resources for the Future).

Mishan, Ezra J. 1971. "Evaluation of Life and Limb: A Theoretical Approach," *Journal of Political Economy* vol. 79, no. 4 (July/August) pp. 687–705.

National Academy of Sciences, Assembly of Life Sciences. 1977. *Drinking Water and Health* (Washington, D.C.).

National Academy of Sciences, Commission on Natural Resources. 1977. *Effects of a Polluted Environment: Research and Development Needs* (Washington, D.C.).

Page, R. Talbot, Robert H. Harris, and Samuel S. Epstein. 1976. "Drinking Water and Cancer Mortality in Louisiana," *Science* vol. 193, no. 4247 (July 2) pp. 55–57.

Peterson, William. 1975. *Population*, 3rd ed. (New York, Macmillan).

Raiffa, Howard, William B. Schwartz, and Milton W. Weinstein. 1977. "Evaluating Health Effects of Societal Decisions and Programs," in National Academy of Sciences, *Decision Making in the Environmental Protection Agency*, vol. IIb, *Selected Working Papers* (Washington, D.C.).

Rosen, Sherwin. 1974. "Hedonic Prices and Implicit Markets: Product Differentiation in Pure Competition," *Journal of Political Economy* vol. 82, no. 1 (January/February) pp. 34–55.

Schelling, Thomas C. 1968. "The Life You Save May Be Your Own," in Samuel B. Chase, Jr., ed., *Problems in Public Expenditure Analysis* (Washington, D.C., Brookings Institution).

Smith, Robert S. 1976. *The Occupational Safety and Health Act: Its Goals and Its Achievements* (Washington, D.C., American Enterprise Institute for Public Policy Research).

Speizer, F. E., Y. Bishop and B. G. Ferris. 1977. "An Epidemiologic Approach to the Study of the Health Effects of Air Pollution," in *Proceedings of the Fourth Symposium on Statistics and the Environment* (Washington, D.C., American Statistical Association).

Thaler, R. H., and S. Rosen. 1976. "The Value of Saving a Life: Evidence from the Labor Market" in N. E. Terleckyj, ed., *Household Production and Consumption* (New York, Columbia University Press).

United Nations. 1973. *Determinants and Consequences of Population Trends* vol. 1 (New York).

U.S. Department of Health, Education and Welfare, National Center for Health Statistics. 1964. *Health Survey Procedure, Vital and Health Statistics Programs and Collection Procedures*. Series 1, no. 2 (Washington, D.C.).

U.S. Department of Health, Education and Welfare. 1970. *Man's Health and the Environment—Research Needs* (Washington, D.C.).

U.S. Department of Health, Education and Welfare. 1977. *Human Health and the Environment—Some Research Needs* (Washington, D.C.).

Viscusi, W. Kip. 1978. "Labor Market Valuations of Life and Limb: Empirical Evidence and Policy Implications," *Public Policy* vol. 26, no. 3 (Summer), pp. 359–386.

Wallace, T. Dudley. 1977. "Pretest Estimation in Regression: A Survey," *American Journal of Agricultural Economics* (August) pp. 431–443.

Willig, Robert D. 1976. "Consumer's Surplus Without Apology," *American Economic Review* vol. 66, no. 4 (September) pp. 589–597.

Zeckhauser, Richard, and Donald Shepard. 1976. "Where Now for Saving Lives?" *Law and Contemporary Problems* vol. 40, no. 4 (Autumn) pp. 5–45.

PART **IV**

# MEASURING THE ROLE
# OF NATURAL RESOURCES
# IN PRODUCTION PROCESSES

# 6

## The Measurement of Raw Material Inputs

Lawrence J. Lau

### 1. Introduction

A growing concern that raw material inputs to production, especially those which are nonrenewable, are being rapidly depleted by rising demands, combined with the degradation of such common property resources as air and water, have led to the question of whether "sufficient" raw materials exist to support a high standard of living in the present as well as the future. "Sufficiency" is a difficult concept to define, especially in such a context, but one may begin by attempting to measure the current usage rates for raw material inputs and estimating their potential availability.

This chapter examines the problems in defining aggregate materials inputs at the plant, industry, and economy levels. Given that such measures have played a key role in conventional neoclassical analyses of the "sufficiency" of raw materials, it is important to establish whether increasing, constant, or decreasing quantities are needed to produce a given set of outputs. This information, coupled with alternative technological scenarios, may be used to evaluate the "sufficiency" of the existing stock of raw materials.

"Sufficiency," of course, depends on many factors. It depends on the standard of living desired, and the degree to which commodities may be substituted to achieve this standard. Not much will be said about this substitution among final consumption demands in this chapter. "Sufficiency" also depends on the levels of technology in both the supplying and using

The author is grateful to Ernst R. Berndt, W. Erwin Diewert, Zvi Griliches, Tjalling C. Koopmans, and V. Kerry Smith for helpful discussions.

sectors. However, while technological progress in the former always increases the availability of raw material inputs, technological progress in the latter may either increase or decrease demand for such inputs. For example, the introduction of synthetic fibers increased the demand for crude oil, whereas the development of more efficient appliances decreased the demand for electricity and hence the demand for fuels; the introduction of large-scale integrated circuits decreased industrial demand for silver, and the introduction of communication by satellites reduced the demand for electric cables and hence the demand for copper.

"Sufficiency" also depends on the stock of initial endowments, which in a strictly physical sense, is given and fixed. However, knowledge of the extent of the initial endowments is far from complete, and every discovery and invention increases the potential use value of the initial endowments. The term "endowments" as used here also includes the environment, and more generally the regenerative ability of the whole ecological system. Thus, it is possible that although the physical quantities of raw materials consumed have declined, to the extent that ecological and environmental qualities have continued to be worsened, the total "endowments" are actually being depleted.

"Sufficiency" is not an issue that can be adequately taken up here. Rather, I wish to focus on the narrower question of measuring the quantity of material inputs used in production. Specifically this chapter is concerned with the following questions:

1. How should one measure the quantities of *specific* raw material inputs used at the plant or industry level? For example, how should one measure the total quantity of iron ore consumed in a smelting plant when ores of different qualities are used? How should one measure the total quantity of crude oil consumed in a refinery when crude oils of different boiling points, densities, sulfur, and wax contents are used? This chapter considers the aggregation of "similar" materials which nevertheless have distinctly different characteristics.

2. How should one measure the quantities of *specific* raw material inputs used at the economy level? For example, how should one measure the total quantity of specific material inputs consumed by all industries taken together? The difficulty arises when ostensibly the same input is used in completely different sectors. Examples are wood in the construction industry and in the paper industry; and crude oil in the electric utility industry and the synthetic textile industry. Thus, the discussion considers the aggregation of "similar" materials *across industries*.

3. Is it possible to construct a quantity index of aggregate material inputs used at the economy level? This involves aggregation across different types of raw material inputs and across all using industries.

4. How should one attempt to measure the "available" quantities of specific materials inputs?

5. Is it possible to construct an index of aggregate quantity of material inputs "available"?

6. How should one attempt to evaluate the "importance" of material inputs?

The problem of measuring usage of materials at the plant level is primarily one of aggregation across "similar" raw materials of different characteristics. The materials all belong to a general class, as can be seen from the examples given earlier. Occasionally, more than one class of raw materials may be involved. The problem of measuring usage of specific materials at the industry level also involves aggregating across production units in the same end use sector. At both the plant and industry level an aggregate quantity index of a specific class of inputs, such as iron ore, is needed to facilitate the derivation of an input-output relationship between, for instance, pig iron and iron ores, with or without taking into account the presence of other inputs. In the industry case, however, one must also take into account differences among the production units in terms of their technologies and endowments of fixed capital stocks. In addition, such an input-output relationship must also reflect the use of nonpriced, "common property" resources in the production process. The ultimate purpose of such measurements is the derivation of an aggregate input-output relationship which can be used to predict the aggregate quantity of raw material required for a given level of output or vector of output levels.

The problem of measuring material *availability* is somewhat more complex. It depends on the relative natural abundance, renewability, and recyclability of the specific material, the current and future state of the exploration, extraction and/or supply technology, the current and future state of the technology of the end use sectors (with respect to both efficiency and substitutability), and the nature and the rate of turnover of the capital stocks in both the supplying and using sectors.

At the economy level, construction of an aggregate measure of usage or availability of raw materials is even more complex because of interindustry transactions. Thus, even though an industry does not use raw material inputs directly, it may use them indirectly through a processed intermediate input whose manufacture requires other materials. Here the substitutability between raw and processed (including recycled) materials inputs becomes very important.

As an example of the type of problems that may arise in attempting to measure availability, consider the measurement of the aggregate quantity of agricultural land. Presumably one can aggregate land *used* in agriculture by an index of quality adjustment that depends on various characteristics of the land. In particular, this aggregation may depend on the composition of agricultural output, relative output and input prices, and the quality of the water input. However, it is much more difficult to determine the aggregate quantity of land *available* for agriculture, inasmuch as there are alternative productive uses for land, and availability for agricultural use depends on technology and prices, among other things.

As mentioned before, in a physical sense, the aggregate quantity of available materials is fixed. What changes over time is the quantity of output that can be produced with the available inputs; thus, availability should be measured in terms of the level of *potential output*. The interest in measuring the actual aggregate quantity of inputs used is based on a desire to determine a relationship between output and material inputs which could be used to estimate the potential output from available materials.

## 2. What Is a Material?

Before taking up the question of how to measure the quantity of raw material inputs, I wish to discuss how one may decide when several distinct materials can be considered a single material. Intuitively, if substances display similar characteristics in their applications, they should be considered as the same material.

First it is necessary to introduce the notion of a characteristic. A characteristic is a property of a material, such as chemical content, density, conductivity, hardness, tensile strength, melting point, boiling point, or solubility which can be quantitatively or qualitatively distinguished and measured. If materials are completely pure and homogeneous, then the definition is more or less straightforward in the case of a single characteristic. Assuming that the characteristic in question is measurable, one can index each material by the value of its characteristic, for example, iron content, which can be represented by a point on a straight line. Of course, the values of the characteristic of two or more materials may coincide and hence may be represented by the same point on the straight line. A natural definition of distinctness is then: two materials are distinct if the values of their characteristic are different. Two materials are considered to be the same if the values of their characteristic are the same. In practice, one may further require that the difference be "noticeable" (or measurable)[1] and that the difference be "relevant," that is, affect the application of the material. For example, in many applications, the color of the material may be "irrelevant."

---

[1] The ability to discriminate, that is, to identify differences, is critical in deciding whether the two materials are distinct.

However, a complication arises if the materials are not completely pure or homogeneous (see Skinner, 1976). In this case, the characteristic of a material can no longer be represented by a single point on a straight line. Instead, it will have to be represented in the form of a probability distribution. For example, the iron content of a particular type of iron ore may lie between 24 and 26 percent, with a mean of 25 percent. A natural extension of the definition of distinctness between two materials consists of specifying the degree of overlap between the two probability distributions. For example, if the overlap is small, the two materials should be regarded as distinct. If the overlap is substantial, the two materials should be regarded as a single one.

So far, so good. But because it is possible to create new materials and to refine and separate and amalgamate naturally occurring materials, one can in effect create "materials" with arbitrary distributions of the values of a specific characteristic. One can thus choose from a continuum of values as well as a continuum of the degree of "purity" (the variance of the distribution over the values of the characteristic).[2]

Some characteristics may depend on external conditions. For example, the conductivity of a material may depend on the ambient temperature. (This may be a disadvantage in some applications, but an advantage in others.) Thus, it is not enough to identify a material by its characteristic in a single state of nature. It is necessary to take into account its characteristics in all possible *relevant* states of nature. In general, it is necessary to deal with more than one characteristic. One can distinguish between materials by the "distance" between them in the space of characteristics.

Another approach to the classification of materials is to make use of their relative natural abundance. Again, let us consider the situation of a single characteristic, say, iron content. One can use empirically observed frequencies to estimate the probability that a piece of randomly chosen naturally occurring rock of a certain fixed volume would have a specified iron content. One can plot the estimated probability density function as in figure 6.1.

In this hypothetical figure, three distinct materials can be identified. If another piece of rock is encountered, its measured iron content can be used to identify whether it is material 1, 2 or 3. This approach can, of course, be extended to the case of many relevant characteristics. In essence, this approach takes every relative peak in the probability density function defined over the space of characteristics as representing a distinct material. In order for this method to work well, the peaks must be sharply defined. This method breaks down if there are substantial flat regions (plateaus) in the probability density function. In this latter case, one can also consider the probability

---

[2] Other moments of the distribution may also matter. In general, one can choose from the space of all probability distributions.

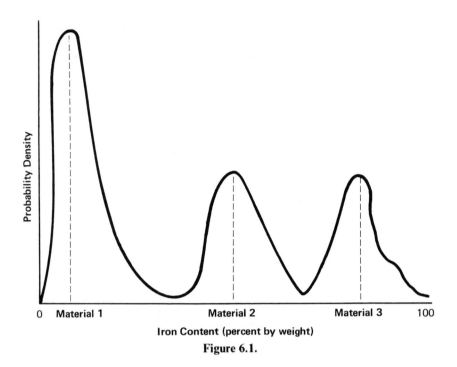

**Figure 6.1.**

density function of the marginal distributions. In other words, one can simply integrate out those characteristics which are not useful in classifying materials or are irrelevant to the application.

The major objection to the relative natural abundance approach is men's ability to create new materials either by simply mixing existing materials or by actually synthesizing new materials, for example, alloys and chemical compounds. Relative abundance has no particular significance any more if it can be changed artificially. Moreover, a rare material, which is not necessarily represented by a local peak in terms of natural abundance, may nevertheless be critically important.

Still another approach to the classification of materials is by end use. If two materials are both used in the production of the same product, for example, cables and wires, then they must share some relevant characteristics, for example, conductivity, and should be regarded as belonging to the same general class of materials, even though they may differ in many other characteristics. The objection to this approach is that these differences in other characteristics imply that they may (at least potentially) be employed for different end uses, especially if the relative prices change. Thus, identical end use, especially at only a limited set of relative prices, is not a reliable criterion for classifying materials. Moreover, the end uses of different materials may change as the technology changes, leading to further difficulties with this approach, as the following example shows.

Suppose we wish to decide when some rocks can be regarded as iron ore and when they cannot. The first criterion has to do with the iron content in the rocks. One can use the percentage content by weight and cut off at some arbitrarily chosen percentage. However, this procedure ignores the economics of recovering the iron. It is possible that iron may be extracted from rocks of low iron content at a lower cost than from rocks of high iron content. Thus, the identification of the rocks as iron ore may depend on the costs of extraction and recovery (see chapter 8). For each type of rock, one can estimate the cost required to extract one unit of iron. This cost number then becomes a characteristic of the rock and a rock is an iron ore if the cost of extraction per unit of iron is below a certain prespecified number. It is easy to see that this latter procedure will be affected by the prices of factors of production, the technology of extraction, and the size and composition of the existing stock of capital.

Material classification is still very much an art, guided by common sense, and a completely unambiguous system of classification has yet to be developed. The following sections rely on a commonsense notion of what constitutes a single material—materials that share some characteristics which are relevant in some common applications.

## 3. Classification of Material Inputs

Material inputs in the production process may be classified broadly into raw and processed materials. Included in the first category are such natural raw materials as wood, livestock, crude oil, and iron ore. Included in the second category are such processed materials as chipboard, leather, synthetic fibers, pig iron, and scrap iron. One may also include in the first category such inputs as clean air and water. This chapter focuses principally on raw materials, which may be further distinguished by whether they are renewable, such as wood, cotton fibers, natural rubber and livestock, or nonrenewable, such as crude oil[3] and iron ore. Moreover, many processed materials are recyclable—for example, glass, paper, scrap iron, and tin—although other processed materials, such as most plastics, are not presently recyclable except perhaps at exorbitant cost. In measuring the quantity of raw material inputs, it is important to recognize the possibility of recycling and changes over time in the technology of recycling, because this will affect the overall relationship between output and raw material inputs on the one hand, and the price re-

---

[3] There are attempts to develop plant varieties that will produce oil.

lationship between output, raw material inputs and other inputs, on the other. With a given, fixed base of raw material inputs, any improvement in recycling technology increases the permanent standard of living that the fixed materials base is capable of supporting. The importance of recycling depends of course on the degree of substitution between raw and recycled materials, and on the durability of the materials embedded in each end use.

Raw materials may be further classified by end use sectors. For example, crude oil, natural gas, and uranium may be employed in generating electricity. Pulpwood, paper, and rags may be employed in paper making. Some raw materials may be employed in more than one end use sector. For example, crude oil may also be used in the textile industry (as feedstock) along with cotton. Classification by end use sectors has the advantage that one can focus on the efficiency and substitution of various raw material inputs from the demand side.[4]

Raw materials may also be classified by production or supply sectors, for example, agriculture or mining. The classification may be further refined so that each sector includes only raw material inputs with similar methods of production and/or extraction. Classification by production sectors thus provides a convenient framework for analyzing the effects of technological change on the supply side.

What are the factors which may alter the usage of raw material inputs? They can be divided into those affecting demand and those affecting supply. Demand side factors include discoveries of new applications for existing raw materials or new processes which substitute raw or processed materials, technological changes in the end use sectors which result in greater efficiency, changes in the composition and durability of the capital plant and equipment in the end use sectors, changes in the durability of products using raw materials, progress in recycling technology, and last but not least, discoveries of harmful side effects of production. Supply side factors include changes in the technology of exploration, extraction, and recovery; development of new plant and animal varieties; introduction of new techniques of planting and animal husbandry; extension of cultivable land; and control of air and water pollution.

## 4. Aggregation by End-Use Sectors

This section considers aggregation of raw material inputs of different types which are employed in the same end use sector. As an example, consider the aggregation of crude oil, natural gas, uranium, and water[5] in the gener-

---

[4] Other examples of multiple end-use sectors include the examples of construction and electric wires and cables mentioned by Koopmans.

[5] Water is needed for hydroelectric power.

ation of electricity. Obviously, aggregation of this type depends on the prevailing level of technology. For example, uranium was probably worthless as a raw material input to the electric utility industry before the invention of the atomic reactor. Its value in generating electricity will change with the introduction of the breeder reactor and finally will probably become worthless again with the introduction some time in the future of the fusion reactor or with improvements in solar energy technology. Aggregation of this type also depends on how capital plant and equipment are distributed by age and by fuel type.[6]

Aggregation is a problem because the raw material inputs used in even a narrowly defined end-use sector are not absolutely homogeneous. They differ according to location and the period over which they are obtained. For example, iron ores may have different iron contents and impurities, and the latter may in turn affect the input-output relationship in iron production. Different processes require different raw material inputs. The purpose of constructing a single aggregate measure of such inputs is to simplify the representation of the input-output relationship *in the aggregate*.

One conventional measurement practice is to aggregate inputs in accordance with a single characteristic—for example, potential calorific values for different fuels and iron content for different iron ores. While this practice may sometimes be satisfactory, it does not work when other characteristics of the raw materials may also affect the nature of the production process, either directly or through interaction with the type and age of the capital stock. For example, in the case of fuels, the actual realizable heat values depend on the nature of the capital plant and equipment.

A second conventional measurement practice is to use relative prices of different raw materials as the weights for forming an aggregate quantity index of inputs. The basic idea is that if different users of the raw material inputs can be assumed to have equal access to all markets, then a higher price is paid only when the quality is higher (abstracting, of course, from transportation costs) if equilibrium prevails in all the related markets. This does not take into account imperfections of the market, existence of prior commitments and contracts, etc. However, it does form a second common point of departure for the aggregation of raw material inputs of different characteristics. An extension of this practice leads to the hedonic price index approach which, strictly speaking, is based on the further assumption that supplies of different raw material inputs are perfectly elastic at given prices. (For a description of this approach in other contexts see Griliches, 1961; Ohta, 1975; and Ohta and Griliches, 1975). These approaches are considered from a theoretical point of view in a very general way, beginning with aggregation at the level of a single plant.

---

[6] The distribution is especially important if the capital plant and equipment is not readily malleable and retrofitting is prohibitively expensive.

Aggregation at the Plant Level

Let us consider a plant with a production function $F(\cdot)$ which employs capital $K$, labor $L$, energy $E$, and raw material input to produce a single output $V$. In addition, it is assumed that the raw material input may be further distinguished by a vector of characteristics $a$, and that the production function may be different for different $a$.[7] Thus:

$$V = F(K,L,E,M,a) \tag{1}$$

where $M$ is the quantity of the raw material input with the vector of characteristics $a$. The production function $F(\cdot)$ is assumed to have the usual neoclassical properties. In particular, it is assumed to be strictly monotonically increasing in $K$, $L$, $E$, and $M$.

Given strict monotonicity of the production function, one may, corresponding to every vector of characteristics $a$, solve equation (1) to obtain the raw material input requirement function:

$$M = f(V,K,L,E,a) \tag{2}$$

If one compares the different quantities of raw material input corresponding to different vectors of characteristics $a$ that are required for the production of output $V$ with capital $K$, labor $L$, and energy $E$, one has:

$$\frac{M_1}{M_2} = \frac{f(V,K,L,E,a_1)}{f(V,K,L,E,a_2)} \tag{3}$$

for all values of $a_1$ and $a_2$. $M_1/M_2$ represents the conversion ratio between the two kinds of raw material inputs for the production of $V$ with the given quantities of capital, labor, and energy. In general, this ratio depends on all these quantities, so that, for example, the two kinds of raw material inputs may substitute at close to a ratio of one to one at low levels of output and capital, but at a ratio of two to one at high levels of output and capital.

Let us see why equation (3) may be a useful relationship. Let us choose to measure all raw material inputs in terms of $M_1$, that is, in terms of quantities of raw material input with the vector of characteristics $a_1$. Thus, whatever the quantity of $M_2$ is, its equivalent quantity in terms of $M_1$ is given by:

$$M_1^* = \frac{f(V,K,L,E,a_1)}{f(V,K,L,E,a_2)} M_2 \tag{4}$$

Now consider the output that can be produced with $M_1^*$ units of the raw

---

[7] In this very general setting one of the components of the vector $a$ may be the composition of the raw material input—which may be made up of two or more different raw materials.

material input with the vector of characteristics $a_1$, which is given by:

$$F(K,L,E,M_1^*,a_1) \tag{5}$$

I shall show that this is precisely equal to $F(K,L,E,M_2,a_2)$.
  *Suppose $F(K,L,E,M_1^*,a_1) = \overline{F}$. Then by using equation (2),*

$$M_1^* = f(\overline{F},K,L,E,a_1) \tag{6}$$

By equation (4)

$$M_1^* = \frac{f(V,K,L,E,a_1)}{f(V,K,L,E,a_2)} M_2 \tag{7}$$

$$= \frac{f(V,K,L,E,a_1)}{f(V,K,L,E,a_2)} f(V,K,L,E,a_2), \text{ by equation (2)}$$

$$= f(V,K,L,E,a_1)$$

However, $f(\cdot)$ is monotonic in output if $F(\cdot)$ is monotonic in inputs. Thus, the equality of equations (6) and (7) implies that $\overline{F} = V$. What this means is that if $M_2$ can be converted into equivalent units of $M_1$, then the production function for the raw material inputs with the vector of characteristics $a_1$ can be used to predict the output. Thus, not only does one have a way of aggregating different kinds of raw material inputs in terms of a standard unit, but these equivalent units can also be used in a production function defined for the standard unit!

This finding may seem too good to be true and indeed there is a difficulty in implementing this approach. In order to make use of the conversion formula in equation (4), one has to know $V$. But in general, it is $V$ which is the variable of interest. Nevertheless, if the conversion function

$$\frac{f(V,K,L,E,a_1)}{f(V,K,L,E,a_2)}$$

is known to depend on $V$, it is still possible to determine $V$ by solving the equation:

$$V = F\left[K,L,E,\frac{f(V,K,L,E,a_1)}{f(V,K,L,E,a_2)} M_2, a_1\right]$$

as an implicit function in $V$ for given $K$, $L$, $E$, $M_2$, $a_1$ and $a_2$.

The analysis is considerably simplified if the conversion function is in fact independent of output. We shall first consider the simplest case, namely, that the conversion function is independent of not only output but also of capital, labor, and energy. In order that the ratio $M_1/M_2$ be independent of $V$, $K$, $L$, and $E$ for all $V$, $K$, $L$, $E$, $a_1$, and $a_2$, that is, in order for there to exist conversion functions between the different types of raw material inputs that depend only on the relative characteristics and not on the quantity of output, capital, labor, or energy, one must have:

$$f(V,K,L,E,a_2) \frac{\partial f}{\partial V}(V,K,L,E,a_1) = f(V,K,L,E,a_1) \frac{\partial f}{\partial V}(V,K,L,E,a_2)$$

$$f(V,K,L,E,a_2) \frac{\partial f}{\partial K}(V,K,L,E,a_1) = f(V,K,L,E,a_1) \frac{\partial f}{\partial K}(V,K,L,E,a_2)$$

$$f(V,K,L,E,a_2) \frac{\partial f}{\partial L}(V,K,L,E,a_1) = f(V,K,L,E,a_1) \frac{\partial f}{\partial L}(V,K,L,E,a_2)$$

$$f(V,K,L,E,a_2) \frac{\partial f}{\partial E}(V,K,L,E,a_1) = f(V,K,L,E,a_1) \frac{\partial f}{\partial E}(V,K,L,E,a_2)$$

or

$$\frac{\partial \ln f}{\partial V}(V,K,L,E,a_1) = \frac{\partial \ln f}{\partial V}(V,K,L,E,a_2)$$

$$\frac{\partial \ln f}{\partial K}(V,K,L,E,a_1) = \frac{\partial \ln f}{\partial K}(V,K,L,E,a_2)$$

$$\frac{\partial \ln f}{\partial L}(V,K,L,E,a_1) = \frac{\partial \ln f}{\partial L}(V,K,L,E,a_2)$$

$$\frac{\partial \ln f}{\partial E}(V,K,L,E,a_1) = \frac{\partial \ln f}{\partial E}(V,K,L,E,a_2)$$

which must hold for all $V$, $K$, $L$, $E$, $a_1$, and $a_2$. However, note that the left-hand sides do not depend on $a_2$ and the right-hand sides do not depend on $a_1$. However, the two sides must be identically equal, so that both sides must be independent of $a_1$ and $a_2$. This implies that:

$$\frac{\partial \ln f}{\partial V}(V,K,L,E,a), \quad \frac{\partial \ln f}{\partial K}(V,K,L,E,a)$$

$$\frac{\partial \ln f}{\partial L}(V,K,L,E,a), \quad \frac{\partial \ln f}{\partial E}(V,K,L,E,a)$$

must be independent of $a$. In other words, the raw material input requirement functions must have the form:

$$M = f(V,K,L,E,a) = f^*(V,K,L,E)A(a)$$

or equivalently, the production function must have the form:

$$V = F[K,L,E,A(a)M] \tag{8}$$

that is, the differences in the raw material inputs with different vectors of characteristics must be expressible in the factor augmentation form. Observe that equation (8) is a drastic specialization of equation (1). In equation (1), the production function is a function of $4 + n$ variables, where $n$ is the number of characteristics distinguished, whereas in equation (8), the production function is a function of only four variables.

Let us interpret what this result means. If we keep constant the quantity of capital, labor, and energy (and whatever other factor inputs), but use raw material inputs of different characteristics in order to produce the *same* output, the ratios of the quantities of these different materials inputs required may depend on the quantities of output, capital, labor, and energy, as well as characteristics of the materials. The conversion ratio depends on the raw material input characteristics when and only when the different types of raw material inputs are convertible into one another by the multiplication of a scalar-valued function of the characteristics. For example, scrap iron as well as iron ores of different grades may be convertible to standard iron ore equivalents by a single scalar function of the characteristics. Moreover, the conversion ratio between any two different raw material inputs is fixed and independent of the prices of output, capital, labor, energy, or the raw material inputs themselves, given their respective characteristics.

Thus, we have proved that a constant conversion ratio between different kinds of raw material inputs is valid *if and only if* the production function has the factor augmentation form in the inputs. This also implies that the different inputs are perfect substitutes. If heat values are used as weights to aggregate different fuels, it is implicitly assumed that there is perfect substitution among the fuels in production. If iron content is used as a weight to aggregate different iron ores, it also implies perfect substitution among iron ores. Notice that although the augmentation assumption is a strong restriction, it does allow the use of a single production function defined in terms of a standard raw material input to predict outputs corresponding to different levels and qualities of inputs.

Given the factor augmentation assumption, the prices of the different raw material inputs $P_M(a_i)$'s should be in proportion to their productivities in the end use sector, and one must have equalization of the effective price of a unit of the standard raw material input. Thus:

$$p_M(a_1)/A(a_1) = p_M(a_2)/A(a_2) \equiv \bar{p}_M$$

so that

$$\ln p_M(a_i) = \ln A(a_i) + \ln \bar{p}_M, \quad \forall\, i \tag{9}$$

where $\bar{p}_M$ is a constant. This provides the basis for estimating a "hedonic price" equation based on the prices paid for the different raw material inputs by the same plant under the augmentation assumption. The function $A(a)$ may be identified if in fact the set of vectors of characteristics $a$ spans the full dimensional space of $a$, that is, if the components of $a$ are capable of independent variations.

Thus far we have made no assumptions about the behavior of the plant management. Now suppose that production is carried out in this plant under conditions of cost minimization. The plant chooses the quantities of capital, labor, and energy, along with the quantities and types of raw material inputs. These choices are made subject to the prices of capital, labor, energy, and the price function of raw material inputs (as a function of the vector of characteristics $a$), as well as to the required level of output. Hence:

$$C[V,r,w,p_E,p_M(a)]^8$$

$$= \min_{K,L,E,M,a} [rK + wL + p_E E + p_M(a)M \,|\, V \geq F(K,L,E,M,a)]$$

where $r$, $w$, and $p_E$ are the prices of capital, labor, and energy respectively Let

$$C^* \equiv \min_{K,L,E,M} [rK + wL + p_E E + \bar{p}_M M \,|\, V \geq F(K,L,E,M,a)]$$

$$= C^*(V,r,w,p_E,\bar{p}_M,a)$$

$C^*(\cdot)$ is thus the cost function, given that the raw material input with vector of characteristics $a$ will be used. Therefore:

$$C[V,r,w,p_E,p_M(a)] = \min_a C^*[V,r,w,p_E,p_M(a),a]$$

Given a raw material input price function $p_M(a)$, if more than one type of raw material input is used simultaneously for the production of the same level of output and at the same set of prices of capital, labor, and energy, then it follows that the costs of production must be identical for a cost-minimizing firm, so that

$$C^*[V,r,w,p_E,p_M(a_1),a_1] = C^*[V,r,w,p_E,p_M(a_2),a_2]$$

where $a_1$ and $a_2$ are the vectors of characteristics of the two raw material inputs that are used. It also follows that the costs of using other raw materials must be at least as great.

Let $g(\cdot)$ be the inverse of the cost function with respect to the raw material input price, so that:

$$p_M(a_i) = g(\bar{C}^*,V,r,w,p_E,a_i), \quad \forall\, i$$

$g(\cdot)$ is homogeneous of degree one in $\bar{C}^*$, $r$, $w$, and $p_E$ because of the homo-

---

[8] This is in fact a functional rather than a function since it is defined on the raw material input price function.

geneity of the cost function. Consider now the ratio of the prices of two different raw material inputs which are both used in production:

$$\frac{p_M(a_1)}{p_M(a_2)} = \frac{g(\overline{C}^*,V,r,w,p_E,a_1)}{g(\overline{C}^*,V,r,w,p_E,a_2)}$$

Because of homogeneity of degree one of $g(\cdot)$ in $\overline{C}^*$, $r$, $w$, and $p_E$, the ratio $p_M(a_1)/p_M(a_2)$ is homogeneous of degree zero, and one may therefore set $\overline{C}^* = 1$ as a normalization. Thus:

$$\frac{p_M(a_1)}{p_M(a_2)} = \frac{g(1,V,r,w,p_E,a_1)}{g(1,V,r,w,p_E,a_2)} \tag{10}$$

Equation (10) then gives the conversion function between the prices of the two different raw material inputs, which, under the assumption of cost minimization, must reflect relative marginal productivities.

If we now make the strong assumption that the price conversion function is independent of $V$, $r$, $w$, and $p_E$, then by a strictly analogous argument as used previously, one has:

$$\frac{\partial \ln g}{\partial V}(1,V,r,w,p_E,a_1) = \frac{\partial \ln g}{\partial V}(1,V,r,w,p_E,a_2)$$

$$\frac{\partial \ln g}{\partial r}(1,V,r,w,p_E,a_1) = \frac{\partial \ln g}{\partial r}(1,V,r,w,p_E,a_2)$$

$$\frac{\partial \ln g}{\partial w}(1,V,r,w,p_E,a_1) = \frac{\partial \ln g}{\partial w}(1,V,r,w,p_E,a_2)$$

$$\frac{\partial \ln g}{\partial p_E}(1,V,r,w,p_E,a_1) = \frac{\partial \ln g}{\partial p_E}(1,V,r,w,p_E,a_2)$$

which implies that:

$$g(\overline{C}^*,V,r,w,p_E,a) = g^*(\overline{C}^*,V,r,w,p_E)A^*(a)$$

so that

$$\frac{p_M(a_1)}{p_M(a_2)} = \frac{A^*(a_1)}{A^*(a_2)}$$

or

$$\frac{p_M(a_1)}{A^*(a_1)} = \frac{p_M(a_2)}{A^*(a_2)} = \bar{p}_M$$

In other words, one unit of raw material input with the vector of characteristics $a_i$ is worth $A^*(a_i)$ units of the standard raw material input. This in turn implies that the cost function has the form:

$$C^* = C^*[V,r,w,p_E,\tilde{p}_M(a_i)/A^*(a_i)]$$

which in turn implies that the production function has the form:

$$V = F[K,L,E,A^*(a)M]$$

This result turns out to be dual to the result derived earlier, since

$$\min_{K,L,E,M} \{rK + wL + p_E E + \tilde{p}_M(a)M \,|\, V \geq F[K,L,E,A(a)M]\}$$

$$= C^*[V,r,w,p_E,\tilde{p}_M/A(a)]$$

so that $A^*(a) = A(a)$.

### Interactions Between Raw Material Inputs and Other Inputs

If, however, there are interactions among the characteristics of the raw material inputs and the other inputs, such as capital, labor, or energy, then the conversion ratios will no longer be independent of the other inputs. This situation can be expected to arise in general—for example, whether crude oil or uranium is used as the raw material input in electricity generation is going to make a difference in the nature of the capital stock; whether cotton or crude oil feedstock is used as the raw material input in the spinning industry is going to make a difference not only in the capital stock but also in the labor used. In general, one has, as the ratio of the raw material input requirement functions:

$$\frac{M_1}{M_2} = \frac{f(V,K,L,E,a_1)}{f(V,K,L,E,a_2)}$$

so that the conversion ratio depends on everything. We consider the special case in which the conversion ratio is independent of output $V$, so that:

$$\ln f(V,K,L,E,a) = \ln f^*(V,K,L,E) + \ln h(K,L,E,a)$$

This implies that:

$$\frac{M_1}{M_2} = \frac{h(K,L,E,a_1)}{h(K,L,E,a_2)}$$

and that the production function has the form:

$$V = F(K,L,E,M,a) = H[K,L,E,h(K,L,E,a)M]$$

where $M$ is the quantity of the raw material input with the vector of characteristics $a$. This, however, implies that in the aggregate quantity index each raw material input must be weighted by an augmentation factor that depends on the quantities of capital, labor, and energy as well as the vector of characteristics.

The corresponding hedonic price equations will include additional independent variables, such as the quantities of capital, labor, and energy as well as the vector of characteristics. If two raw materials with characteristics $a_1$ and $a_2$ are both used in production, then cost minimization considerations require:

$$\frac{p_M(a_1)}{h^*(K,L,E,a_1)} = \frac{p_M(a_2)}{h^*(K,L,E,a_2)} \equiv \bar{p}_M$$

Thus:

$$\ln p_M(a_i) = \ln h^*(K,L,E,a_i) + \ln \bar{p}_M$$

However, the validity of this hedonic price equation now depends, not only on the assumption of a *perfectly elastic supply* facing the user, but also *on perfect price discrimination* on the part of the suppliers of the raw material inputs.

The above analysis does not make full use of the cost-minimization assumption. If, as before, one assumes cost minimization, then

$$\frac{p_M(a_1)}{p_M(a_2)} = \frac{g(1,V,r,w,p_E,a_1)}{g(1,V,r,w,p_E,a_2)}$$

If the price conversion ratio is assumed to be independent of the output $V$, then

$$g(1,V,w,p_E,a) = g^*(1,V,r,w,p_E)h^*(1,r,w,p_E,a)$$

so that the cost function becomes:

$$C^* = G[V,r,w,p_E,h^*(r,w,p_E,a)\bar{p}_M] \tag{11}$$

When two or more raw material inputs are employed at the same set of $r$, $w$, and $p_E$, it must be the case that:

$$h^*(1,r,w,p_E,a_i)\bar{p}_M = p_M(a_i)$$

so that once more one has the hedonic price equation:

$$\ln p_M(a_i) = \ln h^*(1,r,w,p_E,a_i) + \ln \bar{p}_M$$

Note that the conversion factors do depend on $r$, $w$, and $p_E$, as well as on $a$.

Note also that, unlike the case in which the factor depends only on the characteristics, aggregation through the production function is now different from aggregation through the cost function. The production function dual to the cost function in equation (11) does *not* generally take the form:

$$V = F[K,L,E,h(K,L,E,a)M] \tag{12}$$

It is obvious that the above analysis extends directly to cases in which there are different types of capital, labor, and energy. Thus, within this framework, one can accommodate substantial interactions between the characteristics of the raw material inputs and other inputs such as capital, labor, and energy. Likewise, the introduction of the possibility of technological change is completely straightforward. Technological change may occur in the main production function, or in the conversion function, or in both. In the latter two cases a time trend variable will appear in the hedonic price function.

### The Possibility of Joint Production

Thus far we have dealt only with the case in which a single output is produced. We now consider the case of joint production, that is, more than one output produced in the same plant. There are two leading joint production cases, which are discussed in turn. In the first, all of the joint outputs are desirable. In the second, one or more of the joint outputs is undesirable.

In the first case, if the conversion ratio is independent of the levels of the different joint outputs, then the previously derived results essentially carry over. The production function takes the form:

$$V_0 = F[V_1, \ldots, V_m, K, L, E, A(K, L, E, a)M]$$

where $V_i$ is the quantity of the $i$th joint output. The cost function takes the form:

$$C^* = C^*[(V_1, \ldots, V_m; r, w, p_E, p_M(a)/A^*(r, w, p_E, a)]^9$$

However, it is precisely the case in which the composition of output affects the conversion ratios that is interesting. For example, if mutton is not produced jointly with wool, then the livestock input need not be specifically distinguished from petrochemical inputs in the production of fibers. But the general joint production case in which the conversion ratio is not independent of the levels of the joint outputs is too complex to handle. If one can assume that there is at least one joint output which does not affect the conversion ratio, then one can proceed as before, adding the quantities of the remaining joint outputs in the conversion function or hedonic price function. However, this procedure cannot be rigorously justified because it arbitrarily singles out one of the joint outputs. Yet trying to treat the problem in full generality does not seem to lead to simple aggregation procedures.

We consider joint production of a single output $V_1$ with a pollutant $V_0$ so that the production function may be represented as:

$$V_1 = F(K, L, E, M, V_0, a)$$

---

[9] Note that this cost function is not in general the dual to the production function above.

We consider the specialization

$$V_1 = F[K,L,E,V_0,A(K,L,E,V_0,a)M]$$

which implies that the hedonic price functions will depend on the quantity of pollutant as well. Thus, in converting the raw material input with a vector of characteristics $a$, the quantity of pollutant jointly produced needs to be taken into account. Notice that the factor augmentation representation of the conversion function is not the most general possible—it does not depend on $V_1$. On the other hand, it does reflect the idea that the effect of the pollutant is influenced by the quantities of other inputs as well as by the characteristics of the raw material input. Given the factor augmentation assumption, the hedonic price equation can in principle be estimated.

The above analysis does not take into account the behavior of the plant management. Suppose that production takes place under cost minimization. Then the cost function is given by:

$$C = C(V_1,r,w,p_E,\bar{p}_M,p_0)$$

where $\bar{p}_M$ is the price of a unit of the standardized raw material input, and $p_0$ is the penalty per unit quantity of pollution. The hedonic price function can be assumed to take the form:

$$\ln p_M(a) = \ln A^*(r,w,p_E,p_0,a) + \ln \bar{p}_M$$

If observations are made over two regimes—one during which there is no (zero) penalty, and one during which there is—it is possible to pool the data and estimate the hedonic function accordingly.

Alternatively, one can consider quantity restrictions on the pollutant. The plant then minimizes cost subject to given quantities of output and pollutant. If the pollutant restrictions are binding, then the plant's behavior may be described by a restricted cost function:

$$C^* = C^*(V_1,V_0,r,w,p_E,\bar{p}_M)$$

There is, under mild regularity conditions, a one-to-one correspondence between $C^*(\cdot)$ and $C(\cdot)$ so that knowledge of one function implies knowledge of the other. The hedonic price function can be assumed to take the form:

$$\ln p_M(a) = \ln A^*(r,w,p_E,V_0,a) + \ln \bar{p}_M$$

It should, however, be noted that the two alternative hedonic functions correspond to different assumptions of the underlying technology.

If historically there has never been a positive penalty, then it may not be possible to estimate the full hedonic price function. In fact, even if the use of one raw material input produces a higher level of pollutant than another, it will not show up in the function as long as the penalty has always been zero.

In any case, we have seen that with the appropriate data it is possible to take into account in the measurement of raw material input the joint production of pollutant through the hedonic price function. In addition, it is possible to define a production function in terms of a standardized unit of raw material input and quantity of pollutant.

### Aggregation Across Production Units

The preceding discussion is based on an analysis of equivalent production by the same plant. We now consider aggregation across plants, beginning with direct aggregation of quantities of outputs and inputs. Let there be $N$ plants, each with production function $F_i(\cdot)$, capital $K_i$, labor $L_i$, and energy $E_i$, and raw material input $A(K_i,L_i,E_i,a_i)M_i$. We wish to determine under what conditions there exists an aggregate production function which is equal to the sum of the outputs from the individual production functions, for all values of $K_i$'s, $L_i$'s, $E_i$'s, and $M_i$'s.

$$F^*\left[\sum_{i=1}^{N} K_i, \sum_{i=1}^{N} L_i, \sum_{i=1}^{N} E_i, \sum_{i=1}^{N} A(K_i,L_i,E_i,a_i)M_i\right]$$

$$= \sum_{i=1}^{N} F_i[K_i,L_i,E_i,A(K_i,L_i,E_i,a_i)M_i]$$

A necessary and sufficient condition for the existence of such an aggregate production function is that

$$F_i[K_i,L_i,E_i,A(K_i,L_i,E_i,a_i)M_i]$$

$$= F_{0i} + \alpha_K K_i + \alpha_L L_i + \alpha_E E_i + \alpha_M A(K_i,L_i,E_i,a_i)M_i$$

where $F_{0i}$, $\alpha_K$, $\alpha_L$, $\alpha_E$ and $\alpha_M$ are constant parameters. In other words, every production function is linear in $K_i$, $L_i$, $E_i$ and effective raw material input $[A(K,L,E,a)M]$ with identical coefficients. This is actually not as restrictive an assumption as it appears, since $A(K_i,L_i,E_i,a_i)$ can embody substantial substitution among capital, labor, and energy. The difficulty of this approach lies in the fact that the measurement of the aggregate quantity of raw material input

$$\sum_{i=1}^{N} A(K_i,L_i,E_i,a_i)M_i$$

requires information on the joint distribution of $K_i, L_i, E_i$ and the characteristics of the raw material input employed by the $i$th plant. It is thus not a very practical way of measuring the aggregate quantity of raw material input.

Next we consider indirect aggregation via the cost functions. Let there again be $N$ plants. Each plant is assumed to minimize cost and is characterized by a cost function, say:

$$C_i = G_i(V_i, r, w, p_E, \bar{p}_M)$$

where $\bar{p}_M$ is the price of a standardized unit of raw material input, and we have assumed that the augmentation factor depends only on $a$.[10] Aggregate cost is given by:

$$C = \sum_{i=1}^{N} G_i(V_i, r, w, p_E, \bar{p}_M)$$

In order that there exists an aggregate cost function that depends on aggregate output, so that

$$C\left(\sum_{i=1}^{N} V_i, r, w, p_E, \bar{p}_M\right) = \sum_{i=1}^{N} G_i(V_i, r, w, p_E, \bar{p}_M)$$

it is necessary that

$$G_i(V_i, r, w, p_E, \bar{p}_M) = G(V_i, r, w, p_E, \bar{p}_M)$$

where

$$G(0, r, w, p_E, \bar{p}_M) = 0.$$

Hence all plants must have identical cost functions. In addition, in order that

$$C\left(\sum_{i=1}^{N} V_i, r, w, p_E, \bar{p}_M\right) = \sum_{i=1}^{N} G(V_i, r, w, p_E, \bar{p}_M)$$

one must have

$$G(V_i, r, w, p_E, \bar{p}_M) = V_i G^*(r, w, p_E, \bar{p}_M)$$

that is, there must be constant returns to scale. Thus, the aggregate cost function must take the form:

$$C\left(\sum_{i=1}^{N} V_i, r, w, p_E, \bar{p}_M\right) = G^*(r, w, p_E, \bar{p}_M)\left(\sum_{i=1}^{N} V_i\right)$$

From the aggregate cost function, one can derive an aggregate production function (or an aggregate input-output relationship) in terms of the aggregate quantities of capital, labor, energy, and the standardized raw material input. Such a production function can be used to predict aggregate output given the aggregate quantities of the standardized raw material input and other inputs. The aggregate quantity of standardized raw material input can be derived from a knowledge of the quantities of the different nonstandardized raw material inputs and the hedonic price function.

[10] All inputs are assumed to be variable.

If we are willing to generalize the concept of an aggregate cost function to include as arguments not only aggregate output but a finite number of "statistics" of the distribution of outputs by plants, then each individual cost function can take the form:

$$C_i = h_1(r,w,p_E,\bar{p}_M)V_i + \sum_{k=2}^{n} h_k(r,w,p_E,\bar{p}_M)g_i(V_i)$$

where $V, g_1(V), \ldots, g_n(V)$ are a set of linearly independent functions. Aggregate raw material input in standardized units then takes the form:

$$M = \frac{\partial h_1}{\partial \bar{p}_M}(r,w,p_E,\bar{p}_M)\left[\sum_{i=1}^{N} V_i\right] + \sum_{k=2}^{n} \frac{\partial h_k}{\partial \bar{p}_M}(r,w,p_E,\bar{p}_M)\left[\sum_{i=1}^{N} g_k(V_i)\right]$$

$[\sum_{i=1}^{N} V_i]$ and $[\sum_{i=1}^{N} g_k(V_i)]$ may be regarded as "statistics" of the distribution of plant outputs.

Still another generalization is to assume that the cost function depends in addition on a vector of plant characteristics $b$. Thus:

$$C_i = G(V_i,r,w,p_E,\bar{p}_M,b_i)$$

Then in order for an aggregate cost function depending on the "statistics" of the joint distribution of output and plant characteristics to exist, each individual plant cost function must take the form:

$$C_i = \sum_{k=1}^{n} h_k(r,w,p_E,\bar{p}_M)g_k(V_i,b_i)$$

where $g_k(0,b_i) = 0$. The aggregate cost function is just the sum of the cost functions of the $N$ plants. It is clear that the aggregate quantity of raw material input depends on the joint distribution of plant output and plant characteristics. (Related discussion of these issues from demand theory can be found in Lau 1977a,b.)

Next we consider the possibility that different capital plant and equipment may be used for processing raw material inputs with different vectors of characteristics. For example, the capital equipment which is required for processing scrap iron may be quite different from that required for processing iron ore, which may be still quite different from that required for processing beneficiated iron ore.

These capital stocks are different because of the interaction between the raw material and the capital equipment. Another source of heterogeneity lies in the degree of flexibility of the capital stock with respect to intermaterial substitution. For example, some capital equipment can burn both natural gas and oil. Such equipment in general will be more expensive, for a given capacity, than equipment which burns only natural gas or oil. To handle this situation, it is necessary to distinguish carefully between the type of capital stock and the quantity of capital stock, which we take to be capacity. The ensuing analysis is predicated on the assumption of a finite number of types of capital stock, where type can encompass differences in the degree of flexibility and in vintage.

Without loss of generality, we denote the type of capital stock by a vector of characteristics $b$. We assume that the production function of the $i$th plant is given by:

$$V_i = F_i[K_i,b_i; L_i,E_i,A(a_i)M_i]$$

where $K_i$ is the quantity of capital stock with the vector of characteristics $b_i$. We assume that each plant maximizes profit subject to given $K_i$ and $b_i$, with respect to $L_i$, $E_i$, $M_i$ and $a_i$. The results of this maximization may be represented by a normalized restricted profit function for each plant.

$$\Pi_i = \Pi_i(K_i,b_i,w,p_E,\bar{p}_M)$$

where $\bar{p}_M$ is the price of a standardized unit of raw material input normalized by the price of output. The aggregate normalized restricted profit for all plants is given by:

$$\Pi = \sum_{i=1}^{N} \Pi_i(K_i,b_i; w,p_E,\bar{p}_M)$$

If we assume constant returns to scale, we can write:

$$\Pi = \sum_{i=1}^{N} G_i(b_i;w,p_E,\bar{p}_M)K_i$$

In general, aggregate raw material input in terms of standardized units is given by $-\partial\Pi/\partial\bar{p}_M$, which depends on each specific $K_i$ and $b_i$. If, however, we assume that the aggregate normalized restricted profit function is expressible as a function of a finite number of "statistics" of the joint distribution of $b_i$ and $K_i$, that is, the joint distribution of quantity and type of capital stock in the end use sector, we have:

$$\Pi[w,p_E,\bar{p}_M,g_1$$

$$\times (K_1,\ldots,K_N; b_1,\ldots,b_N),\ldots,g_n(K_1,\ldots,K_N; b_1,\ldots,b_N)]$$

$$= \sum_{i=1}^{N} \Pi_i(K_i,b_i; w,p_E,\bar{p}_M)$$

where the $g_i(\cdot)$'s, being functional representations of the "statistics" of the joint distribution, must be symmetric in the subscripts of its arguments. This implies that

$$\Pi_i(K_i,b_i,w,p_E,\bar{p}_M) = G(K_i,b_i,w,p_E,\bar{p}_M) + g_i(w,p_E,\bar{p}_M)$$

In other words, the normalized restricted profit functions must be identical up to the addition of a function which is independent of all $K_i$'s and $b_i$'s. If in addition we make the assumption that aggregate normalized restricted profit is zero if the aggregate quantity of capital stock is zero, we have:

$$\Pi_i(K_i,b_i,w,p_E,\bar{p}_M) = G(K_i,b_i,w,p_E,\bar{p}_M)$$

that is, all normalized restricted profit functions are identical across all plants (but note that $b_i$ is allowed to vary across plants).

In addition, the existence of the aggregate normalized restricted profit function further implies that:

$$G(K_i,b_i,w,p_E,\bar{p}_M) = \sum_{k=1}^{n} h_k(w,p_E,\bar{p}_M) g_k^*(K_i,b_i)$$

so that the aggregate normalized restricted profit function becomes:

$$\Pi = \sum_{k=1}^{n} h_k(w,p_E,\bar{p}_M) \left[ \sum_{i=1}^{N} g_k^*(K_i,b_i) \right]$$

The aggregate demand for raw material input in standardized units is then given by:

$$\frac{\partial \Pi}{\partial \bar{p}_M} = \sum_{k=1}^{n} \frac{\partial h_k}{\partial \bar{p}_M}(w,p_E,\bar{p}_M) \left[ \sum_{i=1}^{N} g_k^*(K_i,b_i) \right]$$

It is clear that the aggregate quantity of raw material input demand depends on the joint distribution of the quantity and type of the capital stock. To the extent that the joint distribution of capital stock changes, the relationship between aggregate, normalized, restricted profit and the price of raw material input, and hence indirectly between output and the quantity of raw material input, will also change.

We note that this analysis can be generalized to the case in which the price conversion function takes the form $A^*(r,w,p_E,b,a)$. In that case, the hedonic price function depends on the characteristics of the capital stock as well. It also generalizes in a straightforward manner to the case in which there are many classes of raw material inputs of different characteristics but used in the same production end-use sector.

## 5. Aggregation Across End-Use Sectors

We now consider aggregation across end-use sectors. We ask whether a price index of aggregate raw material input exists under successively more general assumptions. It is clear that direct aggregation as considered in section 4 is not worth pursuing since it implies linear production functions.

First, we dispose of two polar cases. If the prices of standardized units of all classes of raw material inputs move together, or if the standardized units of all classes of raw material inputs are always used in fixed proportions relative to one another, then an aggregate quantity index of raw material inputs always exists. This is known in the literature of aggregation as Hicks aggregation and Leontief aggregation respectively. We consider the more general case in which proportionality does not hold exactly on either the price or the quantity side.

First consider an economy with only two end-use sectors. Both use the "same" class of raw material inputs, although within the class there are many different material inputs corresponding to different vectors of characteristics. Moreover, it is assumed that the conversion functions are the same for the two end-use sectors.

We have three cases. First, suppose that neither sector uses the output of the other sectors as an input. The aggregate cost function for the economy is then given by:

$$C = C_1(V_1, r, w, p_E, \bar{p}_M) + C_2(V_2, r, w, p_E, \bar{p}_M)$$

The aggregate quantity of standardized raw material input is given by:

$$M = \frac{\partial C_1}{\partial \bar{p}_M}(V_1, r, w, p_E, \bar{p}_M) + \frac{\partial C_2}{\partial \bar{p}_M}(V_2, r, w, p_E, \bar{p}_M)$$

where $V_1$ and $V_2$ are the net (equal to gross) outputs of the two sectors respectively.

Next suppose that output of sector 1 is used in the production of output in sector 2, but not vice versa. Then the aggregate cost function for the economy is given by:

$$C = \min_{X_1} [C_1(V_1 + X_1, r, w, p_E, \bar{p}_M) + C_2^*(V_2, X_1, r, w, p_E, \bar{p}_M)]$$

where $C_2^*(\cdot)$ is the minimum variable cost function of sector 2, given the quantity of output of sector 1 used by sector 2 as an input, $X_1$. Again, the aggregate quantity of standardized raw material input is given by:

$$\frac{\partial C}{\partial \bar{p}_M}(V_1, V_2, r, w, p_E, \bar{p}_M)$$

Finally, suppose that the outputs of each sector are used as inputs in the output production of the other sector. Then the aggregate cost function for the economy is given by:

$$C = \min_{X_1, X_2} [C_1^*(V_1 + X_1, X_2, r, w, p_E, \bar{p}_M)$$
$$+ C_2^*(V_2 + X_2, X_1, r, w, p_E, \bar{p}_M)]$$

where $C_i^*(\cdot)$ is the minimum variable cost function for producing one unit of the output of the $i$th industry, given the quantities of the interindustry inputs used and the prices of the variable factors of production. $C_i^*(\cdot)$ can be derived from a knowledge of the ordinary minimum cost function $C(V_i + X_i, p_j, r, w, p_E, \bar{p}_M)$ where $p_j$ is the price of the interindustry input. Again, the aggregate quantity of standardized raw material input is given by $\partial C/\partial \bar{p}_M$ $(V_1, V_2, r, w, p_E, \bar{p}_M)$. This aggregate quantity will in general depend on the relative composition of the joint outputs.

So far the problem is relatively simple because only one class of raw material inputs is distinguished. We now suppose there are two classes of raw material inputs, each with price $\bar{p}_{Mi}$ per unit of the standardized input. We now investigate whether the aggregate cost function can be written in the form:

$$C[V_1, V_2, r, w, p_E, h(\bar{p}_{M1}, \bar{p}_{M2})]^{11}$$

that is, whether the aggregate cost function is homothetically separable in the raw material input prices. If this were the case, then one could construct a single aggregate quantity index of raw material inputs from the quantities of the two classes of raw material inputs.[12]

As before, we consider three separate cases corresponding to the three assumptions on interindustry transactions. First, if neither sector uses the output of the other sector as an input, then the aggregate cost function for the economy is given by:

$$C = C_1(V_1, r, w, p_E, \bar{p}_{M1}, \bar{p}_{M2}) + C_2(V_2, r, w, p_E, \bar{p}_{M1}, \bar{p}_{M2})$$

In order that $C$ be separable in the raw material input prices, one must have the ratio:

$$\frac{\dfrac{\partial C_1}{\partial \bar{p}_{M1}} + \dfrac{\partial C_2}{\partial \bar{p}_{M1}}}{\dfrac{\partial C_1}{\partial \bar{p}_{M2}} + \dfrac{\partial C_2}{\partial \bar{p}_{M2}}}$$

be independent of $V_1$, $V_2$, $r$, $w$, and $p_E$. First, since $V_1$ and $V_2$ are arbitrary, one can set each $V_i$ equal to zero. Since $C_i(0, r, w, p_E, \bar{p}_{M1}, \bar{p}_{M2}) = 0$, one concludes immediately that in order for there to be separability in the aggregate cost function, one must have separability in the individual industry cost functions, so that:

$$C = C_1[V_1, r, w, p_E, h_1(\bar{p}_{M1}, \bar{p}_{M2})] + C_2[V_2, r, w, p_E, h_2(\bar{p}_{M1}, \bar{p}_{M2})]$$

Now in order that the aggregate cost function depend on only one index, it must be the case that

---

[11] Because of homogeneity of degree, one of the cost functions in the variable input prices, $h(\cdot)$ can always be chosen so that it is homogeneous of degree one. See Lau (1969) and Diewert (1973).

[12] See the excellent survey paper on aggregation by Diewert (1977).

$$\frac{\partial}{\partial r} \left( \begin{array}{c} \dfrac{\partial C_1}{\partial h_1} \dfrac{\partial h_1}{\partial \bar{p}_{M1}} + \dfrac{\partial C_2}{\partial h_2} \dfrac{\partial h_2}{\partial \bar{p}_{M1}} \\[2mm] \dfrac{\partial C_1}{\partial h_1} \dfrac{\partial h_1}{\partial \bar{p}_{M2}} + \dfrac{\partial C_2}{\partial h_2} \dfrac{\partial h_2}{\partial \bar{p}_{M2}} \end{array} \right) = 0$$

or

$$\left( \frac{\partial C_1}{\partial h_1} \frac{\partial h_1}{\partial \bar{p}_{M2}} + \frac{\partial C_2}{\partial h_2} \frac{\partial h_2}{\partial \bar{p}_{M2}} \right) \left( \frac{\partial^2 C_1}{\partial h_1 \partial r} \frac{\partial h_1}{\partial \bar{p}_{M1}} + \frac{\partial^2 C_2}{\partial h_2 \partial r} \frac{\partial h_2}{\partial \bar{p}_{M1}} \right)$$

$$= \left( \frac{\partial C_1}{\partial h_1} \frac{\partial h_1}{\partial \bar{p}_{M1}} + \frac{\partial C_2}{\partial h_2} \frac{\partial h_2}{\partial \bar{p}_{M1}} \right) \left( \frac{\partial^2 C_1}{\partial h_1 \partial r} \frac{\partial h_1}{\partial \bar{p}_{M2}} + \frac{\partial^2 C_2}{\partial h_2 \partial r} \frac{\partial h_2}{\partial \bar{p}_{M2}} \right)$$

which upon using the fact that $C_1(\cdot)$ and $C_2(\cdot)$ are separable in $\bar{p}_{M1}$ and $\bar{p}_{M2}$ leads to:

$$\frac{\partial C_1}{\partial h_1} \frac{\partial h_1}{\partial \bar{p}_{M2}} \frac{\partial^2 C_2}{\partial h_2 \partial r} \frac{\partial h_2}{\partial \bar{p}_{M1}} + \frac{\partial C_2}{\partial h_2} \frac{\partial h_2}{\partial \bar{p}_{M2}} \frac{\partial^2 C_1}{\partial h_1 \partial r} \frac{\partial h_1}{\partial p_{M1}}$$

$$= \frac{\partial C_2}{\partial h_2} \frac{\partial h_2}{\partial \bar{p}_{M1}} \frac{\partial^2 C_1}{\partial h_1 \partial r} \frac{\partial h_1}{\partial \bar{p}_{M2}} + \frac{\partial C_1}{\partial h_1} \frac{\partial h_1}{\partial \bar{p}_{M1}} \frac{\partial^2 C_2}{\partial h_2 \partial r} \frac{\partial h_2}{\partial \bar{p}_{M2}}$$

$$= \frac{\partial C_1}{\partial h_1} \frac{\partial^2 C_2}{\partial h_2 \partial r} \left( \frac{\partial h_1}{\partial \bar{p}_{M2}} \frac{\partial h_2}{\partial \bar{p}_{M1}} - \frac{\partial h_1}{\partial \bar{p}_{M1}} \frac{\partial h_2}{\partial \bar{p}_{M2}} \right)$$

$$= \frac{\partial C_2}{\partial h_2} \frac{\partial^2 C_1}{\partial h_1 \partial r} \left( \frac{\partial h_2}{\partial \bar{p}_{M1}} \frac{\partial h_1}{\partial \bar{p}_{M2}} - \frac{\partial h_2}{\partial \bar{p}_{M2}} \frac{\partial h_1}{\partial \bar{p}_{M1}} \right)$$

Either

$$\frac{\partial h_1}{\partial \bar{p}_{M2}} \frac{\partial h_2}{\partial \bar{p}_{M1}} - \frac{\partial \tilde{h}_1}{\partial \bar{p}_{M1}} \frac{\partial h_2}{\partial \bar{p}_{M2}} = 0$$

which implies that

$$h_2(\bar{p}_{M1}, \bar{p}_{M2}) = f[h_1(\bar{p}_{M1}, \bar{p}_{M2})]$$

or:

$$\frac{\partial C_1}{\partial h_1} \frac{\partial^2 C_2}{\partial h_2 \partial r} = \frac{\partial C_2}{\partial h_2} \frac{\partial^2 C_1}{\partial h_1 \partial r}$$

or

$$\frac{\partial \ln \dfrac{\partial C_1}{\partial h_1}}{\partial r} = \frac{\partial \ln \dfrac{\partial C_2}{\partial h_2}}{\partial r}$$

so that

$$\frac{\partial C_1}{\partial h_1} \bigg/ \frac{\partial C_2}{\partial h_2}$$

is independent of $r$ (and $w$ and $p_E$), and hence is a function of only $V_1$, $V_2$, and $h_1$, $h_2$. Thus:

$$\frac{\partial C_i}{\partial h_i} = k(r,w,p_E)g_i(V_i,h_i)$$

or

$$C_i = k(r,w,p_E)G_i[V_i,h_i(\bar{p}_{M1},\bar{p}_{M2})] + k_i(r,w,p_E,V_i), \quad i = 1,2 \tag{13}$$

which implies that the aggregate cost function takes the form:

$$C = k(r,w,p_E)\{G_1[V_1,h_1(\bar{p}_{M1},\bar{p}_{M2})] + G_2[V_2,h_2(\bar{p}_{M1},\bar{p}_{M2})]\}$$
$$+ k_1(r,w,p_E,V_1) + k_2(r,w,p_E,V_2)$$

Thus, we have proved that under the assumption of zero interindustry transactions, the aggregate cost function is separable in the prices of raw material inputs if and only if either each individual sector cost function is separable with identical $h(\cdot)$ functions, or it takes the special form of equation (13). What this means is that either the two classes of raw materials are substitutable in the same way in *all* sectors, or the technology of each sector has to take a special form.

Next, if only the output of sector 1 is used in the production of output in sector 2, but not vice versa, then the aggregate cost function for the economy is given by:

$$C = \min_{X_1} [C_1(V_1 + X_1,r,w,p_E,\bar{p}_{M1},\bar{p}_{M2}) + C_2^*(V_2,X_1,r,w,p_E,\bar{p}_{M1},\bar{p}_{M2})]$$

We note that if one assumes differentiability of the cost functions $C_1(\cdot)$ and $C_2^*(\cdot)$, a necessary condition for a minimum is:

$$\frac{\partial C_1}{\partial X_1} + \frac{\partial C_2^*}{\partial X_1} = 0$$

Now consider:

$$\frac{\dfrac{\partial C}{\partial \bar{p}_{M1}}}{\dfrac{\partial C}{\partial \bar{p}_{M2}}} = \frac{\dfrac{\partial C_1}{\partial \bar{p}_{M1}}(V_1 + X_1^*, r,w,p_E,\bar{p}_{M1},\bar{p}_{M2}) + \dfrac{\partial C_2^*}{\partial \bar{p}_{M1}}(V_2, X_1^*,r,w,p_E,\bar{p}_{M1},\bar{p}_{M2})}{\dfrac{\partial C_1}{\partial \bar{p}_{M2}}(V_1 + X_1^*, r,w,p_E,\bar{p}_{M1},\bar{p}_{M2}) + \dfrac{\partial C_2^*}{\partial \bar{p}_{M2}}(V_2, X_1^*,r,w,p_E,\bar{p}_{M1},\bar{p}_{M2})}$$

where $X_1^*(V_1,V_2,r,w,p_E,\bar{p}_{M1},\bar{p}_{M2})$ is the aggregate cost-minimizing value of interindustry input. In order for separability to hold, this partial derivative must be independent of $V_1$, $V_2$, $r$, $w$, and $p_E$. Again, since $V_1$ and $V_2$ are arbitrary, one may choose $V_i = 0$ successively. If $V_2 = 0$, then the aggregate cost-minimziing quantity of $X_1$ must be equal to zero. Hence

$$C = C_1(V_1,r,w,p_E,\bar{p}_{M1},\bar{p}_{M2})$$

We conclude that $C_1(\cdot)$ must be separable in $\bar{p}_{M1}$ and $\bar{p}_{M2}$. If $V_1 = 0$, then the condition for minimum aggregate cost implies:

$$\frac{\partial C_1}{\partial X_1}[X_1,r,w,p_E,h_1(\bar{p}_{M1},\bar{p}_{M2})] + \frac{\partial C_2^*}{\partial X_1}(V_2,X_1,r,w,p_E,\bar{p}_{M1},\bar{p}_{M2}) = 0$$

which implies that

$$X_1^* = X_1^*[V_2,r,w,p_E,h_1(\bar{p}_{M1},\bar{p}_{M2}),\bar{p}_{M1},\bar{p}_{M2}]$$

Separability then implies that:

$$C_2^*\{V_2,X_1^*[V_2,r,w,p_E,h_1(\bar{p}_{M1},\bar{p}_{M2}),\bar{p}_{M1},\bar{p}_{M2}],r,w,p_E,\bar{p}_{M1},\bar{p}_{M2}\}$$

depends on only a single index. A sufficient but not necessary condition is that $\bar{p}_{M1}$ and $\bar{p}_{M2}$ enter $C_2^*(\cdot)$ as an aggregate $h_1^*(\bar{p}_{M1},\bar{p}_{M2})$. If, however, it is assumed that production is subject to constant returns in all sectors, then the price of $X_1$ must be equal to unit cost, $c_1[r,w,p_E,h_1(\bar{p}_{M1},\bar{p}_{M2})]$. The cost function of $V_2$, $C_2$ [not to be confused with $C_2^*(\cdot)$], is given by:

$$C_2 = C_2(V_2,p_1,r,w,p_E,\bar{p}_{M1},\bar{p}_{M2})$$
$$= c_2\{c_1[r,w,p_E,h_1(\bar{p}_{M1},\bar{p}_{M2})],r,w,p_E,\bar{p}_{M1},\bar{p}_{M2}\}V_2$$

which in order for it to be separable, implies

$$\frac{\partial}{\partial p}\left(\frac{\dfrac{\partial c_2}{\partial c_1}\dfrac{\partial c_1}{\partial h_1}\dfrac{\partial h_1}{\partial \bar{p}_{M1}} + \dfrac{\partial c_2}{\partial \bar{p}_{M1}}}{\dfrac{\partial c_2}{\partial c_1}\dfrac{\partial c_1}{\partial h_1}\dfrac{\partial h_1}{\partial \bar{p}_{M2}} + \dfrac{\partial c_2}{\partial \bar{p}_{M2}}}\right) = 0, \quad p = r,w,p_E$$

which leads to:

$$\left(\frac{\partial c_2}{\partial c_1}\frac{\partial c_1}{\partial h_1}\frac{\partial h_1}{\partial \bar{p}_{M2}} + \frac{\partial c_2}{\partial \bar{p}_{M2}}\right)\left[\frac{\partial^2 c_2}{\partial c_1 \partial p}\frac{\partial c_1}{\partial h_1}\frac{\partial h_1}{\partial \bar{p}_{M1}} + \frac{\partial c_2}{\partial c_1}\frac{\partial^2 c_1}{\partial h_1 \partial p}\frac{\partial h_1}{\partial \bar{p}_{M1}}\right.$$
$$\left. + \frac{\partial^2 c_2}{\partial p \partial \bar{p}_{M1}} + \frac{\partial^2 c_2}{\partial c_1 \partial \bar{p}_{M1}}\frac{\partial c_1}{\partial p}\right] - \left(\frac{\partial c_2}{\partial c_1}\frac{\partial c_1}{\partial h_1}\frac{\partial h_1}{\partial \bar{p}_{M1}} + \frac{\partial c_2}{\partial \bar{p}_{M1}}\right)$$
$$\times \left[\frac{\partial^2 c_2}{\partial c_1 \partial p}\frac{\partial c_1}{\partial h_1}\frac{\partial h_1}{\partial \bar{p}_{M1}} + \frac{\partial c_2}{\partial c_1}\frac{\partial^2 c_1}{\partial h_1 \partial p}\frac{\partial h_1}{\partial \bar{p}_{M2}}\right.$$
$$\left. + \frac{\partial^2 c_2}{\partial p \partial \bar{p}_{M2}} + \frac{\partial^2 c_2}{\partial c_1 \partial \bar{p}_{M2}}\frac{\partial c_1}{\partial p}\right] = 0$$

This equation simplifies into:

$$\frac{\left(\dfrac{\partial c_2}{\partial c_1}\dfrac{\partial c_1}{\partial h_1}\dfrac{\partial h_1}{\partial \bar{p}_{M2}} + \dfrac{\partial c_2}{\partial \bar{p}_{M2}}\right)}{\left(\dfrac{\partial c_2}{\partial c_1}\dfrac{\partial c_1}{\partial h_1}\dfrac{\partial h_1}{\partial \bar{p}_{M1}} + \dfrac{\partial c_2}{\partial \bar{p}_{M1}}\right)} = \frac{\dfrac{\partial^2 c_2}{\partial p \partial \bar{p}_{M2}} + \dfrac{\partial^2 c_2}{\partial c_1 \partial \bar{p}_{M2}}\dfrac{\partial c_1}{\partial p}}{\dfrac{\partial^2 c_2}{\partial p \partial \bar{p}_{M1}} + \dfrac{\partial^2 c_2}{\partial c_1 \partial \bar{p}_{M1}}\dfrac{\partial c_1}{\partial p}}$$

Unfortunately it is not possible to characterize the cost function further, except to say that it is sufficient that the same $h(\cdot)$ index enters both cost functions.

Finally, for the general case in which both sectors use the other sector's output, one has for the aggregate cost function

$$C = \min_{X_1,X_2} [C_1^*(V_1^* + X_1;X_2,r,w,p_E,\bar{p}_{M1},\bar{p}_{M2})$$
$$+ C_2^*(V_2 + X_2,X_1,r,w,p_E,\bar{p}_{M1},\bar{p}_{M2})] = C(V_1,V_2,r,w,p_E,\bar{p}_{M1},\bar{p}_{M2})$$

It has not been possible to determine the necessary conditions on the individual industry cost functions in order that the aggregate cost function be separable.

It appears unlikely that at the aggregate economy level aggregate cost functions are separable in the prices of the raw material inputs. If that is the case, one cannot meaningfully measure the aggregate quantity of raw material inputs used and therefore perhaps one should not attempt to construct an overall index of the quantity of aggregate raw material inputs.

Finally, if we make use of the nonsubstitution theorem, we can write:

$$p_i = d_i(r,w,p_E,\bar{p}_{M1},\bar{p}_{M2}), \quad i = 1,2$$

where $d_i$ is used to denote the fact that it is different from the cost functions that have been considered earlier. The aggregate "cost" may be written as the value of the net joint outputs:

$$C = d_1(r,w,p_E,\bar{p}_{M1},\bar{p}_{M2})V_1 + d_2(r,w,p_E,\bar{p}_{M1},\bar{p}_{M2})V_2$$

In order for this function to be separable, we need:

$$d_i = d_i[r,w,p_E,h(\bar{p}_{M1},\bar{p}_{M2})], \quad i = 1,2$$

We emphasize that the $d_i(\cdot)$'s are not the same as the individual industry unit cost functions $c_i(\cdot)$'s.

## 6. Raw Material Inputs at the Economy Level

Thus far I have considered the measurement of raw material inputs only from the point of view of demand. I have not considered measurement of supply. The analysis, of course, can be interpreted to include the presence of processed materials which can substitute for raw materials. For example, one or more of the interindustry inputs can be interpreted as processed materials and their substitution possibilities in relation to raw materials can be fully captured by the individual industry cost functions. These substitution possibilities, however, may make the separability assumption untenable.

Moreover, the analysis in section 5 is unfortunately not completely re-solved—it will be purely fortuitous if the different classes of raw material inputs together form an aggregate for *all* the end-use sectors. If the supply side is added, so that the sectors producing the raw material inputs are also included, the situation is even more complex. The prices of the different classes of raw material inputs become endogenous to the system and may in partic-ular depend on the vector of joint outputs. It is not clear what meaning can be attached to the notion of an aggregate quantity of raw material inputs under such circumstances.

One thing that conceivably can be done is the following. The supply sectors of the raw material inputs may be reasonably assumed to face some capacity constraints. The effect of variations of these capacity constraints on the re-sulting system of prices and quantities of final outputs can be investigated. This will provide some measure of the importance of limitations in the supply of raw materials. By varying these capacity constraints proportionally, it is possible to obtain some measure of the importance of the limitations in the aggregate. However, this is a far cry from having an aggregate quantity of raw material inputs which can be used in an input-output type relationship such as a production function.

There are, in fact, additional complications. I have considered only a static economy. What happens if the analysis is extended to a dynamic context? In this case, the time structure and the type of capital investment for specific industries will make a difference to the current and future use values of dif-ferent classes of raw material inputs. The possibility of recycling must be introduced. There will be sectors producing scrap metals and waste paper. The durability of both consumer goods and capital investments (possibly raw material-specific) will make a difference. In addition, the hedonic price equations must be modified to take into account the lack of perfect and in-stantaneous adjustments in response to raw material input prices because of the sunk costs of the existing capital stocks.

With the introduction of these additional complexities, it appears even more unlikely that a single aggregate quantity index of raw material inputs can be rigorously justified. However, this does not mean that one should give up measuring raw material inputs. It is possible that with suitable aggregation it may be possible to represent the economy with only a few classes of raw material inputs.[13] This is something which requires a more intense empirical investigation.

Finally, I wish to address the question of "importance" of raw material inputs. In a way the question is not well posed as stated. Since the production of almost every physical commodity requires physical inputs to some degree

---

[13] Of course, if the prices of the raw material inputs within each class always move together, then such a representation of the economy is always possible. But we hope to be able to define aggregates even when the prices of the constituent raw material inputs do not move together exactly proportionally.

(even plants require water), it is easy to see that raw material inputs are definitely essential. Nor is there any real danger that aggregate raw material input will be exhausted (especially in light of the conservation laws of physics). What may happen is, of course, the potential exhaustion of certain specific raw materials. What is relevant is how crucial they are to a given standard of living. It is here that considerations of efficiency of use; of substitutability among capital, labor, energy, and aggregate raw material inputs; and of intermaterial substitutability enter. These are areas which deserve further careful empirical research.

The cost share of raw materials in total cost or gross national product is not a good measure of the "importance" of such inputs. A large share may well be the result of a low marginal productivity with abundant use. A small share may well be consistent with a high marginal productivity with resulting low utilization. For example, consider the use of catalysts in chemical processes and the use of doping "impurities" in the manufacture of semiconductors. The cost shares of the catalysts and "impurities" are very small, but the two inputs are vitally "important" in the respective manufacturing processes.

Probably the most reliable measure of the change in relative "importance" of raw material inputs is their real (relative) prices. These reflect the true marginal productivities. To the extent that there are positive or negative externalities associated with the use of raw material inputs but not reflected in the market prices, the market prices should be adjusted downward or upward, as the case may be. Likewise, nonpriced, common property resources can become relatively more or less "important" as their relative scarcity values change. Relative "importance" thus depends on the production technology not only of market commodities but also of nonmarket commodities and their interactions.

The current economic value of the aggregate raw material inputs base—the values of mines, mineral rights, oil wells, land, etc.—may provide a reasonable index of the "importance" of raw material inputs. It reflects existing and expected future technologies. To the extent that there is adequate pollution legislation, the current economic value should also reflect the negative externalities of depletion or exhaustion of the nonpriced raw material inputs. Strictly speaking, however, the validity of such an index is predicated on the existence of complete and perfect markets. In reality, complete and perfect markets do not exist, and an index based on current aggregate economic value may not reflect the true importance of raw material inputs.

A more useful exercise is to examine the effects curtailments in the materials inputs base would have on the stream of current and future final consumption goods. Such an accounting should include ecological and environmental quality as inputs and should measure consumption goods with negative values, such as medical care to counteract health impairments. This may provide some insight into the issue of "sufficiency."

## 7. Conclusions

On the basis of an admittedly incomplete analysis, I conclude that it is possible to construct an aggregate quantity of raw material inputs for specific end-use sectors. Further research is necessary to establish the precise conditions under which an aggregate quantity of raw material inputs can be constructed for the economy as a whole where there are nonzero interindustry transactions. It is likely that these conditions will be quite restrictive. However, this does not necessarily rule out the possibility that the role of raw material inputs in the economy may be represented by several suitably chosen classes of inputs rather than just a single aggregate.

How these classes should be chosen is an empirical question which deserves to be further investigated. The point of departure of such an investigation may be the cost functions of individual end use sectors, in which the prices of the interindustry inputs are explicitly included. From the analysis of such cost functions, one can also obtain information on the degree of substitutability between raw material inputs and processed material inputs, and in particular on those processed material inputs which are obtained through recycling. For each end-use sector, and for each class of raw material inputs, one can also attempt to estimate a hedonic price function. This function will provide the information necessary for aggregating raw material inputs within the end-use sector. In addition, information should be developed on the distribution of capital stock by size, type, and vintage within each end-use sector. This is relevant to the way in which raw material inputs with different characteristics should be aggregated within an end-use sector. Finally, as one introduces dynamic elements in the analysis, additional considerations such as the effects of technological change, changes in durability of both capital stocks and consumer goods, and changes in investment behavior will also become relevant.

Investigations on the validity of the hedonic price equations under conditions of elastic supply will also contribute to an understanding of the aggregation problems involved.

These are only a few of the many questions that may be raised about raw material inputs. It is believed that these questions are the most urgent, and when they are resolved, the ability to analyze the role of raw material inputs in the economy will be significantly enhanced.

## References

Diewert, W. E. 1973. "Functional Forms for Profit and Transformation Functions," *Journal of Economic Theory* vol. 6, no. 3 (June), pp. 284–316.

———. 1974a. "Applications of Duality Theory," in M. Intriligator and D. Kendrick, eds., *Frontiers of Quantitiative Economics* vol. 2 (Amsterdam, North-Holland).

———. 1974b. "Functional Forms for Revenue and Factor Requirements Functions," *International Economic Review* vol. 15, no. 1 (February), pp. 119–130.

———. 1976. "Exact and Superlative Index Numbers," *Journal of Econometrics* vol. 4, pp. 115–145.

———. 1977. "Aggregation Problems in the Measurement of Capital," Discussion Paper No. 77-09, Department of Economics, University of British Columbia (mimeographed).

Griliches, Zvi. 1961. "Hedonic Price Indexes of Automobiles: An Econometric Analysis of Quality Change," *The Price Statistics of the Federal Government*, *General Series No. 73* (New York, National Bureau of Economic Research).

Lau, L. J. 1969. "Duality and the Structure of Utility Functions," *Journal of Economic Theory* vol. 4, no. 1 (December), pp. 374–396.

———. 1977a. "Existence Conditions for Aggregate Demand Functions: The Case of a Single Index," Technical Report No. 248, Institute for Mathematical Studies in the Social Sciences, Stanford University.

———. 1977b. "Existence Conditions for Aggregate Demand Functions: The Case of Multiple Indices," Technical Report No. 249, Institute for Mathematical Studies in the Social Sciences, Stanford University.

Ohta, M. 1975. "Production Technologies of the U.S. Boiler and Turbogenerator Industries and Hedonic Price Indexes for their Products: A Cost-Function Approach," *Journal of Political Economy* vol. 82, no. 1 (February), pp. 1–26.

———. and Zvi Griliches. 1975. "Automobile Prices Revisited: Extensions of the Hedonic Hypothesis," in N. E. Terleckyj, ed., *Household Production and Consumption* (New York, National Bureau of Economic Research).

Skinner, B. J. 1976. "A Second Iron Age Ahead?" *American Scientist* vol. 64, pp. 258–269.

# 7

## The Perceived Role of Materials in Neoclassical Models of Production Technology

### Raymond J. Kopp and V. Kerry Smith

This paper reports the findings of a series of experiments conducted to appraise the usefulness of neoclassical economic models for measuring the degree of factor substitution possible in production activities. Large-scale, engineering, process analysis models of iron and steel production were used to represent the "true" characterization of production processes for this technology. We evaluate the effects of the following on the substitution possibilities perceived by the neoclassical model: (1) The definition of natural resource inputs; (2) the qualitative features of the engineering technology; and (3) the presence of exogenous constraints on economic optimization (that is, cost minimization). This appraisal was undertaken because factor substitution is an important mechanism in ameliorating the limitations imposed on economic growth by exhaustible natural resources.

Concern over the supply of natural resources is at least as old as economic analysis itself, with recurring attention given to Malthusian scenarios of all types. In the United States, these episodes of concern have been repeated several times during the twentieth century, each one following closely on the heels of heavy demands on available materials resources.[1] Before the current

This research was supported by the National Science Foundation's Directorate for Applied Research under Contract No. NSF-C-ERS77-15083. Some of the results reported here are based on work in R. J. Kopp and V. Kerry Smith, "Measuring Factor Substitution with Neoclassical Models: An Experimental Evaluation," *Bell Journal of Economics* vol. 11 (Autumn 1980) pp. 631–655. Thanks are due Mary Kokoski for most capable research assistance and to William J. Vaughan for his contribution to related research on the performance of process analysis models. The authors also wish to thank Ernst Berndt and John Moroney for their careful review and constructive comments on an earlier draft of this paper.

[1] Barnett and Morse (1963) offer a detailed history of the conservation movement to the time of the publication of their book. It should be noted that their effort was motivated in part

resurgence of interest, the most influential evaluation of the implications of resource availability for economic well-being was *Scarcity and Growth*, by Harold Barnett and Chandler Morse. Their analysis of the long-term trends in scarcity indexes for natural resources led them to conclude that there was no natural resource problem in a limitational sense. Resource substitution within existing technologies, along with technological change, had apparently relaxed any genuinely pressing supply constraints.[2]

Since then, an extensive new literature has developed on the role of natural resources for economic activities sparked, in part, by energy and environmental "crises" of the recent past.[3] In many respects this new work has repeated in more formal terms already familiar conclusions about the importance of natural resources in maintaining economic welfare over time. Indeed, Solow's (1974) Ely lecture comes close to paraphrasing some of the earlier Barnett-Morse conclusions by observing (page 10) that:

> The seriousness of the resource-exhaustion problem must depend in an important way on two aspects of the technology: first, the likelihood of technical progress, especially natural-resource-saving technical progress, and, second, the ease with which other factors of production, especially labor and reproducible capital, can be substituted for exhaustible resources in production.

In the context of a simple growth model with an aggregate production function that has constant elasticity of substitution and a constant population, Dasgupta and Heal (1979) have demonstrated that whether or not a constant level of consumption can be permanently sustained depends on whether the elasticity of substitution between reproducible capital and the exhaustible natural resource is greater or less than unity.[4]

---

by the reports of the Cooke and Paley commissions. Indeed, Resources for the Future was established as a result of the recommendations of the second of these presidential commissions (see Resources for the Future, 1977 for a brief history).

More recently, there has been continuous interest in issues related to resource availability since the 1973 oil embargo, with studies by a variety of special groups. The most recent among these was the President's Commission on Critical Supplies and Shortages.

[2] Barnett and Morse (1963) described the natural resource problem as one of adjustment to change and not the lack of natural resources. Specifically, they noted (page 244) that:

> The resource problem is one of continual accommodation and adjustment to an ever-changing economic resource quality spectrum. The physical properties of the natural resource base impose a series of initial constraints on the growth and progress of mankind, but the resource spectrum undergoes kaleidoscopic change through time. Continual enlargement of the scope of substitutability—the result of man's technological ingenuity and organizational wisdom—offers those who are nimble a multitude of opportunities for escape. In fact the constraint does not disappear, it merely changes character. New constraints replace the old, new scarcities generate new offsets.

[3] For a detailed review of the literature on economics of natural resources to 1977, see Peterson and Fisher (1977). A companion study for environmental economics is available in Fisher and Peterson (1976).

[4] If the elasticity of substitution is exactly unity, the CES function reduces to a Cobb–Douglas specification and the elasticities of productivity of the natural resource and capital determine whether the exhaustible resource poses a problem for a constant level of consumption.

Much of the current empirical analysis of the role of natural resources in production processes has focused on Solow's two questions: To what degree can we substitute away from exhaustible natural resources in production? What can we expect from resource-saving technological innovation? Most often these analyses have adopted neoclassical economic models of production rather than some alternative modeling structures.[5] Unfortunately, the neoclassical model contains several restrictive assumptions which are often overlooked when the model's results are interpreted. An example is the assumption that input substitution can proceed at the rate implied by the substitution elasticity over all ranges of input use.[6] Considering the physical laws underlying production activities, this assumption seems implausible. Dasgupta and Heal (1979, page 206) acknowledge that:

> The main analytical novelty that exhaustible resources present in the analysis of growth possibilities open to an economy is that one has to be particularly conscious about the properties of production functions at the "corners." The banality of this observation is matched only by the problems this poses in obtaining empirical estimates . . . the assumption that the elasticity of substitution is independent of the capital-resource ratio may be a treacherous one to make. Past evidence may not be a good guide for judging substitution possibilities for large values of K/R (capital to natural resource) [parenthetical note added].

This conclusion implies that proper interpretation of neoclassical models cannot stop with measures of whether substitution *can* take place. Rather, it requires an understanding of *how* that substitution occurs.

An understanding of how substitution takes place requires a greater familiarity with the engineering processes of production than most economists normally acquire in modeling production activities. Neoclassical models perceive the production function as a "black box" into which inputs enter and from which outputs miraculously emerge. As such, they gloss over important engineering details crucial to a thorough understanding of the activities themselves. This judgment should not be misconstrued. The black box approach may well be useful for a variety of theoretical exercises. However, it does not necessarily provide a reliable empirical description of all engineering technologies. The measurement of either substitution or complementary

---

[5] Several alternatives to neoclassical economic modeling exist. Engineering process analysis models are just one example.

[6] Cummings and Schulze (1977) were the first to identify this limitation and observed (pages 1 to 2) that:

> Current treatments of the Ramsey problem with limited resource availability ignore a fundamental restriction, however, which arises naturally from the problem itself: the conservation of mass-energy. Most of these works make use of Cobb–Douglas production functions . . . wherein it is implicitly assumed that capital stocks are perfectly substitutable for the rate of natural resource availability. The conservation of mass requires that the mass of output be no greater than the mass of inputs . . . Since the nature of capital and labor's contribution to the production process is that of altering the resource mass or converting energy content to material or work output, the relevant balance restriction concerns output and resource use.

relations between pairs of inputs in specific production processes requires more than using a data-fitting criterion to judge whether the technologies can be summarized with a specific neoclassical function. Rather, such models must not only summarize the broad features of the engineering technology, they must also reveal a quite subtle aspect of that technology—input association through the curvature features of the estimated functions.[7]

This chapter proposes to evaluate the reliability of neoclassical production models as instruments for gauging the potential for factor substitution in production processes. An examination of the "how" of input substitution requires that the specific processes permitting the substitution be enumerated. This provides the basis for the definition of each relevant input. Conventional micro theory stops with the statement that factor inputs are homogeneous sets of goods or services. It does not address directly the dimensions in which each input must be homogeneous. For example, one might define fuel as an input to a given production process. If the amount of latent energy in terms of Btus were the only characteristic of the fuel relevant to the production process in question, then it would not be necessary to identify fuel types such as natural gas, fuel oil, or coal as separate factor inputs. By contrast, if sulfur content, ash content, specific gravity, and even such indirect attributes as storage requirements were important to the production processes, then a fuel input defined solely in terms of Btus would likely be misleading.[8] This example suggests that the characteristics of the input that are relevant to the given production activities provide the basis for an appropriate definition of the set of goods or services which can be included in a single factor input. Moreover, substitution between inputs defined in this way is possible because of differences in their mixes of such "valued" characteristics.

Accordingly, what is perceived as input substitution and the processes through which it takes place depends not only on the production technology but also on the definition of the factor inputs. These issues are important for applied econometric estimates of production models since these efforts often must rely upon data collected to serve other objectives. These data will reflect input definitions and levels of aggregation that may not be consistent with accurately approximating the features of the underlying technology (or technologies) within a neoclassical framework.

An equally important issue arises in estimating the features of a production technology. For the most part, these features are revealed by the behavior of firms. That is, we do not directly observe the outcomes of production choices removed from the individual firm's objectives and constraints. This is the basis of duality theory. A knowledge of these behavioral motives and constraints

---

[7] Fisher, Solow, and Kearl (1977) in their study of aggregate production functions remarked "The elasticity of substitution—a curvature parameter—is not well-determined by the data" (page 317).

[8] Berndt (1978) has recently used these concepts to consider the appropriate properties for an index of the quantity of energy used and its price.

can be used to advantage in estimating the features of the technology. However, if these conditions are incompletely or inaccurately described, they will also affect how the characteristics of the underlying production processes are perceived.

While these issues are certainly not new ones for economic analysis, there has been no attempt to systematically evaluate their effects on the neoclassical model's perceptions of the prospects for input substitution within a framework that reflects the complexities of an engineering technology.[9]

The results in this chapter are based on experimental methods in which data derived from three, large-scale, process analysis models of iron and steel production are used to evaluate the effects of the input definition, the engineering characteristics of the technology, and the presence of exogenous constraints (i.e., limitations on residuals discharges) on neoclassical models. As we detail in what follows, our findings relate to the estimation of an *ex post* technology at the micro level. This orientation may seem at odds with the earlier quotes from Solow and Dasgupta and Heal, whose analyses were based on aggregate, long-run models. However, these authors would be among the first to acknowledge that the information necessary to use the reasoning inherent in these models must originate at the micro level.

The next section outlines the methods for our evaluation in more specific terms. The second section discusses the design of the experiments and the specification of the estimating forms used. Section 3 summarizes the results for our benchmark case—the neoclassical model applied under "ideal" conditions. In the fourth section we focus on four different aggregations of materials inputs and the implications of the different data transformations implied for the estimated features of the production technology. Section five reviews the effects of constraints on residuals discharges on our overall results, and the last details the implications of these experiments for the appropriate use and interpretation of estimates of production technology based on neoclassical methods.

## *Methods of Analysis*

The most important element in the neoclassical model of production is the production function itself, which is used to represent the configuration

---

[9] Capturing the complexity of production processes requires the recognition of heat and materials balances present within the production process. For example, any description of production activities requires that there be a taxonomic enumeration of the goods and services used in those activities to produce the intended outputs. The goods and services contributing to these production processes are generally designated the factor inputs. Conventional theory defines the outputs as the desired goods or services that motivated production in the first place. However, there are also by-products that are not desired which result from the production transformations. Both types of outputs must be accounted for if the model is to accurately represent the production activities.

of processes involved in transforming a given set of factor inputs into desired outputs. It is, therefore, a compact summary of the technology under study and, for practical purposes, should be judged in terms of its ability to approximate the features of that technology. This ability will not be independent of the ways in which the factor inputs are defined and measured. In terms of the example cited in the introduction, if measures of fuel are available only in total Btu terms and the underlying technology is affected by other characteristics of the fuel, then quite independent of the functional specification and other attributes of the application, measurements of substitution prospects will be affected by this definition of fuel.

### Analytical Background

Issues concerned with the measurement of inputs and aggregation across heterogeneous inputs and production activities are not new to economic analysis. Indeed, two sets of results are especially relevant to the findings presented here. The first of these relates to the work of Houthakker (1955), which illustrated how aggregation across independent production activities can introduce perceived input substitution. Specifically, his analysis demonstrated that aggregating a fixed coefficient technology (where the micro elasticities of substitution between factors were zero) with a Pareto distribution of capital intensities yielded an aggregate Cobb–Douglas function with an elasticity of substitution between the aggregated factors of unity.[10]

The second set of results concerns the aggregation of inputs for a given technology. Here the past literature has concentrated on cases that can be described either exactly or approximately by some specified production function.[11] In this context it is possible to define the properties of alternative procedures for aggregating inputs into indexes. Diewert's (1976) definition of a superlative quantity index is one example. His framework identifies such an index as one that is an *exact* measure of the quantity for any function that provides a second-order approximation to a linear homogeneous function.[12]

Unfortunately, neither of the lines of research, though extensively developed, are relevant for a complex, *interdependent* process analysis technology that is more compatible with real world production activities. In such a

[10] This literature has been extended in several important ways by recent authors including Johansen (1972), Levhari (1968), and Sato (1975) for the theoretical work. Sato's (1975) book provides a summary of the state of understanding of the implied relationships between micro and aggregate representations of the technology.

[11] Diewert (1976) has recently provided a review of these results utilizing duality theory to illustrate their implications with cost and indirect utility functions.

[12] Applications of this methodology have been increased, with work of Fuss (1977) and Pindyck (1979) as examples.

framework, the micro processes are not independent and additive. They are interdependent, with a cumulative sequence of processing activities reflecting the steps necessary for the inputs to be transformed into the final outputs. These processing steps involve several intermediate products which are not primary inputs, but which may be substituted for such inputs. The presence of these intermediate products further complicates the measurement of factor substitution. Moreover, in such a system substitution is not smooth, as would be implied in a differentiable functional representation. Often, when inputs are rigorously defined according to the characteristics essential to a given production process, there is very limited, if any, scope for substitution. Rather, substitution arises from the definition of the factor inputs and the technological unit of analysis. Figure 7.1a provides an example in simple terms.

Suppose we consider the production of molten iron from two inputs—iron ore and coke. It may be possible to have two different combinations of iron ore and coke where the quantity of ore is defined specifically as composed of given Fe and sulfur concentrations and coke is also assumed to be defined in precise terms by its level of impurities. These two combinations are given by $A$ and $B$. Each yields the same quantity of molten iron (by assumption). In this setting the scope for substitution is limited. However, suppose we define several types of iron ore (i.e., grades with differing levels of Fe and sulfur concentrations) as iron and follow the same practice with coke. The apparent process density increases with the expansion in the definition of each input. In terms of our example, this can be illustrated with the introduction of new input combinations such as $C$, $D$, $E$, and $F$ in figure 7.1b. The shape of the isoquant now appears closer to that of a conventional neoclassical mode (i.e., $TT'$ in figure 7.1b versus $OO'$ in figure 7.1a). Of course, this comparison implicitly assumes that the measurement problems for the iron and coke aggregates can be resolved without distorting the perceived substitution properties of the technology. This is an index number problem in terms quite comparable to those we discussed earlier. However, in this case, the issue concerns whether an index of characteristics can be developed that will accurately depict the substitution possible in the technology.[13]

Unfortunately, in order to apply the available results in the existing aggregation literature, we would need to assume conditions for the inputs (i.e., smoothly changing characteristics) that are incompatible with our objectives. Moreover, the complexity of most engineering processes seems to defy analytical derivations of the sort developed by Houthakker. Therefore, to evaluate the performance of neoclassical models as approximations for such underlying technologies, we adopt an experimental method of analysis. This strategy requires the definition of an engineering, process analysis model

[13] There is a direct parallel to the hedonic literature of consumer behavior. Berndt (1978) discusses the implications of this parallel in more detail in his analysis of an appropriate measure of an aggregate energy input.

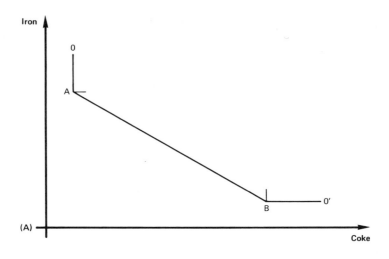

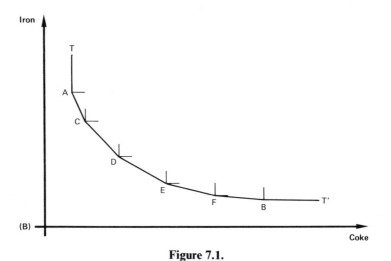

**Figure 7.1.**

that will constitute our "true" production technology.[14] With it we can generate the types of information used in neoclassical studies of the features of the production technology and evaluate, under controlled conditions, the authenticity of the neoclassical model's representation.

[14] Our approach is similar in logic to the work of: Fisher (1971); Fisher, Solow, and Kearl (1977) for evaluating the estimation of an aggregate production function; or Gapinski (1973), Gapinski and Kumar (1974), and Thursby and Lovell (1978) on the effects of alternative methods and/or functional specifications for estimating a micro production technology.

However, there are two important distinctions: (a) our experiments do not include stochastic errors and (b) there is no closed functional representation of production activities. It is defined as a sequence of processing activities.

Our specification of the neoclassical models utilizes cost functions and relies upon the McFadden (1979)–Shepard (1970)–Uzawa (1962) duality theorems to relate the estimated features of these functions to the characteristics of a neoclassical production technology. We consider three classes of influences which can affect the performance of neoclassical methods in accurately depicting substitution possibilities. These include: (1) the complexity of the process alternatives in the underlying engineering technology, (2) the level of aggregation of a subset of the factor inputs (i.e., the materials inputs), and (3) the presence and degree of additional constraints to productive activities in the form of limitations on discharges of atmospheric and waterborne residuals.

## A Description of the Engineering Technology

Implementing this experimental method requires selecting a well-developed, engineering, process analysis model that is compatible with an optimizing framework (in our case cost minimization) and that reflects the complexity of actual production activities. The necessary complexity arises from a full enumeration of the processing steps in transforming inputs into outputs and the need to reflect heat (energy) and materials balances at each processing step. Our choice of model is the Russell–Vaughan (1976) linear programming, process analysis model of iron and steel plants. This model was developed as part of RFF's industry studies to evaluate the residuals generated by selected industrial activities.[15] As a result, it is structured to use heat and materials balances to identify the residual by-products of each processing step in the technology. Moreover, it can be used to represent three distinct types of steel plants, each associated with a different steelmaking furnace—the basic oxygen (BOF), open hearth (OH), and electric arc (ARC) furnaces. These models identify between 480 and 541 structural activities (or columns), depending on the steelmaking technology.

While a complete description of the models is beyond the scope of a single chapter (and is already available in Russell and Vaughan, 1976), in order to appreciate the ensuing sequence of steps in our analysis, some rudiments of the technology must be reviewed. Figure 7.2 outlines in general terms the processing stages in converting inputs to one of these plants into finished steel products. The essential feature distinguishing each of these technologies is heat. The BOF and OH furnaces correspond to the hot metal technologies for producing molten steel. This classification implies that these furnaces indirectly process iron ore by manufacturing a reductant, coke (in the process designated coking), smelting a type (or a mix of types) of this ore with the coke and fluxes to produce molten iron (as indicated by the *blast furnace*

---

[15] See Bower (1975) for a summary of the research associated with these studies of selected industries.

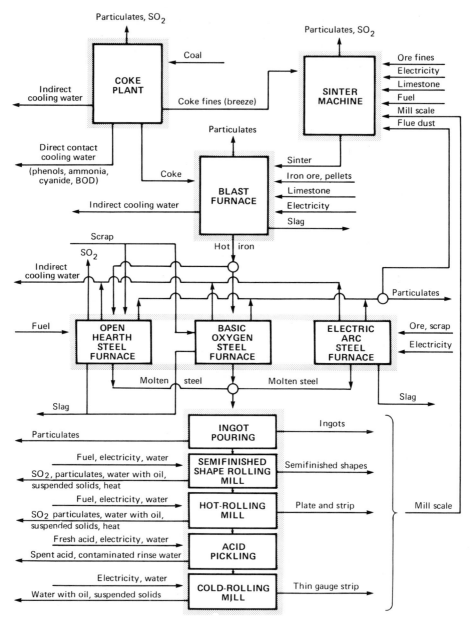

**Figure 7.2.** A simplified schematic view of iron and steel production. From C. S. Russell and W. J. Vaughan, *Steel Production: Processes, Products, Residuals* (Baltimore, Md., Johns Hopkins University Press for Resources for the Future, 1976) p. 22. A circle at a junction indicates a major choice point.

activity in the figure), and then further refining it by oxidizing the unnecessary silicon, manganese, phosphorus, and carbon in either the BOF or OH steel-making furnaces. The molten steel then undergoes a similar configuration of refining activities to produce ingots, semifinished shapes, plate and strip, and thin-gauge strip steel products.

One of the most important differences between these furnaces has to do with the source of heat in the refining stage for molten iron. In the case of the BOF furnace, the molten iron and oxidation reactions are the principal sources of heat. This limits the furnace to a narrow range of refining temperatures and, in turn, constrains the proportions of cold metal (scrap) to hot that can be used to produce molten steel. By contrast, the OH furnace permits the use of auxiliary heat in the refining process, making possible a corresponding wider range of refining temperatures and wider mix of cold to hot metal combinations. It seems clear that these differences will result in quite different patterns of substitution between scrap and iron ore, or coal and other fuels with these two technologies.

More subtle considerations require a recognition that the coking process yields gas and liquid by-products, which can, with selected treatment, be used as a source of auxiliary heat in the OH furnace or to generate the electricity necessary for the finishing activities in all three technologies. Unfortunately, not all of these connecting links can be represented in figure 7.2 and would require a detailed study of the technology matrices for the models. However, once it is recognized that they are present, it is possible to understand how coal used to produce a reductant might indirectly substitute for purchased sources of auxiliary heat. It would displace the purchased sources of heat once the treatment activities are used to process the by-product fuels (gaseous and liquid) from coking. The range of these possibilities differs with technology and will be reflected in the apparent process density of each technology.[16]

The electric arc is designed primarily for production of molten steel directly from scrap. It is generally designated as a cold metal technology, whose source of heat is an electric arc. This production of steel directly from scrap has important implications for the range of other activities required at the steel mill. For the most part, the ARC furnace does not require coking, sintering, and blast furnace activities, since they are associated with reducing iron ore. This reduces the number of intermediate products and both valuable and nonvaluable by-products which could be recovered at various processing stages. As we shall note later, the absence of these activities will be important to the ARC's ability to respond to constraints on discharges of residuals.

---

[16] Smith and Vaughan (1978) have discussed the implications of alternative process analysis models for each of the types of plants studied here. In addition, Russell and Vaughan (1976) detail in their table 2.1 (pages 30–31) the mechanisms giving rise to process density at each stage in their models.

## An Outline of the Methods

Given each of these models, our experiments require that the models be confronted with alternative sets of factor prices and residual discharge constraints and solved for the cost-minimizing factor demands. Each solution constitutes a data point for the next stage of our analysis in which samples of such solutions for each model will be used to evaluate the perceived neoclassical technology.

While the general logic of the process is direct, there are a number of specific details in the analysis that must be considered at greater length. The first of these concerns the treatment of capital inputs in the production activities of each plant. We distinguish two types of capital—productive plant and equipment, and pollution abatement equipment. For all the analysis that follows, the productive capital (plant and equipment) is treated as an invariant, fixed factor, with the capacity of each plant held at the same level—2,000 short tons of finished steel products per day. The linear technology implies constant returns to scale and therefore reduces interest in how the output effects of an *ex ante* formulation of the models might be perceived. Pollution abatement capital is assumed to be a variable factor and capable of being retrofitted on the existing plants.[17]

A second consideration in the development of our results relates to the definition of factor inputs. One of the mechanisms for increasing the detail in a process analysis model of any technology is to classify inputs and their associated uses according to their characteristics. Thus, there are a number of types of coal, iron ore, scrap, etc. that can be selected by each model, with each choice implying different sets of processing activities. As noted at the outset, input definition in any model is associated with perceived substitution possibilities. Therefore our definition of the initial or base level of inputs, from which we will subsequently aggregate, must be consistent with identifying the perceived substitutions between them. In order to satisfy this constraint, we define nine factor inputs—iron ore, coal, fuel oil, natural gas, scrap, labor, maintenance, pollution abatement capital, and all other operating inputs, and vary the prices of all the constituent elements within each input class proportionately in all the experiments.[18]

---

[17] This assumption introduces some difficulty in calculating the unit cost of pollution abatement capital and also serves to illustrate some of the problems that would arise with *ex ante* models for these plants. Specifically, the actual unit cost cannot be calculated without knowledge of the level of air or water flow through the treatment equipment. However, these flow levels are choice variables. We resolved this endogeneity by specifying the unit costs as corresponding to the design rates of flow through the equipment. Nonetheless, this could pose a more significant problem in modeling real world *ex ante* decisions within a linear technology if one chooses not to incorporate the discrete features of the capital equipment into the model.

[18] This corresponds to the Hicksian (1939) composite commodity concept usually employed in indifference curve analysis of consumer behavior. Leontief (1936) developed a similar concept

## A Framework for Evaluation of the Estimates

The final technical issue relates to a standard of comparison for the results of neoclassical analysis of these data. That is, the process analysis models do not have parametric representations that are directly compatible with the neoclassical models. Substitution arises because different mixes of processes are utilized in response to changes in the relative factor prices. However, in order to gauge the adequacy of these neoclassical tools, it is necessary to summarize compactly the prospects for substitution depicted by each model. This summary provides the benchmark for evaluating performance of the neoclassical structure under ideal conditions and each set of less than ideal conditions discussed earlier. Moreover, the nature of this comparison will be quite different from the evaluations in other experimental analyses, such as those appraising the properties of an estimator or test statistic.[19] That is, we are not comparing the estimates from alternative neoclassical models with the "true" values of specific parameters. Rather, the comparisons seek to evaluate the judgments that would be made on the prospects for substitution using a neoclassical model relative to indexes of the substitution possibilities present in the underlying engineering model. Therefore, the indexes of substitution in these process analysis models cannot be the basis for direct numerical comparisons with the neoclassical estimates.

Our proposed indexes of the prospects for substitution are defined to assure that substitution and complementary associations between inputs are always identified correctly. We have designated them as *derived arc elasticities of substitution* to distinguish them from traditional arc elasticities of substitution. Our index is given in equation (1).

$$\sigma_{ij}^{A} = \frac{1}{C_{j2}} \frac{\left[ \dfrac{Q_{2i} - Q_{1i}}{Q_{2i} + Q_{1i}} \right]}{\left[ \dfrac{P_{2j} - P_{1j}}{P_{2j} + P_{1j}} \right]} \tag{1}$$

where  $C_{j2}$ is cost share of the $j$th factor input at $P_{2j}$ prices

$Q_{2i}$ is quantity of $i$th factor demanded at a price $P_{2j}$ for the $j$th factor and all other prices and output held constant

---

for quantity aggregation as well. In order to adopt Hicks's composite commodity approach to aggregation, prices must vary in the same proportion. The Leontief scheme does not require price proportionality because it assumes quantity proportionality, so the weights in these relations can be used to derive the appropriate price index. Gorman (1959) proposed the approach most often used today with separability restrictions. Katzner (1970) provides a brief summary of each approach.

[19] The stochastic nature of other experimental studies requires that sufficient replications of each experiment be conducted to permit estimating the sampling distributions for each parameter. The Fisher, Solow, Kearl (1977) paper provides a good example of its implications for evaluating the features of estimated aggregate production functions.

$Q_{1i}$ is quantity of $i$th factor demanded at a price $P_{1j}$ for the $j$th factor and all other prices and output held constant

In contrast to conventional (Allen, 1938) partial elasticities of substitution, these elasticities will not necessarily be symmetrical. Moreover, this definition of arc elasticities is consistent with the generalization of the elasticity of substitution to an $n$-factor input technology.[20] These derived arc elasticities offer no more than a summary of the substitution possibilities inherent in the engineering model's optimal responses to a price change in a single factor. Consequently, when they are used to evaluate the neoclassical estimates, it is important to recognize that this involves a comparison of one measure of the substitution possibilities inherent in a given technology with another. While both transform the process analysis model's responses into neoclassical terms, the elasticity estimates based on a neoclassical cost function restrict the measured optimal responses to conform to a given functional relationship. By contrast, the derived arc elasticities do not restrict the possible responses to conform to such a specification.

Accordingly, we cannot judge the neoclassical model's performance relative to this standard using a set of quantitative criteria. Nonetheless, these comparisons can offer information on the properties of neoclassical models as tools for analyzing the features of the underlying technology if a consistent typology of errors in representing the optimal responses of the process technology is defined.

Our framework identifies three types of errors according to the magnitude of the "true" prospects for substitution relative to the judgments that would be made from neoclassical estimates. We have tried to gauge the magnitude of these errors in qualitative terms. The first type of error, and what will be regarded as the most serious one, is *false association*. Simply stated, these errors occur when neoclassical estimates of the Allen elasticities of substitution lead to a conclusion that is the direct opposite of the actual case. For example, if two inputs are judged (using the neoclassical estimates) to be complements when they are actually substitutes in the underlying technology, a false association error is recorded. Of course, before proceeding, it is necessary to define what is implied by "judging the elasticities to reflect a particular association." For our purposes, this implies that the estimates are first "screened" with a type of "significance test;" thus the sign of an elasticity

---

[20] See Morrissett (1953) for a discussion of the limitations of the early approaches based on relationships as:

$$\sigma_{ij} = \left[ \frac{\left(\dfrac{X_2}{X_1}\right)_A - \left(\dfrac{X_2}{X_1}\right)_B}{\left(\dfrac{X_2}{X_1}\right)_A + \left(\dfrac{X_2}{X_1}\right)_B} \right] \Bigg/ \left[ \frac{\left(\dfrac{P_1}{P_2}\right)_A - \left(\dfrac{P_1}{P_2}\right)_B}{\left(\dfrac{P_1}{P_2}\right)_A + \left(\dfrac{P_1}{P_2}\right)_B} \right]$$

A more recent discussion is available in Bever et al. (1978).

estimate is considered as a measure of input association only when the ratio of the estimated elasticity to its estimated asymptotic standard error is greater than two. Otherwise, the estimated elasticities are regarded as *noninformative*. This significance test can be interpreted as a test of the hypothesis that the estimated elasticity is not significantly different from zero. Such an interpretation could lead one to conclude that these inputs are used in fixed proportions. In the analysis that follows we adopt the alternative interpretation that the neoclassical model is incapable of establishing a "reliable" estimate of the association.

Clearly, this standard is arbitrary. The properties of the ratio of the estimated coefficient to estimated standard error for neoclassical models using the flexible functional forms and Zellner system estimators are not well understood for small samples.[21] Nonetheless, these issues are not directly limiting to our analysis. We are attempting to mimic the ways in which the neoclassical tools are used, regardless of whether the statistical foundations of the use patterns are well defined.[22] Thus, what is of interest in our appraisal is how the estimates of the technology based on a neoclassical cost function would be used in describing the underlying technology.[23]

The second type of error is also related to the measured association between inputs and will be designated a *nonassociation* error. This error can arise from two types of neoclassical estimates. The first of these would lead to noninformative estimates when the underlying association between the inputs would be clearly one of substitution or complementarity. The second type of error in this class yields a measured association in the neoclassical estimates (i.e., an informative estimate) when there is no clear underlying association between the inputs. While we might argue that the latter is more serious than

[21] The experimental literature on the performance of estimators for the production technology using flexible functional forms is quite limited. Guilkey and Lovell (1978) and Hazilla (1978) provide some evidence for cases involving the translog specification to estimate other specified production or cost functions.

[22] As we observed earlier, our application is nonstochastic. The only source of the errors in the models estimated (which are described in the next section) is the degree of approximation of the neoclassical cost function to that implied by the process analysis technology. This view is consistent with that developed by Marsden, Pingry, and Whinston (1974). They observe (pages 136–137) that:

A basic dichotomy in the emphasis of the engineering and economic production functions becomes readily apparent here. When models of the type introduced earlier in the paper [mass-energy-balance relationships] are applied to processes including significant relative amounts of labor, it becomes increasingly difficult to meaningfully quantify equations of the form (3) [an explicit relationship for reaction rates] . . . in the more highly technical processes, which are becoming more and more prevalent, where labor does not enter as a substitutable input, the engineering formulation is directly applicable. Indeed, we argue that this approach is preferable since it provides a basis for important direct technical analysis.

[23] Nearly all recent evaluations of the production technology using the flexible functional forms have used these approximate tests to interpret their results. Examples would include: Binswanger (1974), Humphrey and Moroney (1975), Moroney and Toevs (1977), Pindyck (1979), Dennis and Smith (1978), and others.

the former, both are involved with incorrect judgments of nonassociation of inputs.

The last class of errors relates to judgments about the magnitude of the prospects for substitution. Since the derived arc elasticities are not "true" parameters, this category, designated *false magnitude*, is necessarily heterogeneous. We have identified three types of comparisons between the neoclassical estimates and the derived arc elasticities as consistent with this type of error:

1. The estimates are rated noninformative when the inputs (or aggregations of inputs) bear consistent association with one another
2. The Allen elasticities grossly overstate or understate the degree of association between inputs
3. The Allen elasticities appear informative (i.e., satisfy the "significance test") when there is ambiguity concerning the association between the inputs

We will use these criteria to extract from our empirical findings general conclusions on the effects of the following on the descriptions of the technology that would be obtained using a neoclassical cost function: the features of the technology, the definition of the inputs (and the associated factor price indexes), and the presence of constraints on residual discharges.

## 2. *Experimental Design and Estimation*

Our data consist of repeated solutions to the cost-minimizing linear programming process models for each of the three steelmaking furnaces described in the previous section. These samples are composed of two types of solutions for each plant: (1) the optimal solutions in response to alternative specified values for each of the factor prices; and (2) the optimal solutions when constraints on the emissions of residuals are varied along with factor prices.[24] The solutions associated with alternative specified values for the

[24] The input prices are set as multiples of the 1973 levels. These multiples are given as follows:

| Input | Low (L) | High (H) |
|---|---|---|
| Natural gas | 0.27 | 1.73 |
| Coal | 0.27 | 1.73 |
| Fuel oil | 0.27 | 1.73 |
| Iron ore | 0.67 | 1.33 |
| Scrap | 0.22 | 1.78 |
| Labor | 0.59 | 1.41 |
| All other operating inputs | 0.50 | 1.50 |
| Maintenance | 0.59 | 1.41 |
| Pollution abatement capital | 0.50 | 1.50 |

factor prices were derived by varying each price individually from a base level (the 1973 values) to a low and a high value. These limits were defined on the basis of two considerations: (1) the monthly variation in the comparable wholesale price index for the factor from 1967 to 1975; and (2) the potential for bias in approximating the piecewise-linear cost surface due to what Griffin (1978) refers to as the nondifferentiability of the production surface. We also included solutions with all factors at their low and high prices. Thus, we have twenty-one solutions for each furnace (BOF, OH, and ARC) as a result of price variation alone.

Constraints on atmospheric and waterborne residuals were each varied as a unit (because of the physical interdependencies between members in each class) over low, medium, and high levels of restrictions. These levels are defined in terms of increments over the minimum technically feasible emission levels. Moreover, they were set uniformly for all three plants to assure comparability among the constraints each faced. Equations (2a) through (2c) define the levels for the constraints.

$$C_{Lj} = TM_j + 0.70 \, (D_{BOFj} - TM_j) \tag{2a}$$

$$C_{Mj} = TM_j + 0.30 \, (D_{BOFj} - TM_j) \tag{2b}$$

$$C_{Hj} = TM_j \tag{2c}$$

where  $C_{kj}$ is constraint at level $k$ ($k = L, M, H$) for discharges into the air ($A$) or water ($W$), $j = A, W$

$TM_j$ is minimum technically feasible discharge level for $j$, $j = A, W$

$D_{BOFj}$ is discharge level of the BOF plant (the dirtiest technology) to receptacle $j$

The intermediate discharge constraint corresponds approximately to the 1977 BPTCA (Best Practicable Technology Currently Available) and the high constraint to the 1983 BATEA (Best Available Technology Economically Achievable). These constraint levels were considered for atmospheric and waterborne residuals individually for each of three price levels (base, low, and high) for all of the factors, thereby providing eighteen additional solutions.

Each solution for each furnace type reports the optimal expenditures on each of the nine factors, given specified factor prices and levels of environmental constraints. Within each of our defined factors there are often subcategories (coal is indexed by sulfur and ash content, iron ore by Fe and sulfur contents as well as size, etc.). Each of these subcategories can, in principle, have a different price. Since the prices of these subcategories of a given factor class all vary by the same proportion, any one of their prices can be selected

**Table 7.1**    The Outline of Factor Aggregations

| Aggregation No. | Number of distinct factors | Number of aggregates | Composition of aggregates[a] |
|---|---|---|---|
| 1 | 7 | 2 | AF11 = coal and iron ore; AF21 = fuel oil and natural gas |
| 2 | 6 | 2 | AF12 = coal, iron ore and scrap; AF22 = fuel oil and natural gas |
| 3 | 5 | 2 | AF13 = maintenance, coal, iron ore and scrap AF23 = fuel oil and natural gas |
| 4 | 4 | 1 | AF14 = maintenance, coal, iron ore, scrap, fuel oil and natural gas |

[a] AFij designates the ith aggregated factor for the jth aggregation scheme.

as an index of the price for that class without affecting the estimates of sub-stitution prospects.[25]

Our evaluation of the neoclassical model will consider five alternative summaries of these solutions for each furnace type. The summaries corre-spond to the disaggregated or benchmark case where each of the nine factors are identified, and four different aggregations of the same solutions are de-fined to correspond to the manner in which the data from these solutions might be available in practice. The specific features of these aggregations are defined in table 7.1. Aggregation 1 corresponds to a case in which ma-terials inputs are differentiated into fuels (fuel oil and natural gas), virgin materials (metallurgical coal and iron ore), and recycled materials (scrap). In the second aggregation, the distinction between virgin and recycled ma-terials is dropped. The third aggregation illustrates the effect of confounding the materials aggregate with maintenance inputs and the last enlarges this materials aggregate by including fuels. In contrast to the original definitions of our factors, each of these aggregations introduces problems with mea-surement of the relevant price index. Since the prices of the components of these aggregates do not change by the same proportion, it is important to examine the effects of a selected price index on the performance of a neo-classical cost function.

Our basic neoclassical model is a cost function. More specifically, we limit our analysis to the properties of the most popular of the currently available flexible functional forms—the translog function.[26] Since all iron and steel

[25] For our empirical work we used scale prices so that the price of each input at the base level was unity and the low and high expressed as multiples of the base. See footnote 24 for the specific values of these multiples.

We also consider quantity weighted prices for each input category as one potential incorrect price index. As one might expect, the results for this case are substantially different from those reported here. These differences are too diverse to summarize in this paper.

[26] Recent papers by Wales (1977) and Blackorby, Primont, and Russell (1978) (chapter 8) consider the advantages and disadvantages of alternative flexible forms. Several forms, notably

outputs are held fixed, this function is a quadratic specification in the logs of the relevant factor prices. Following conventional practice, we estimate the parameters of the function using models composed of alternative sets of restricted cost share equations. Equation (3) is an example of one of these equations.[27]

$$\frac{P_i X_i}{C} = \alpha_i + \sum_{j=1}^{n} \beta_{ij} \ln P_j + \epsilon_i \tag{3}$$

where  $P_i$  is price of the $i$th factor input

$X_i$  is optimal level of use of the $i$th factor input

$C$  is total variable cost $\left( \text{i.e., } C = \sum_{i=1}^{n} P_i X_i \right)$

$n$  is total number of factor inputs in each model

$\epsilon_i$  is error for the $i$th equation

Each of these systems of cost share equations was estimated with Zellner's (1962) seemingly unrelated regressions estimator subject to linear homogeneity and symmetry restrictions.[28] Two different price indexes were con-

---

the generalized Box-Cox, seem to offer advantages over the translog. However, the translog remains the most popular format, and forthcoming work by by Griffin (1982) suggests that the differences in approximating cost functions with pseudodata (using the Russell–Vaughan, 1976, model) are not pronounced. Indeed, he concludes that the translog is likely to be preferred.

[27] It should be noted that the errors ($\epsilon_i$'s) for each cost-share equation arise because of the approximation process and are *not* due to any inherent stochastic elements in the data. Each aggregation of the factor inputs yields a different number of cost-share equations for estimation. The most detailed system, our benchmark case, is a system of eight-share equations. The number of equations estimated is always one less than the number of distinct factors identified in table 7.1. The cost share for the factor "all other operating inputs" is omitted in the estimation of all models.

[28] The majority of applications using systems of cost-share equations to estimate a translog model have relied upon an iterative version of the restricted Zellner estimator (see Berndt et al., 1974, for further discussion). This preference is based on the finding that iterative application of the Zellner estimator yields estimates numerically equivalent to the maximum likelihood estimates.

Unfortunately in our case the computational costs of such an iterative estimator prevented its application to the models with a large number of factor inputs. Theory suggests that selecting the one-step version of the Zellner estimator can lead to less efficient estimates and may result in the estimates being sensitive to the cost-share equation that was omitted. We have adopted a compromise solution to accommodate these computational constraints which called for: (a) adopting the iterative estimator with estimates based on all the translog price aggregations in order to give maximum advantage to the estimation of the price indexes; (b) application of the one-step Zellner estimator for the largest models (the benchmark cases); and (c) use of the one-step estimator for the share-weighted aggregates with selective comparisons of the implications of this choice. That is, we estimated all four aggregations for the OH furnace using both the one-step and the iterative Zellner estimators for the case of share-weighted prices. Our comparisons indicate very marginal changes in the coefficient estimates, largely in the fourth decimal place and some slight reduction in the $t$-ratios for the one-step estimated coefficients (the latter being due to a difference in the degrees of freedom adjustment used with the program to calculate the one-step estimator). Since the changes would not be large enough to change our analysis of the estimated elasticities of substitution, we concluded that the compromises required by computational costs were unlikely to impinge upon our further findings.

sidered for each of the aggregations. The first is a simple share-weighted average of the prices for the factors in each aggregate. Equation (4) provides an example of this method for the case where two factors are aggregated.[29]

$$P_{Ai} = W_{1i}P_{1i} + W_{2i}P_{2i} \qquad (4)$$

where $P_{ji}$ is price of the $i$th factor for $j$th solution ($j = 1,2$)

$P_{Ai}$ is price index for the aggregate of goods 1 and 2 for the $i$th solution

$W_{ji}$ is $\dfrac{P_{ji}X_{ji}}{\displaystyle\sum_{j=1}^{2} P_{ji}X_{ji}}$

$X_{ji}$ is optimal quantity of the $j$th factor for the $i$th solution

The second approach assumes that the price index can be represented by the translog unit cost function that would underlie a linear homogeneous subfunction for the aggregate. Diewert (1976) has shown that the Tornqvist approximation to the Divisia index would be an exact price index for this case. Equation (5) provides the translog price index comparable to the two-factor example given in equation (4).

$$\ln P_{Ai} = \alpha_i + \sum_{j=1}^{2} \beta_j \ln P_{ji} + \tfrac{1}{2} \sum_{j=1}^{2} \sum_{k=1}^{2} \gamma_{jk} \ln P_{ji} \ln P_{ki} \qquad (5)$$

The parameters of this index (except the scale parameter, $\alpha_i$) can be estimated using cost-share equations. In this case the shares relate to the cost of each component relative to the full costs of the aggregate (see Fuss, 1977, or Pindyck, 1979, as examples). Once again the parameters in these share equations are estimated subject to the restrictions of linear homogeneity in prices and symmetry.

To summarize, four factors differentiate our empirical results. They are the technology used in generating the sample, the form of the materials inputs (i.e., their level of aggregation), the sample composition (constrained or unconstrained cost-minimizing solutions), and the index used to measure the price of each of the aggregated factors. All the possible variations on each of these features were considered in appraising the performance of the translog form of the neoclassical cost function as a method for estimating the substitution possibilities in an engineering technology.

We begin our analysis by comparing the estimated elasticities of substitution under the best circumstances, our benchmark case, with what is known

[29] Fuss (1977) describes this method as a Pasche value-weighted index. It is frequently used in the construction of price and quantity indexes for both Canadian and U.S. data series.

of the features of the underlying technology for each type of steelmaking furnace. With this information, it is possible to compare the findings for this benchmark case with the estimates from the various aggregates and price indexes we have considered.

## 3. Neoclassical Models Applied to the Benchmark Samples

Tables 7.2 through 7.4 present the estimated Allen elasticities of substitution based on the application of the translog cost function (using cost-share equations) to the cost-minimizing solutions for each steelmaking furnace.[30] Only the "informative" estimates are reported in each table. The dashes represent those cases where the absolute magnitude of the ratio of the estimated elasticity to estimated asymptotic standard error was less than two.[31] Our engineering description of the three steelmaking technologies would lead to judgments that the ARC furnace was the least able to substitute among materials, the OH was the most able, and the BOF of intermediate ability.

---

[30] The Allen partial elasticities of substitution for a translog cost function are given as:

$$\sigma_{ij} = [\beta_{ij} + S_i S_j]/S_i S_j$$

where $\beta_{ij}$ is the parameter for ln $P_j$ in the $i$th cost share equation [see equation (3) in the text]

$S_i$ is cost share for the $i$th factor

All estimates were evaluated at the mean cost shares for the sample. This procedure corresponds to most conventional practices (see Moroney and Toevs, 1977; Humphrey and Moroney, 1975; Atkinson and Halvorsen, 1976; Smith, 1978; and Halvorsen, 1977 as examples). There are, of course, cases where these elasticities were calculated for specific observations, either years (Berndt and Wood, 1975) or countries in a cross-sectional sample (Griffin and Gregory, 1976 and Pindyck, 1979).

Our objective is to judge the ability of neoclassical methods to represent substitution possibilities in general, so the mean cost shares are adopted as indicative of conventional practice. It is certainly reasonable to expect that extensions to our analysis will consider the differential fit at each of the sampled points.

This issue becomes especially important for the samples composed of unconstrained cost-minimizing solutions.

[31] The asymptotic variance for $\hat{\sigma}_{ij}$ is defined as

$$\text{var}\,(\hat{\sigma}_{ij}) = \frac{\text{var}\,(\hat{\beta}_{ij})}{(S_i S_j)^2}$$

$S_i$ and $S_j$ are evaluated at the mean cost shares corresponding to the point where the $\hat{\sigma}_{ij}$ are evaluated. This estimate corresponds to conventional practice (see Binswanger, 1974 for an example).

There is an important distinction between our application and the use of this asymptotic test statistic in the literature. Our sample is not affected by random errors. One must maintain that the approximation errors are stochastic in order to formally interpret the test criterion as a "significance test." While this assumption may itself be subject to question, the verdict on it is not crucial to our analysis. Our objective is to mimic conventional practices in applying neoclassical models to production data derived from engineering process models.

**Table 7.2.** Informative Allen Partial Elasticities of Substitution: ARC Furnace, Unconstrained Residual Discharges, Nine-Factor Benchmark Case

| Inputs | Maint. | Capital | Coal | Gas | Oil | Ore | Scrap | Labor | Other |
|---|---|---|---|---|---|---|---|---|---|
| Maint. | −0.4264 | — | — | — | — | — | 0.0527 | — | — |
| Capital | | −1134.4 | — | — | — | — | — | — | 11.9182 |
| Coal | | | −14.4 | — | — | — | — | — | — |
| Gas | | | | −39.608 | 28.925 | — | — | — | — |
| Oil | | | | | −22.284 | — | — | — | — |
| Ore | | | | | | −10.033 | — | — | — |
| Scrap | | | | | | | — | 0.2851 | 0.6244 |
| Labor | | | | | | | | −0.6739 | — |
| Other | | | | | | | | | — |

**Table 7.3.** Informative Allen Partial Elasticities of Substitution: BOF Furnace, Unconstrained Residual Discharges, Nine-Factor Benchmark Case

| Inputs | Maint. | Capital | Coal | Gas | Oil | Ore | Scrap | Labor | Other |
|---|---|---|---|---|---|---|---|---|---|
| Maint. | −0.3030 | — | — | — | — | 0.2149 | — | — | — |
| Capital | | −205.71 | −2.3151 | 305.5 | — | 4.9354 | 6.7345 | −3.2972 | 6.6085 |
| Coal | | | −2.2626 | — | 19.1371 | 0.7679 | 1.1381 | −0.2865 | 0.2620 |
| Gas | | | | −31173.0 | — | — | — | — | — |
| Oil | | | | | −415.84 | — | — | — | — |
| Ore | | | | | | −1.1098 | 0.9112 | 0.3346 | — |
| Scrap | | | | | | | −17.248 | — | — |
| Labor | | | | | | | | −0.3758 | — |
| Other | | | | | | | | | — |

A detailed judgment on the ability of neoclassical models to represent these technologies requires at least two types of comparisons. The first of these is an informal overview of the estimated elasticities for each furnace type relating the findings to known features of each technology. While this review may be informative, it involves considerable judgment. Accordingly, we also compare the sign and magnitude of the estimated Allen elasticities with the derived arc elasticities.

Turning to the first of these evaluations and to the ARC furnace, the neoclassical results do mimic the technology rather closely. Excluding the cases involving substitution with the factor of other operating inputs (designated "other" in the tables) where it is difficult to evaluate the effects of price changes, only three elasticities would be judged as "informative." These are the substitutions between: maintenance and scrap, scrap and labor, and natural gas and fuel oil. The last of these results suggests a high degree of substitution between fuel oil and natural gas. This finding is completely consistent with the engineering features of the ARC plant. The plant includes fossil fuel-fired steam-generating electric turbines. While these turbines are identified by the fuel used, including purchased fuel oil or natural gas, and when relevant, by-product coke oven gases, sludge, forerunnings, and tar, the ARC furnace does not generate by-product fuels, so the primary fuels available for its electricity (an important intermediate product in ARC production activities) are fuel oil and natural gas. The columns representing the turbines for these fuels indicate comparable heat contents (in terms of Btus/lb) for these fuels and thus comparable performance in the unconstrained solutions for the two factors. Accordingly, the model should suggest a very high degree of substitution between them as a direct result of their respective roles in electricity generation.

The scrap-maintenance and scrap-labor substitutions are quite low and most likely reflect the changes in labor and maintenance inputs that are required by different types of scrap inputs (e.g., No. 1 heavy melting, No. 1 factory bundles shredded, or No. 2 bundles of scrap).

The second furnace, BOF, also provides equally plausible estimated Allen elasticities of substitution. One should recall, however, the importance of by-product fuels in this technology. The coke oven gases, sludge, forerunnings, and tar (as well as other recoverable by-products) that are not available with the ARC technology are present with the BOF furnace to a large degree. This is because of coking and blast furnace activities in a BOF plant (see figure 7.2). The estimated substitution elasticities in the capital (by-product recovery capital) and coal rows of table 7.3 result from the uses of coal and residual treatment equipment to recover by-products under a strictly cost-minimizing criterion. Thus, the two factors are seen as complements. Capital and natural gas are highly substitutable because capacity in treatment equipment enables the coke oven gases and other fuels to displace the purchased sources of heat

**Table 7.4.** Informative Allen Partial Elasticities of Substitution OH Furnace, Unconstrained Residual Discharges, Nine-Factor Case

| Inputs | Maint. | Capital | Coal | Gas | Oil | Ore | Scrap | Labor | Other |
|---|---|---|---|---|---|---|---|---|---|
| Maint. | −0.2681 | | | | | 0.2166 | | | |
| Capital | | −379.26 | −3.9804 | −82.856 | −34.484 | 7.6487 | | −4.8003 | 14.7329 |
| Coal | | | −3.321 | 6.7856 | 7.9171 | 0.4426 | 1.8918 | −0.1887 | |
| Gas | | | | −259.94 | | | | | |
| Oil | | | | | −85.586 | | | | |
| Ore | | | | | | −2.0378 | 2.8356 | 0.2397 | |
| Scrap | | | | | | | −12.559 | 0.4425 | |
| Labor | | | | | | | | −0.3505 | |
| Other | | | | | | | | | 0.3117 |

**Table 7.5.** Derived Arc Elasticities of Substitution for the ARC Furnace[a]

| Inputs | | Maint. | Capital | Coal | Gas | Oil | Ore | Scrap | Labor | Other |
|---|---|---|---|---|---|---|---|---|---|---|
| Maint. | L | 0.152 | | | | 0.0112 | | | | 0.0 |
| | H | −0.115 | | | | 0.0 | | | | −0.0 |
| Capital | L | 0.589 | 1.283 | | | −11.0 | | | | 0.0 |
| | H | 0.107 | −0.448 | | | 0.3 | | | | 21.728 |
| Coal | L | −0.0 | 0.1 | 0.00002 | | −0.0 | | | | −0.106 |
| | H | 0.0 | −0.0 | −0.340 | | 0.0 | −0.152 | 0.025 | −0.089 | 0.0 |
| Gas | L | −0.0 | 0.452 | 0.0 | 80.901 | 71 | | | | −0.0 |
| | H | 429.488 | −5.7 × 10^8 | −1371 | 147 | 2.2 × 10^9 | −615 | 103 | −359 | −428 |
| Oil | L | −0.0 | 1.365 | 0.0 | 0.0 | | 0.0 | −0.0 | 0.0 | 0.0 |
| | H | 0.0 | −0.979 | 0.0 | 0.0 | | −0.0 | 0.0 | −0.0 | −0.0 |
| Ore | L | −0.0 | −1.587 | 0.0 | 0.0 | −0.0 | 0.0 | 0.0 | 0.0 | 0.0 |
| | H | 0.0 | | −0.0 | 0.0 | 11.112 | −0.0 | −0.0 | −0.0 | −0.0 |
| Scrap | L | −0.0 | 0.077 | 0.0 | 0.0 | −0.0 | 28.849 | | 0.0 | 0.0 |
| | H | 2.279 | −0.235 | 28.661 | 0.0 | 0.0 | 0.0 | | 3.752 | 12.853 |
| Labor | L | −0.0 | 0.218 | 0.0 | 0.0 | −0.0 | −0.0 | −0.0 | 0.0 | 0.0 |
| | H | 0.0 | −0.157 | −0.0 | 0.0 | 0.0 | −0.0 | 0.0 | −0.0 | −0.0 |
| Other | L | −0.0 | 0.237 | 0.0 | 0.0 | −0.0 | 0.0 | 0.0 | 0.0 | 0.0 |
| | H | 0.128 | 28.177 | −0.0 | 0.0 | 0.394 | −0.0 | 0.0 | −0.0 | −0.0 |

[a] L Designates evaluated at factor's low price and H at the factor's high price.

for electricity generation. The same explanation would hold for the fuel oil–coal substitution.

The by-product recovery capital also recovers mill scale, ore fines, and flue dust. As a result, this equipment provides the mechanism for substituting recycled sources of iron for virgin sources. Ore-scrap and coal-scrap substitution arise from the furnace's limited ability to accommodate different steelmaking practices (in terms of hot to cold metal ratios). Similar explanations can be offered for each of the remaining elasticities that are consistent with what is embedded in the technology matrix of the model.

Unfortunately, the neoclassical estimates are not as consistent with the underlying technology for the open hearth furnace. This technology was described as the one most capable of accommodating substitution and thus these findings seem contradictory. However, it is important to distinguish potential for substitution from clarity in the input associations. Among the most visible of these apparent contradictions is the complementarity between residual treatment capital and fuel oil (or natural gas). We know from the engineering relations that this capital is similar to that employed by the BOF furnace (namely, to recover by-product fuels that will substitute for purchased fuels in electric power generation and other activities). There is, however, an important distinction. The range of activities affected by these by-product fuels now includes the steelmaking furnace, since the OH furnace permits supplementary heat to be utilized in the refining process. This heat can be provided through the use of these recovery products. Thus, there is a two-way causation. The steelmaking practice adopted affects the by-product heat that is available by influencing the hot metal produced. However, the more heat used in the OH steelmaking furnace, the less the need for hot metal. When these considerations are joined with other uses of the treatment capital (e.g., for recovery of substitutes for virgin ore sources), it is difficult to hypothesize *a priori* the appropriate relation between capital and the purchased fuels, and thus we have an explanation for the apparent anomalies with the OH estimates. All other informative estimates are consistent in sign with those for the BOF furnace and seem in reasonable proximity to the features of the underlying technology.

The second component of our comparison is an evaluation of the relationship between our derived arc elasticities and the estimated Allen elasticities. Here it should be acknowledged at the outset that the comparison is *not* between the true value of a parameter and the estimate. It is a matter of judging the consistency of one approximation with another. Since the process models do not embody substitution effects comparable to those maintained to be present in neoclassical models, any comparison will be approximate.

Tables 7.5, 7.6, and 7.7 provide the derived arc elasticities for each furnace. Each pair of inputs has four estimated elasticities corresponding to the low and high values of each factor's price within the substitution pair, while all

**Table 7.6.** Derived Arc Elasticities of Substitution for the BOF Furnace[a]

| Inputs | | Maint. | Capital | Coal | Gas | Oil | Ore | Scrap | Labor | Other |
|---|---|---|---|---|---|---|---|---|---|---|
| Maint. | L | | 0.674 | -0.209 | 0.0 | 0.0 | 0.4618 | 0.0 | -0.2020 | 0.1254 |
| | H | | -0.0 | -0.0 | 0.0 | 0.0 | 0.0 | -0.0 | 0.0 | 0.0 |
| Capital | L | -1.321 | | -1.105 | 0.0 | -885.1 | 4.4459 | 0.0 | -1.506 | 6.887 |
| | H | 9.966 | | -14.112 | 0.0 | 12214.0 | 28.7006 | -0.0 | -9.114 | 102.211 |
| Coal | L | -0.6412 | -6.025 | | 0.0 | -33.036 | 2.2647 | 3.8358 | -1.295 | -0.0383 |
| | H | 0.1075 | -4.99 | | 0.0 | 19.740 | 0.0655 | -0.0 | -0.2226 | 0.2465 |
| Gas | L | -1 | 44 | 65 | | 0.0 | 4 | 0.0 | 6 | 0 |
| | H | 0 | -4368 | -249 | | -1343 | 382 | -1683 | 184 | -798 |
| Oil | L | -0.0 | 4 | 15 | 0.0 | | 0.0 | 0.0 | 1 | 1 |
| | H | 0.0 | -4368 | -249 | 0.0 | | 382 | -1683 | 184 | -798 |
| Ore | L | 0.1286 | 15.680 | 0.1734 | 0.0 | 0.0 | | 3.0138 | 0.2631 | -0.2164 |
| | H | 0.1499 | 5.526 | 0.2326 | 0.0 | 24.448 | | -0.0 | 0.2290 | -0.1193 |
| Scrap | L | 0.1507 | 47.796 | 0.8583 | 0.0 | 0.0 | 0.1876 | | 0.3605 | -0.9787 |
| | H | 0.1674 | 16.478 | 1.4330 | 0.0 | 0.0 | 1.596 | | 0.4459 | -0.1650 |
| Labor | L | -0.1739 | -5.085 | -0.2604 | 0.0 | -29.040 | 0.5805 | 0.0 | | 0.1368 |
| | H | -0.0007 | -5.718 | -0.6768 | 0.0 | 22.354 | 0.0525 | -0.0 | | 0.1501 |
| Other | L | -0.0834 | 22.095 | 0.2606 | 0.0 | 0.0 | -0.0535 | 0.0 | -0.0251 | |
| | H | 0.1181 | 8.167 | 0.0314 | 0.0 | 31.184 | -0.0867 | -0.0 | 0.0286 | |

[a] L Designates evaluated at factor's low price and H at the factor's high price.

other factors were held at their base prices. In each row the identified factor's price changes first to the low value and then to the high. Thus, for example, the derived arc elasticities of substitution between maintenance and capital for the ARC furnace were 0.152, 0.115, 0.589, and 0.107. The first two correspond to the elasticities for the low and high prices of maintenance and the second two to the low and high for capital.

A review of these tables suggests that the informational value of these derived arc elasticities as a guide to each furnace's technology may not be great. Two factors may bear quite different paired associations at the various factor prices considered. Equally important, the magnitudes of the elasticities vary rather substantially. These factors may explain the large number of noninformative estimates with the translog models. Nonetheless, there is one important area of general agreement for two of the furnaces. In terms of our error taxonomy, the ARC and BOF furnaces are not subject to false-association errors. The primary discrepancies arise for these furnaces in judging where the inputs are neither substitutes nor complements (nonassociation) and in gauging the order of magnitude of that association. Moreover, with the ARC furnace, these latter errors are all associated with the translog estimates judged to be noninformative. The same observation is true for the BOF furnace, with two exceptions—capital and natural gas, and coal and fuel oil. With these exceptions the translog estimates are judged noninformative and the derived arc elasticities seem to suggest some association may exist.[32]

The open hearth furnace offers the least correspondence between the derived arc and the translog estimates of the elasticities of substitution. Here two false association errors (for coal and ore, and ore and labor) are apparent if the derived arc elasticities are compared with those estimated using the translog model. The balance of the errors arise with translog estimates judged to be noninformative.

Overall, these comparisons suggest a few broad observations on the use of neoclassical cost functions (as represented by the translog cost function model) to estimate the production technology under "ideal' conditions (in terms of the degree of input aggregation). The neoclassical models perform remarkably well when the evaluation is based on estimates after some "significance" test. They generally seem to identify the nature of the associations between inputs correctly. Where the association between two inputs is unclear, they would lead to noninformative estimates.

Unfortunately, we can say much less about the magnitude of the measured

---

[32] This conclusion may not be entirely warranted for the translog model since the comparison is between a single point estimate of $\sigma_{ij}$ from the neoclassical model (i.e., at the mean cost shares) versus the derived arc elasticities at each observation. Since both the translog's estimate of $\sigma_{ij}$ and the estimated standard error will change with the values for $S_i$ and $S_j$, the verdict may well be different with a more complete comparison.

**Table 7.7.** Derived Arc Elasticities of Substitution for the OH Furnace[a]

| Inputs | | Maint. | Capital | Coal | Gas | Oil | Ore | Scrap | Labor | Other |
|---|---|---|---|---|---|---|---|---|---|---|
| Maint. | L | | $-0.208$ | $-0.0701$ | $21.147$ | $2.655$ | $0.274$ | $-0.0$ | $-0.123$ | $-0.1208$ |
| | H | | $-0.001$ | $0.0049$ | $0.917$ | $-0.010$ | $0.0$ | $0.0$ | $-0.0004$ | $-0.005$ |
| Capital | L | $-1.358$ | | $-4.203$ | $-20$ | $-28.9$ | $11.759$ | $-0.0$ | $-3.090$ | $26.884$ |
| | H | $-0.0$ | | $0.001$ | $0.0$ | $-0.0$ | $-0.0$ | $0.0$ | $-0.001$ | $0.0$ |
| Coal | L | $-0.4424$ | $-34.560$ | | $38.615$ | $4.401$ | $0.7489$ | $10.619$ | $-1.715$ | $-0.344$ |
| | H | $0.1623$ | $-0.458$ | | $-10.343$ | $10.862$ | $-0.638$ | $2.545$ | $-0.252$ | $0.122$ |
| Gas | L | $-0.0$ | $-288$ | $12$ | | $58$ | $2$ | $-0.0$ | $1$ | $5$ |
| | H | $3.7 \times 10^6$ | $4.8 \times 10^6$ | $-1.9 \times 10^7$ | | $4.5 \times 10^7$ | $-10296$ | $1187$ | $2.5 \times 10^6$ | $3.1 \times 10^7$ |
| Oil | L | $-0.0$ | $-100$ | $-11.146$ | $111$ | | $0.667$ | $-0.0$ | $0.72$ | $2.2$ |
| | H | $-13311$ | $-4 \times 10^5$ | $485$ | $7 \times 10^9$ | | $179$ | $1187$ | $-343$ | $-9375$ |
| Ore | L | $0.0350$ | $-0.307$ | $-0.352$ | $11.749$ | $0.153$ | | $7.144$ | $-0.224$ | $0.084$ |
| | H | $-0.0785$ | $29.731$ | $-1.327$ | $6.071$ | $0.447$ | | $8.247$ | $-0.068$ | $-0.454$ |
| Scrap | L | $0.255$ | $2.652$ | $2.645$ | $-9.76$ | $0.552$ | $4.596$ | | $0.466$ | $-0.147$ |
| | H | $0.646$ | $8.286$ | $8.340$ | $-109.63$ | $-5.215$ | $10.467$ | | $2.520$ | $1.488$ |
| Labor | L | $-0.175$ | $-23.381$ | $-0.940$ | $4.233$ | $-0.835$ | $-0.666$ | $6.510$ | | $0.457$ |
| | H | $-0.003$ | $-0.001$ | $0.002$ | $0.459$ | $-0.004$ | $-0.0$ | $0.0$ | | $-0.002$ |
| Other | L | $-0.544$ | $-0.080$ | $0.276$ | $62.828$ | $4.424$ | $0.001$ | $-0.0$ | $-0.037$ | |
| | H | $0.131$ | $37.907$ | $0.110$ | $2.603$ | $1.373$ | $-0.248$ | $0.0$ | $0.064$ | |

[a] L Designates evaluated at factor's low price and H at the factor's high price.

elasticities. With the exception of the estimates identified above, the translog model seems to err on the conservative side of the association, by understating the magnitude of the association (whether it be one of substitution or complementarity). Finally, it would seem that the greatest errors occur in gauging associations between inputs involved in complex intermediate output relationships. The most notable examples would be those that occur with by-product recovery capital, coal, and purchased fuels.

The next two sections of this chapter compare these benchmark results with those derived with increasing levels of input aggregation.

## 4. Implications of Aggregation for Perceived Substitution: The Unconstrained Solutions

Tables 7.8 through 7.10 trace the impact of aggregation on the perceived elasticities of substitution for each furnace and price index. These tables focus on the elasticities for the materials inputs as the definition expands from the most disaggregated, nine-factor case (our benchmark estimates) to progressively more expansive definitions, to the case where the aggregate includes all materials inputs (aggregate 4). Following the practices we defined at the outset, only the elasticities that would be judged "informative" are reported.

What is of primary interest in the comparisons across aggregation is the impact of input definition on the perceived input substitution and the extent to which the results are affected by the aggregate price index selected. Considering the most and the least flexible technologies (OH and ARC furnaces), we see that progressive input aggregation tends to reduce the neoclassical model's ability to precisely identify input relationships. That is, the number of noninformative estimates increases. A casual review of the cases seems to support the use of neoclassical models since many of the noninformative aggregate estimates arise where there are conflicts in the associations (mixtures of substitution and complementarity) between each constituent of the aggregate and the relevant factor. This response is more clear-cut in the furnaces with a substantive number of informative elasticity estimates at the most disaggregated level (the OH and BOF furnaces) and less apparent with the ARC furnace.

There are, however, several cases where the estimated elasticities change in ways that bear no apparent relation to the underlying disaggregated elasticities. The substitution measured between capital and the maintenance-coal-ore-scrap aggregate using a translog price index with the OH furnace is one notable example. Accordingly, it is important to review all the changes in the estimates and classify any such discrepancies. This is the ob-

**Table 7.8.** Overview of Informative Allen Elasticities of Substitution Across Aggregations: Unconstrained ARC Furnace

| Inputs | $\sigma_{ij}$ | Aggregation 1 Share Agg. | Aggregation 1 TL Agg. | Aggregation 2 Share Agg. | Aggregation 2 TL Agg. | Aggregation 3 Share Agg. | Aggregation 3 TL Agg. | Aggregation 4 Share Agg. | Aggregation 4 TL Agg. |
|---|---|---|---|---|---|---|---|---|---|
| Coal-Ore | — | | | | | | | | |
| Oil-Gas | 28.92 | | | | | | | | |
| Scrap-Coal | — | — | 2.030 | | | | | | |
| Scrap-Ore | — | | | | | | | | |
| Scrap-Oil | — | 0.511 | 0.515 | | | | | | |
| Scrap-Gas | — | | | | | | | | |
| Maint.-Coal | — | — | — | | | | | | |
| Maint.-Ore | — | | | 0.174 | 0.185 | | | | |
| Maint.-Scrap | 0.0527 | | | | | | | | |
| Maint.-Oil | — | — | — | — | — | | | | |
| Maint.-Gas | — | | | | | | | | |
| Capital-Coal | — | — | — | — | — | | | | |
| Capital-Ore | — | | | | | 1.105 | 5.919 | | |
| Capital-Scrap | — | | | | | | | 1.102 | — |
| Capital-Maint. | — | | | | | | | | |
| Capital-Oil | — | — | — | — | — | — | — | | |
| Capital-Gas | — | | | | | | | | |
| Labor-Coal | — | | | 0.165 | 0.231 | | | | |
| Labor-Ore | — | | | | | 0.493 | — | | |
| Labor-Scrap | 0.2851 | | | | | | | 0.522 | 0.139 |
| Labor-Maint. | — | | | | | | | | |
| Labor-Oil | — | — | — | — | — | — | 21.363 | | |
| Labor-Gas | — | | | | | | | | |
| Coal-Oil | — | | | | | | | | |
| Coal-Gas | — | — | — | | | | | | |
| Ore-Oil | — | | | 0.265 | — | | | | |
| Ore-Gas | — | | | | | 0.522 | — | | |
| Scrap-Oil | — | | | | | | | | |
| Scrap-Gas | — | | | | | | | | |
| Maint.-Oil | — | | | | | | | | |
| Maint.-Gas | — | | | | | | | | |

[a] Share-weighted aggregate price index.
[b] Translog aggregate price index.

jective of our error typology. Using the three types of errors defined in section 1—false association, nonassociation, and false magnitude—it is possible to organize the information. It should, however, be recognized that these standards are not demanding of the neoclassical methodology. Our inherent inability to define the "true" values of the neoclassical elasticities prevents any precise quantitative appraisal of performance. Nonetheless, these criteria are broadly consistent with many of the uses of neoclassical estimates. Often the precise magnitudes of the elasticities are not as important as judging the nature of the input association and identifying whether it is "strong" or relatively "limited." Our standard is sufficient to meet these needs.

Table 7.11 summarizes the results of a complete review of all of the estimated elasticities over technology, aggregation scheme, and price index.

**Table 7.9.** Overview of Informative Allen Elasticities of Substitution Across Aggregations: Unconstrained BOF Furnace

| Inputs | $\sigma_{ij}$ | Aggregation 1 | | Aggregation 2 | | Aggregation 3 | | Aggregation 4 | |
|---|---|---|---|---|---|---|---|---|---|
| | | Share Agg. | TL Agg. | Share Agg. | TL Agg. | Share Agg. | TL Agg. | Share Agg. | TL Agg. |
| Coal-Ore | 0.768 | | | | | | | | |
| Oil-Gas | — | | | | | | | | |
| Scrap-Coal | 1.139 | 1.234 | — | | | | | | |
| Scrap-Ore | 0.911 | | | | | | | | |
| Scrap-Oil | — | — | — | | | | | | |
| Scrap-Gas | — | | | | | | | | |
| Maint.-Coal | — | — | — | | | | | | |
| Maint.-Ore | 0.215 | | | — | — | | | | |
| Maint.-Scrap | — | | | | | | | | |
| Maint.-Oil | — | — | — | — | — | | | | |
| Maint.-Gas | — | | | | | | | | |
| Capital-Coal | −2.315 | — | — | | | | | | |
| Capital-Ore | 4.935 | | | — | — | 1.751 | 386.942 | | |
| Capital-Scrap | 6.735 | | | | | | | 1.585 | — |
| Capital-Maint. | — | | | | | | | | |
| Capital-Oil | — | — | — | — | — | — | — | | |
| Capital-Gas | 305.5 | | | | | | | | |
| Labor-Coal | −0.287 | — | — | — | — | | | | |
| Labor-Ore | 0.335 | | | | | — | −144.4 | | |
| Labor-Scrap | — | | | | | | | — | — |
| Labor-Maint. | — | | | | | | | | |
| Labor-Oil | — | — | — | — | — | — | 1.245 | | |
| Labor-Gas | — | | | | | | | | |
| Coal-Oil | 19.137 | 10.502 | 14.029 | | | | | | |
| Coal-Gas | — | | | — | 16.483 | | | | |
| Ore-Oil | — | | | | | | | | |
| Ore-Gas | — | | | | | — | — | | |
| Scrap-Oil | — | | | | | | | | |
| Scrap-Gas | — | | | | | | | | |
| Maint.-Oil | — | | | | | | | | |
| Maint.-Gas | — | | | | | | | | |

[a] Share-weighted aggregate price index.
[b] Translog aggregate price index.

Several overall conclusions emerge. Our experimental evidence suggests that neoclassical cost functions applied to data consistent with cost minimization will not, as a rule, indicate a false association between inputs. That is, they will not lead to conclusions that two inputs are complements when they are, in fact substitutes. This finding holds for both rigid technologies and more flexible ones. Aggregation with either price index has no apparent effect on this property.

In addition, it seems that there is no advantage to using the superlative indexes (such as the translog aggregator function proposed by Diewert, 1976) with any of the aggregations or technologies we considered. If aggregation of the inputs is improper in an engineering sense, neither index does appre-

**Table 7.10.**  Overview of Informative Allen Elasticities of Substitution Across Aggregations: Unconstrained OH Furnace

| Inputs | $\sigma_{ij}$ | Aggregation 1 Share Agg. | Aggregation 1 TL Agg. | Aggregation 2 Share Agg. | Aggregation 2 TL Agg. | Aggregation 3 Share Agg. | Aggregation 3 TL Agg. | Aggregation 4 Share Agg. | Aggregation 4 TL Agg. |
|---|---|---|---|---|---|---|---|---|---|
| Coal-Ore | 0.443 | | | | | | | | |
| Oil-Gas | — | | | | | | | | |
| Scrap-Coal | 1.892 | 2.808 | 2.555 | | | | | | |
| Scrap-Ore | 2.836 | | | | | | | | |
| Scrap-Oil | — | — | — | | | | | | |
| Scrap-Gas | — | | | | | | | | |
| Maint.-Coal | — | — | — | | | | | | |
| Maint.-Ore | 0.217 | | | — | — | | | | |
| Maint.-Scrap | — | | | | | | | | |
| Maint.-Oil | — | — | — | — | — | | | | |
| Maint.-Gas | — | | | | | | | | |
| Capital-Coal | −3.980 | — | — | | | | | | |
| Capital-Ore | 7.649 | | | — | — | — | 273.6 | | |
| Capital-Scrap | — | | | | | | | — | — |
| Capital-Maint. | — | | | | | | | | |
| Capital-Oil | −34.3 | −38.9 | −78.8 | −37.3 | −88.2 | −37.7 | — | | |
| Capital-Gas | −82.8 | | | | | | | | |
| Labor-Coal | −0.189 | — | — | | | | | | |
| Labor-Ore | 0.240 | | | — | — | 0.273 | −18.9 | | |
| Labor-Scrap | 0.443 | | | | | | | 0.264 | — |
| Labor-Maint. | — | | | | | | | | |
| Labor-Oil | — | — | — | — | — | — | 1.075 | | |
| Labor-Gas | — | | | | | | | | |
| Coal-Oil | 7.917 | | | | | | | | |
| Coal-Gas | 6.786 | 3.802 | 3.033 | | | | | | |
| Ore-Oil | — | | | 2.093 | 2.508 | | | | |
| Ore-Gas | — | | | | | 1.428 | — | | |
| Scrap-Oil | — | | | | | | | | |
| Scrap-Gas | — | | | | | | | | |
| Maint.-Oil | — | | | | | | | | |
| Maint.-Gas | — | | | | | | | | |

[a] Share weighted aggregate price index.
[b] Translog aggregate price index.

ciably better in mitigating the distortions that result. While the mix of errors associated with share-weighted and translog price indexes is often different, the frequency and apparent magnitude of the errors are comparable.

The open hearth furnace seems to be least affected by the aggregation of the three steelmaking technologies. This technology is also the most flexible and may well be in closest correspondence to the smooth substitution features assumed in neoclassical models.

A review of the factor inputs involved in the errors of nonassociation and false magnitude suggests that four factors—capital, coal, and the two fuels (fuel oil and natural gas)—account for a substantial fraction of the errors in aggregation. Moreover, errors involving these factors are most likely to occur with the BOF and OH furnaces. One explanation for this finding may rest with the neoclassical model's inadequate treatment of intermediate products produced by the plant. In this case, the adoption of the treatment activities for airborne and waterborne pollution can lead to valuable by-products such as ammonia, phenol, coke oven gases, etc. These treatment activities involve what we have defined as pollution abatement capital. It is used by plants under certain configurations of factor prices regardless of constraints on discharges. Thus, coal may substitute for natural gas because the existence of a given level of abatement capital permits coke oven and blast furnace gases to substitute for natural gas as a heat source in both the steel-making furnace and in electricity generation.

The inputs involved in the errors are also those most likely to be affected by these by-product recovery activities. While this conclusion is somewhat conjectural, it is consistent with the Russell–Vaughan (1976) general discussion of by-product treatment in steelmaking.

Several qualifications to table 7.11 should also be noted. One reason why the ARC furnace appears better than either the BOF or the OH furnaces relates to the benchmark elasticity estimates. With the ARC furnace these are, in large measure, noninformative. Thus, there is little scope for confounding estimated aggregate substitution relations as a result of diversity in the substitution relations for factors within the aggregate relative to those outside it. This is not the case for either the BOF or OH technologies. In addition, the scope for such errors declines with progressive aggregation. Thus the lower frequency of errors with aggregation 4 (for all furnace types) relative to aggregation 2 is not necessarily a confirmation of aggregation 4. It reflects, in part, the diminished opportunities for conflicts.

A final observation concerning these findings relates to the effects of progressive aggregation on the perceived substitution possibilities between factors outside the aggregate. With both the BOF and OH furnaces, the neoclassical model fails to identify the capital-labor input association in all four aggregations, regardless of the price index utilized for the aggregated variables. On the other hand, the ARC furnace model performs very well, producing only a single nonassociation error between capital and scrap.

## 5. Constraints on Residuals Discharges and Perceived Substitution

We discuss here two aspects of the estimated Allen elasticities of substitution using mixed samples consisting of unconstrained cost-minimizing

**Table 7.11.** Errors in Perceived Substitution in Neoclassical Models Without Discharge Constraints[a]

| | Technology | | | | | |
|---|---|---|---|---|---|---|
| | ARC | | BOF | | OH | |
| Aggregation/Errors | Share Agg. | TL Agg. | Share Agg. | TL Agg. | Share Agg. | TL Agg. |
| 1. False-assoc. | None | None | None | None | None | None |
| Nonassoc. | Scrap-(Oil-gas)[b] | Scrap-(Coal-ore)[b]; Scrap-(Oil-gas)[b]; Capital-scrap[b] | Capital-scrap; Capital-(Oil-gas); Capital-labor | Capital-scrap[b]; Capital-(Oil-gas); Labor-maint.; Capital-labor | Capital-maint.[b]; Labor-scrap | Capital-maint.[b]; Labor-scrap; Labor-maint.; Capital-labor |
| False magnitude | None | None | None | None | None | None |
| 2. False-assoc. | None | None | None | None | None | None |
| Nonassoc. | (Coal-ore-scrap) | None | Capital-(Oil-gas); (Coal-ore-scrap)-(Oil-gas); Capital-labor | Capital-(Oil-gas); Capital-labor | Capital-labor | Capital-labor |
| False magnitude | None | None | None | None | None | None |
| 3. False-assoc. | None | None | None | None | None | None |
| Nonassoc. | Capital-(Maint.-coal-ore-scrap); Labor-(Maint.-coal-ore-scrap); (Maint.-coal-ore-scrap)-(Oil-gas) | Capital-(Maint.-coal-ore-scrap); Labor-(Oil-gas) | Capital-(Maint.-coal-ore-scrap); Labor-(Maint.-coal-ore-scrap); Capital-labor | Capital-(Maint.-coal-ore-scrap); Labor-(Maint.-coal-ore-scrap) | Labor-(Maint.-coal-ore-scrap); Capital-labor | Labor-(Maint.-coal-ore-scrap); Labor-(Oil-gas); (Maint.-coal-ore-scrap)-(Oil-gas) |
| False magnitude | None | None | None | None | None | Capital-(Maint.-coal-ore-scrap) |
| 4. False-assoc. | None | None | None | None | None | None |
| Nonassoc. | Capital-(Maint.-coal-ore-scrap-oil-gas); Labor-(Maint.-coal-ore-scrap-oil-gas) | Labor-(Maint.-coal-ore-scrap-oil-gas) | Capital-labor | Capital-labor; Capital-(Maint.-coal-ore-scrap-oil-gas) | Capital-labor; Labor-Maint.-coal-ore-scrap-oil-gas) | Capital-labor |
| False magnitude | None | None | None | None | None | None |

[a] The benchmark estimates used to determine the aggregation errors are drawn from a nine-factor model estimated from the twenty-one constrained observation sample.
[b] Indicates that the perceived aggregate relationship was consistent with the noninformative benchmark estimate. Thus, under a weaker criterion for judging informative estimates, these errors would not arise.

**Table 7.12.**  Informative Allen Partial Elasticities of Substitution: ARC Furnace, Constrained Residuals Discharges, Nine-Factor Case

| Inputs | Maint. | Capital | Coal | Gas | Oil | Ore | Scrap | Labor | Other |
|--------|--------|---------|------|-----|-----|-----|-------|-------|-------|
| Maint. | −0.3466 | — | — | — | — | — | 0.1712 | 0.2214 | — |
| Capital | | — | — | — | — | — | — | — | — |
| Coal | | | −10.438 | — | — | — | 1.4046 | — | — |
| Gas | | | | −39.555 | 20.948 | — | — | — | — |
| Oil | | | | | −22.722 | — | — | — | — |
| Ore | | | | | | −8.6705 | — | — | — |
| Scrap | | | | | | | −0.0712 | 0.2140 | 0.4457 |
| Labor | | | | | | | | −0.5923 | — |
| Other | | | | | | | | | |

solutions and those for cost minimization subject to discharge constraints. The first dimension relates to a comparison of the estimates based on mixed samples relative to those discussed in our benchmark case. Here the mixed sample estimates attempt to represent two distinct behavior patterns. Tables 7.12 through 7.14 report the estimated elasticities for the nine-factor case with each furnace.

Our results here are clear-cut. The introduction of the constrained solutions reduces the neoclassical model's ability to identify input relationships. There is a reduction in the number of informative estimates that seems to be concentrated in the BOF and OH furnaces and is largely associated with the capital input. The estimates for the ARC furnace are not greatly altered.

To understand this finding, it is necessary to reconsider the engineering features of the technology. Recall that capital refers to treatment equipment for the residuals generated in production activities. These activities can, as noted in the previous section, lead to usable by-products that serve as intermediate inputs in further production activities. Moreover, they substitute for purchased inputs (primarily fuels). We argued in the previous section that these activities were responsible for the perceived substitutions among a number of factor inputs, such as metallurgical coal and natural gas in the open

**Table 7.13.**  Informative Allen Partial Elasticities of Substitution: BOF Furnace, Constrained Residuals Discharges, Nine-Factor Case

| Inputs | Maint. | Capital | Coal | Gas | Oil | Ore | Scrap | Labor | Other |
|--------|--------|---------|------|-----|-----|-----|-------|-------|-------|
| Maint. | −0.3286 | — | — | — | — | — | — | — | — |
| Capital | | −197.06 | — | — | — | — | — | — | 6.1939 |
| Coal | | | −2.3808 | — | 19.243 | 0.6211 | 1.4978 | — | — |
| Gas | | | | −31754 | — | — | — | — | — |
| Oil | | | | | −454.13 | — | — | — | — |
| Ore | | | | | | −0.8646 | — | — | — |
| Scrap | | | | | | | −16.433 | — | — |
| Labor | | | | | | | | −0.4096 | — |
| Other | | | | | | | | | |

**Table 7.14.**  Informative Allen Partial Elasticities of Substitution: OH Furnace, Constrained Residuals Discharges, Nine-Factor Case

| Inputs | Maint. | Capital | Coal | Gas | Oil | Ore | Scrap | Labor | Other |
|---|---|---|---|---|---|---|---|---|---|
| Maint. | −0.3042 | — | — | — | — | — | — | — | — |
| Capital | | — | — | — | — | — | — | — | — |
| Coal | | | −3.2372 | — | 7.0547 | 0.3596 | 2.2199 | — | — |
| Gas | | | | −309.17 | — | — | — | — | — |
| Oil | | | | | −78.375 | — | — | — | — |
| Ore | | | | | | −1.9723 | 2.8635 | — | — |
| Scrap | | | | | | | −12.709 | 0.5372 | — |
| Labor | | | | | | | | −0.4495 | 0.2565 |
| Other | | | | | | | | | |

hearth and basic oxygen furnaces. Moreover, we found that input associations resulting from the role of these intermediate outputs tended to be confounded with aggregation.

Our present estimates using the mixed samples seem to reinforce the need to understand these intermediate outputs. Discharge constraints in the BOF and OH furnace induce the plants to utilize treatment equipment to a far greater extent than would be required by the value of the by-products these processes generate. Thus, the translog estimates suggest that substitution relations with this capital cannot be detected because the responses are not in conformity with unconstrained cost-minimizing solutions. The outputs of treated residuals can have values independent (by virtue of the imposed constraints) of the usable by-product fuels.

The second aspect of our results compares the effects of aggregation and discharge constraints on the estimated substitution elasticities by furnace and price index. The comparison, however, in this case is between the estimates with the mixed samples at each level of aggregation versus the benchmark estimates with the unconstrained samples. Table 7.15 repeats our summary of the results by type of error, furnace, input aggregation, and price index. Since both aggregation and constraints on discharges are reflected in these estimates, it is not surprising that clear patterns seem elusive.

Several general observations can be made. In these cases, false association errors arise with aggregations 2 through 4. They are associated with the ARC and OH furnaces using the share aggregation schemes. This finding contrasts with the results for the estimates based on samples with unconstrained solutions where neoclassical methods never resulted in false association errors.

It also seems that a substantial number of the remaining errors can be related to the role of treatment capital and those inputs yielding or substituting for the usable by-products produced with discharge treatment. However, there are a number of other errors present as well, so that this pattern does not seem as clear as with the unconstrained solutions.

Overall, we find that discharge constraints affect our estimates of substitution possibilities in a significant and disturbing way. In addition, for certain technologies they seem to increase the severity of the errors associated with aggregation of materials inputs.

## 6. Summary and Implications

Previous evaluations of the viability of neoclassical models for estimating the features of production technology have consistently maintained that the "true" technology is described by some smooth neoclassical production function.[33] As a result, they have focused attention on the effects of different types of error structures, approximation procedures, and estimation methods (direct or indirect) on how well the features of that technology can be measured. The analysis in this chapter began by questioning the maintained assumptions that the "true" technology is a smooth production function. We have begun with the premise that it is best considered an interrelated configuration of production activities or processes. Substitution in such a framework arises because of differences in the inputs used or the processes adopted to transform inputs into intermediate and/or final goods. It is generally not smooth, as would be hypothesized in a neoclassical framework. Therefore, neoclassical models must be considered as one of several means to compactly approximate its features.

Our investigation was motivated by the need to understand how substitution in production activities takes place. We observed at the outset that recent analyses of the role of exhaustible natural resources in simple economic growth models suggest that the assumed ability to substitute factor inputs at extreme factor ratios is important to the conclusions of the models. Thus, to evaluate whether neoclassical models are robust in their description of input substitution in these regions of input usage, we must consider the activities permitting that substitution and the ability of neoclassical models (as approximations) to accurately reflect their properties.

Our analysis was conducted in an experimental framework that used large-scale, cost-minimizing process analysis models for three different technologies for iron and steel production to evaluate the performance of neoclassical cost functions in describing these technologies. Our findings consider the effects of technological characteristics, input aggregation, and residual discharge constraints on the measured levels of substitution for the materials inputs in these technologies. While experimental analyses are always subject to the caveat that they are necessarily specific to the features of the experiments, several tentative conclusions can be derived from our work. They

---

[33] See Gapinski and Kumar (1974) and Gapinski (1973) as examples.

**Table 7.15.** Errors in Perceived Substitution in Neoclassical Models with Discharge Constraints[a]

Technology

| Aggregation/Errors | ARC — Share Agg. | ARC — TL Agg. | BOF — Share Agg. | BOF — TL Agg. | OH — Share Agg. | OH — TL Agg. |
|---|---|---|---|---|---|---|
| 1. False assoc. / Nonassoc. | None<br>Maint.-labor[b]<br>Scrap-(Oil-gas)<br>(Coal-ore)-(oil-gas)[b] | None<br>Maint.-labor[b]<br>Scrap-(Oil-gas)<br>Labor-(Oil-gas) | None<br>Maint.-labor[b]<br>Maint.-(Oil-gas)<br>Capital-scrap<br>Capital-(Oil-gas)<br>Capital-labor | None<br>Capital-scrap<br>Capital-labor<br>Capital-(Oil-gas) | None<br>Maint.-labor[b]<br>Capital-labor<br>Labor-scrap<br>Capital-(Oil-gas) | None<br>Maint.-labor[b]<br>Capital-labor<br>Capital-(Oil-gas)<br>Capital-scrap |
| False magnitude | None | None | None | None | None | None |
| 2. False assoc. | None<br>Maint.-(Coal-ore-scrap) | None | None | None | None | None |
| Nonassoc. | Maint.-(Oil-gas)<br>Labor-(Oil-gas)<br>Labor-(Coal-ore-scrap)[b]<br>(Coal-ore-scrap)-(Oil-gas)[b] | Labor-(Oil-gas) | Maint.-labor[b]<br>Capital-Labor<br>Maint.-(Oil-gas)<br>Labor-(Oil-gas)<br>Capital-(Oil-gas) | Maint.-labor<br>Maint.-(oil-gas)<br>Labor-(Oil-gas)<br>Capital-(Oil-gas)<br>Capital-labor | Maint.-labor[b]<br>Capital-Labor<br>Capital-(Oil-gas)<br>Labor-(Coal ore-scrap) | Capital-labor |
| False magnitude | None | None | None | None | None | None |
| 3. False assoc. | None | None | None | None | None | None |
| Nonassoc. | Labor-(Maint.-coal-ore-scrap) | Labor-(Maint.-coal-ore-scrap)<br>(Maint.-coal-ore)-(Oil-gas) | Capital-labor<br>Labor-(Oil-gas)<br>Capital-(Oil-gas) | Capital-labor<br>Labor-(Oil-gas)<br>Capital-(Oil-gas) | Capital-labor<br>Labor-(Oil-gas) | Capital-labor<br>Labor-(Maint.-coal-ore-scrap)<br>Capital-(Maint.-coal-ore-scrap)<br>(Maint.-coal-ore-scrap)-(Oil-gas)<br>Capital-labor |
| False magnitude | None | None | None | None | None | None |
| 4. False assoc. | None | None | None | None | None | None |
| Nonassoc. | Labor-(Maint.-coal-ore-scrap) | Capital-labor<br>(Maint.-coal-ore)-(Oil-gas) | Capital-labor | Capital-labor | Capital-labor | Capital-labor |
| False magnitude | None | None | None | None | None | None |

[a] The benchmark estimates used to determine the aggregation errors are drawn from a nine-factor model estimated from the thirty-nine constrained observation sample.

[b] Indicates that the perceived aggregate relationship was consistent with the noninformative benchmark estimate. Thus, under a weaker criterion for judging informative estimates, these errors would not arise.

are offered as guidelines for further inquiry into the modeling of production technologies rather than as definitive observations that are expected to hold for all production processes.

First, our estimation strategies in using neoclassical cost functions, where estimates are interpreted together with some approximate significance test in describing a technology, provide remarkably good descriptions of the features of all three technologies in the benchmark cases. In these cases, the correct input prices are identified, factors are fully disaggregated, and all solutions are consistent with cost minimization. The neoclassical models' elasticities of substitution always identify correctly the direction of association between each pair of inputs. While there is some difficulty in correctly estimating the substitution prospects when there are conflicting associations (substitutability and complementarity) at different input prices, these errors are limited to two of the three furnace types (ARC and BOF). Moreover, they generally lead to the conclusions that the neoclassical model cannot isolate a "precise" association between the inputs involved, rather than a precise false association.

With the open hearth furnace (OH), these problems are a bit more serious. It appears that neoclassical models applied to this furnace with inputs in their disaggregate form (the benchmark case) oversimplify the nature of the associations between inputs that can arise from changes in production processes. That is, the OH furnace realizes its flexibility in input usage through varying the refining temperatures over a wider range and thereby accommodating a greater variety of hot to cold metal practices. These process changes have important implications for the production of by-products and, in turn, for the ability of the OH plant to substitute these intermediate outputs for purchased inputs. As a consequence, the final association between any two inputs can be affected by what might be labeled direct and indirect influences. The former would refer to input substitution occurring directly in some process, such as iron ore for scrap in the steelmaking furnace.[34] The latter arises from the by-products generated in activities necessary for direct substitution, but which can affect its ability to be realized. In our example, iron ore does not substitute directly for scrap; it must first be reduced to molten iron. These reduction activities generate by-product fuels, which if applied to the OH furnace, reduce the need for molten iron. In the presence of such complexities, it is difficult to gauge the nature of the input associations. Our results suggest that neoclassical estimates can indicate that they are too simple when the underlying technology is consistent with a quite different conclusion. Interestingly, however, as the inputs involved in these complex relations are ag-

[34] An analogy can be drawn between substitution in these process steps and how it is reflected in the aggregate. For the case of independent microtechnologies, the recent work of Sato (1975) offers analytical findings. When these activities cannot be assumed independent, the task becomes more difficult.

gregated (using either share or translog price aggregates), the performance of the model improves.[35]

The second general set of conclusions relates to the effects of aggregation. All three technologies exhibit sufficiently interdependent production activities for the inputs we defined that it would not be possible to identify any subset of them as separable from the remainder.[36] Thus, aggregation of the materials inputs cannot be justified in principle.[37] Equally important, their prices in our samples do not vary in the same proportion. As a consequence, any aggregation of the nine-factor inputs identified for each type of furnace can be expected to distort perceptions of the underlying technology. Our findings suggest that selecting a member of the class of "ideal" price indexes does not reduce the scope or magnitude of errors introduced through aggregation.

With these technologies, aggregation of the materials inputs tends to lead to a greater number of noninformative estimates of the substitution elasticities. This implies that associations in which there is some conflict in the substitution relations between inputs that are constituent elements in the aggregate, with those external to the aggregate, are resolved with a loss of information (a noninformative estimate). In cases where no such conflicts exist, the magnitude of the measured elasticities may not be consistent with the inherent capabilities of the system. While the majority of our estimates lead to understatements, there are several cases of substantial overstatement. Thus, overall conclusions on the direction of these errors are difficult to deduce. As we observed earlier, these errors were somewhat less pronounced with the more flexible technologies (OH and BOF).

The final dimension of our inquiry was an examination of the implications of constraints on residuals discharges for the perceived possibilities of input substitution. These results focus on effects of additional constraints on resource allocation that are not reflected in the neoclassical model of the technology. Our findings suggest that they tend to distort measured substitution relations at the "ideal" level and all aggregations. The errors lead to misperceived patterns of association between pairs of inputs, a reduction in the ability to obtain informative estimates, and errors in the magnitude of the measured prospects for substitution. Interestingly, despite the differences in the levels of residuals generated by each of the three steelmaking furnaces, there was no clear-cut pattern, in terms of severity of their impact, across the furnaces.

[35] This finding is partly because the complex associations between inputs, through their individual associations with unmeasured intermediate products, are submerged in the aggregate factor input.

[36] The separability of two factors from a set of remaining inputs would require that the marginal technical rate of substitution between these two factors not be affected by changes in the use levels of any of the remainder.

[37] Of course, in practice the justification for aggregation is often only one of convenience in that it is required by virtue of the sample size available or the form of the data. See Pindyck (1979) and Fuss (1977) as examples.

There are a number of qualifications that can be raised with respect to generalizing these findings beyond the confines of our experiments. As noted at the outset, these conclusions cannot be assumed to hold across other technologies and may well be limited in their applicability to actual steel furnaces.[38] They relate to the properties of the neoclassical tools under a quite favorable set of conditions for approximating the production technology.

Nonetheless, one might conjecture the implications of these conclusions in evaluating the relevance of elasticities of substitution between materials (or natural resource) inputs and other factors estimated in recent neoclassical econometric studies. First, these studies have, as a rule, dealt with *ex ante* technology, considering capital a variable factor input. Our analysis related to the *ex post* technology in that productive capital is fixed.[39] This difference does limit the comparability between the two cases. However, if we can assume that the *ex ante* technology only serves to expand the set of processes that can be adopted without necessarily reducing their interdependence, we might use the OH furnace results to offer such conjectures. Specifically, our findings would question the measured prospects for materials substitution using an aggregate materials input (as in the Berndt–Wood, 1975, and Humphrey–Moroney, 1975, analyses). Efforts to disaggregate both the industry and the character of the materials inputs (as in the more recent Moroney–Toevs, 1977, and Moroney–Trapani, 1978, analysis) have greater prospects for success, but may still be at too high a level of input aggregation to effectively gauge the limits to input substitution that are imposed by physical laws in the underlying technologies.

[38] This qualification arises because one might reasonably question the accuracy of the model's depiction of these technologies. If such questions were well founded, then the results would nonetheless be of interest because of their evaluation of neoclassical techniques for an "abstract" process analysis model.

As it happens, appraisals of these models' ability to track the movements in unit costs relative to unpublished industry data (at the firm level) by William J. Vaughan when he was at the Council on Wage and Price Stability suggest they do remarkably well in explaining price movements. They do, however, tend to understate the companies' reported unit costs. This difference is approximately a constant and may reflect the treatment of productive capital costs as well as accounting conventions.

[39] Strictly speaking, the optimal planning models also relate to the *ex ante* technology. However, these restrictions are usually not formalized. Nonetheless, it may well be argued that an *ex post* analysis and the adjustments consistent with it are the ones largely relevant for policy purposes.

## References

Allen, R. G. D. 1938. *Mathematical Analysis for Economists* (London, Macmillan).

Atkinson, S. E., and Robert Halvorsen. 1976. "Interfuel Substitution in Steam Electric Power Generation," *Journal of Political Economy* vol. 84 (October) pp. 959–978.

Ayres, A. U., and A. V. Kneese. 1969. "Production, Consumption and Externalities," *American Economic Review* vol. 59 (June) pp. 282–297.

Barnett, H. J., and Chandler Morse. 1963. *Scarcity and Growth* (Baltimore, Md., Johns Hopkins University Press for Resources for the Future).

Berndt, E. R. 1976. "Reconciling Alternative Estimates of the Elasticity of Substitution," *Review of Economics and Statistics* vol. 58 (February) pp. 59–68.

———. 1978. "Aggregate Energy, Efficiency, and Productivity Measurement," *Annual Review of Energy* vol. 3, pp. 225–273.

———, and M. S. Khaled. 1977. "Energy Prices, Economies of Scale and Biased Productivity Gains in U.S. Manufacturing, 1947–1971," Discussion Paper No. 77-23, Department of Economics, University of British Columbia, August.

———, and D. O. Wood. 1975. "Technology, Prices and the Derived Demand for Energy," *Review of Economics and Statistics* vol. 57 (August) pp. 259–568.

———, and ———. 1977. "Engineering and Econometric Approaches to Industrial Energy Conservation and Capital Formation: A Reconciliation," MIT Energy Laboratory Working Paper No. MIT-EL-77-040.

———, B. H. Hall, R. E. Hall, and J. A. Hausman. 1974. "Estimation of Inference in Nonlinear Structural Models," *Annals of Economic and Social Measurement* vol. 3, no. 4, pp. 653–665.

Bever, R. C., J. R. Marsden, V. S. Fumas, and Andrew Whinston. 1978. *Interim Report on Methodology of Process Models* (Purdue University).

Binswanger, H. P. 1974. "A Cost Function Approach to the Measurement of Factor Demand Elasticities of Substitution," *American Journal of Agricultural Economics* vol. 56 (May) pp. 377–386.

Blackorby, Charles, Daniel Primont, and R. Robert Russell. 1978. *Duality, Separability and Functional Structure: Theory and Economic Applications* (Amsterdam, North-Holland).

Bower, B. T. 1975. "Studies in Residuals Management in Industry," in E. S. Mills, ed., *Economic Analysis of Environmental Problems* (New York, National Bureau of Economic Research).

Cummings, Ronald, and W. D. Schulze. 1977. "Ramsey, Resources, and the Conservation of Mass-Energy," paper presented at Conference on Natural Resource Pricing, Trail Lake, Wyoming.

Dasgupta, Partha, and G. M. Heal. 1979. *Economic Theory and Exhaustible Resources* (Cambridge, Mass., Cambridge University Press).

Dennis, Enid, and V. K. Smith. 1978. "A Neoclassical Analysis of the Demand for Real Cash Balances by Firms," *Journal of Political Economy* vol. 86 (October) pp. 793–814.

Diewert, W. E. 1976. "Exact and Superlative Indexes," *Journal of Econometrics* vol. 4 (May) pp. 115–146.

Fisher, A. C., and F. M. Peterson. 1976. "The Environment in Economics: A Survey," *Journal of Economic Literature* vol. 14 (March) pp. 1–33.

Fisher, F. M. 1971. "Aggregate Production Functions and the Explanation of Wages: A Simulation Experiment," *Review of Economics and Statistics* vol. 53 (November) pp. 305–326.

———, R. M. Solow, and J. M. Kearl. 1977. "Aggregate Production Functions: Some CES Experiments," *Review of Economic Studies* vol. 44 (June) pp. 305–320.

Fuss, M. A. 1977. "The Demand for Energy in Canadian Manufacturing: An Example of the Estimation of Production Structures with Many Inputs," *Journal of Econometrics* vol. 5 (January) pp. 89–116.

Gapinski, J. H. 1973. "Putty-Clay Capital and Small Sample Properties of Neoclassical Estimators," *Journal of Political Economy* vol. 81 (January/February) pp. 145–147.

———, and T. K. Kumar. 1974. "Nonlinear Estimation of the CES Production Parameters: A Monte Carlo Study," *Review of Economics and Statistics* vol. 56 (November) pp. 563–567.

Gorman, W. M. 1959. "Separable Utility and Aggregation," *Econometrica* vol. 27, pp. 469–481.

Griffin, J. M. 1977. The Econometrics of Joint Production: Another Approach," *Review of Economics and Statistics* vol. 59 (November) pp. 389–397.

———. 1978. "Joint Production Technology: The Case of Petrochemicals," *Econometrica* vol. 46 (March) pp. 379–398.

———. 1979. "Statistical Cost Analysis Revisited," *Quarterly Journal of Economics* vol. 93 (February) pp. 107–130.

———. 1982. "Pseudo Data Estimation with Alternative Functional Forms," in V. Kerry Smith, ed., *Advances in Applied Micro-Economics*, vol. 2 (Greenwich, Conn., JAI Press, forthcoming).

———, and P. R. Gregory. 1976. "An Intercountry Translog Model of Energy Substitution Responses," *American Economic Review* vol. 66 (December) pp. 845–857.

Guilkey, D. K., and C. A. K. Lovell. 1980. "On the Flexibility of the Translog Approximation," *International Economic Review* vol. 21 (February) pp. 137–147.

Halvorsen, Robert. 1977. "Energy Substitution in U. S. Manufacturing," *Review of Economics and Statistics* vol. 59 (November) pp. 381–388.

Hazilla, Michael. 1978. "The Use of Economic Theory in Econometric Estimation: Inference in Linear Constrained Models," (unpublished Ph.D. thesis, State University of New York at Binghamton).

Hicks, J. R. 1939. *Value and Capital* (London, Oxford University Press).

Houthakker, H. S. 1955–56. "The Pareto Distribution and the Cobb-Douglas Production Function in Activity Analysis," *Review of Economic Studies* vol. 23, pp. 27–31.

Humphrey, D. B., and J. R. Moroney. 1975. "Substitution among Capital, Labor, and Natural Resource Products in American Manufacturing," *Journal of Political Economy* vol. 83 (February) pp. 57–82.

Johansen, Leif. 1972. *Production Functions* (Amsterdam, North-Holland).

Katzner, D. W. 1970. *Static Demand Theory* (New York, Macmillan).

Leontief, Wassily. 1936. "Composite Commodities and the Problem of Index Numbers," *Econometrica* vol. 4, pp. 39–59.

Levhari, David. 1968. "A Note on Houthakker's Aggregate Production Function in a Multifirm Industry," *Econometrica* vol. 36 (January) pp. 151–154.

Marsden, J. R., David Pingry, and Andrew Whinston. 1974. "Engineering Foundations of Production Functions," *Journal of Economic Theory* vol. 9, pp. 124–140.

McFadden, D. L. 1979. "Cost, Revenue and Production Functions," in M. A. Fuss and D. L. McFadden, eds., *Production Economics: A Dual Approach to Theory and Applications* (Amsterdam, North-Holland).

Moroney, J. R., and Alden Toevs. 1977. "Factor Costs and Factor Use: An Analysis of Labor, Capital and Natural Resource Inputs," *Southern Economic Journal* vol. 44 (October) pp. 222–239.

———, and J. M. Trapani. 1978. "Options for Conserving and Substituting for Non-Fuel, Nonrenewable Resources in the United States," unpublished paper, Tulane University.

Morrissett, Irving. 1953. "Some Recent Uses of Elasticity of Substitution: A Survey," *Econometrica* vol. 21 (January) pp. 41–62.

Peterson, F. M., and A. C. Fisher. 1977. "The Exploitation of Extractive Resources: A Survey," *Economic Journal* vol. 87 (December) pp. 681–721.

Pindyck, R. S. 1979. *The Structure of World Energy Demand* (Cambridge, Mass., MIT Press).

Resources for the Future. 1977. *The First 25 Years: 1952–1977* (Washington, D.C., Resources for the Future).

Russell, C. S., and W. J. Vaughan. 1976. *Steel Production: Processes, Products, and Residuals* (Baltimore, Md., Johns Hopkins University Press for Resources for the Future).

Sato, Kazuo. 1975. *Production Functions and Aggregation* (Amsterdam, North-Holland).

Shephard, R. W. 1970. *Theory of Cost and Production Functions* (Princeton, N.J., Princeton University Press).

Smith, V. Kerry. 1978. "The Ames-Rosenberg Hypothesis and the Role of Natural Resources in the Production Technology," *Explorations in Economic History* vol. 15 (July) pp. 257–268.

———, and W. J. Vaughan. 1981. "Strategic Detail and Process Analysis Models for Environmental Management: An Econometric Analysis," *Resources and Energy* vol. 3, no. 1, pp. 39–54.

Solow, R. M. 1974. "The Economics of Resources or the Resources of Economics," *American Economic Review* vol. 64 (May) pp. 1–14.

Thursby, J. G., and C. A. K. Lovell. 1978. "An Investigation of the Kmenta Approximation to the CES Function," *International Economic Review* vol. 19 (June) pp. 363–378.

Uzawa, Hirofumi. 1962. "Production Functions with Constant Elasticities of Substitution," *Review of Economic Studies* vol. 29 (October) pp. 291–299.

Wales, T. J. 1977. "On the Flexibility of Flexible Functional Forms: An Empirical Approach," *Journal of Econometrics* vol. 5 (March) pp. 183–193.

Zellner, Arnold. 1962. "An Efficient Method of Estimating Seemingly Unrelated Regressions and Tests for Aggregation Bias," *Journal of the American Statistical Association* vol. 57 (June) pp. 348–368.

PART **V**

# GEOLOGICAL AND ECONOMIC MODELING OF RESOURCE AVAILABILITY

# 8

## The Assessment of Long-term
## Supplies of Minerals

DeVerle P. Harris and Brian J. Skinner

### 1. Introduction

An assessment of long-term supplies of mineral resources demands an
unfamiliar blend of geology and economics. *Mineral resources* consist of that
portion of the earth's total mineral endowment that can be profitably recovered. Mineral resource is an economic term, not a geological one. The
*mineral endowment* is a fact of nature independent of, and unrelated to, any
economic system. Assessing mineral *endowment* is a geological task. Ideally,
such an assessment would provide full information about the way the mineral
endowment is distributed in the earth as well as an estimation of its overall
magnitude. Assessing mineral *resources* is largely an economic task because
the fraction of the mineral endowment that can be recovered is influenced
by social and financial conditions.

This chapter attempts to address some of the issues involved in the two
kinds of assessment from the point of view of a geologist and a mineral
economist. A number of common terms are defined in order to reduce am-
biguities.

Geological Definitions

The word mineral is used so loosely in everyday conversation that it can
mean such diverse things as all the inorganic solid substances found in the
earth as well as the metallic elements found in living matter. This semantic
confusion is only one among many that contribute to the difficulty of communication between disciplines.

247

*Minerals* are solid, crystalline, chemical elements or chemical compounds that are formed by the inorganic processes of nature; each mineral has a characteristic crystal structure and a specific chemical composition. *Mineraloids* are amorphous substances that resemble minerals but lack both a characteristic crystal structure and a specific composition. Quartz, diamond, mica, and magnetite are minerals; natural glass (obsidian), pitch, amber, petroleum, and opal are mineraloids. *Rocks* are natural aggregations of one or more minerals and/or mineraloids; granite, limestone, coal, and rock salt are familiar examples.

Among the myriad natural substances dug out of the earth, there are plentiful examples of minerals, mineraloids, and rocks. Each substance, regardless of designation, is found in localized deposits. A given deposit will be exploited either because it is especially rich in the desired material or, if the substance is relatively common and used in large amounts, because it is located close to potential markets and transportation costs are low. *Mineral deposits* are local accumulations of specific minerals. Unfortunately the term mineral deposit is sometimes loosely applied to rocks or mineraloids. This semantic lapse causes a good deal of confusion (regretfully contributed to by some geologists, as in Lindgren, 1932, page 9). When deposits of rocks or mineraloids are being discussed, the product should be used as an adjective. Coal is mined from coal deposits; slate, granite, and gravel from their respective deposits; and rock phosphate from phosphate deposits.

The advantage for the geologist in sticking with narrowly defined terms becomes apparent when the origins and modes of occurrence of rocks, minerals, and mineraloids are discussed. Mineral deposits, for example, can be readily classified by origin so that generalized genetic relationships become apparent, and this in turn provides a foundation for estimating deposit abundances. Rocks can be classified by origin and this in turn clarifies the genetic relationships among the rock families. Unfortunately, genetically based classification systems cannot be readily transposed to classifications of the ways materials are actually used.

*Mineral endowment* is a relatively new term that has been introduced into the geological literature in response to the needs of resource analysts. Each occurrence of a given mineral has measurable characteristics such as size, associated minerals, concentration, host material, depth, geometric form, and geologic association. The sum of all characteristics for all occurrences defines the distribution of that mineral in the earth. However, the sum is so large it is unworkable to use it in practice, so instead a few key characteristics, such as concentration, size, and depth are selected. Then some lower boundary value for each characteristic is selected and the mineral endowment is defined as the sum of all occurrences exceeding the defined boundary values. The lower boundary values are usually set far below the values that would interest the miner. Thus, mineral endowment is a purely physical measure and is not dependent on economics or technology.

### Resource Definitions and Perspectives

We have already defined mineral resources as that portion of the earth's total mineral endowment that can be profitably recovered. Mineral resources do not have absolute numbers. As Zimmerman (1964) remarked, "Resources are not, they become." This succinct statement expresses the single most important, but all too often overlooked feature of a mineral resource, its dynamics. While mineral endowment changes only with depletion, mineral resources are created as well as destroyed by economic circumstances. Favorable price/cost ratios expand resources. Similarly, high costs or unfavorable governmental policies reduce resources.

The term mineral resources conveys little information without additional qualification; at best, it identifies the general subject to be materials that are sources of one or more minerals. Mineral resources can usually be estimated once a mineral endowment is known, but we must always remember that resources exist only with respect to an economic and technological framework.[1] To be useful, a statement on mineral resources must also include specific economic conditions and technological capabilities, as well as the state of nature.

The economic and technological conditions selected for a given set of mineral resources need not be those that currently prevail. Specification of current economic conditions and current technology of processing thus identifies a subset of mineral deposits that could be mined at a profit. The sum of all materials that could be recovered from these deposits is referred to as the *economic resource.*

At any given time there is only partial knowledge of resources and economic resources and qualifiers are needed to convey the degree of knowledge. Paper communication requires a correct and liberal use of these qualifiers. When the term resources is used without a qualifier, it is to be interpreted as referring to known and unknown, economic and subeconomic resources.

---

[1] While there is nothing in the definition of mineral endowment that stipulates that the collections of mineral occurrences which are defined as resources are subsets of endowments, such a relationship is assumed in the use of the term in this chapter: mineral endowment includes resources. The term is particularly useful when an inventory of occurrences with specific physical characteristics is estimated as an initial step in appraising resources and potential supply. Given this, it makes little sense to define the physical characteristics of an endowment so narrowly that resources for a given set of economic and technologic conditions exceed the mineral endowment.

**Table 8.1.**    A Tabulation of Reserve–Resource Terminology

| Terms | Aspects | | |
| --- | --- | --- | --- |
| | Occurrence | Economic | Technological |
| Reserves | Known | Present cost level | Currently feasible |
| Resources | Known and unknown | Any cost level specified | Currently feasible and probable future feasibility |
| Resource base | Known and unknown | Irrelevant | Feasible and infeasible |

*Source:* From Sam H. Schurr, Bruce Netschert, Vera F. Eliasberg, Joseph Lerner, and Hans H. Landsberg, *Energy in the American Economy, 1850–1975* (Baltimore, Md., Johns Hopkins University Press for Resources for the Future, 1960) table 91, p. 298.

Known economic resources are commonly referred to as ore reserves. This general category is subdivided into classes, for example, proved, probable, and possible, to indicate degree of certainty about the estimated quantity and grade of ore. A comprehensive treatment of ore reserve and resources terminology has been provided by Schanz (1975).

The relations of economics, technology, and degree of knowledge to categories of resources were summarized in a table by Schurr et al. (1960) (See table 8.1.) This table captures the important dynamics of resources: a change in product price or factor prices, or an improvement in technology of production causes a change in resources.

The most widely cited resource classification scheme is attributed to Vincent E. McKelvey (1973), past director of the U.S. Geological Survey (figure 8.1). The diagram of this classification has become known as the "McKelvey box." While the McKelvey box is a refinement of the Schurr–Netschert table in that it defines a greater number of categories of resources, it is a less complete representation of resource relations than the table. For example, technology, factor prices, and product price are all lumped into one effect, economics. Furthermore, closing the box at the base of submarginal resources leaves out of this classification some of the material included by Schurr and Netschert. The term *resource base*, meaning all of a given metal in the crust, regardless of mineralogical location, was originated and defined by Netschert (1958). The term is a physical one, unaffected by economics or technology. Material which has a sufficient concentration of the element or compound sought, but for which there is no existing or near-feasible production technology, is not a resource according to the definition provided by Schurr et al. (1960, pages 296–297) but it is a part of the resource base. Since the McKelvey box does not specify a nonresource category, it does not include this material. This is not an oversight on McKelvey's part. McKelvey is a geologist and as we will see in the next section, geologists view resource base as a misleading and pointless term.

Economics and technology impart a special character to the concept of resources, for the economic structure and the employable technology of a

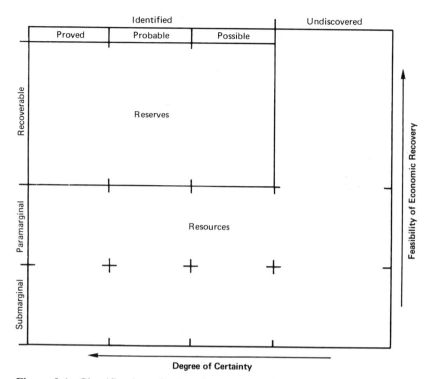

**Figure 8.1.** Classification of mineral reserves and resources according to the "McKelvey Box." Degree of certainty increases from right to left, and feasibility of economic recovery increases from bottom to top. From V. E. McKelvey, "Mineral Resource Estimates and Public Policy," in *United States Mineral Resources*, U.S. Geological Survey Professional Paper 820 (Washington, D.C., GPO, 1973).

nation are dynamic—they change with time. Consequently, a noneconomic resource today may be an economic resource five years from now. This can result from increased demand and higher prices, a decline in the real cost of labor and capital, the adoption of new technology, or all of these factors. In a sense, resources can be created by man's economic activities and his scientific and engineering genius. Similarly, they can be destroyed by unfavorable economics (which includes the availability of foreign supplies that cost less than those obtained from domestic mining and processing) and government policy on taxation, trade, environmental protection, mineral leasing, etc. As the amount of economic resources changes with economic conditions and technological improvement, the conditions for their identification and appraisal also change.

An appraised resource consists of all the minerals or metals that could be recovered if all deposits were known. Generally, this estimate considers neither the cost of exploration nor the fact that only some fraction of the deposits expected to occur would be found by current exploration methods. The term *potential supply* is therefore used to refer to the quantity of material in known deposits plus that in deposits expected to be discovered. In establishing a proper perspective for potential supply, it is helpful to imagine that exploration is conducted by one large firm, so that exploration of the same ground is not repeated, but that unit costs and efficiency of exploration otherwise are typical of the average firm. Then, given the specified status of technology and factor prices and given that markets are unlimited at the specified product price, the optimum amount of exploration would be the sum of the nonnegative *net* present values of deposits that constitute the resource and would be discovered. Under the specified conditions there is clearly an optimum exploration expenditure. To contribute to potential supply, deposits must be of such a quality that their exploitation covers discovery and production costs. Allocating to each deposit discovered its share of the exploration effort ($EX$) gives a net present value (net of exploration and production costs). Naturally, more deposits can be discovered if the exploration effort is increased to a higher level than the optimum, but since the effort is allocated to deposits discovered, increasing it beyond the optimum loses more economic and discoverable resources than are gained. For a given exploration technology and at any progression of exploration, the deposits which remain to be discovered require a greater expenditure per unit of resource than those already discovered. In exploration models, this effect sometimes is expressed through modeling exploration by "saturation" types of functions, such as $1 - e^{b \cdot EX}$, in which the probability approaches 1 as $EX$ approaches infinity ($b$ is a constant).

From the definition of the optimum exploration expenditure, it is apparent that the potential supply is the material contained in the resource deposits that would be discovered by the optimum exploration expenditure and which could be produced economically, including exploration as well as production costs. Like a mineral resource, a potential supply consists of an inventory made under specified conditions. Conceptually the resource and potential supply can be equal, but equality requires that the geographical region be completely explored. Since exploration incurs a cost and is less than perfectly effective, the potential supply is generally less than the resource. The relationship between the terms commonly used by resource analysts can be demonstrated diagrammatically, as shown in figure 8.2.

### Aims of this Paper

It should already be apparent from the preceding definitions and discussions of their significance that a considerable problem exists in translating

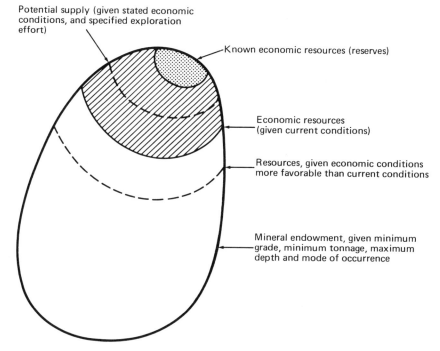

Resource Base > Mineral Endowment > Resources > Potential Supply > Reserves

**Figure 8.2.** Resource terminology and relations. From D. P. Harris, "Undiscovered Uranium Resources and Potential Supply," in National Academy of Sciences, *Workshop on Concepts of Uranium Resources and Probability* (Washington, D.C., NAS, 1978).

the geologists' stock inventories into a form useful to the economist. In order to estimate production and extraction costs for deposits yet to be found, the geologist is asked to supply information exceeding that currently available. The so-called McKelvey box is an attempt to lump all of the uncertainties together, but instead of clarifying, it confuses. In the McKelvey box inference, opinion and measurement are mixed in such a way that original data cannot be recovered.

It is not yet known how to construct a scheme that allows a ready flow of information between geology and economics without loss of clarity or unnecessary mixing of hard data and inference. Nevertheless, we believe it is possible to clarify some of the issues that have caused confusion in previous attempts. We begin with a discussion of the geology of mineral deposits and how their occurrence influences the way materials are recovered. We follow with discussions of exploration for mineral deposits and attempts to appraise mineral endowments, mineral resources, and potential supplies.

## 2. Geological Concepts: The Way Materials Occur and Are Used

Because we are discussing those mineral substances actually used, which are a small fraction of the many minerals, mineraloids, and rocks found on earth, it is convenient to begin the discussion of the geological perspective with a summary of material uses.

### Uses of Natural Materials

The most convenient way to discuss the use of natural materials is through the property or properties exploited. All metals, for example, have properties such as ductility and high thermal and electrical conductivity, which allow the materials from which they are derived to be assigned to a use category. There is only a rough and inexact correspondence between the four use categories and geological classifications of mineral occurrence. Despite this, the correspondence makes it possible to determine the classes of materials within which shortages are most likely to occur.

1. *Materials used for the extraction of metals.* With a very few exceptions, such as the brines used as a source of magnesium, all of the materials in this group are minerals. Some minerals are far more desirable as sources of metals than others. The key factors are the ease with which the mineral in question is concentrated and smelted to yield the desired end product. For example, siderite ($FeCO_3$) is readily smelted to yield iron, but fayalite ($Fe_2SiO_4$), which contains several percent more iron than siderite, is so difficult to smelt that it is entirely unsuitable for the production of iron.

The so-called ore minerals, from which metals can be extracted, are sought and exploited wherever they can be found and conveniently mined. For most metals, transportation costs are an important but not controlling factor in production. It is in this category of materials that many of the perceived future supply limitations lie.

2. *Materials used for their chemical and fertilizer properties.* Most of the materials in this category are also minerals, but they are separated from the metallic minerals because they are generally used for their intrinsic properties as compounds. Sodium carbonate ($Na_2CO_3$), for example, is used as sodium carbonate, not as a source of sodium (Na) or carbon dioxide ($CO_2$).

Many of the chemical and fertilizer materials are used in large tonnages and have relatively low values. Transportation is a key factor in the production and use of phosphatic fertilizers, sodium chloride, and many other members of this category. For a very few chemical and fertilizer materials there may be eventual supply limitations, but for the majority, supplies are extremely large and factors other than abundance, principally transportation, control their use.

3. *Materials used for their special or aggregate physical properties.* This diverse group ranges from building materials, such as sand, gravel, cut stone, and cement, most of which are rocks, to special abrasives such as tripoli, and to gemstones, which can be minerals, mineraloids, or rocks. With the exception of gemstones, there are very few limitations on abundance, and in addition a great deal of substitution is possible among members of the group, especially in the building materials. Production is strongly influenced by transportation costs, however, so local supply problems often arise.

4. *Materials used as sources of energy.* The materials from which energy is obtained by combustion are either rocks, such as coal, oil shales or tar sands, or mineraloids, of which petroleum is the prime example. The two nuclear fission fuels, uranium and thorium, are recovered mainly from minerals, so questions of nuclear fuel abundance are approached, at least in part, in the same way as questions of mineral abundance in groups 1 and 2.

### Supplies of Natural Materials

Rocks of all kinds occur in huge amounts because they are formed as a result of processes that affect vast volumes of the earth's crust. Consequently, there are no real limits on supply. This statement is correct even for comparatively rare rocks such as coal and phosphorite (rock phosphate), which require extremely unusual formation conditions. The earth's crust is not homogeneous, however, so there are marked geographic limitations on the supplies of some rocks. Coal is an example because more than 90 percent of all coal deposits occur in North America, Europe, and Asia. An important general conclusion can be drawn concerning the distribution of rocks: the more abundant the rock type, the less restricted it is in its geographic range or, to state the converse, the rarer a rock type, the more restricted its geographic range. Despite local restrictions on availablility, supplies of all useful rocks are apparently so large that little effort has been expended on estimates of abundance. The estimates that have been made are rather imprecise and almost surely err on the low side.

Mineral and mineraloid abundances present an entirely different picture. Because this chapter does not address the question of petroleum abundance, and because petroleum is the most important mineraloid, we will concentrate solely on minerals.

Minerals are selectively mined, as mentioned, either for their intrinsic physical or chemical properties, or for their metallic contents. A great many physical properties are of interest; for example, hardness and toughness are important for grinding and polishing materials, color and/or transparency are important in gemstones and many other applications, flexibility of fibers is required for the asbestos minerals, absorbency (as by certain clays) is needed for many cleaning and separating operations, and slipperiness is essential for lubrication. Certain minerals are better than others for satisfying physical property requirements, but for most circumstances substitutes or synthetic equivalents can be readily identified. Even diamond, the hardest of all grinding materials, can now be manufactured in sizes and shapes suitable for all but gemstone use. Thus, *the use of minerals for their physical properties is not an area in which supply limitations seem to offer insurmountable technological challenges.*

Where the chemical properties of minerals are concerned, the possibilities for substitutes and synthetic materials are more limited than they are for physical properties so the potential for long-term supply problems seems to be larger. Fortunately, a close examination of the individual minerals of interest shows that the problem is not a major one, for two reasons. First, most of the chemical elements present in the chemical-supply minerals are rather common, so the minerals tend to be common too. Second, most of the minerals are soluble in water and so their mineral deposits are formed by evaporation of sea or lake water. Deposits formed by evaporation are called evaporites and the individual minerals are referred to as evaporite minerals. When the U.S. Geological Survey discussed U.S. mineral resources in the volume edited by Brobst and Pratt (1973), the authors of the chapter on evaporites concluded that, for the world as a whole, "within the next several hundred or few thousand years, no evaporite resource will be exhausted" (page 197). Included in the category of evaporite resources are materials such as potassium and magnesium salts, sodium chloride, calcium sulfate, calcium chloride, sodium carbonate, sodium sulfate, nitrate compounds, the salts of boron, strontium, bromine, and iodine. Other chemical-supply minerals, such as fluorite ($CaF_2$, the main source of fluorine) and sulfur, which are not found as evaporite minerals, are also judged to be free of long-term supply problems by U.S. Geological Survey experts.

The remaining minerals belong to the group of minerals recovered for their metallic content. Because some of the metals are intrinsically rare elements (the average content of lead in the earth's crust, for example, is only 0.0010 percent), it is hardly surprising that minerals containing a given rare metal should also be intrinsically scarce. Nor should it be too surprising that most of the potential mineral shortages perceived by geologists should also fall in this group. This chapter, therefore, deals principally with problems associated with supplies of minerals recovered for their metallic or other elemental contents.

Crustal Abundances and the Resource Base

The crustal abundance of a chemical element is the average content of that element in earth's crust expressed as a percentage by weight. There is also an old and now rarely used unit, the clarke, which is numerically equal to crustal abundance. Geologists draw a distinction between the crust that underlies the ocean and that beneath the continent because small but distinct differences are present in their bulk compositions. The discussion here concentrates on the continental crust.

Even when chemical elements have very low crustal abundances, their total mass in the crust is exceedingly large because the crust is itself so large. Indeed, the calculated mass of any element is so large by comparison with the quantities mined and used that a suggestion has been made, and widely accepted in some circles, that the crust itself could be considered a mineral resource, even though it is not yet known how to recover all of its materials nor is there any conception of the technology that would allow this. Indeed, this far-fetched notion gave rise to the definition of the resource base (Netschert, 1958) as all of a given metal or chemical element in the crust, regardless of mode of occurrence. Clearly, the resource base of a given element is simply the mass of the crust multiplied by the crustal abundance. Unfortunately, resource base, as so many other terms, has become confused by semantic diversification and, because it ignores the way minerals actually occur and hence will be mined, most geologists view the term as misleading at best and downright distorting most of the time.

For all practical purposes, society is certainly restricted to the crust of the earth for its material resources. Those deeper portions of the earth, 40 km or more below the surface, which contain rocks and minerals different from those in the crust, are inaccessible to mining because of intense heat and high pressures. Realistically, however, not even the entire crust can be considered accessible. The deepest drill holes (in soft and favorable rocks) are only 9 km, and the present deepest mine opening (again, in a favorable region with a low thermal gradient) is only 3.8 km. The most optimistic depth that should be considered is only 10 km and most practical mining engineers place it at much less than this.

Given an earth radius of 6,371 km, continental crust covering 30 percent of the earth's surface, and an average crustal density of 2.8 $gm/cm^3$, the mass of continental crust to a depth of 10 km is $4.3 \times 10^{18}$ metric tons. The element carbon is used here to point out the kind of confusion geologists find in the concept of a resource base. Since the crustal abundance of carbon is 0.02 percent (Taylor, 1964), the resource base to a depth of 10 km is $4.3 \times 10^{18} \times 0.0002$ or $860 \times 10^{12}$ metric tons. By comparison, about $5 \times 10^9$ metric tons of carbon are used each year as a fuel. However, comparison of the two numbers is completely misleading if it leads to the conclusion that all of the carbon resource base is usefully recoverable under some imagined set of economic conditions. Because carbon is used as a combustion fuel, it is meaningless to use $860 \times 10^{12}$ metric tons as a resource base. For example, approximately half of the carbon is already oxidized to carbonate and so is not available for combustion. It is even misleading to suggest that $430 \times 10^{12}$ metric tons of reduced carbon, which is the form necessary for combustion, is a resource base.

Consider how carbon occurs in the crust. There are several identifiable reservoirs—coal, oil, and gas (approximately half of which can be recovered by present technology), viscous oils in tar sands, and solid organic matter in the common sedimentary rocks. Averitt (1974) estimated that the world contains about $16 \times 10^{12}$ metric tons of coal. Assuming an average of 80 percent carbon, the coal reservoir contains $12.8 \times 10^{12}$ metric tons of carbon. Assuming the crust contains as much as $4,000 \times 10^9$ barrels of petroleum (meaning oil and equivalent calorific amounts of gas), and an average carbon content of 83 percent, the petroleum reservoir contains $0.44 \times 10^{12}$ metric tons of carbon. If the amount of heavy viscous oil is a liberal $2,000 \times 10^9$ barrels, for another $0.22 \times 10^{12}$ metric tons of carbon, the remaining reduced carbon is all present as dispersed solid material in sedimentary rocks, mainly in the fine, fragmental rock called shale. When shale is heated to a high temperature, the solid organic matter is converted to gaseous hydrocarbons, most of which can then be condensed to an oily and combustible liquid. The amount of energy needed to treat and heat a metric ton of shale in order to effect a distillation is equivalent to that obtained by burning 40 liters of oil. Thus, organic-rich shales that yield 40 or more liters of distillate per ton can be separated from the much more common varieties that yield less than 40 liters, which cannot be processed for their combustion energy. One estimate of the distillable oil from shales is $2,000 \times 10^9$ barrels, equivalent again to about $0.22 \times 10^{12}$ metric tons of carbon. Thus, by elimination, it can be deduced that approximately $416 \times 10^{12}$ metric tons of reduced carbon are present at unrecoverably low grades in ordinary shales. Approximately $14 \times 10^{12}$ metric tons of reduced carbon, or 1.63 percent of the total carbon resource base, is all that is potentially usable as a combustion fuel. Similar analyses of occurrence can be made for any element.

## Crustal Abundance and the Distribution of Minerals

The total number of minerals identified to date is only 2,400. Considering that 88 different chemical elements have been identified in the crust, and that combinations between those 88 elements could produce an astronomically large number of stable compounds, the number of minerals seems surprisingly small. The reason for the seeming disparity lies in the crustal abundance of elements, nine of which account for 99.0 percent by weight of the entire continental crust. These are oxygen, 45.2 weight percent; silicon, 21.2; aluminum, 8.0; iron, 5.8; calcium, 5.1; magnesium, 2.8; sodium, 2.3; potassium, 1.7, and titanium, 0.9. The remaining 79 elements total only 1.0 percent of the crust and are therefore present in essentially trace amounts.

The most abundant element is oxygen, which readily serves as an anion and forms complex anions with silicon. Earth's crust is, therefore, 99 percent by weight a mass of oxide and silicate minerals in which aluminum, iron, calcium, magnesium, sodium, and potassium are the cations combined with oxygen and silicon. There are, to be sure, other kinds of minerals, but quantitatively they are minor constituents of the crust. The most important of the minor mineral families, based on the next two most abundant anions, carbon (0.02 percent) and sulfur (0.03 percent), are the carbonates, sulfides, and sulfates. The most common carbonate, sulfide, and sulfate minerals are, however, all formed by combinations with the six most common cations. The general chemistry of the crust is therefore largely the chemistry of silicate minerals, with a leavening of a few oxide minerals plus the carbonates of calcium, magnesium, and iron; the sulfides of iron; and the sulfates of calcium. When the chemistry of other minerals is considered, as it must be when mineral deposits are discussed, it is the chemistry of quantitatively minor and necessarily limited materials.

The late V. M. Goldschmidt, who is sometimes called the father of geochemistry, elucidated a number of rules governing mineral composition. One of the rules provides an explanation for the restricted number of minerals. When two cations have similar charges, one can substitute for the other in a mineral without producing a change in the geometry of the crystal structure and therefore without producing a new mineral. The extent of substitution is partly a function of temperature and pressure, but is predominantly a function of the closeness in size of the substituting cations. If the radii of the cations differ by less than about 15 percent, complete substitution is usually possible. Thus, $Fe^{+2}$ with a radius of 0.76 angstroms (Å) and $Mg^{+2}$ with a radius of 0.65 Å can substitute freely for each other in many different minerals. Examples are olivine $(Mg,Fe)_2SiO_4$ and pyroxene $(Mg,Fe)SiO_3$. [The parentheses around (Mg,Fe) indicate that they substitute freely for one another in the structure.] Coupled substitutions to maintain charge balances are also possible. Two cations such as $Na^{+1} + Si^{+4}$ can jointly substitute for two others, such as $Ca^{+2} + Al^{+3}$, having similar ionic radii and the same total charge. When the differences in ionic radii are greater than 15 percent, some substitution is still possible, but there are definite limits beyond which the addition of much larger or much smaller cations will cause mineral structures to change to accommodate the new cations or, more commonly, for a separate mineral to form in which the substituting element becomes the major charge-balancing cation.

Because most chemical elements occur in such tiny amounts in the crust, they can be readily accommodated by substitutions in common oxide and silicate minerals without the saturation point being reached and therefore without separate minerals being formed. The only way minerals of the scarce elements can form is for some geological process to cause a local enrichment of one of the scarce elements so that substitution limits are exceeded. The major rock-forming processes, which are weathering and sedimentation to form sedimentary rocks, melting and fractional crystallization to form igneous rocks, and mineral regrowth by heat and pressure to form metamorphic rocks, rarely cause sufficiently large local enrichments, so separate minerals of the scarce elements rarely (and for most, never) form in common rocks. Consider lead, for example. The crustal abundance is 0.0010 percent. Rock-forming processes produce enrichments in the lead content of some rocks to as much as 0.02 percent, or twenty times the crustal abundance, but the minerals present are still not saturated in lead, so no lead mineral forms. Instead, the lead (radius 1.20 Å) substitutes for potassium (radius 1.33 Å) in common minerals such as mica and feldspar.

No hard or definite rules can be drawn as to the concentration level that any given element must reach before a separate mineral can form. Obviously the level depends in part on the presence or absence of compatible ions with which substitution is possible. A rough rule of thumb is that most elements will start to form separate minerals when a concentration of 0.1 percent is reached. There are many exceptions, however. Gold, uranium, and molybdenum are three elements that have ionic radii and/or ionic charges such that possible substitutions are limited, so they often form minerals at much lower concentrations than 0.1 percent. Gallium, however, is twice as abundant in the crust as lead but it is so close in size to aluminum ($Ga^{+3} = 0.62$ Å; $Al^{+3} = 0.57$ Å) that the substitution limit is much greater than 0.1 percent and is practically never exceeded; gallium minerals are therefore among the rarest of all minerals.

Metals can be roughly divided into three groups. The first consists of five metals—silicon, iron, aluminum, titanium, and magnesium—which have crustal abundances in excess of 0.1 percent and form minerals in a great many kinds of rocks. The same generalization can of course be extended to other geochemically abundant elements, but since they are not useful for their metallic properties, they are not discussed here. For the five abundant metals, there are no perceived shortages or limitations in supply. Even though bauxite, the most desired ore of aluminum, is limited in abundance, there are many alternative ore minerals.

The second group of elements has crustal abundances between 0.01 and 0.1 percent. They lie in an abundance range such that many rock-forming processes produce the concentration necessary for separate minerals to form, and this second group is therefore also present as minerals in many common rocks. The group includes barium, chlorine, fluorine, manganese, phosphorus, sulfur, vanadium and zirconium, but only two, manganese and vanadium, are metals of sufficiently great industrial importance to warrant attention. While high-grade deposits of manganese and vanadium are certainly limited and thus shortages must be anticipated, the general availability of the two metals is not likely to be restricted because many rock types constitute low-grade deposits.

The third group contains all of those metals with crustal abundances below 0.1 percent. They rarely form separate minerals and therefore rarely form distinct mineral deposits. It is in this group, which we refer to as being geo-chemically scarce, that both absolute and local shortages may appear.

### Influence of Geochemistry on Mining and Metallurgy

Production of geochemically scarce metals involves two distinct and sep-arate operations: the first is mining the deposit and separating the desired ore mineral to form a pure concentrate; the second is chemical processing (usually called smelting) of the concentrate to free and purify the metal. The two operations are presented here in terms of the energy needed to release the metal. As an example, consider the mining of an average copper ore as presented by Kellogg (1974).

A typical copper ore mined from an open pit consists of a mass of valueless silicate minerals mixed with a small quantity of a copper sulfide mineral. In order to mine the ore, approximately 2.5 tons of waste rock must be removed for every ton of ore recovered. The energy used in mining (including the en-ergy equivalent of materials used in the process) is 40,000 Btu/ton using a conversion factor of 10,500 Btu/kWh for those parts of the process using electricity. For a typical ore deposit containing 0.7 percent Cu, this amounts to 10,000 Btu/lb of copper in the mined ore. The mined ore must then be crushed and the copper sulfide mineral separated from the valueless silicate minerals by some process based on a difference in physical properties, such as flotation or density. Typically, a concentrate of chalcopyrite ($CuFeS_2$) will contain as much as 30 percent Cu and the concentration 'process will recover 80–90 percent of the copper in the ore. Assuming an 80 percent re-covery, Kellogg calculated the energy needed for mining plus concentration to be 33,040 Btu/lb of copper.

Smelting and refining a chalcopyrite concentrate consume an additional 20,000 Btu/lb of copper, and give a total energy consumption of 53,040 Btu/lb of pure copper. If ores with lower copper contents are used, mining and concentration energy used simply increases proportionally to the content of copper in the ore, but the energy needed for smelting the concentrate re-

**Table 8.2.**  Energy Used to Mine and Process a Copper Ore in Which Copper Is Present as the Mineral Chalcopyrite (CuFeS$_2$)

| | Energy used (Btu/lb of copper) | | |
|---|---|---|---|
| Grade, percent Cu | 0.07 | 0.1 | 0.01 |
| Mining plus concentration | 33,040 | 231,280 | 2,312,800 |
| Smelting and refining | 20,000 | 20,000 | 20,000 |
| Total | 53,040 | 251,280 | 2,332,800 |
| Equivalent thermal energy in bituminous coal, in pounds of coal | 4.1 | 19.3 | 180 |

*Note:* An overburden stripping of 2.5 tons of waste rock per ton of ore is assumed, and concentration is 80 percent efficient.
*Source:* Data from H. H. Kellogg, "Energy Efficiency in the Age of Scarcity," *Journal of Metals* vol. 26 (June 1974).

mains the same.[2] Table 8.2 presents the energy consumption for sulfide ores of three different grades.

Consider now the circumstance where metals are to be freed from entrapment in silicate minerals. The one case where this already has been done, aluminum, can be used as a guide. Aluminum is traditionally prepared by mining and concentrating bauxite (an impure aluminum hydroxide), then processing the bauxite chemically to produce pure Al$_2$O$_3$, followed by electrolysis of a solution of Al$_2$O$_3$ in a suitable flux. Since bauxites are limited in extent, considerable research effort has been devoted to the preparation of an Al$_2$O$_3$ concentrate from silicate minerals in common rocks, minerals such as clays [ideally Al$_2$Si$_2$O$_5$(OH)$_4$] and anorthite (CaAl$_2$Si$_2$O$_8$). Data by which the two kinds of ore can be compared are presented by Bravard et al. (1972). They calculated the case for a clay-ore containing 15.9 percent Al. The important part of their calculations for our purposes is that 43,170 Btu/lb of aluminum are required to produce the Al$_2$O$_3$ from the clay.

Using the information for aluminum recovered from a clay, together with the optimistic assumptions that (1) no overburden need be removed and (2) the concentration process is 100 percent efficient, the energy requirements for copper production can be estimated from silicate ores. These estimates are given in table 8.3. Thus, switching from sulfide to silicate ores at some future date does not seem to be difficult at first glance. The magnitude of the problem only becomes apparent when another geochemical fact is added. The approximate lower limit of copper in sulfide ores is about 0.1 percent (COMRATE, 1975). The upper limit for copper in large bodies of common rock is still unknown, but it is certainly below 0.1 percent. Thus, transfer from a sulfide curve to a silicate curve will probably be somewhat like the situation shown in figure 8.3.

[2] Such use of lower grade ores also implies an increase in the residual by-products of production. That is, in order to obtain a given quantity of copper (with specified quality), a large volume of ore will need to be processed. On the basis of simple mass balance calculations, the waste and tailing per unit of refined copper will increase.

**Table 8.3.**   Energy Used to Mine and Process a Copper Ore in Which All Copper Is Present in Biotite

| | Energy used (Btu/lb of copper) | | |
|---|---|---|---|
| Grade, percent Cu | 0.7 | 0.1 | 0.01 |
| Mining plus concentration | 19,300 | 135,000 | 1,350,000 |
| Preparation of a copper salt | 326,858 | 2,288,010 | 22,880,100 |
| Smelting | 20,000 | 20,000 | 20,000 |
| Total | 366,158 | 2,443,010 | 24,250,100 |
| Equivalent thermal energy in bituminous coal, in pounds of coal | 28 | 188 | 1,866 |

*Note:* No overburden need be stripped, and concentration and smelting are assumed to have 100 percent recovery.

The data in figures 8.3 and 8.4 are derived for copper, but can equally well be applied to most metals now used. Some, such as aluminum, already plot on the upper, or energy-intensive curve. Most others plot on the less energy-intensive, or "sulfide ore" curve, despite the fact that in many cases, such as iron, the ore minerals are not sulfides. The locations of some common minerals are shown in figure 8.5.

It is quite clear from our present knowledge of geochemistry that every metal with a crustal abundance below 0.01 percent will reach the same kind of mineralogical barrier as that shown for copper in figure 8.3. It is possible (but still unproved) that the size of the mineralogical barrier may even be a function of the crustal abundance of an element, being largest for the scarcest element.

The exact path that will be followed by each metal as grades and ores change in the future is not entirely clear. In the case of copper, for example, the existence of ferromanganese nodules and metal-rich clays on parts of the deep ocean floor, both of which contain copper in solid solution, allow an optimistic future to be suggested.

Unfortunately, a similarly optimistic future cannot be predicted for most metals. The way the future will actually unfold is not, of course, solely dependent on energy; the question of economics also enters. Figures 8.4 and 8.5 should not, therefore, be simply translated into plots of cost versus grade. Questions of royalties, labor, capital, and politics must all be considered and each metal and each mineral deposit must be separately evaluated. For the long-term future it seems highly unlikely that meaningful cost analyses can be made, especially when the possible influence of new and presently unknown technologies must be taken into account.

Despite the many uncertainties, the information in figure 8.3 suggests that a completely different kind of technology and energy balance must be assumed if we are ever to consider recovering most metals from ordinary silicate minerals. Where the imaginable future is concerned for most metals, therefore, speculation must be realistically limited to long-term supplies of the

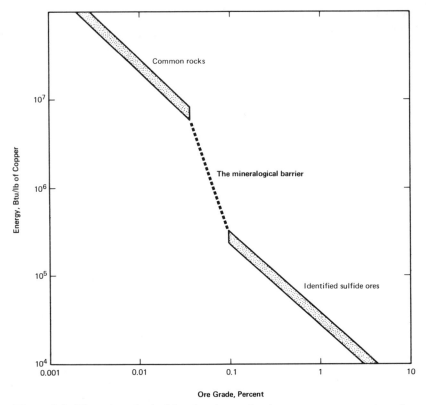

**Figure 8.3.** The mineralogical barrier that technology must overcome in order to produce copper from ordinary rocks after all sulfide ores are used. All geochemically scarce metals present the same challenge.

beneficiable ores that can be mined, concentrated, and smelted analogously to the case presented for chalcopyrite in table 8.2. Considering the entire crust, or any large portion of it, as a resource for future development simply cannot be countenanced with any hope that it will come to pass. From the geological viewpoint, the question of long-term mineral supplies thus reduces to the following:

1. Are there possible kinds of mineral deposits which are still unfamiliar or which are unknown and which might reasonably be worked?
2. How much and how easily found is the material in mineral deposits that can be processed?

To these can be added a nongeological question:

3. Are there possible unconventional extraction technologies that might be applicable to deposits that cannot now be worked because of high costs?

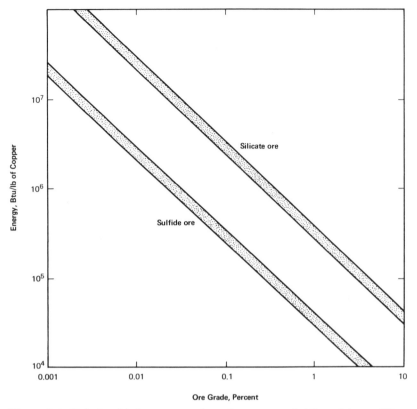

**Figure 8.4.** Relationship between grade and energy needed for mining, milling, and smelting copper ores. Data are given in tables 8.2 and 8.3.

We feel that the last question cannot be tackled in this chapter and should most appropriately be considered by an expert in extraction metallurgy. The first question requires the short answer in the following section. The second is more involved and occupies the remainder of this chapter.

### Unconventional and Presently Unrecognized Sources of Metals

There is a long history of successful discoveries of new and previously unexpected kinds of mineral deposits. Beryllium, for example, traditionally has been recovered from the beryllium-aluminum silicate mineral beryl, but in recent years unexpectedly large deposits of another beryllium mineral, bertrandite, have also been discovered. Niobium and tantalum offer another example: traditionally recovered from the small amounts of their oxide minerals found in a type of rock called pegmatite, they are now recovered in much larger amounts from another rock type, called a carbonatite, which was not even recognized as a distinct rock until after World War II.

Despite the successes quoted—and they are only two among a much larger group—it is not realistic to expect that all or even many metals have new and unexpected kinds of mineral deposits waiting to be found. We make this statement because the large-scale sampling and analysis programs now used as prospecting methods (commonly called geochemical prospecting) have not demonstrated the existence of many unsuspected kinds of deposits. Where mineral deposits have been found by such methods, they have usually been the kinds of deposits with which geologists are already familiar. One could argue that only those areas likely to contain conventional deposits are prospected, but the argument becomes continually less compelling as larger and larger areas are subjected to chemical analysis. It can also be argued that testing is highly selective and tends to be concentrated on a few elements such as copper, lead, zinc, and uranium, and that some metals, whose chemistry in the crust is less well understood, have not been tested at all. This is a valid assertion and it points to a neglected area for research. Knowledge of the geochemistry of many metals (for example, tungsten, tin, and tantalum) is so limited that it simply is not possible to make an accurate assessment of the way the metals are distributed in the crust and, therefore, systematic prospecting programs cannot be designed. Deposits tend to be found by accident.

There is only one general scientific conclusion that can be drawn concerning the question of unsuspected kinds of deposits. Chemical elements which have such distinctive chemistries that the possibilities for atomic substitution are limited are more likely to be concentrated in unsuspected hiding places than are elements with less distinctive chemistries. Examples of the former are tin, tungsten, niobium, tantalum, beryllium, uranium, gold, and antimony. Examples of some elements less likely to form unsuspected kinds of deposits are copper, lead, zinc, nickel, and chromium. From this line of argument one can conclude that most of the mineral deposits still to be found will be similar to deposits that have already been discovered, or will prove to have been formed by similar deposit-forming processes.

## 3. Properties of Mineral Deposits

### Geochemically Abundant Metals

In the second section we pointed out that metals can be divided into three groups on the basis of crustal abundance and geochemical behavior. The first two groups, with crustal abundances greater than 0.1 percent and falling between 0.01 and 0.1 percent respectively, commonly form separate minerals in ordinary rocks. Elements falling into these groups are referred to as the geochemically abundant elements. The difference between the two groups is a matter of degree rather than basic differences in geochemical behavior.

Mineral deposits of the geochemically abundant elements tend to be compositional extremes of ordinary rocks and to be very large—some may be as large as $10^{10}$ tons. The deposits that are worked are also so rich that only a small degree of concentration is needed to produce a product for the smelter. Indeed, in many cases, the ore can be shipped and used without concentration. The ore minerals sought are, for the most part, oxides, hydroxides, or carbonates, though in the case of aluminum it is apparent that some silicate minerals (e.g. clays and feldspars) are almost as useful as the presently used hydroxides.

Because ore minerals of the geochemically abundant metals are so common, only the very richest deposits are considered when resource estimates are made. The low-grade deposits contain such astronomically large tonnages of metal that supplies can always be assured. Consider iron, for example. The principal ore minerals of iron are the oxides and hydroxides, and because the oxide and hydroxide minerals are formed by weathering and sedimentation, by igneous processes and by metamorphism, the ore minerals of iron are present in essentially all rocks. Standard petrographic descriptions of ordinary rocks routinely report the presence of almost 2 percent by volume, or 3 percent by weight, of opaque iron ore minerals. Assuming that the ore minerals contain 67 percent Fe by weight (magnetite, the most common oxide, contains 72 percent Fe), this suggests that ordinary rocks of the crust are iron ores amenable to beneficiation with an average grade of 2 percent Fe. That is, they are ores that lie on the lower curve of figure 8.5. Considering that the crustal abundance of iron is 5.80 percent, this simple calculation suggests that about 30 percent of all the iron in the crust could be recovered without any change in technology and without having to jump a mineralogical barrier, by simply mining lower and lower grade ores until ordinary rocks such as granites and gneisses are being processed to yield an oxide or hydroxide concentrate. The continental crust therefore contains $7.5 \times 10^{16}$ metric tons of recoverable iron to a depth of 10 km. Even if this calculation is wrong by a factor of 10, the principle does not change and the amount of recoverable iron is still enormous.

### Geochemically Scarce Metals

The third group, the geochemically scarce metals, all have crustal abundances below 0.01 percent and their geochemical behavior differs sharply from the geochemically abundant ones. The geochemically scarce metal group

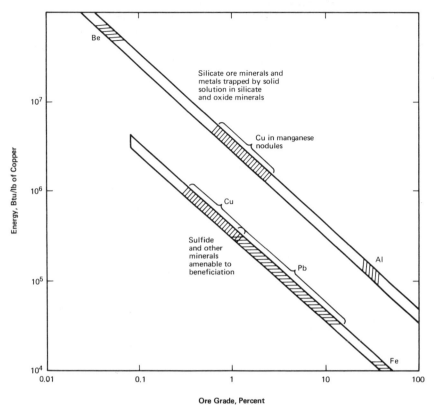

**Figure 8.5.** Ore minerals of common metals (except those produced from placer deposits) fall on either the high-energy or low-energy curve. Positions of the present-day ores of a few common metals are indicated.

substitutes for abundant metals in common silicate minerals. A few of the scarce metals—copper, zinc, and chromium—have been reported to form rare mineral grains in some rocks, but most of the group never form separate minerals in ordinary rocks. The only time the group forms separate minerals is when some special, localized, and rare set of circumstances produces a geochemically unusual environment in which an extreme concentration of one or more of the scarce metals occurs. The two most important concentrating processes are magmatic differentiation, in which separation of liquids, gases, or solids during cooling and crystallization of magma produces locally extreme compositions, and hydrothermal differentiation in which hot, saline fluids react with rocks, selectively scavenge scarce metals, transport their dissolved load, and then by any of several possible processes, deposit the scarce metals as sulfide, oxide, or even pure elemental minerals in an open fracture or a porous rock. The combination of processes needed to produce mineral deposits means that the deposits are relatively rare features in the crust, relatively small in size (ranging from $10^1$ to $10^9$ metric tons), and not homogeneously distributed.

From a general geochemical argument, it can be deduced that only a small percentage—between 0.01 and 0.001 percent—of the amount of a scarce metal in the crust is present in ore minerals (Skinner, 1976). This means that the recoverable amount of any given scarce metal in the crust must be roughly proportional to its crustal abundance. Unfortunately, general geochemical arguments have not yet led to any predictive models concerning the size, grade, frequency, and geographic distribution of mineral deposits. Since it is these factors that control, to a large extent, how deposits are mined and prospected and this in turn controls long-term mineral supplies, we must briefly consider some of the empirical data concerning mineral deposits.

## Mineralogy and the Grouping of Metals

The most important ore minerals of the scarce metals are sulfides, oxides, and pure elements. Not all of the compounds are simple oxides or simple sulfides. The ore minerals of beryllium, for example, are silicates, which are complex oxides. Table 8.4 lists the chemical families of the most important geochemically scarce metals. Note that only one element, nickel, has minerals of major importance that fall into two different families (sulfides and oxides).

The reasons for the limited range of ore minerals lie, of course, in the chemistries of the minerals and the processes by which they are concentrated. There are many similarities between the chemistries of sulfide minerals, for example, and in one property in particular they are very similar. All of the sulfide minerals have very low solubilities in hydrothermal solutions. Not surprisingly, therefore, it is usually a sulfide compound that precipitates from a hydrothermal solution rather than a carbonate or sulfate or some other possible, but more soluble, mineral. The chemical similarities among the sulfide minerals lead to an important factor in their occurrence—almost all sulfide mineral deposits are enriched in more than one geochemically scarce metal. In many deposits one, two, or three metals predominate (for example, lead and zinc are very commonly found together), while several others are present in small but significant amounts so that during processing they can be recovered as by-products. Indeed, a number of metals (such as gallium, germanium, and cadmium) are produced mainly as by-products and are rarely mined as separate entities. Similar metal associations are also observed in the oxide minerals and elemental metals. The principal metal associations, together with the kinds of deposits in which they are found, are listed in table 8.5.

**Table 8.4.** Chemical Families of the Important Geochemically Scarce Metals

| Chemical family | Major importance | Minor importance |
|---|---|---|
| Sulfides | Antimony | Platinum group metals |
| | Arsenic | Tin |
| | Bismuth | Vanadium |
| | Cadmium | |
| | Cobalt | |
| | Copper | |
| | Gallium | |
| | Germanium | |
| | Indium | |
| | Lead | |
| | Mercury | |
| | Molybdenum | |
| | Nickel | |
| | Silver | |
| | Zinc | |
| Oxides | Beryllium | Copper |
| | Chromium | Zinc |
| | Lithium | |
| | Nickel | |
| | Niobium | |
| | Tantalum | |
| | Thorium | |
| | Tin | |
| | Tungsten | |
| | Uranium | |
| | Vanadium | |
| | Zirconium | |
| Elements | Gold | Copper |
| | Platinum group metals | Silver |

It is apparent from table 8.5 that certain metals such as silver, cobalt, and cadmium are produced mainly as by-products. Unless large deposits are known from which such metals can be produced as primary products, therefore, it is clear that production will be controlled by the host metal. This is already true for silver and cadmium. For a number of other metals, production now depends on a very few deposits plus by-production and it is apparent that future production will change rapidly as the few large deposits are depleted. Examples of metals falling in this category are gold, mercury, and tin.

### Sizes and Grades of Deposits

The size of a mineral deposit multiplied by its average grade indicates how much metal is present and potentially recoverable. Unfortunately, many factors intervene in obtaining accurate data for all kinds of deposits. Testing

**Table 8.5.**  Major Classes of Mineral Deposits and the Metal Associations Observed Within Them

| | |
|---|---|
| Deposits formed | |
| by magmatic processes | |
| Pegmatites | Niobium + tantalum + (tungsten + tin) |
| | Beryllium + lithium |
| | Tungsten + tin + (niobium + tantalum) |
| | Uranium + thorium |
| Carbonatites | Niobium + tantalum + (uranium + thorium) |
| | Copper |
| Layered intrusives | Nickel + copper + (platinum group metals) |
| | Platinum group metals + (copper + nickel) |
| | Chromium |
| | Vanadium |
| Deposits formed | |
| by hydrothermal processes | |
| Stratabound deposits | Lead + zinc + (silver + copper + cadmium) |
| | Copper + (lead + zinc + silver + cobalt) |
| | Uranium + (vanadium) |
| Veins and stockworks | Copper + molybdenum + (silver + gold) |
| | Copper + (lead + zinc + silver + cobalt) |
| | Molybdenum |
| | Lead + zinc + (silver + bismuth) |
| | Silver + (gold) |
| | Gold + (silver) |
| | Mercury |
| | Tin + tungsten + (silver) |
| | Uranium |
| | Antimony + (tungsten) |
| Massive deposits in | Copper + (lead + zinc) |
| volcanic rocks | Copper + lead + zinc + (silver + gold) |
| Contact metamorphic | Copper + (molybdenum + lead + zinc) |
| deposits | Lead + zinc |
| | Tin + tungsten |
| | Tungsten |

*Note:* Where two or more metals are listed, deposits will usually, but not necessarily, contain all of them. Metals listed within parentheses are usually present in minor amounts and will be recovered only as by-products.

deposits is an expensive process, so tests are usually carried just far enough to assure stable continuity of mining. As an example of the changing perception of recoverable metal, consider the data in table 8.6, which shows the development and production history of the Bingham Canyon Mine, Utah. It is not possible to know exactly how much metal is present until a deposit is completely worked out. Nevertheless, it is possible to make good estimates of metal content based on a combination of testing and geological inference. From such estimates, research geologists working for AMAX produced the information presented in figure 8.6 (COMRATE, 1975).

The data in figure 8.6 strongly suggest that specific types of deposits have distinct ranges of size and grade. It might be argued that the lower grade limit is not an accurate representation of the true lower limit because low-grade,

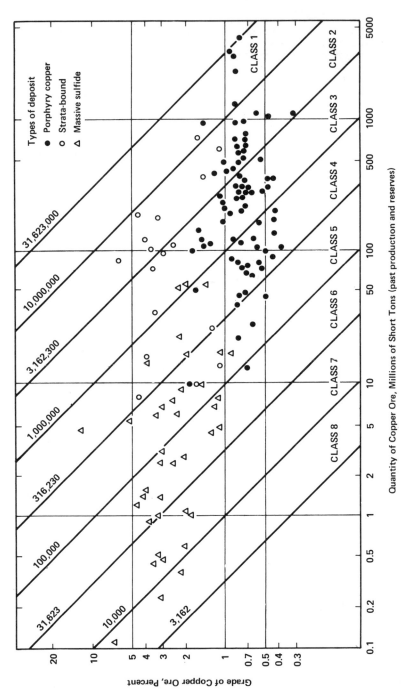

**Figure 8.6.** Size and grade characteristics of copper deposits of the three main geological types. Based on U.S. Geological Survey, Presentation at COMRATE Colloquium, Estes Park, Colo., 1973. (Diagonal lines show tons of copper metal contained per deposit. Classes refer to distribution of world copper deposits by metal contained.)

uneconomic deposits have not been tested and developed. The argument can be only partly correct. Both massive sulfide and strata-bound deposits could be worked to lower grades if lower grade and larger tonnage deposits were available. Thus, the only deposit class in which large, low-grade deposits might remain unknown is in the porphyry coppers and there, for the geochemical reasons stated earlier, the lower grade boundary would be about 0.1 percent Cu anyway, so the region of figure 8.6 that is left for exploration is not large.

It can be seen from figure 8.6 that a small fraction (29 percent) of the deposits contains the vast preponderance (85 percent) of the copper. This is not an unusual situation because exactly the same property is displayed by two other closely studied commodities—petroleum and coal. Although it has not yet been demonstrated for other materials, it is generally assumed that the same kind of distribution holds true for all mineral deposits. To a first approximation, therefore, it should be possible to test the success of modern mineral exploration by the frequency with which deposits of size classes 1 and 2 are discovered. Unfortunately, data have not yet been gathered in a sufficiently convenient manner for this task to be carried out. They do lead to the general geochemical observation (Skinner, 1976) that the largest known deposit for a given metal and the total number of discovered deposits falling in a given size range are both proportional to the crustal abundance of the metal. Thus, if larger and larger deposits are found, or if deposits equal in size to the largest continue to be found, one could safely conclude that prospecting is meeting society's needs. It is surely significant, and not very encouraging, that the largest deposits of most metals being mined today were discovered many years ago; when new deposits are opened for mining they tend to be smaller than the "older giants."

### Geological versus Geographic Distribution of Deposits

The formation of mineral deposits requires specific and rare combinations of geological processes. The frequency of geological processes is not uniform throughout the crust, nor have they been uniform in importance throughout the earth's history. The distribution of specific kinds of deposits is therefore not likely to be uniform throughout the crust. This is indeed observed to be true. In theory, of course, a sufficiently large portion of the crust should contain rocks of all kinds and ages and hence all kinds of mineral deposits should be present. In practice, no country, with the possible exception of the U.S.S.R., controls a large enough portion of the crust to be sure that deposits of all kinds are contained within its borders. Thus, geographic inhomogeneity in the distribution of mineral deposits ensures that no country except the U.S.S.R. is likely to be able to develop self-sufficiency in all its mineral requirements.

Problems of Exploration for New Deposits

The search for new deposits is guided by perceptions of the geological environment in which the search is conducted. These in turn are conditioned by knowledge of how mineral deposits form. With the exception of carbonatites, no new classes of magmatic mineral deposits have been identified for at least fifty years. A different situation exists for hydrothermal deposits. Remember that formation of any hydrothermal deposit requires the confluence of several different processes—the circulation of a hydrothermal solution; the collection of metals in the solution by any of several possible mechanisms; transport by flow in some confined channel or aquifer; then precipitation of the dissolved load by cooling, by evaporation, by pressure drop, by chemical reactions, or by a combination of events. Specific combinations of processes and events are characteristic of specific geological environments. Specific classes of mineral deposits are also characteristic of specific geological environments. Because the possible combinations of events, and of environments, is very large, new environments for hydrothermal deposits are being identified all the time. How many remain to be found is an open question, but each time a new type of deposit is discovered (usually by accident), a spate of prospecting follows. The primary factor influencing prospecting is, therefore, knowledge of the way mineral deposits form.

Once an area has been identified from general geological mapping as likely to contain certain kinds of mineral deposits, prospecting will begin. The actual details of success in prospecting are discussed in later sections. Here we simply point out that government encouragement or discouragement of prospecting can play as important a role as geological factors. Nongeological factors do not, of course, influence mineral endowment, but they do play a vital role in the ability to assess the endowment and to identify the fraction that is a mineral resource.


## 4. Exploration for Mineral Deposits


Practice and Effectiveness

As mineral deposits with surface exposure are depleted, the ability to find hidden deposits becomes an increasingly important factor in the potential supply of a region. In the United States, for example, the productivity of conventional prospecting for most metals, except for uranium and except in Alaska, had declined to low levels by 1940 because most mineralized outcrops had been examined by that time (Bailly, 1978). In the future, domestic mineral supplies will primarily come from hidden deposits.

**Table 8.6.**    Production and Development History of Bingham Canyon Mine, Utah
(tons of copper)

| Development history | Production |  |  |  |
|---|---|---|---|---|
|  | 1899 | 1915 | 1930 | 1970 |
| Cumulative production from start of mining, 1904 | — | 498,696 | 2,296,078 | 10,851,559 |
| Reserves developed ahead of mining | 247,700 | 4,966,000 | 6,822,000 | 12,588,000 |
| Estimated grade, percent copper | 2.0% | 1.45% | 1.06% | 0.71% |

*Source:* Based on data from the Commission on Mineral Resources and the Environment, "Resources of Copper," in *Mineral Resources and the Environment* (Washington, D.C., National Academy of Sciences, 1975) chapter VI.

As the productivity of conventional prospecting has declined, improved technology has made it possible to prospect beneath surficial cover. This includes improved knowledge of the way mineral deposits form, new geophysical and geochemical sensing systems, plus direct sampling by drilling. The effectiveness of these technologies varies with the mineral sought, its mineralogical associations, and the geological environment in which the deposit occurs. It is the consideration of these factors in combination with measures to decrease the probability for failure, the so-called gambler's ruin, which gives rise to exploration strategies.

Tables 8.7 and 8.8 show the distributions of metal discoveries by year of discovery and primary method for the United States and Canada, respectively. Especially noteworthy for the United States is the fact that conventional prospecting has not produced a discovery in a decade. Discoveries by geophysical technologies and by geological inference have remained fairly constant, and discoveries by geochemistry have been sporadic and limited in number. Clearly, in the United States during this period, geological inference has been the most important exploration method.

**Table 8-7.**    Discoveries of U.S. Metal Mines, 1951–70

| Year of discovery | Principal exploration method |  |  |  |  |  |  |  | Total No. |
|---|---|---|---|---|---|---|---|---|---|
|  | Conventional prospecting |  | Geologic inference |  | Geophysical anomaly |  | Geochemical anomaly |  |  |
|  | No. | % | No. | % | No. | % | No. | % |  |
| 1951–55 | 1 | 8 | 9 | 75 | 2 | 17 | — | — | 12 |
| 1956–60 | 2 | 13 | 10 | 67 | 2 | 13 | 1 | 7 | 15 |
| 1961–65 | — | — | 13 | 87 | 2 | 13 | — | — | 15 |
| 1966–70 | — | — | 15 | 79 | 2 | 11 | 2 | 10 | 19 |
| 1951–70 | 3 | 5 | 47 | 77 | 8 | 13 | 3 | 5 | 61 |

*Source:* P. A. Bailly, "Changing Rates of Success in Metallic Exploration," Paper presented at the GAC-MAC-SEG-CGU Annual Meeting, Vancouver, British Columbia, April 25, 1977.

**Table 8-8.**    Discoveries of Canadian Metal Mines Through 1975

| | Principal exploration method | | | | | | | | |
|---|---|---|---|---|---|---|---|---|---|
| Year of discovery | Conventional prospecting | | Geologic inference | | Geophysical anomaly | | Geochemical anomaly | | Total |
| | No. | % | No. | % | No. | % | No. | % | No. |
| Pre-1920 | 26 | 93 | 2 | 7 | — | — | — | — | 28 |
| 1920–29 | 12 | 80 | 3 | 20 | — | — | — | — | 15 |
| 1930–39 | 13 | 87 | 2 | 13 | — | — | — | — | 15 |
| 1940–50 | 13 | 76 | 4 | 24 | — | — | — | — | 17 |
| 1951–55 | 16 | 46 | 14 | 40 | 5 | 14 | — | — | 35 |
| 1956–60 | 6 | 25 | 4 | 17 | 14 | 58 | — | — | 24 |
| 1961–65 | 4 | 27 | 4 | 27 | 5 | 33 | 2 | 13 | 15 |
| 1966–70 | 2 | 10 | 4 | 20 | 13 | 65 | 1(?) | 5 | 20 |
| 1951–70 | 28 | 30 | 26 | 28 | 37 | 39 | 3 | 3 | 94 |
| 1971–75[a] | 1 | 4 | 4 + 1(?) | 19 | 15 | 58 | 3 | 11 | 26 |

*Sources:* Pre-1920 through 1964: D. R. Derry, "Exploration Expenditure, Discovery Rate and Methods," *CIM Bulletin* vol. 63, no. 362 (1970). For 1965 through 1975: D. R. Derry and Booth, "Mineral Discoveries and Exploration Expenditure—A Revised Review 1965–1976," Paper presented at 1977 CIM Symposium.

[a] No principal exploration method was given for two discoveries during 1971–75.

The record for Canada covers a much longer time and it shows clearly the changing productivity of differing technologies employed in exploration. Especially apparent is the decline of conventional prospecting to only 4 percent of all discoveries in the period 1971–75. As with the United States, the productivity of geological inference has been rather constant since about 1940. It is noteworthy that as discoveries by conventional prospecting decreased during 1956–60, those by geophysics increased rapidly, and geophysics has continued to be a very productive exploration technology.

Geochemistry first produced a discovery in 1961–65 and seems to offer promise of increased productivity in the future.

The very different yields between the United States and Canada reflect several things. One of the most important is the fact that during the period reported, Canada was, and still is, much less well explored than the United States, so more deposits with surface exposure remained to be detected by prospecting teams. Additionally, the relatively high incidence of massive sulfide deposits made the productivity of geophysical technology very high by comparison with the United States, where massive sulfide deposits occur relatively less frequently.

Although advancing technologies increase the ability to detect buried deposits, this ability declines rapidly with depth, as is demonstrated by the estimates of experts in exploration. Figure 8.7 shows the opinion expressed in a recent CRA(1978) report on the discoverability of a porphyry copper deposit having 150,000,000 short tons of mineralized rock averaging 0.7 percent Cu, given a cutoff grade of 0.2 percent. Note how rapidly the ability to detect this deposit, using today's technology, deteriorates with depth. If

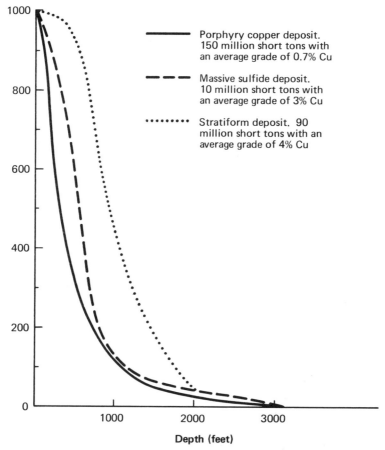

**Figure 8.7.** Discoverability of copper deposits using current technology. A discoverability of 1,000 implies certainty of discovery given best-practice technology. From Charles River Associates, *Economics and Geology of Mineral Supply: An Integrated Framework for Long Run Policy Analysis*, Publication prepared for the National Science Foundation, Washington, D.C., November 1978.

the deposit were partially exposed, current exploration would be certain to discover it, but under only 300 feet of burial, discoverability is reduced to 0.5. If the deposit were to be buried beneath 3,000 feet of cover, it would be virtually undiscoverable, unless there were some unusual circumstance, such as its association with another deposit nearby or some recognizable geological feature.

Figure 8.7 also shows the opinion of this same expert about the discoverability of a massive sulfide copper deposit and of a stratabound or stratiform copper deposit. The massive sulfide deposit envisioned in these statements of discoverability is one of 10,000,000 short tons of mineralized rock having an average grade of 3 percent Cu or Cu equivalent. The stratabound or stratiform deposit is of 90,000,000 short tons of rock having an average grade of 4 percent Cu or Cu equivalent. Since most North American massive sulfide and stratabound copper deposits occur in Canada, their discoverability reflects exploration in geologic environments and under terrain conditions characteristic of that country. Conversely, the discoverability for a porphyry copper deposit represents exploration experience primarily in the southwestern United States and northern Mexico.

Massive sulfide mineral deposits are commonly mineralized with copper, lead, and zinc, and sometimes with silver and gold in varying amounts. In some instances, copper mineralization will be dominant; in others, it may be lead and zinc. Therefore, discoverability of a massive lead or zinc deposit would be very similar to that for a massive copper deposit. The effect of depth of cover on discoverability varies considerably for these three reference deposits. Discoverability of the porphyry copper deposit deteriorated rapidly with depth of cover, while that for a stratabound-stratiform deposit deteriorated the least, discovery still being a certainty beneath 300 feet of cover and reduced to only 0.9 at 600 feet.

Discoverability reflects more than just depth and the expert's opinion reflects his personal weighting of all factors. Other important factors generally include the kind of cover, the geological environment, the mineralogy, and the size and grade of the deposit. The effect of size and grade on discoverability of copper deposits was explored in some detail using expert estimates of discoverability under a variety of assumptions for these factors. Statistical analysis of these responses showed that according to expert experience, for porphyry copper deposits the tonnage of mineralized rock is not a significant factor in discoverability, but the average concentration of copper is significant (CRA, 1978). An interpretation of this result is that porphyry copper deposits typically are large and of low grade; thus variation of size, while it is typically large, has little effect, the converse being true for grade. In the discoverability of massive sulfide copper deposits, grade is not significant while size is significant, probably because grades typically are high and size typically is small. Both grade and size were considered to be important factors in the discoverability of stratabound and stratiform copper deposits.

An additional useful study that examined the concept of discoverability should be mentioned. Donald (1974) also relied on the opinion of explorationists about copper exploration and surveyed the nine major mining firms conducting exploration in the Northern Sonora of Mexico. He included questions about regional exploration for favorable areas and target detection by each of three geophysical techniques (including polarization, airborne

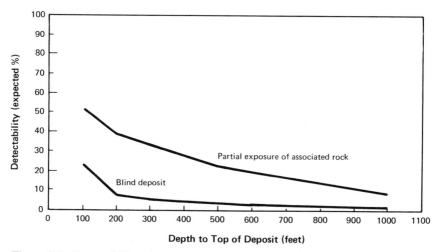

**Figure 8.8.** Detectability of a Northern Sonoran deposit. Note that a detectability of 100 implies certain discovery by best-practice exploration. From Charles River Associates, *Economics and Geology of Mineral Supply: An Integrated Framework for Long Run Policy Analysis.* Publication prepared for the National Science Foundation, Washington, D.C., November 1978.

magnetic, and ground magnetic), by geology, and by geochemistry. The probability for the joint events of area recognition and target detection was computed using the averaged responses of the nine explorationists for a hidden copper deposit and for a deposit which, although not exposed, does exhibit clues in outcrop rock such as alteration and mineralization typically associated with such a deposit. The results of this analysis are shown in figure 8.8. The experience of the nine explorationists is that the probability for the discovery of a hidden copper deposit in the Sonora of Mexico deteriorates rapidly with depth of cover, from 0.23 at a depth of 100 feet to 0.123 at a depth of 200 feet, after which the rate of deterioration decreases considerably; at a depth of 1,000 feet of cover, the probability for discovery is 0.012. For the deposit with an outcrop of mineralization or alteration, the probability for detection is 0.573 at a depth of 100 feet, 0.424 at a depth of 200 feet, 0.25 at a depth of 500 feet, and approximately 0.10 at 1,000 feet. Thus, the presence of an outcrop of associated mineralization or alteration is extremely beneficial to exploration; without it, the probability for discovery is low, especially for cover in excess of 200 feet.

The main point to be drawn from these studies of experience in copper exploration is that while technologies of geology, geochemistry, and geophysics have offset to some degree the depletion of surface deposits by providing man with the capability to look beneath the surface, this ability is limited by the depth of cover.

In a very general sense, the history of metals exploration technology can be summarized in three phases:

1. Conventional prospecting of surface indicators.
2. The detection of shallowly covered deposits through instrumental sensing of associated physical and chemical signatures.
3. The use of integrated geological models to make geological inferences about favorable areas and deposit occurrences.

Evidence indicates that unless some major improvements are made in the technologies of geophysics and geochemistry, every country must adopt the techniques of stage three. The United States is already in this phase. According to Bailly (1978), geologic thinking is without any doubt the deepest penetrating tool, the most effective of the remote sensing capabilities. In essence, exploration will have to become much more an exercise of geoscience concepts, theory, and fact than prospecting and the direct sensing of the physics and chemistry of minerals or elements present in or associated with the deposit. The Committee on Mineral Resources and the Environment of the National Academy of Sciences (COMRATE) (1975, page 147) summarizes this third phase of exploration as follows:

> The third generation exploration effort consists of using geological occurrence models (sometimes with genetic content) of deposits and of their settings. Such models allow the formulation of predictions about mineral provinces and mineral occurrences in the absence of mineralized outcrops and in the absence of anomalies resulting from instrumental surveys. This conceptual approach has not yet produced many reserves, but it is expected that it will in the future, thanks to the major improvements in recent times in the conceptual, genetic content of the science of ore deposition.

Clearly, the future presents a challenge to the technologies of geological inference, geophysics, and geochemistry. Because of the depletion of surface and near-surface deposits and because of the rapid decrease in the detectability of deposits as depth of cover (burial) increases, unless there are significant improvements in these exploration technologies, the costs of discovery of future metal deposits will increase significantly. Another proposition seems indicated: Unless the low detection ability of current technology is improved in the future, as those deposits closest to the surface are depleted and as exploration is directed to deeper deposits, there will have to be increased reliance on direct search by drilling. When the opportunity costs of missed deposits plus the costs of identifying false anomalies exceed those of drilling false anomalies in barren ground, the use of drilling as a primary search technology will be justified. There are those who think that the point has been reached already (Ridge, 1974). Ridge and others argue that the mistakes due to the use of geology, geophysics, and geochemistry, when combined with the cost to society of redundant exploration (more than one firm may gather the same basic geoscience data), more than justify grid drilling. As yet, there has not been a thorough and unequivocal economic justification for such a claim. However, the failure of predrilling technology to improve the detectability of deep deposits may one day make drilling the preferred exploration technology and improvement of the technology would hasten such an event. In the case of uranium exploration, the amount of information which now is obtained from records of dry holes has increased exploratory drilling in spite of large increases in costs of drilling; the improved benefits outweigh these costs (Bonner, 1978).

A proposition of a totally different kind springs from the rapid decrease in detectability as depth increases. The proposition is, simply, that for those geological environments where deposits have been discovered and in which a deposit is equally likely to occur at any depth within the upper crust of the earth, a large number of deposits remain to be discovered. The proposition is not true for all classes of deposits, but for deposits such as massive sulfides in volcanic terrains, the proposition follows from the fact that our detection ability deteriorates so rapidly with depth of cover. Of course, the cost per pound of metal produced from deeply buried deposits may be quite high, reflecting not only the high costs of discovery, but the increased production costs resulting from the thickness of cover of the deposit. The proposition is not a suggestion to predicate resource assessment upon the assumption of equal deposit occurrence with depth. In some environments such a proposition is acceptable while in others it is not. Furthermore, even if equal frequency of occurrence with depth is indicated, the average grade and the distribution of grades may be very different for a deposit which is near enough to the surface to be oxidized and enriched than one which contains only the original, unenriched mineralization.

### Costs

An exploration technology that is ineffective in the detection of covered deposits, when considered jointly with a declining discovery rate of surface and near surface deposits, leads to an expectation for rising costs of discovery. Only technical changes in exploration can enhance the ability to add to known deposits. Analysis of historical discovery costs invariably shows that they have been increasing. Technical change in exploration methods has not been rapid enough to offset these costs. However, there is some disagreement as to how much discovery costs have actually increased.

The most definitive studies on exploration costs and effectiveness have been drawn from Canadian experience. Roscoe (1971) implied a tenfold increase in discovery costs from 1951 to 1969, but the large increase was not verified by a careful study by Cranstone and Martin (1973), who claim that Roscoe did not take into account deposit size and grade and did not include all discoveries made during that period. Cranstone and Martin examined exploration over the period 1946–71 and concluded that if deposits "on the shelf" (deposits found by previous exploration but held in inventory either because of adverse economics or the expectation of discoveries of higher quality deposits) are considered, and account is given to the sizes and grades of the deposits discovered, the real cost of discoveries per pound of aggregate metal approximately doubled during this twenty-five year period. This amounts to an annual rate of increase in real discovery costs of approximately 3 percent.

Bailly (1978), using the Canadian data of Cranstone and Martin, defined three measures:

$$EFT = \frac{\text{Value of discoveries}}{\text{Expenditures for all exploration projects}}$$

$$= \text{exploration effectiveness}$$

$$PE = \frac{\text{Value of discoveries}}{\text{Expenditure for project}} = \text{project effectiveness}$$

$$SR = \frac{\text{Expenditure for successful projects}}{\text{Expenditure for all projects}} = \text{success ratio}$$

These measures are related: $EFT = (PE)(SR)$. The trends of these measures for Canada from 1951 to 1970 are shown in figure 8.9. Exploration effectiveness declined from 160 to 55. The decline is due to a moderate decrease in project effectiveness and a large decrease in success ratio: Today, less than 7 percent of expenditures on exploration result in economic discoveries. Because of the large contribution of drilling to total exploration expenditures on successful projects, Bailly (1978) proposes that cost-effective improvements in drilling technology could at least slow, if not reverse, the decrease in project effectiveness.

The single most important factor in the decline of overall exploration effectiveness must be the declining discovery rate for surface and near-surface deposits and the ineffectiveness of sensing (geophysics and geochemistry) technologies in identifying anomalies associated with deeper mineral deposits. This ineffectiveness means that a greater number of anomalies are drilled on average in relation to discovery of economic deposits at some depth. In spite of improvements in the integrated use of these technologies, one is forced to conclude that real discovery costs have certainly increased and have perhaps doubled.

Data are not available to support an in-depth study of discovery costs for the United States, but such a study would probably support the conclusions drawn from the Canadian data. If anything, since mining is at a more mature

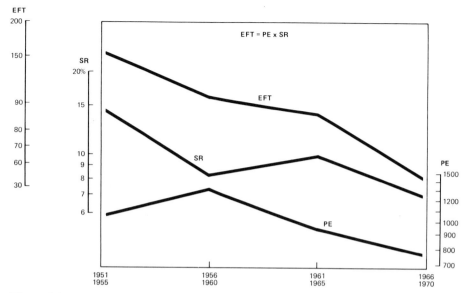

**Figure 8.9.** Trends in discovery. Note that *EFT* is exploration effectiveness; *PE*, project effectiveness; and *SR*, success ratio. From P. A. Bailly, "Today's Resource Status—Tomorrow's Resource Problems: The Need for Research on Mineral Deposits." Paper presented at the GSA–GAS–MAC Joint Annual Meeting, Toronto, Oct. 23, 1978.

stage of development in the United States, it seems likely that a decline in discovery rates is even more advanced in the United States than it is in Canada, meaning that discovery costs per pound of metal are probably higher.

The doubling of exploration costs per unit of metal extracted certainly is not unexpected, but is an intriguing result when viewed against the historical pattern of total exploration expenditures as a percentage of annual production. This percentage has been generally reported to be in the range of 3 to 5 percent (Bailly, 1978; Brant, 1968). Figure 8.10 shows the trend in this percentage for Canada from 1951 to 1970 and the projections of Martin, Cranstone, and Zwartendyk (1976) of what the percentage will have to be to meet future metal requirements. As indicated in figure 8.10, the percentage has been rather constant at 4 percent until the 1966–70 period, in which it increased to 5 percent. Since real metal prices during this period declined overall, the maintenance of this nearly constant percentage in the face of the failure of exploration technology to compensate for fewer discoveries presumably means that the productivity of capital and labor downstream in the exploration-exploitation cycle (mining, processing, and refining) has offset, not only the effects of depletion on mining and processing, but also some of the decline in discoveries.

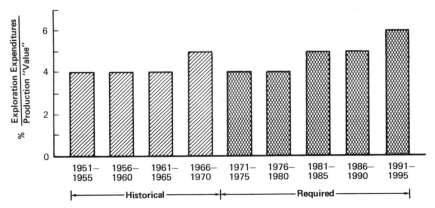

**Figure 8.10.** Exploration expenditure expressed as a percentage of production "value," 1951–1995. Based on H. L. Martin, D. A. Cranstone, and J. Zwartentyk, *Metal Mining in Canada, 1976–2000*, MR 167 (Ottawa, Energy Mines and Resources, 1976).

It is probable that the balance between increasing productivity and decline in discoveries is only a temporary one and that metal prices must eventually rise. The increased demand for new metal in the future will force a search for the more deeply covered deposits. If this search uses a technology that exhibits as rapid an attenuation of discoverability with depth of cover as it does with the current technology, it is highly likely that productivity gains in the production of metals will not be able to compensate for the large increases in discoverability costs. This would increase metal prices for a given demand. Of course, the greater depths of the deposits exploited in the future could increase mining costs as well, unless the force of technical change is sufficient to overcome them, and the price rise might be even greater.

## 5. Appraisal of Resources

The many exercises which are loosely referred to as "resource appraisals" are in fact a number of highly varied techniques reflecting different goals, premises, and motivations. In large part, the variation can be explained by the task itself—appraising unseen, postulated, mineral deposits. Obviously, appraisal of the unseen requires a model of some kind and models can be generated in different ways. Some appraisal models, for example, are heavily predicated on the geological associations of mineral deposits, while others ignore geology entirely and model the behavior of the "finding" (or exploration) process. Not surprisingly, such different approaches yield different results because not only do they differ in model structure, they are actually describing different things.

Most of the so-called resource appraisals that have been published actually assess potential supply, not resources and certainly not mineral endowment. Unfortunately, the potential supply assessed is usually vaguely defined and on examination can be seen to represent a mix of current and past technology and economics. To clarify this unfortunate confusion, we review the different resource appraisal methodologies that have been employed, and offer our opinions on the utility or inadequacy of each method.

### Geological "Resource" Estimates and Methods

The natural place to turn to for data on mineral availability is the U.S. Geological Survey. The most recent and most comprehensive publication on mineral availability is the Survey's Professional Paper 820 edited by Brobst and Pratt (1973).This fine volume contains a wealth of information, but unfortunately it does not meet the requirement for describing mineral availability in a long-term supply model. At best, it provides estimates of conditional and speculative resources, either for economic conditions similar to current conditions or for some unspecified set of economic conditions. Furthermore, the quantities reported generally are tons of metal. Little information is provided concerning the sizes and grades of ore deposits, grade distributions, or the depths of the deposits containing the tonnages of metal in each of the resource categories. Without such information, it is not possible to assess the impacts of future economic and technological factors, which differ considerably from those of the past and present.

The methodology most often used in the past by geologists to make "resource" estimates employs geological analogy. As customarily applied, analogy usually estimates potential supply directly. This becomes apparent upon examining the mechanics of the model.

*Estimation by geological analogy: a simplified description.* This method requires the identification of one or more control areas (well-explored, producing regions) that are similar in geology to the area being appraised (study area). Some unit of mineral density (cumulative production plus reserves per unit of area or volume) is determined for the control area, and this is multiplied by the area or volume of the study area to provide an initial estimate of undiscovered resources of the study area. The estimate may be adjusted for differences in the geology of control and study areas and the depth and size of the deposits expected to occur in the study area.

The geological analogy method has been used, and is still being used, to appraise potential supplies of uranium, and the method certainly has the appeal of reasonableness and a certification of tradition. What after all, could be more logical than to compare an unknown area with a known one, the control area? But geological analogy, as currently applied, turns out not to be totally satisfactory as an appraisal methodology for potential uranium supplies. One of the primary sources of dissatisfaction is the mixing of economics and geoscience. In essence, the geologist directly estimates potential supply. He never really estimates endowment. The obvious criticism is that such a procedure (mixing economics and geology) places too much of a burden on the geologist. As a scientist, the geologist's contribution should be the exercise of his geoscience. A related, but more subtle, criticism is that geological analogy, as currently practiced, actually inhibits the full exercise of geoscience by the appraiser by resorting to analogy at an early stage of analysis.

Finally, it is becoming increasingly important that the estimation methodology be one with a "track" that others can follow in evaluating the estimate. The implicit, judgmental mixing of geology and economics makes it impossible for anyone to examine assumptions and those factors which are critical in the appraisal.

*Limitations of estimates by geological analogy.* There are two major limitations to the appraisal of potential supply by geological analogies as described above. The first is that the estimate of potential supply that customarily results does not provide the parameters needed to assess the impact of lower or higher costs and prices and of technological improvements on resources and potential supply. For an appraisal to be useful in this regard, it must describe endowment in terms of deposit characteristics, such as grade, tonnage of ore, and depth, as was done in the appraisal of New Mexico uranium (Ellis, Harris, and VanWie, 1975). While such modification is an improvement, it exposes a limitation of another kind: geologists generally do not feel that they can reliably estimate endowment in deposits having grades below those currently being exploited. Thus, the endowment in subeconomic deposits may have to be inferred by some auxiliary means, such as the cumulative tonnage-average grade relationship (see Ellis, Harris, and VanWie, 1975, and Harris, 1977, section 7 of part II). Only by modifying the methods traditionally used by geologists, therefore, can bias be reduced and appraisals made useful for answering political and economic questions concerning energy supply and use in resource extraction.

The second major limitation of geological analogy as customarily applied is that it is useful only for estimating potential supply from deposits with familiar modes of occurrence. It has been repeatedly observed that explorationists find what they are looking for. It follows that if a mineral occurs in modes not currently recognized, the resources contained in those deposits will not be represented in estimates of potential supply which have been made by geological analogy. While this seems like a glaring weakness of the geological analogy method, one must be careful not to overcriticize such estimates for two reasons:

1. Even though resources may exist in deposits of unknown modes, those resources do not constitute potential supply until the identity of the modes and their geological characteristics are known. Therefore, such resources are important only for very long-term planning.
2. Only one alternative appraisal method (crustal abundance-geostatistical) provides for the presence of endowment in unknown modes, and this methodology has problems of a different kind.

*Use of geologic analogy by DOE.*   The U.S. Department of Energy (DOE) and its predecessors (the Energy Research and Development Administration and the Atomic Energy Commission) have routinely estimated "potential" uranium resources. Since the estimates were made using a formalized version of geologic analogy, the methodology used by DOE merits brief examination. Specifically, $P$, the "potential" (potential supply) for a "base" forward cost is estimated by the following equation:

$$P = N \cdot F \cdot U \cdot T$$

where $P$ is potential of area being evaluated

$N$ is number of square miles (or other unit) of favorable ground in area being evaluated

$F$ is geological favorability factor

$U$ is percent of unexplored favorable ground in area being evaluated

$T$ is mineralization factor (tons $U_3O_8$ per square mile or other unit measure)

The geological favorability factor, $F$, is estimated as a score by listing geological attributes present in the area being evaluated relative to a control area (producing region). The resulting factor is modified as necessary to describe the favorability of the region. The mineralization factor, $T$, is computed on the control area. Where appropriate, this may also be judgmentally modified.

*Possible bias and its source.*   Typically, mineral resource appraisals have been made by geologists using some variant of geological analogy, and typically these estimates have been proven by history to have been conservative. This historical fact seems to have been forgotten in recent times in the wake of the drastic downward revision by the U.S. Geological Survey of estimated undiscovered, recoverable oil resources in the coterminous United States.

*The search for alternative methods.* The fact that resource estimates made by geologists with apparently equal expertise have often differed by large factors, and that geological estimates were predicated upon so many judgmental factors, motivated the search for other, more objective, approaches to resource appraisal. Three such approaches are (1) the life cycle of production and discovery rates, (2) discovery rates versus cumulative drilling effort, and (3) crustal abundance relations. These approaches are described briefly in subsequent sections.

### Life Cycle and Discovery Rate Analysis

The life cycle and discovery rate methods were popularized by M. King Hubbert (1967) in his analysis of U.S. oil resources. More recently, M. A. Lieberman (1976) employed similar methods, using Hubbert as a guide, to estimate ultimately recoverable uranium resources in the United States. The objective character of these models and their supposed capability of estimating "undiscovered, recoverable" resources without bothering with difficult geological analysis give the models a strong appeal. Not only is the appraisal based upon quantitative analysis of data and therefore reproducible (provided the same procedure is followed), but it can be done quickly and easily.

There are two principal propositions in the methodology first employed by Hewitt (1929) and developed more recently by Hubbert (1967) and by Lieberman (1976):

1. The production (i.e., extraction and processing) of a mineral or mineraloid is sufficiently regular in the time domain that its life cycle can be determined from historical data and meaningfully extrapolated to estimate $Q_\infty$, the total recoverable resources.

2. The quantity of a mineral or energy resource discovered in an aggregate of resource regions per foot of drilling (discovery rate) declines according to the exponential law as drilling accumulates, and the area under the exponential, which has been fitted to data on discovery rates, provides an accurate estimate of $Q_\infty$.

Hubbert and Lieberman stipulated further that the life cycles of oil and uranium, respectively, conform to the first derivative logistic, a curve possessing symmetry and exhibiting a bell-like shape.

*A brief comment on the life-cycle model and estimates.* Basically, the use of life cycles to estimate the potential supply from undiscovered deposits amounts to estimating potential supply by extrapolating a time series of production far into the future. For such extrapolation to be accurate, there must be strong assumptions about the continuation of trends in economics and technology as well as the state of nature.

Hubbert's analysis of discovery and production trends and his basically accurate forecast of the peaking of oil production was most skillfully done. This work is especially impressive in view of the fact that at the time he was espousing an unpopular position. So far, production is pretty well tracking his predicted life cycle. He deserves and receives wide recognition for these achievements.

It does not necessarily follow, however, that Hubbert's use of the life-cycle model, coupled with the discovery-rates model, provides an accurate estimate of undiscovered, recoverable oil resources. There is a considerable chasm separating intermediate production forecasting from the estimation of undiscovered, recoverable resources by extrapolating to infinity the perceived life cycle of production. Similarly, the fact that a turning point in production could be predicted by Hubbert from a time series of discoveries which led production by twelve years does not make a case for the life cycle as an absolute resource appraisal tool. Problems attendant on the use of the model are vividly demonstrated by Lieberman's attempt to use it to appraise undiscovered, recoverable resources of uranium.

Lieberman candidly admits to an aborted estimation of undiscovered uranium resources through use of the first derivative logistic curve as a model of the life cycle of uranium production or discovery (1976, page 434). "In both cases the fit of the data to the logistic curve was not especially good, and equally satisfactory fits could be obtained over a range of values of $Q_\infty$." Lieberman's best fits to the discovery and production time series indicated a $Q_\infty$ of 534,000 and 550,000 short tons of uranium oxide ($U_3O_8$), respectively. These values are absurd as estimates of $Q_\infty$: 534,000 short tons is less than the sum of cumulative production and reserves of 543,000 short tons, and 550,000 are only slightly larger.

*The discovery-rate model.*   Lieberman certifies his methodology for the analysis of undiscovered, recoverable uranium resources by citing the success with which this model was employed by Hubbert on oil resources. Insight on Lieberman's work is obtained by examining Hubbert's use of the exponential decline of discovery rates.

HUBBERT'S USE OF THE EXPONENTIAL.   An in-depth critique of Hubbert's methodology is provided in the journal, *Materials and Society* (Harris, 1977b). The reader is referred to this article for details; only a few relevant findings are summarized here. Figure 8.11 (from Hubbert, 1969) shows the pattern of $dQ/dh$ versus $h$ for oil. An exponential curve was fitted to these data by pivoting the curve on the discovery rate of the last increment of drilling and swinging the curve until the area under it equaled the total amount of oil discovered. Subsequently, the mathematical expression of this curve was integrated from $h = 0$ to $h = \infty$ to provide an estimate of $Q_\infty$.

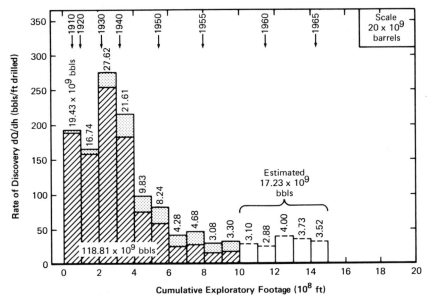

**Figure 8.11.** Crude oil discoveries per foot of exploratory drilling versus cumulative exploratory footage in the United States, exclusive of Alaska, 1860–1967. From M. K. Hibbert, "Energy Resources," in *Resources and Man* (San Francisco, Calif., W. H. Freeman, 1969) figure 8.16.

Subtracting the sum of cumulative production, known reserves, and estimated reserve additions from $Q_\infty$ yields an estimate of undiscovered, recoverable oil resources. Hubbert's estimate of $Q_\infty$ was $168 \times 10^8$ bbls of oil, a quantity which implies much smaller undiscovered, recoverable resources than estimates made by the U.S. Geological Survey.

Consider applying this same procedure when only five increments of $10^8$ feet of drilling had been completed, then for those from 6 through 15. What would have been the resulting estimates of $Q_\infty$? This situation was simulated by using the data of figure 8.11 and estimating $Q_\infty$ successively for each increment of $10^8$ feet of drilling from 5 to 15. The resulting estimates of $Q_\infty$ are plotted in figure 8.12 (solid line).

Hubbert (1974) redid his analysis using updated reserves and discovery data for 1971. Figure 8.13 shows the plot of discovery rates for 1971 data, and the broken line graph of figure 8.12 shows the recomputed estimates of $Q_\infty$ for drilling increments 13 through 15 based upon the 1971 revised data on reserves and discovery rates. Additionally, estimates of $Q_\infty$ for the newly completed drilling of increments 16 and 17 are shown in figure 8.12.

Three observations are especially noteworthy:

1. There is a strong upward trend in these successive estimates; as more drilling accumulated, higher estimates of $Q_\infty$ resulted.

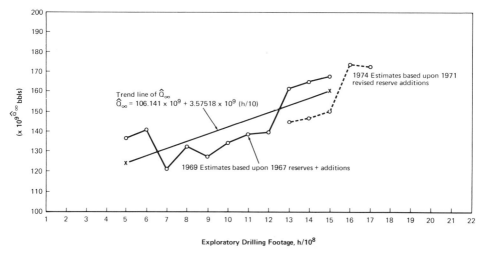

**Figure 8.12.** Successive estimates of $Q_\infty$ by Hubbert's method as drilling is accumulated from $5 \times 10^8$ feet to $17 \times 20^8$ feet.

2. The sum of cumulative production and measured, indicated, and inferred *reserves* (quantities in known deposits) in 1975 *exceeds* all estimates of $Q_\infty$ except those made for the last two increments of drilling.
3. The total reserves to be accredited to drilling increments 16 and 17 may be overstated, as they were in 1969 for increments 13 through 15. Thus, the only estimates of $Q_\infty$ which exceed the sum of cumulative production and reserves in 1975 appear to be based upon very uncertain data.

In a nutshell, the estimates of $Q_\infty$ that would have resulted by applying Hubbert's analysis earlier appear to have a positive trend and a negative bias.

REASONS FOR THE NEGATIVE BIAS.   There are two principal reasons for the negative bias in the estimation of $Q_\infty$ by Hubbert's methodology:

1. The negative exponential is not an appropriate model of discovery rates for the aggregate of regions.
2. The relationship of $dQ/dh$ to $h$ overstates depletion where drilling has been progressively directed to deposits at increasing depths and data are aggregated across resource regions, each of which is at a different stage of exploration.

The second reason is an overriding one. This point is most easily made by looking at a hypothetical boundary condition: If $Q_\infty$ were infinite, but the deposits that comprise $Q_\infty$ were distributed over a finite geographic area and

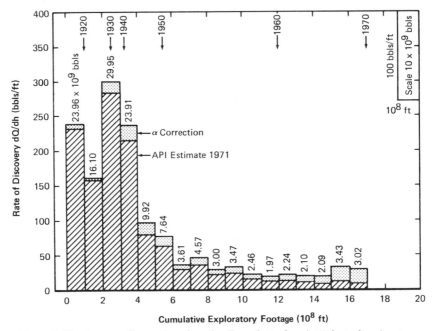

**Figure 8.13.** Average discoveries of crude oil per foot of each 10 feet of exploratory drilling in conterminous United States from 1860 to 1971. From M. K. Hubbert, *U.S. Energy Resources, A Review As of 1972.* Paper presented at the request of Henry M. Jackson, Chairman, U.S. Senate Committee on Interior and Insular Affairs, 93 Cong., 2 sess.

evenly to infinite depth, the simple fact that greater drilling depths would be required for additional resources would result in a decline in $dQ/dh$, and application of the Hubbert methodology would provide some finite value for $Q_\infty$ when it actually is infinite. Obviously, conditions with respect to uranium resources are very different from those of this hypothetical situation; nevertheless, it serves to demonstrate the overstatement of depletion which arises from drilling to successively greater depths.

The first reason really covers a minor issue and a major one. The minor issue is that even if $dQ/dh$ versus $h$ were an appropriate statement of the effectiveness of exploration, the exponential curve which has been fitted to this measure appears to decay more rapidly for larger values of $h$ in the case of oil than do the data. The major issue is that there are no theoretical grounds for the negative exponential as the appropriate model. Even if analysis were restricted to deposits of a common depth and explorationists were able to select preferentially the largest targets first, about all that can be established generally without imposing additional conditions is that $dQ/dh$ would decline monotonically with $h$, but not necessarily exponentially.

ISSUES UNIQUE TO LIEBERMAN'S ANALYSIS.    Unlike Hubbert, Lieberman based his analysis on discovery rates of a current dollar cost category of discoveries (Hubbert employed a physical measure of discovery rate). This fact raises a host of economic and resource issues and data analysis problems. A full and proper description of these is beyond the scope of this chapter; consequently, they are only summarized in the following paragraphs. (For a more comprehensive treatment see Harris, 1976b.)

Lieberman's plot of discovery rates and cumulative footage does not represent accurately what it was intended to do: determine the effectiveness of exploration in finding new deposits. Annual additions of reserves to old deposits were incorrectly treated as discoveries and credited to the exploration drilling of the year prior to that in which they were reported. Furthermore, it is widely recognized that some development drilling is reported by industry as exploration drilling.

Basing the analysis of undiscovered, recoverable resources of $U_3O_8$ on discovery rates defined by a single, somewhat arbitrary, set of price and cost conditions which we shall designate as $8, raises several economic and data issues: (1) the effect of inflation on discovery rates, (2) the effect of improved productivity and future development drilling on discovery rates, and (3) the appropriate multiplier to be applied to undiscovered $8 resources to infer the quantity of undiscovered $30 resources. Contrary to Lieberman's claim, the inflation of costs has significantly eroded $8 reserves from the very initiation of that category of reserves. Annual rates of losses of reserves due to inflation have averaged approximately 4 percent for the seven years prior to 1974. The effect of inflation can be appreciated by considering the hypothetical situation in which the resource is infinite and a constant amount of exploration drilling is allocated each year. In this case, rates of discovery of reserves having a specified grade would be constant. However, if discovery rates were based upon reserves of a specified cost, and if these costs were to inflate at an annual rate of 4 percent, discovery rates would decline exponentially, as drilling progressed, at a rate equal to the rate of inflation.

Improvements in productivity would have an effect on discovery rates opposite to that of inflation. The manner in which inflation and productivity improvements should be treated varies, depending upon whether the immediate objective is to comment upon the effectiveness of exploration in finding new deposits having a constant economic quality (cost) or a constant physical quality (grade). Irrespective of which choice is made for the analysis of data, a comprehensive resource analysis ultimately requires the assessment of productivity improvements as well as physical depletion, for the issue of primary importance to society is the *economic* scarcity of uranium resources. Lieberman does not comment upon these issues.

Since undiscovered, recoverable $30 resources are determined by scaling up the estimate of undiscovered, recoverable $8 resources, the result is subject to all of the aforementioned frailties plus uncertainty about the appropriate ratio. Conceptually, it is clear what this ratio should be: the ratio of *undiscovered* $30 *resources* to *undiscovered* $8 *resources*. Obviously, this ratio is not known. While using, as Lieberman did, the ratio of $30 reserves and production to $8 reserves and production may appear to give a prudent estimate, this ratio probably considerably understates the undiscovered $30 resources. The proportion of all undiscovered resources of $U_3O_8$ which are recoverable at a forward cost of $30 most likely is a lot greater than the proportion of reported reserves recoverable at $30. An overriding issue in this judgment is that data on $30 reserves are very incomplete (underreported); these data represent primarily the $30 reserves in deposits having $8 reserves. The $30 reserves of many deposits having no $8 reserves are not included in the inventory of $30 reserves. Other issues spring from the fact that exploration has been progressively directed to targets at greater depth. The greater effectiveness of exploration in finding high-grade than low-grade deposits at increased depths and the increase in mining costs with depth imply a greater proportion of undiscovered resources in the $30 forward-cost category than is the case for current reserves and past production.

*Concluding statement about life-cycle and discovery rate estimates.* Three facts emerge from Lieberman's work. The first of these is that the life-cycle model is essentially meaningless for the appraisal of undiscovered, recoverable resources of $U_3O_8$, and there is reasonable doubt about its usefulness for the appraisal of undiscovered, recoverable resources of any kind for a large region, such as the entire United States, which contains considerable unexplored ground. The second fact is that the discovery-rate model as used by Hubbert and Lieberman is predisposed to underestimate undiscovered, recoverable resources. The third fact is that both of the models constitute an economic forecast as well as a statement about resource depletion, but, since the economics is implicit to the data and model form, neither the implied economic conditions nor the implied physical endowment are known or stated. Accepting an estimate of undiscovered, recoverable resources made by these models is accepting a prognostication of future economic conditions which are unstated, together with an implied but unstated endowment.

### Estimates by Crustal Abundance

In the discussion of resource appraised by geological analogy, it was pointed out that two limitations of the methods are the estimation of resources in deposits of known modes but subeconomic grades and the estimation of resources in unknown or unfamiliar modes of occurrence. The first of these limitations can be mitigated somewhat by supplementary models and analysis. But the second of these limitations, that of unfamiliar modes of occurrence, has no ready solution within the scope of geological methods as customarily applied.

One appealing feature of the crustal abundance models, given that their assumptions can be accepted, is that endowment, resources, and potential supply in deposits of known and unknown modes having subeconomic grades is easily estimated. Those who use these models defend their use in spite of strong, and in some cases questionably appropriate assumptions, because of the utility of being able to generalize beyond present experience regarding resources. Generally, the European school views the official estimates of U.S. uranium resources as too conservative, because they do not include uranium occurrences in unfamiliar modes. Conversely, it is argued by some that the structure of the models by which such inference is made is so unrealistic and so unsupported by data and experience that such estimates are of little value, and in fact, may be misleading.

*The abundance-reserve relationship of McKelvey.*  McKelvey (1960) plotted recoverable reserves for various metals in the U.S. against the crustal abundance of the metals and proposed that there is a general relationship of reserve abundance to crustal abundance: The more abundant the element, the larger its reserves. This appeal to intuition can be justified, with certain caveats, from geochemical and geological principles.

Erickson (1973), restricting attention to just those elements which form the chief constituents of their ores, took lead as a standard, meaning that he assumed that all deposits of lead were known. He thus normalized the relationship on lead:

$$R = 2.45 \times A \times 10^6$$

where $A$ is crustal abundance
$R$ is metric tons of recoverable metal resources

While this relationship is an interesting one and has stimulated thinking about crustal abundance and resources, it is not satisfying as a resource appraisal tool. First of all, the fact that the relationship is based upon reserves known at some point in time defeats some of the purposes of basing a methodology upon crustal abundance. Of course, the relationship could be redetermined using cumulative production plus reserves. While this would help, it would still understate resources. In the case of lead, it would show no resources other than those which are known. The estimate of undiscovered resources for all other metals reflects that metal's crustal abundance, the deviation of that metal from the reserve abundance relationship, and the greater or lesser degree of exploration and exploitation compared with lead.

History has shown (at least it appears so at present) that the crustal abundance perspective of greatest interest for resource appraisal is not the relationship across metals of crustal abundance to reserve abundance, but the statistical distribution of the concentrations of a *given* metal in portions of the earth's crust of various sizes.

The following sections describe two crustal abundance–geostatistical models as they have been used to estimate mineral "resources."

*Crustal abundance–geostatistical models.*    There are two crustal abundance-geostatistical models that have been or are being used to estimate mineral resources. One was developed by J. W. Brinck for Euratom, and the other was developed by the Programmes Analysis Unit (PAU) of Great Britain in collaboration with the Geological Institute of Great Britain. Both of these models have three assumptions in common:

1. The crust of the earth to some specified depth in a region is comprised totally of mineral deposits.
2. The average concentration of the metal in the crust of the earth is the average grade of all deposits in a region.
3. The distribution of grades of deposits is lognormal.

The following sections provide only a general, nontechnical description of these models. For a full description and critique, see Harris (1977a, parts II and III).

BRINCK'S MODEL AND ESTIMATES.    Suppose that a metal were distributed randomly throughout the earth's crust. Suppose further that the crust were partitioned into blocks of some specified, uniform size and that the amount of metal in each block were known. Then, a histogram showing the amount of rock in the region having metal concentrations within each of a number of grade intervals could be constructed. If the ordinate scale were divided by $T$, the total tonnage of rock in the region, the histogram would show the fraction of the total rock of the region having grades in each of the grade intervals. It is assumed in Brinck's model that a smooth curve fitted to this histogram would be symmetrical and of normal shape, provided that the grade axis is in the logarithmic scale.

Such a distribution is represented in figure 8.14. Suppose that the parameters of this distribution are known. Then, the first step in estimating undiscovered endowment in deposits of the size and shape typical of those currently known and having grades above a cutoff of $q'$ is the computation of $P_{q'}$, the probability represented by the area under the curve to the right of $\ln q'$. The tonnage of mineralized rock having grades of at least $q'$ is simply the product of $P_{q'}$ and $T$ (the tonnage of rock in the earth's crust to some specified depth within the region being considered): $t_{q'} = P_{q'} T$. A quantity

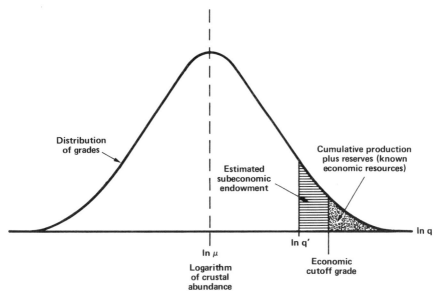

**Figure 8.14.** Brinck's use of the lognormal distribution of element concentration ($q$).

$m_{q'}$, the total endowment (undiscovered resources plus reserves plus cumulative production) of metal in deposits having grades above $q'$, is computed as the product of $t_{q'}$ and $\bar{q}_{q'}$, the average grade of the material comprising $t_{q'}$: $m_{q'} = t_{q'}\bar{q}_{q'}$. $q_{q'}$ is computed from the grade distribution of figure 8.14.

The picture becomes a bit more complicated when these concepts are applied, for the histogram cannot be determined in the manner described. In practice, the distribution of grades is assumed to be lognormal, having as its mean the logarithm of crustal abundance. Generally, some published estimate of crustal abundance is taken as a known quantity. Thus, all that remains is to estimate the variance of the distribution. This is done by assuming that reserves plus cumulative production of the region represent all material that occurs in deposits of the size and shape typical of known and produced deposits and having grades of at least economic cutoff grade. Given these assumptions, the logarithmic variance can be calculated directly. Finally, given $\ln \mu$ (the logarithm of crustal abundance) and $\sigma^2$, the estimated logarithmic variance, the tonnage of rock having grades of at least $q'$ can be computed mathematically for any value of $q'$, including grades far below current cutoff grades. Similarly, $\bar{q}_{q'}$ and $m_{q'}$ can be computed mathematically. Thus, so long as there is no reason to change the block size or shape from that typical of known deposits, endowment is easily computed.

However, if it is desired to know the endowment for a specified cutoff grade but for blocks of some size or shape different from typical, known deposits, a new variance must be computed. This is done by employing the Matheron–DeWijs formula, which relates variance to the volume and shape of the block. This relationship is very important to Brinck's approach, for it not only allows the estimation of endowment in any specified size and shape of block, but it also allows the estimation of the parameters of the lognormal distribution by an alternative means: a geochemical survey. Where geochemical samples of the region have been obtained, the mean and variance of the logarithms of concentrations serve as estimates of $\ln \mu$ and $\sigma^2$. Then by use of the Matheron–DeWijs formula, the variance of grade for blocks of any specified size, instead of geochemical samples, can be computed from the variance of the samples. Figure 8.15 demonstrates schematically this procedure of inference.

Brinck's later work substituted the logbinomial for the lognormal, on the premise that they are asymptotically equivalent. In addition, Brinck derived cost functions for exploration and exploitation of the deposits defined by the endowment model. Exploration cost was defined as a function of the size and shape of a block and the frequency of occurrence of such a deposit in the environment. The frequency of occurrence was defined by Brinck to be a function of size, shape, and grade. Capital and operating costs were defined as a function of size. Through a cash flow analysis, costs were ascribed to the deposits described by the endowment model. Thus, estimates can be made of potential supply from blocks of any specified size and shape, and at any specified cost.

A COMPARISON OF ESTIMATES BY BRINCK'S MODEL.    Ellis et al. (1975) compared an estimate by Brinck's method of the initial uranium endowment of New Mexico (meaning reserves, cumulative production, and $U_3O_8$ in undiscovered deposits) in deposits having grades of at least 0.10 percent $U_3O_8$, with the estimate which resulted from the subjective probability survey of geologists and the subsequent extrapolation of the cumulative tonnage-average grade relationship:

| Method | Endowment | |
|---|---|---|
| | Tonnage of mineralized rock (short tons) | Tonnage of $U_3O_8$ (short tons) |
| Brinck | $8.43 \times 10^8$ | $1.10 \times 10^6$ |
| Subjective probability | $6.09 \times 10^8$ | $1.26 \times 10^6$ |

As indicated, these estimates of initial endowment of $U_3O_8$ are very similar. The estimate of undiscovered endowment would be obtained by subtracting the quantity of cumulative production plus reserves.

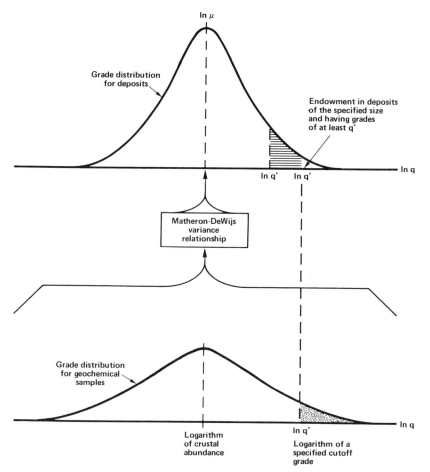

**Figure 8.15.** Inference from the grade distribution of geochemical samples to minable deposits.

It is instructive to compare the estimate of endowment by these methods for a cutoff grade of 0.01 percent $U_3O_8$, instead of 0.10 percent:

| *Method* | *Endowment* | |
| --- | --- | --- |
| | Tonnage of mineralized rock (short tons) | Tonnage of $U_3O_8$ (short tons) |
| Brinck | $3.0 \times 10^{12}$ | $4.4 \times 10^8$ |
| Subjective probability | $3.8 \times 10^9$ | $1.4 \times 10^6$ |

Thus, for a cutoff grade of 0.01 percent $U_3O_8$, the estimated endowment of $U_3O_8$ for New Mexico by Brinck's model is approximately 300 times greater than the estimate made by geologic analysis and the extrapolation of a grade-tonnage relationship. This divergence is especially striking in view of the fact that the estimates by the two methods were essentially the same for the endowment in deposits having grades of at least 0.10 percent $U_3O_8$. Is the endowment indicated by Brinck's model present? No one really knows. The data on uranium in New Mexico that are available primarily reflect sandstone deposits and indicate a narrow range of grades, with little hope for large quantities of low-grade uranium. This does not preclude the presence of low-grade endowment in other modes of occurrence, although currently there is no indication of this endowment.

SOME QUALIFICATIONS ABOUT BRINCK'S MODEL.   Some general qualifications are in order concerning estimates from Brinck's model. First, given acceptance of the foundations of the model, estimates are probably conservative, for the parameters of the model are estimated by assuming that the current inventory of known reserves plus cumulative production represents the totality of endowment of the region in deposits having grades of at least the current economic cutoff grade. This simply is not so in most cases: In most regions there are undiscovered deposits having grades of at least the current economic cutoff grade.

Viewed from a more general perspective, estimates by this model may be very optimistic with respect to the use of the inferred resources, for the model assumes that there is a continuity of grades down to and beyond crustal abundance. This assumption has been challenged. For example, Skinner (1976) suggests that the distribution may be bimodal: The bulk of the earth's crust consists of common rock in which elements occur in silicate lattices; this is represented by the major peak. The amount of the crust in which an element occurs as a major constituent in a mineral is represented by the second peak. At present, the bimodality hypothesis can be neither proved nor disproved. So far, surveys have not disclosed two modes for uranium. But, it is not known whether that is because there is no second mode or because there are not enough samples to demonstrate the presence of a second mode.

Finally, even if all of these assumptions are met, until the modes of occurrence of the low-grade endowment can be identified, it is not a usable resource; consequently, great care must be exercised in interpreting and using these estimates. There are many particulars of this model that are worth comment; for these, the reader is referred to Harris (1977a, section 8 of part II).

THE PAU MODEL AND ESTIMATES.   Like Brinck, the Programmes Analysis Unit (PAU) of Great Britain considers a specified depth of the earth's crust within a region to consist entirely of deposits. But, unlike Brinck,

PAU specifies that deposit size (tonnage of mineralized rock) is distributed lognormally and is independent of deposit grade, which is also distributed lognormally. Thus, while in Brinck's model deposits are blocks of some specified uniform size, in the PAU model there is an entire distribution of deposit sizes.

Another departure from Brinck's methods arises in the procedure for quantifying the PAU model. In estimating the unknown parameter, the variance, by the reference distribution approach, Brinck had to consider all resources having grades above economic cutoff to have been discovered; PAU views the data on deposit tonnage and grades as merely a sample from the truncated region of a bivariate population (deposit tonnage and grade), although PAU describes the sample as biased with respect to size (deposit tonnage). The truncation boundary which defines the truncated region describes those combinations of size and grade that yield the maximum cost for which production is economic. Contrary to the approach employed by Brinck, PAU makes no assumption, in estimating the parameters of the bivariate lognormal distribution, about how much of the resources in the deposits of the truncated region have been discovered.

Figure 8.16 schematically represents the PAU model and the estimation of its parameters. A contour represents combinations of tonnage and grade having equal probability density, and the line that crosses the contour represents the truncation effect of a specified cost in which cost is jointly determined by deposit size and grade. The shaded region connotes that part of the bivariate distribution which is in the truncated region and which is represented by data on deposits produced in the past and deposits that are currently being mined.

PAU derived a mathematical procedure for estimating the unknown parameters of the complete distributions for deposit size and grade, given (1) crustal abundance; (2) statistical averages from known deposits of grade, tonnage of ore, and tonnage of $U_3O_8$; and (3) an estimate of the cost relationship. The mathematics is rather complex and will not be described here. (For a more complete description of the PAU model, see Harris, 1977a, section 2 of part III and section 1 of part IV, or Drew, 1977.)

The results of the data analysis described by PAU are estimates of the four unknown parameters of two independent lognormal distributions [two parameters for grade $q$ and two parameters for deposit tonnage $t$]:

$\ln \mu_q \ln \mu_t$

$\sigma_q \sigma_{t'}$

PRODUCTION COSTS AND RESOURCES.  As a prerequisite to the estimation of the four unknown parameters, PAU had to define a simple cost

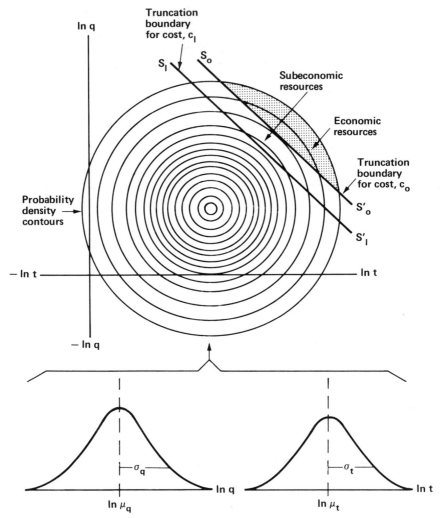

**Figure 8.16.** The PAU model. Note that $q$ is the deposit average grade; and $t$, deposit tonnage.

function which described production cost $c$ as a function of deposit tonnage $t$ and grade $q$:

$$c = \alpha_0 t^{\alpha_1} q^{\alpha_2}$$

alternatively,

$$\ln c = \ln \alpha_0 + \alpha_1 \ln t + \alpha_2 \ln q$$

Essentially, if $c_0$ is specified as the current cost level, then this equation can be used to define all combinations of deposit tonnage and grade that can be produced at a cost of no more than $c_0$. Those deposits having tonnages and grades greater than those implied by the cost relationship lie in the truncated region of figure 8.16.

Given the cost function and the estimated parameters of the two lognormal distributions, resources can be estimated for any specified level of costs. For example, suppose that a production cost of $c_1 > c_0$ is specified. For $c_1$, a new truncation boundary $S_1 - S_{1'}$, can be defined, as indicated in figure 8.16. This new truncation boundary defines a larger truncated region; $rs_{c_1}$, resources for the maximum cost of $c_1$, are estimated by forming the product of two quantities:

$$rs_{c_1} = t_{c_1}\overline{q}_{c_1}$$

where $t_{c_1}$ is the total mineralized material that could be produced at a cost
no greater than $c_1$
$\overline{q}_{c_1}$ is the average grade of $t_{c_1}$

The quantity of $t_{c_1}$ is estimated by multiplying the probability (volume) of the truncated region (the region bounded on the lower left by boundary $s_1 - s_{1'}$) by $T$, the total tonnage of rock in the region:

$$t_{c_1} = p_{c_1}T$$

Similarly, $\overline{q}_{c_1}$ is the average grade of all deposits lying in the truncated region.

EXPLORATION AND POTENTIAL SUPPLY.   Potential supply is estimated by multiplying the probability for discovery, $p_{c_1}$, by $rs_{c_1}$:

$$ps_{c_1} = \rho_{c_1}rs_{c_1}$$

The probability for discovery is defined by PAU as a function of exploration effort and average deposit size:

$$\rho_{c_1} = 1 - e^{-b\overline{t}_{c_1}E}$$

where $E$ is exploration effort, which is specified as some part of profits
$\overline{t}_{c_1}$ is the average size of deposits in the truncated region
$b$ is a parameter to be estimated

As previously pointed out, many deposits in the truncated region have larger tonnages and higher grades than those associated with $c_1$. Therefore, these deposits have a production cost lower than $c_1$. It must follow that $\overline{c}$, the average production cost per pound $U_3O_8$ for all deposits of the truncated region, must be less than $c_1$. Profit per pound $U_3O_8$, $\pi$, is defined as the difference $c_1 - \overline{c}$: $\pi = c_1 - \overline{c}$. PAU conceptualized exploration as being driven by this profit. Thus, given $b$ and the fraction of profit invested in exploration, potential supply can be estimated for any specified cost level. But $b$ must first be estimated.

PAU estimated $b$ by considering the ratio of cumulative production plus reserves to $rs_{c_0}$ to be $\rho$ and by taking the historical average exploration cost per pound as $E$. Then, since $t_{c_0}$ was obtained from statistical data on known deposits, estimation of $b$ required only a simple algebraic solution. Finally, given $b$, the four estimated parameters, the cost function, and the fraction of profits to be allocated to exploration, resources, and potential supply could be estimated for any specified maximum cost.

ESTIMATES BY THE PAU MODEL.   PAU applied their model to the appraisal of uranium resources and potential supply for various cost levels and exploration expenditures. According to PAU's analysis, U.S. resources of $U_3O_8$ producible at a cost of \$30 (1975), if the deposits were known, are approximately $20 \times 10^6$ short tons. PAU estimates that if 100 percent of profits were to be invested in exploration, U.S. potential supply of $U_3O_8$ would be approximately $11 \times 10^6$ short tons. But, if only 40 percent of profits were to be invested (according to PAU, this is the historical average), the potential supply of $U_3O_8$ would be reduced to approximately $5 \times 10^6$ short tons.

QUALIFICATIONS OR UNRESOLVED ISSUES WITH THE PAU MODEL. The fact that crustal abundance is specified as the arithmetic mean of the postulated lognormal distribution of concentration and that the earth's crust in the region is considered to consist entirely of deposits gives the PAU model some of the same characteristics as Brinck's model. Expectedly, some of the qualifications or unresolved issues identified with regard to Brinck's model also are relevant to the PAU model, for example, assumption of grade continuity to and beyond crustal abundance. Here, comment is restricted to those features of issues that are unique to the PAU model. One of these is the assumption of statistical independence of deposit grade and deposit tonnage.

There is evidence that deposit grade and tonnage may be statistically independent for the sandstone deposits of New Mexico (Harris, 1977a, sections 2 and 3 of part III). Furthermore, independence may exist for other modes of occurrence, although this has not been proven. Even if independence were to exist separately for each of the modes of occurrence of uranium, a case is not necessarily established for independence of deposit size and grade *across all modes*, as is assumed by the PAU model. The proposition that deposit grade and tonnage are statistically independent across all modes is difficult to test objectively because of limited data and bias in the statistical data caused by the economics of exploration and exploitation.

As with Brinck's estimates, caution is in order in interpreting PAU's estimates of potential supply for high cost levels because some of the material which constitutes this potential supply may exist in unfamiliar types of deposits.

## Modeling and Informational Issues with Regard to Resource Adequacy and Long-Term Mineral Supply

### An Ideal Model

Because of the complexities of economic issues and of long-term economic dynamics, it is natural to attempt to construct models as a means of exploring the issues. The most useful model would contain a description of the mineral resources by quantity and quality, plus the exploitation of the resources through defined technologies within a comprehensive economic system, which contains both the allocative mechanisms of a market economy and the general economic dynamics. Such a model is complex and presents many obstacles and challenges. It requires the interfacing of separate models which are of very different forms and for which the data may not be available. Or, stated differently, the data available may not be in the appropriate form.

For example, the model ideally would describe, not the mineral resources of a region, but rather the mineral endowment. In the endowment inventory, each deposit would be given a depth of cover (burial), total tonnage of mineralized rock, the average grade, and the fractions of the deposit having various grades. The exploration and exploitation modules would act upon this inventory, as dictated by the market allocation model through expectation relations, to identify the deposits discovered and the mining plan that optimizes the expected present value of projected production levels. During any period of time, the rent from producing deposits would fund exploration and development. Periods of oversupply due to diminished demand or new production capability would result in decreased exploration because of the lower price required to clear the market and the resulting decrease in rent. Similarly, because of depletion of producing deposits and the short-run inelasticity of supply to price, a shift to greater demand would increase price and rent, which would fund more exploration and ultimately result in the development of new production capacity.

The exploration model would yield discoveries in response to the level of activity indicated and the degree of discovery depletion. To do this credibly, it must account for differences in discoverability resulting from size, grade, and depth of cover and the error in exploration decisions. Every discovery would be examined in the exploitation module to determine if it is producible or whether it should be held on the shelf awaiting more favorable economics.

Since every discovery would be described by a total tonnage and a grade distribution, the exploitation modules could imitate development decisions by searching for that combination of plant size, cutoff grade, and production rate which maximizes profits for expected demand and product and factor prices. Thus, a large mineral deposit situated at considerable depth and having a wide range of grades may yield only a small ore body, given the technology, capital costs, and expectations for price and factor costs prevailing at the time of the development decision. Much of the mineral deposit would be left in the ground or placed on the dump because its grade would be too low to cover milling costs.

A system of this kind explicitly describes the partial irreversibility of the mining decision with respect to time. That is, a deposit developed later and at a higher price would have yielded more ore than an identical deposit developed earlier at a low price. Sometimes the material left behind is so low in grade and is situated in such a manner that it may never be produced, or if it is, it will require a very high price. In other situations, as the deposit is extracted, higher prices or lower production costs justify expanding the initial plant in order to mine previously excluded material. Thus, the exploitation module must allow for this expansion as well as the resources that cannot be used at all.

If the technologies of the exploration and exploitation modules are explicitly described, the effects of technological improvements, capital costs, and factor prices can be evaluated.


The Resource Model

*Preferred form.*   The ideal foundation for a long-term supply model is a mineral endowment inventory. Clearly, this inventory includes producing deposits, prospects, and unknown but postulated deposits. In many cases the latter component, the unknown deposit, makes up by far the greatest part of the endowment. Consequently, there is great uncertainty attendant on the estimates of the endowment, for this part of the inventory often must be estimated without any direct information about the presence of a deposit. Estimation must be based upon some kind of model. Therefore, the preferred endowment inventory is probabilistic.

A useful probabilistic description of the mineral endowment inventory would deal with each kind (mode) of deposit separately, for example, porphyry copper, and would consist of four probability distributions:

1. Probability distribution for number of deposits or for that fraction of the earth's crust which consists of mineralized rock

2. A bivariate dependent distribution of deposit tonnage and of the deposit average grade
3. A probability distribution for grades, conditional upon deposit tonnage and deposit average grade
4. A probability distribution for depth to the deposit

The first three of these distributions would be conditional upon the cutoff grade and minimum size specified for the description of the endowment. This cutoff grade would be specified at a level that eliminates metal locked up in the crystal lattices of silicate minerals.

*Inadequacies of past efforts.* Section 5 commented upon resource estimates which have been made and the methods employed to make them. With respect to the preferred methodology, one which can support a long-term supply model, all resource estimates made to date are inadequate. Clearly, a resource appraisal method that directly yields potential supply cannot support a long-term supply model which is specified in the comprehensive manner just described, for it denies the description of the physical features of mineral deposits and the interaction of technology and economics with these features. Thus, resource estimates made by geological analogy as traditionally applied are not useful. Estimates by life cycle or discovery rate models are even less useful, for not only are the physical features of the endowment suppressed, but economic conditions and technology are prescribed by unstated trends in the response variables arising from unstated levels, which are associated with total depletion.

The appraisal methods which are capable of supporting the ideal resource model must describe the mineral endowment, not resources or potential supply. Basically, there are only two classes of methods which have this potential: (1) comprehensive geological analysis within a probabilistic framework, and (2) improved and more comprehensive crustal abundance-geostatistical models. While both of these classes have potential, the remainder of this section explores the issues and problems of supporting the ideal resource model by comprehensive geologic analysis.

There are several reasons for limiting our discussion to this analytical method. There is, for the United States, a great deal of geological data and knowledge, and unless it can be shown that such information is useless with respect to the appraisal of unknown endowments, estimates should be improved by the use of this information. The geological approach is the method which is being adopted by the U.S. Geological Survey and the U.S. Department of Energy. Finally, geological analysis has not yet been fully developed or applied as a means of resource appraisal; geology and the geologist have not yet been fairly put to the task.

The Challenge to Geology

The proposition was advanced at the beginning of this section that the preferred resource model would consist of four probability distributions for each mode of occurrence of a metal (or nonmetal) for each resource region—distributions for number of deposits, tonnage and average grade per deposit, depth to deposit, and grades within the deposit. The magnitude of the task of providing these may be appreciated by considering the fact that some resource regions may have no known deposits and that the only information existing for the region may be geological and geophysical maps. Clearly, compiling such a comprehensive probabilistic description of endowment is extremely difficult and will require the integration of geoscience, statistical inference, and geological and statistical data on the deposits. Where data on representative deposits exist, the task may be simplified by determining the probability distributions for deposit size and average grade and the distribution of grades within the deposit from these data. This would reduce the task for the geologist to one of describing probabilistically, conditional upon the geologic information, either the number of deposits in the region by depth or the fraction of the earth's crust which contains deposits. Even so, the challenge to geology is great.

There are those who question whether the science of economic geology is sufficiently advanced to perform this task credibly. Most of those who place little stock in geological estimates do so, not because they believe that there is no relationship between earth processes and the formation of mineral deposits, but because (1) man's understanding of this relationship is very limited, or (2) man's ability to infer correctly the states of the earth's processes from geological data is limited. The large variation in estimates by geologists is often cited as evidence of these limitations. Conceivably, both of the limitations could be so severe that use of the geological premise may be perceived as providing no real information about endowment. Under such circumstances, abandoning geological analysis for some other approach seems to be indicated. Are matters this bad? It clearly is difficult to assess how bad or good they are. It really is not relevant to point to a few regions where geological estimates have been very bad to make a case against them, or to point to a few regions where they have been good to give credence to this approach.

A fair statement seems to be that it is too early to pass judgment on the contribution that can be made by geology to the appraisal of undiscovered mineral deposits. Until the oil embargo, few people were concerned about estimates of mineral or energy resources. Resource appraisal had not been perceived as an important function of geology. Consequently, the occasional and superficial efforts of the past may not be a good indication of what geology and the geologist can contribute. A sustained national effort to organize and integrate data and to evaluate it with respect to a comprehensive theoretical framework of mineral endowment may yield considerable rewards. The challenge is not just a data problem. Improved estimates of mineral endowment require a more comprehensive statement of resource theory, as well as the generation of more and better data. The following sections survey rather briefly efforts that have been or are at present directed to the appraisal of mineral endowment.

*Number of deposits.*    Estimation of a probability distribution for the number of deposits which occur in a region, given only the geology of that region and some minimum grade and tonnage, forces the geologist to work with both probability and the geology of deposit occurrence. Research efforts are evident in both areas and challenging questions are arising in both. One question is the extent to which the geologist should predicate his occurrence models upon earth processes or upon directly observable geological features.

*Geology and deposit occurrence.*    The justification for appraising mineral endowment by geology rests on the proposition that mineral deposits were formed by some of the same earth processes that caused associated, observable, geological features. The utilization of this premise requires inferences from observable geological features to earth processes of an earlier duration and from implied earth processes to the development of mineral deposits. In this philosophy, a mineral deposit (not an ore deposit) is a geological phenomenon.

Under ideal conditions of full information about these relationships, even when dealing with concealed deposits, it would be possible to reason from observable geological conditions to earth processes and hence to endowment. Some geologists may attempt to do this, even without complete information, but many do not. Rather, they adopt certain short-cuts. Sometimes they actually have paid little attention to this relationship; instead, they have taken a few statistical measures and inferred directly to resources or potential supply. Others have resorted to geographic extrapolation and by-passed geology almost totally.

The challenge to geoscience is to improve understanding of the inference from geology to earth processes and of the relationships of earth processes to the formation of mineral deposits. Current work by the U.S. Geological Survey and the U.S. Department of Energy is directed to these issues and their efforts to develop genetic-geologic models are examples of such work.

*Genetic–geologic models (DOE-USGS).*    An evaluation of the potential U.S. supply of uranium is to be undertaken by the Department of Energy and the U.S. Geological Survey. This program, referred to as JOINUP, is to employ a new appraisal methodology, one which separates economic considerations from the geoscience analysis.

The first step in estimating endowment will be the identification and description of genetic–geologic models. Essentially, a genetic model of a particular kind of deposit identifies those earth processes that are required for the formation of that deposit and specifies process and mineralization interrelations. These models describe the synthesis of the geology, geochemistry, and geophysics of uranium environments.

The motivation for building genetic models is that once the "fingerprint" of each uranium environment is described in a genetic model, the geologist can use these fingerprints to identify regions in the United States which are uranium environments. This procedure is basically geoscience combined with pattern recognition.

Given a conviction that a region under study belongs to a specific geological environment, as indicated by its geology and the genetic model, the geologist must then ascribe a uranium endowment to that region. Unquestionably, this is the most difficult stage of the evaluation. It is not sufficient to use a mineralization factor, for that describes what has been found and is economic to produce. The objective of the new procedure is to estimate what is there, the endowment. While it may never be possible to estimate endowment without using an analogy at some point, this implementation of the new approach is far more demanding of geological data on uranium deposits than geological analogies.

*The probability dimension: multivariate models.*    The fact that the occurrence of a mineral deposit reflects the combined influences of a number of earth processes suggests that multivariate probability theory and multivariate statistical models would be useful in defining the probability distribution of endowment.

Some interesting research has been devoted to the use of multivariate techniques for resource appraisal (Harris, 1965; Agterberg, 1978; Singer, 1972). In particular, the work of Agterberg (1978) in developing a logit probability model is encouraging.

In spite of the promise of multivariate models, their application to estimates of mineral endowment at present is limited. The development and application of multivariate models makes heavy demands on resource theory, data, and time. Scientists are still many years away from being able to apply multivariate models credibly in estimates of mineral endowment on a national level. It is necessary to improve (1) the quantity and quality of geological data, (2) the ability to formalize the geology-endowment theory, (3) the ability to meaningfully quantify the geological data, and (4) the coordination of data and model structure. Because of the magnitude of this task, current appraisals of mineral endowment and those in the near future are employing and will continue to employ subjective methods.

*Subjective assessment.*   Current research in the subjective assessment of the probability distribution for mineral endowment is directed at a number of issues, among which are bias in subjective assessment, consistency in assessment, formalizing inference rules, decision aids, and the manner of elicitation. The following description of research in progress at the University of Arizona demonstrates the focus of some current research. A similar effort is in progress at the Stanford Research Institute.

The research at the University of Arizona employs subjective probabilities; however, it is very different from previous surveys of this sort because the probabilities given by a geologist are for the explication of the earth processes that cause endowment, not for endowment *per se.*

To put the approach in perspective, it is helpful to visualize the end product, which is the use of the appraisal methodology to estimate the uranium oxide ($U_3O_8$) endowment of a region. Imagine a geologist seated at a desk upon which there are all relevant geological maps of the region. On his right, and easily accessible to him, is a computer terminal through which he can communicate in an interactive mode with a program in the main computer installation. This program is very special because it expresses that geologist's previously determined endowment model. In other words, it describes what the geologist considers to be the earth processes involved in the formation of uranium deposits. The geologist uses this program as an aid in making a probabilistic appraisal of endowment. He examines all of his geological data and, based upon his examination, conveys to a derived computer algorithm his assessment of the probabilities that each of the earth processes relevant to the formation of deposits will take on different states (i.e., outcomes). The algorithm combines the probability distributions for each process to derive a probability distribution for the outcome of interest—a deposit of uranium oxide.

The computer program contains more than the identity of the processes and their interrelationships. It also describes the probability that the intensity or magnitude of each process (in various combination with other processes) will result in the formation of uranium deposits. The identity of the processes, their interrelations, and the probabilities collectively constitute the geologist's inference net. This inference net is a statement of the geologist's perception of the geology-endowment function—it represents the geoscience and uncertainty of uranium occurrence, as he sees it. It is important to understand that the elements of the inference net are processes, such as leaching and oxidation, not physical characteristics, such as oxidized sandstone. Of course, there are many processes and many geological conditions, so that the task is much more complex than the simple analog described here to demonstrate the essential concepts.

Research into the use of a geologist as an integral part of an endowment estimation system is embryonic. Future developments in this field promise to be very interesting and, it is hoped, useful.

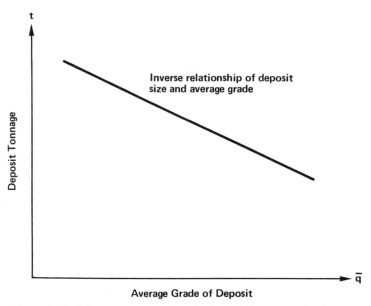

**Figure 8.17.** Diagram representing the belief of many geologists concerning the still speculative relationship of deposit size and average grade.

*The tonnage-grade relation.*    There are several relations which are loosely referred to as a tonnage-grade relation. The one at issue here is correlation between the total tonnage of rock in a mineral deposit and the average grade of that rock. The nature of this relation is important to the economics of long-term mineral supply because if it is found that for a given metal the tonnage and average grade are inversely correlated, some of the concern about the depletion of high-grade deposits is alleviated. While an inverse correlation does not alter this depletion, it does affect its economic consequences. This is because as lower grade deposits are mined, they will most likely be, on average, of larger size, which would permit economies of scale in mining to offset to some degree the economic costs of refining lower grades.

It has been, and still is, commonly believed that there is an inverse relation between tonnage and average grade for many types of deposits (see figure 8.17). The experience has been that as the high-grade deposits are depleted, lower grade but much larger deposits have been found.

In the case of copper deposits in this country, history documents the early exploitation of high-grade vein deposits, primary and enriched, and the later transition to the low-grade prophyries, generally with a larger tonnage of ore than was contained in the high-grade veins. Technological advances made this transition to lower grade ores possible without increases in copper prices;

in fact, real prices continued to decline during and after this transition. In effect, technology created copper resources by allowing the exploitation of a different kind of deposit. Another striking example of the effect of technology in expanding resources is the application of concentrating and pelletizing technologies to low-grade taconite material, which created a usable source of iron for the blast furnace. With experience such as the foregoing, it is hardly surprising that mineral scientists and engineers commonly believe that as cutoff grade decreases, deposits of larger size can be expected. The nature and strength of this relation are not easily identified, for experience as well as data reflect economic influences. For example, the perception of this relation reflects the sizes and average grades of known deposits, and those deposits which are well enough known to permit estimates of tonnage and average grade are primarily economic deposits. If a very low-grade deposit is to be economic, it must on average be of large size; therefore, the sample would be biased in favor of large sizes for lower grades. Even if deposit size and average grade were unrelated, the filtering performed by economic choice would impart an inverse correlation.

The investigation of this relation is even further complicated by the fact that if any data are available on size and average grade, they usually are for the ore, not the mineral deposit. The importance of this fact can be appreciated by imagining two identical deposits, one at the surface and the other at 1,000 feet below ground. Mining economics would require a higher cutoff grade for the deposit at 1,000 feet; this would result in the reporting of a smaller tonnage of ore, but at a higher average grade. In other words, the data have been both filtered and translated (see figures 8.18 and 8.19).

Straightforward statistical analysis of ore deposit data reflects the economic effects of truncation and translation less than it does the actual correlation of deposit size and average grade, depending upon the relative gradients of the cost surface and the correlation relation (see figure 8.20). It is virtually impossible to find a set of data which are free from filtering and translation. Two approaches can be taken to investigate this relation. One is to ignore the filtering effect of exploration, which biases the data to large size and to a lesser degree to high grade (see the discussion on discoverability in the section on exploration), and to analyze data on only those deposits which have been completely drilled. Unfortunately, there are not many deposits that have been completely drilled. More to the point, such data are not publicly available. An alternative is to obtain subjective estimates based upon geologic analysis of the undrilled or unproven parts of the ore body and add these to reported reserves plus cumulative production.

The second approach is, in effect, to purge the filtering and translation effects from the data. This requires modeling grade and tonnage, exploration, and exploitation in an integrated system. Then, the parameters of the grade

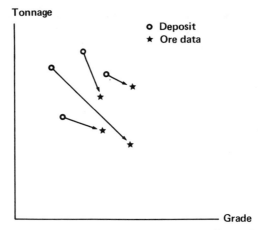

**Figure 8.18.** Representation of the effect of economics and technology in translating deposit data to ore data. From D. P. Harris, "Undiscovered Uranium Resources and Potential Supply," in National Academy of Sciences, *Workshops on Concepts of Uranium Resources and Producibility* (Washington, D.C., NAS, 1978).

and tonnage models and relations are determined indirectly by searching for those values which cause the system to yield the measures which match the statistics computed on the actual ore data.

Neither of these two approaches has been fully employed. A very incomplete variation of the second approach was used to explore the tonnage-grade relation on uranium deposits in the San Juan Basin of New Mexico (Harris, 1977a). That study employed a mining cost model to define the truncation grade for each of a number of tonnage classes. The frequency distribution of grades of deposits within each tonnage class was treated as a truncated sample; it was truncated at the minimum grade economic for deposits of that size, as defined by the cost function. After the parameters of the grade distribution were estimated from the truncated samples, the relationship between grade and tonnage was investigated by using the estimated parameters for the full, nontruncated grade populations. These parameters were regressed on the midtonnages of the tonnage classes. Although in the original data, tonnage and grade were inversely correlated, statistical analysis revealed no significant relation between grade and tonnage. This suggests, within limits of the analysis, that the correlation in the original data reflected primarily economies of scale in mining.

The first approach has been employed by the U.S. Geological Survey to the extent that data and information permit. The most complete investigation

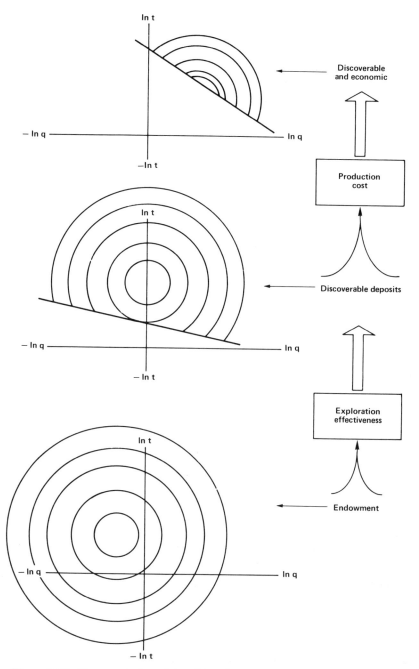

**Figure 8.19.** Representation of the effect of economics and technology on ore versus mineral endowment.

315

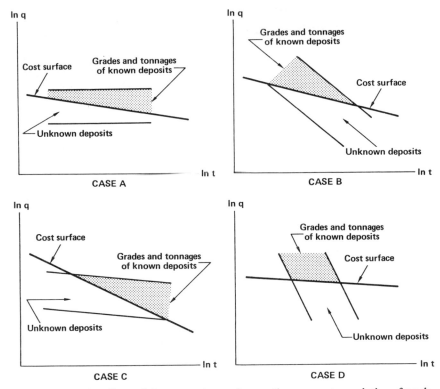

**Figure 8.20.** The effects of the truncation surface on the apparent correlation of grade and tonnage. From D. P. Harris, *Mineral Endowment, Resources, and Potential Supply: Theory, Methods for Appraisal, and Case Studies* (Tucson, Ariz., MIN-RESCO, 1977).

has been applied to copper deposits. Prior to statistical analysis, cumulative production and its average grade were combined with reported ore reserves data on tonnage and average grade. Where possible, experts were asked to estimate the quantity of mineralized rock in addition to the ore reserves and their average grade, given a cutoff grade of 0.1 percent Cu. These data and estimates were combined to give a single tonnage and average grade for each deposit. Estimates of additional mineralized rock were available on only part of the deposits; consequently, the data were not uniform. Statistical analyses of the data showed that the correlation of size and grade is not statistically significant for porphyry or stratabound-stratiform deposits, but is so for massive sulfide deposits. This is an interesting result in view of the fact that most experts considered (and many still do) tonnage and average grade to be inversely correlated for porphyry deposits.

In a survey of the copper resources of Sonora, Mexico, Harris (1973) found that each geologist interviewed believed that average grade and tonnage were inversely related for each mode of mineral occurrence: vein and porphyry. Their belief was strongly expressed in probabilities for total occurrences, but when the probability for *all geologists* was aggregated for a given mode of occurrence, there was so much disagreement that for the group as a whole there was no statistically meaningful relationship between deposit size and grade within the prophyry class. However, for the group as a whole, there was a strong relationship when grade and deposit size were examined *across* both modes of occurrence.

Independent studies by industry members (personal communications to D. Harris) showed that within the porphyry class of deposits there was no statistically significant relationship between deposit size and deposit grade. Singer et al. (1975) argued that geological reasoning dictates that deposit size and deposit grade are statistically independent because they are controlled by different geological processes. This reasoning makes the fact that the statistical analysis of the mixed population (porphyry, massive sulfide, and stratabound) showed a significant negative correlation all the more intriguing. Is this simply the economic effect? Or is it more? Is it possible that when size and grade are viewed across the entire spectrum of modes that size and grade are correlated, while they are not within a given mode? Since concentration requires complex sequential enrichment-depletion processes, there is some appeal, albeit weak, to the suggestion that it is less likely for such complexity to apply on a large scale than on a small one. These questions cannot be answered without better data and a more comprehensive analysis which allows for filtering and truncating effects.

A note of caution is in order. Even if there is an inverse correlation across all modes of occurrence, the use of this relation is limited to concentrations greater than that barrier grade which separates concentrations in ore minerals from concentrations of the metal in common rock. The results to date of U.S. Geological Survery investigations of the tonnage-grade relation and size and grade models are summarized in table 8.9.

*Intradeposit grade variation.*    Most, if not all, resource models which include undiscovered resources and their discovery have represented the postulated deposits by a tonnage and an average grade, which usually have been assigned to the postulated deposits using models developed from data on known deposits. Typically, these models describe the relative frequency of occurrence of ore deposits of various sizes and average grades. For a model with a very long-term time framework, such a representation is inadequate in two respects: (1) it does not describe the total amount of material in the deposit, and (2) it does not describe how the total material in the deposit is distributed by grade. Without this information, the effects of future prices, costs, and technology cannot be explored fully with the long-term supply model. The representation of a mineral deposit as a quantity of material which

**Table 8.9.** Grade and Tonnage Models

| Deposit type | Tonnage and grade variables (units in parenthesis) | Number of deposits used in developing model | Correlation coefficient of listed variable with variable on line with it in column 2 | 90 percent of deposits have at least | 50 percent of deposits have at least | 10 percent of deposits have at least |
|---|---|---|---|---|---|---|
| Porphyry Copper | Tonnage of ore (millions of tons) | 41 | | 20 | 100 | 430 |
| | Average copper grade (percent) | 41 | With tonnage of ore* −0.07 NS | 0.1 | 0.3 | 0.56 |
| | Average molybdenum grade (percent Mo) | 41 | | 0.0 | 0.008 | 0.031 |
| Island Arc Porphyry Copper | Tonnage of ore (millions of tons) | 41 | | 20 | 100 | 430 |
| | Average copper grade (percent) | 41 | With tonnage of ore* −0.07 NS | 0.1 | 0.3 | 0.56 |
| | Average molybdenum grade (percent Mo) | 41 | | 0.0 | 0.008 | 0.031 |
| | Average gold grade—locally significant but not determined | | | | | |
| Porphyry Molybdenum | Tonnage of ore (millions of tons) | 31 | | 1.6 | 24 | 340 |
| | Average molybdenum grade (percent Mo) | 31 | With tonnage of ore* −0.06 NS | 0.065 | 0.13 | 0.26 |
| Podiform Chromite | Tonnage of $Cr_2O_3$ (tons) | 268 | | 15 | 200 | 2,700 |
| Copper Skarn | Tonnage of ore (millions of tons) | 38 | | 0.08 | 1.4 | 24 |
| | Average copper grade (percent) | 38 | With tonnage of ore* −0.44** | 0.96 | 1.7 | 3.5 |
| | Average gold grade—locally significant but not determined | | | | | |
| Mafic Volcanogenic | Tonnage of ore (millions of tons) | 37 | | 0.24 | 2.3 | 22.0 |
| | Average copper grade (percent) | 37 | With tonnage of ore* −0.13 NS | 1.1 | 2.2 | 4.1 |
| | Average zinc grade excluding deposits without reported grades (percent) | 19 | With tonnage of ore* 0.03 NS | 0.3 | 1.3 | 5.5 |
| | Average gold grade—locally significant but not determined | | | | | |

| Deposit type and statistic | | | | |
|---|---|---|---|---|
| **Felsic and Intermediate Volcanogenic Massive Sulfide** | | | | |
| Tonnage of ore (millions of tons) | 89 | 0.19 | 1.9 | 18.0 |
| Average copper grade (percent) | 89 | 0.54 | 1.70 | 5.40 |
|   With tonnage of ore* −0.41** | | | | |
| Average zinc grade excluding deposits without reported grades (percent) | 41 | 1.40 | 3.80 | 10.00 |
|   With tonnage of ore* 0.25 NS | | | | |
| Average lead grade excluding deposits without reported grades (percent) | 14 | 0.20 | 0.96 | 4.80 |
|   With tonnage of ore* −0.02 NS | | | | |
| Tonnage contained gold excluding deposits without reported gold (tons) | 38 | 0.27 | 2.90 | 32.00 |
|   With tonnage of ore* 0.78** | | | | |
| Tonnage contained silver excluding deposits without reported silver (tons) | 46 | 5.00 | 80.00 | 1,300.00 |
|   With tonnage of ore* 0.82** | | | | |
| **Nickel Sulfide** | | | | |
| Tonnage of ore (millions of tons) | 48 | 0.23 | 1.20 | 5.90 |
|   With tonnage of ore* −0.03 NS | | | | |
| Average nickel grade (percent) | 48 | 0.32 | 0.61 | 1.20 |
|   With tonnage of ore* 0.03 NS | | | | |
| Average copper grade (percent) | 48 | 0.18 | 0.47 | 1.20 |
|   With nickel grade* 0.04 NS | | | | |
| **Mercury** | | | | |
| Tonnage of contained mercury (tons) | 165 | 0.09 | 3.10 | 120.00 |
| **Vein gold** | | | | |
| Tonnage of contained gold (tons) | 43 | 0.29 | 3.30 | 30.00 |
| **Skarn/Tactite Tungsten** | | | | |
| Tonnage of ore (millions of tons) | 31 | 0.024 | 0.63 | 17 |
| Average tungsten grade (percent W) | 31 | 0.24 | 0.51 | 1.10 |
|   With tonnage of ore* −0.34 NS | | | | |

*Note:* Tabulated data occur on line from column to column. All data in metric units. NS, not significant; * significant at 5 percent level; ** significant at 1 percent level.

**Table 8-10.**    Drill Sample Intradeposit Grade Variance for 17 U.S. Porphyries

| Deposit | $\gamma$ | $\alpha$ |
|---------|----------|----------|
| 1  | 0.8785920 | 0.05669277 |
| 2  | 0.7772585 | 0.0532021 |
| 3  | 0.8163445 | 0.05759983 |
| 4  | 0.7714428 | 0.04682515 |
| 5  | 0.7578219 | 0.04096632 |
| 6  | 1.024631  | 0.06750213 |
| 7  | 1.163332  | 0.093053 |
| 8  | 0.6201824 | 0.04394351 |
| 9  | 1.378149  | 0.1207513 |
| 10 | 0.9608156 | 0.05951382 |
| 11 | 0.6607206 | 0.04673675 |
| 12 | 0.8703854 | 0.05510846 |
| 13 | 1.199441  | 0.7675494 |
| 14 | 0.8776399 | 0.05486309 |
| 15 | 0.6781007 | 0.4328024 |
| 16 | 0.6291886 | 0.0409957 |
| 17 | 0.8196854 | 0.06358891 |

*Source:* Charles River Associates, *Economics and Geology of Mineral Supply: An Integrated Framework for Long-Run Policy Analysis*, Publication prepared for the National Science Foundation, Washington, D.C., November 1978.

is homogeneous and has a grade throughout equal to the average grade denies a realistic evaluation.

As indicated in the previous section, available data limit what can be done. Information on the intradeposit grade variation is especially meager. Mining companies do have the data which would permit the construction of models of this grade variation, but usually the information is closely guarded because of its implication for production economics. The information is so important to the improvement of long-term supply models, however, that an effort should be made to enlist the cooperation of industry in the construction of models of the intradeposit grade variation for each important mode of occurrence of each metal.

Information important for modeling purposes includes (1) the shape of the distribution of material by grade and its parameters, (2) whether or not the form and parameters of this distribution are dependent upon (correlated with) the size and average grade of the deposit, and (3) the variation in the distribution by mode of occurrence for a given metal.

Recently, Agterberg (1978) and Charles River Associates (1978) attempted to explore some of these questions for copper. Because of limited data, both of these efforts assumed that the material distributed by grade in copper deposits is of lognormal form. This assumption reduced the task to estimating the two parameters of this distribution. The study by Charles River Associates investigated these parameters for porphyry and stratiform copper deposits.

**Table 8.11.** Parameters and Statistics for Intradeposit Grade Variance of Strataform Deposits

| Name of ore body | Stanton's statistics $\bar{\chi}(\%)$ | $S_\chi$ | Estimated parameters $\mu_q$ | $v_1$ | $\gamma$ | $v_2$ |
|---|---|---|---|---|---|---|
| Rothmere I., Nfld. | 1.30 | 0.63 | 0.15 | 0.40 | 1.41 | 0.21 |
| Oriental II, Nfld. | 0.76 | 0.31 | −0.39 | 0.28 | 0.78 | 0.15 |
| B.M. & S6, N.B. | 0.49 | 0.81 | −1.20 | 0.77 | 0.44 | 1.32 |
| B.M. & S12, N.B. | 0.37 | 0.34 | [a] | [a] | [a] | 0.61 |
| Kennco, N.B. | 1.13 | 1.43 | [a] | [a] | [a] | 0.96 |
| Texas, Gulf & Sulfur, N.B. | 0.51 | 0.47 | [a] | [a] | [a] | 0.61 |
| Health Steele "A", N.B. | 0.69 | 0.96 | −1.10 | 1.06 | 0.57 | 1.08 |
| Health Steele "B", N.B. | 0.67 | 0.66 | (−0.74)[a] | [a] | [a] | 0.68 |
| Health Steele "C", N.B. | 0.87 | 0.76 | (−0.42)[a] | [a] | [a] | 0.57 |
| Vermillion, Ont. | 1.51 | 1.74 | −0.14 | 1.05 | 1.48 | 0.85 |
| Errington, Ont. | 1.57 | 1.68 | −0.10 | 1.12 | 1.58 | 0.76 |
| East Avoca, Eire | 0.46 | 0.41 | −1.34 | 0.95 | 0.42 | 0.59 |
| West Avoca, Eire | 0.68 | 0.66 | −0.87 | 1.03 | 0.70 | 0.66 |
| Captains Flat, N.S.W. | 0.74 | 0.42 | −0.44 | 0.27 | 0.74 | 0.28 |

*Sources:* Charles River Associates, *Economics and Geology of Mineral Supply: An Integrated Framework for Long-Run Policy Analysis*, Publication prepared for the National Science Foundation, Washington, D.C., November 1978. Stanton's statistics are from R. L. Stanton, "Abundance of Copper, Zinc, and Lead in Some Sulfide Deposits," *Journal of Geology* vol. 66, no. 5 (1958) pp. 484–502.

[a] No histogram was reported for these deposits. Those values in parentheses are estimates using $v_2$ and $\bar{\chi}$: $\mu_q = \ln(\bar{\chi}) - v_2/2$.

In the case of the porphyry study, the only data available were estimates for seventeen porphyry deposits of the total material and two average grades for two different cutoff grades. Using this information, a search was made for the parameters of the assumed lognormal distribution. Table 8.10 shows the intradeposit grade variance estimated in this fashion for each of these deposits. The investigation of the intradeposit grade variance for stratabound deposits was based upon sample statistics estimated by Stanton (1958) using sparse sample data for fourteen deposits. The statistics estimated were the arithmetic mean grade and the variance of grade for each deposit. Using lognormal theory, the parameters of the assumed lognormal distribution were estimated from the arithmetic mean grade and variance. Table 8.11 shows the resulting estimates of $\mu_q$ and $v$, the parameters of the lognormal distribution which is required to reproduce the sample statistics.

Agterberg (1978) performed a similar analysis of statistics reported by Hazen and Meyers for nineteen ore bodies. Table 8.12 shows the resulting estimates of the intradeposit grade variance, $v$. Clearly, these results are preliminary, representing an attempt to learn from available data. What is needed now is a cooperative effort with mining companies which are able to provide the primary data for statistical analysis and the exploration of model form.

**Table 8-12.**  Hazen's and Meyer's (1966) Statistics for Sets of Copper Exploration Data for 19 Ore Bodies in the United States

| Name of ore body | $n$ | $\overline{X}$ | $s_X$ | $v$ |
|---|---|---|---|---|
| Copper King, Wyo. | 105 | 0.31 | 0.18 | 0.30 |
| Cape Rosier, Maine | 68 | 1.77 | 2.53 | 1.10 |
| Keystone-St. George, Ariz. | 58 | 1.62 | 1.99 | 0.92 |
| Reward Zinc, Ariz. | 84 | 0.18 | 0.32 | 1.42 |
| Reward Zinc, Ariz. | 203 | 0.33 | 0.60 | 1.49 |
| South Hecla, Utah | 13 | 3.88 | −4.22 | 0.77 |
| Majuba Hill, Nev. | 141 | 2.05 | 2.36 | 0.85 |
| Shamrock, Ore. | 114 | 1.95 | 2.21 | 0.83 |
| Shamrock, Ore. | 21 | 0.37 | 0.46 | 0.92 |
| Shamrock, Ore. | 21 | 1.99 | 2.48 | 0.95 |
| Mertic Lode, Alaska | 23 | 3.33 | 4.52 | 1.04 |
| Metric Lode, Alaska | 12 | 0.65 | 0.31 | 0.20 |
| Stillwater, Mont. | 61 | 1.06 | 3.41 | 2.43 |
| Stillwater, Mont. | 76 | 0.22 | 0.20 | 0.61 |
| Stillwater, Mont. | 81 | 0.32 | 0.28 | 0.48 |
| American Eagle, Calif. | 64 | 0.07 | 0.08 | 0.92 |
| Collier, Calif. | 22 | 0.17 | 0.17 | 0.71 |
| North Keystone, Calif. | 60 | 0.88 | 2.01 | 1.82 |
| Khayyam, Alaska | 24 | 2.19 | 2.02 | 0.62 |

*Source:* F. P. Agterberg, "Regional Mineral Appraisal: An Analytical Approach." Paper presented at the National Science Foundation Symposium on Methods for Broad Mineral Resource Appraisal, College of Mineral and Energy Resources, University of West Virginia, Morgantown, W. Va., May 15–18, 1978.

## 7. Summary

Discovery, development, and production of mineral commodities are complex issues. Assessments of undiscovered deposits and future production are even more complex and results are much less certain. A number of conclusions can be drawn from this discussion (some of them are better described as judgments):

1. It is apparent from a study of geochemistry and mineralogy that for the five common metals—iron, aluminum, titanium, magnesium, and silicon—the distribution of common ore minerals is such that there is an inverse relation between grade and tonnage of their ores. As lower grade ores are sought and used, larger tonnages are available. The only limit to this relation is the size of earth's crust because the relation extends to common rocks.

For a second group of metals—manganese, barium, vanadium, zirconium (plus the nonmetals sulfur, phosphorus, chlorine, and fluorine)—limits to an inverse grade-tonnage relation are present, but are so far removed from present-day ores that the metals can be considered similar to the abundant five as far as future supplies are concerned. In the case of all of these metals, technology will not face abrupt challenges from unfamiliar deposits.

2. For all other metals (the geochemically scarce metals), such as copper, lead, zinc, molybdenum, and gold, there are clearly limits to the grade above which ore minerals occur and below which the metals are locked in solid solution in silicate minerals. All conventional ores have grades above the appearance of ore minerals. If mining is to continue after all conventional ores have been discovered and mined, technology will face abrupt changes and its evolution will be a step process, not a smooth one.

3. Discovery (exploration) of conventional mineral deposits (meaning those above the grade at which ore minerals appear) follows three distinct phases:
  (a) conventional prospecting of surface indications
  (b) detection of shallowly covered deposits by geochemical or geophysical sensing
  (c) the use of integrated geological models to draw inferences as to favorable areas and deposit occurrence at depth.
For the United States, stages (a) and (b) have passed, at least far as present technology is concerned, because deposits are essentially undetectable beneath 1,000 feet or more of cover.

Exploration effectiveness is declining and exploration costs are rising. So far, however, productivity of capital and labor in mining, processing, and refining has offset discovery depletions. Thus, while discoveries are declining, material supplies are apparently being maintained by improvements in productivity in areas such as capital and labor in mining, processing, and refining and possibly too by the substitution of abundant metals for scarce ores, of scrap for primary metal, and of nonminerals for minerals. This is probably a temporary situation, however, and metal prices will eventually rise.

4. None of the present methods of assessing mineral resources or making an inventory of mineral endowment is satisfactory. By making assumptions, approximate assessments can be made, but all are biased because data are biased. An ideal model for a given region or a given commodity would include a description of the mineral endowment by quantity and quality for each deposit, plus the exploitation of each deposit by explicitly stated technology within a comprehensive economic system containing both the allocative mechanisms of a market economy and general economic dynamics. No geologist or group of geologists has so far come close to attaining the goals of an ideal model, but we believe that geologists are far from reaching their potential in resource assessment.

## References

Agterberg, F. P. 1978. "Regional Mineral Appraisal: An Analytical Approach," Paper presented at National Science Foundation Symposium on Methods for Broad Mineral Resource Appraisal, College of Mineral and Energy Resources, University of West Virginia, Morgantown, W. Va., May 15–18.

——, C. F. Chung, A. G. Fabbri, A. M. Kelley, and J. S. Springer. 1972. *Geomathematical Evaluation of Copper and Zinc Potential of the Abitibi Area, Ontario and Quebec* (Ottowa, Geological Survey of Canada).

Averitt, P. 1974. "Coal Resources of the United States, January 1, 1974," Bulletin 1412, U.S. Geological Survey (Washington, D.C., USGS).

Bailly, P. A. 1977. "Changing Rates of Success in Metallic Exploration," Paper presented at the GAC-MAC-SEG-CGU Annual Meeting, Vancouver, British Columbia, April 25.

——. 1978. "Today's Resource Status—Tomorrow's Resource Problems, The Need for Research on Mineral Deposits," Paper presented at the GSA-GAC-MAC Joint Annual Meeting, October 23, Toronto.

Bonner, J. A. 1978. "The Changing U.S. Uranium Exploration Industry," *Uranium Resources—An International Assessment*, Topical Symposium on Uranium Resources, Las Vegas, Nev., September 10–13; sponsored by American Nuclear Society and the U.S. Department of Energy, pp. 225–245.

Brant, A. A. 1968. "The Pre-Evaluation of the Possible Profitability of Exploration Prospects," *Mineralium Deposita* vol. 3, no. 1 (March) pp. 1–17.

Barvard, J. C., H. B. Flora, and C. Portal. 1972. "Energy Expenditures Associated with the Production and Recycling of Metals," Oak Ridge National Labs. Report ORNL-NSF-EP-24. Oak Ridge, Tennessee.

Brinck, J. W. 1967. "Note on the Distribution and Predictability of Mineral Resources," *Euratom 3461*, Brussels.

——. 1971. "MIMIC," *Eurospectra* vol. X, no. 2.

Brobst, D. A., and W. P. Pratt. 1973. "United States Mineral Resources," U.S. Geological Survey Professional Paper 820 (Washington, D.C., USGS).

Charles River Associates (CRA). 1978. *Economics and Geology of Mineral Supply: An Integrated Framework for Long Run Policy Analysis*, Prepared for National Science Foundation, Washington, D.C., November.

Commission on Mineral Resources and the Environment (COMRATE). 1975. "Resources of Copper," chapter VI, *Mineral Resources and the Environment* (Washington, D.C., National Academy of Sciences).

Cranstone, D. A., and H. L. Martin. 1973. "Are Ore Discovery Costs Increasing? *Canadian Mineral Exploration and Outlook*, MR 137, published by the Mineral Resources Branch, Department of Energy, Mines and Resources, Ottawa, pp. 5–13.

Derry, D. R. 1970. "Exploration Expenditure, Discovery Rate and Methods," CIM Bulletin 362.

——, and Booth. 1977. "Mineral Discoveries and Exploration Expenditure—A Revised Review 1965–1976," Paper prepared for 1977 CIM Symposium.

Donald, P. G. 1974. "Investment Decisions in Nonferrous Metals Exploration in Mexico: An Economic Analysis of Discovery Probabilities, Expected Financial Returns and Tax Policy," Unpublished doctoral dissertation, Department of Mineral Economics, The Pennsylvania State University, University Park, Pa.

Drew, M.W. 1977. "U.S. Uranium Deposits; A Geostatistical Model," *Resources Policy* (March) pp. 60–70.

Ellis, J. R., D. P. Harris, and N. H. Van Wie. 1975. *A Subjective Probability Appraisal of Uranium Resources in the State of New Mexico*, GJO-110(76), the U.S. Energy Research and Development Administration, Grand Junction Office, Grand Junction, Colorado.

Erickson, R. L. 1973. "Crustal Abundance of Elements and Mineral Reserves and Resources," *United States Mineral Resources*, Professional Paper 820, U.S. Geological Survey (Washington, D.C., USGS) pp. 21–25.

Harris, D. P. 1965. "An Application of Multivariate Statistical Analysis to Mineral Exploration," Ph.D. dissertation, The Pennsylvania State University, University Park, Pa.

———. 1973. "A Subjective Probability Appraisal of Metal Endowment of Northern Sonora, Mexico," *Economic Geology* (March–April) pp. 222–242.

———. 1976a. "The Estimation of Uranium Resources by Life-Cycle or Discovery-Rate Models: A Critique," GJO-112(76), U.S. Energy Research and Development Administration, Grand Junction Office, Grand Junction, Colorado.

———. 1976b. "A Critique of the NURE Appraisal Procedure as a Basis for a Probabilistic Description of Potential Resources and Guides to Preferred Practice," Unpublished manuscript.

———. 1977a. *Mineral Endowment, Resources, and Potential Supply: Theory, Methods for Appraisal, and Case Studies*, MINRESCO, 3330 N. Jackson Ave., Tucson, Arizona.

———. 1977b. "Conventional Crude Oil Resources of the United States: Recent Estimates, Methods for Estimation, and Policy Considerations," *Materials and Society* vol. 1, pp. 263–286.

———. 1978. "Undiscovered Uranium Resources and Potential Supply," *Workshop on Concepts of Uranium Resources and Producibility* (Washington, D.C., National Academy of Sciences) pp. 51–81.

Hewett, D. F. 1929. "Cycles in Metal Production," American Institute of Mining and Metallurgical Engineering, Yearbook, pp. 65–98.

Hubbert, M. K. 1967. "Degree of Advancement of Petroleum Exploration in the United States," *Bulletin of the AAPG* vol. 51, no. 11, pp. 2207–2227.

———. 1969. "Energy Resources," in *Resources and Man* (San Francisco, W. H. Freeman) pp. 157–239.

———. 1974. *U.S. Energy Resources, A Review as of 1972*, A background paper prepared at the request of Henry M. Jackson, chairman, Committee on Interior and Insular Affairs, U.S. Senate, 93rd Congress, 2nd session, Washington, D.C.

Kellogg, H. H. 1974. "Energy Efficiency in the Age of Scarcity," *Journal of Metals* vol. 26 (June) pp. 25–29.

Liberman, M. A. 1976. "U.S. Uranium Resources—An Analysis of Historical Data," *Science* vol. 192, pp. 431–436.

Lindgren, W. 1932. *Mineral Deposits*, 4th ed. (New York, McGraw-Hill).

Martin, H. L., D. A. Cranstone, and J. Zwartendyk. 1976. *Metal Mining in Canada, 1976–2000*, MR 167 (Ottawa, Energy, Mines and Resources).

McKelvey, V. E. 1960. "Relations of Reserves of the Elements to their Crustal Abundance," *American Journal of Science* vol. 258-A (Bradley volume) pp. 234–241.

———. 1973. "Mineral Resource Estimates and Public Policy," *United States Mineral Resources*, Professional Paper 820, U.S. Geological Survey (Washington, D.C., USGS) pp. 9–19.

Netschert, Bruce C. 1958. *The Future Supply of Oil and Gas* (Baltimore, Md., Johns Hopkins University Press for Resources for the Future).

Programmes Analysis Unit (PAU). 1976. "A Deposit Distribution Model for Uranium," Unpublished manuscript. Some of this was published later by M. W. Drew, "U.S. Uranium Deposits—A Geostatistical Model," *Resources Policy* (March 1977) pp. 60–70.

Ridge, J. D. 1974. "Mineral Resource Appraisal and Analysis," *Professional Paper 921*, U.S. Geological Survey (Washington, D.C., USGS).

Roscoe, W. E. 1971. "Probability of an Exploration Discovery in Canada," *Canadian Mining and Metallurgical Bulletin* vol. 64, no. 707, pp. 134–137.

Schanz, J. J. 1975. *Resource Terminology: An Examination of Concepts and Recommendations for Improvement* (Palo Alto, Calif., Electric Power Research Institute).

Schurr, S. H., Bruce Netschert, Vera F. Eliasberg, Joseph Lerner, and Hans H. Landsberg. 1960. *Energy in the American Economy, 1850–1975* (Baltimore, Md., Johns Hopkins University Press for Resources for the Future).

Singer, D. A. 1972. "Multivariate Statistical Analysis of the Unit Regional Value of Mineral Resources," Unpublished doctoral dissertation, The Pennsylvania State University, University Park, Pa.

———, P. Cox, and L. J. Drew. 1975. "Grade and Tonnage Relationships Among Copper Deposits," *Professional Paper 907A*, U.S. Geological Survey (Washington, D.C., USGS).

Skinner, B. J. 1976. "A Second Iron Age Ahead?" *American Scientist* vol. 64, no. 3, pp. 258–269.

Stanton, R. L. 1958. "Abundance of Copper, Zinc, and Lead in Some Sulfide Deposits," *Journal of Geology* vol. 66, pp. 484–502.

Taylor, S. R. 1964. "Abundance of Chemical Elements in the Continental Crust: A New Table," *Geochimica Cosmochimica Acta* vol. 28, pp. 1273–1285.

Zimmerman, E. W. 1964. *Introduction to World Resources* (New York, Harper & Row).

# 9

## Measures of Natural Resource Scarcity Under Uncertainty

### Shantayanan Devarajan and Anthony C. Fisher

Are the resources on which modern industrial economies are based nearing exhaustion? While the authors of the widely publicized volume, *The Limits to Growth* (1972), apparently believe this to be the case, others have questioned this "doomsday" prediction on the basis that the indicator of resource scarcity used (the ratio of reserves to annual consumption) is inappropriate. Not surprisingly, this has led to a debate on what *is* an appropriate measure of scarcity, which appears to have reached the following consensus: the behavior of rent—the shadow price of the resource in the ground—comes closest to signaling impending exhaustion (see Brown and Field, 1978; Fisher, 1977; and Pindyck, 1978).

Unfortunately, rents are ordinarily not observable. However, the works cited show that they bear a close relation to discovery costs, which *are* observable. This has led to the suggestion that rent be estimated from discovery cost data. However, this is a problem. Discovery costs may reflect, not just the difficulty of finding a new source of some mineral, but attempts by mining firms to deal with uncertainty about the relation between discovery inputs and outputs.

This is, in part, the subject of our chapter: supposing one could estimate discovery costs, *how might the estimate be biased by the presence of an uncertainty that is fundamental to the discovery process?* In considering this

Production of this paper was partially supported by grant SOC76-19700A02 from the National Science Foundation to the University of California, Berkeley, administered through the Center for Research in Management.

The authors received helpful suggestions from Kenneth Arrow, Harold Barnett, Geoffrey Heal, William Hogan, John Moroney, and Chandler Morse. Finally, they benefited greatly from several discussions with Hayne Leland.

question, we inevitably shed some light on another, which is important in its own right: *how does uncertainty affect the exploration and extraction behavior of mining firms?* Results reported in this chapter represent only a first pass at these questions. Clearly, much remains to be learned, and a major purpose here is to set an agenda for future research.

Section 1 surveys the debate on measures of scarcity, and summarizes the arguments for the use of resource rent as an indicator. Section 2 focuses on the relationship between rent and discovery cost and identifies the various types of uncertainty which might affect this relationship. A simple, two-period model of optimal resource exploration and extraction is presented in section 3. With the aid of the model, we examine explicitly the conditions under which uncertainty in the exploration process affects patterns of exploration and extraction. Results here also indicate how, and under what conditions, discovery cost systematically deviates from rent. Section 4 contains some qualifications of our results based on both alternative motives for exploration by firms and on institutional restrictions. These qualifications lead quite naturally to suggestions for future research.

## 1. Measures of Scarcity

Before proceeding with a discussion about measures of scarcity, the purpose of such an inquiry should be clear. As Stiglitz (1979) has explained, its purpose is to forecast future resource costs and prices and to say something about how they will affect the standard of living. In other words, will rising prices hold back growth?

This question is different from another one more commonly asked by economists: are resources being depleted too rapidly—or too slowly—by one or another form of market or government arrangement? The two questions are distinct. The country might be facing much higher resource prices and a consequent slowing of growth in the near future, yet no intervention by government would be warranted in the absence of market failure. Conversely, intervention could be indicated even though future prospects remain bright. The forecasting exercise need have no policy implications, whereas the efficiency analysis normally does.

A counter argument to this point, however, might run as follows. If the welfare of future generations is a public good, as Marglin (1963) and others have suggested, everyone might be better off if the government took steps to promote conservation and reduce the anticipated drag on growth. Put a bit differently, the government might intervene to promote intergenerational equity even if the market were allocating resources efficiently (from the standpoint of the present generation).

It is not our intention to consider such questions here. We wish only to shed some light on issues that arise in forecasting resource scarcity. As it turns out, the model we develop can be adapted to deal with some of the efficiency questions as well, but that is another story.

To return, then, to measures of scarcity. Rent is not the only possible measure of impending exhaustion, or increasing scarcity. In fact, many discussions, including that in *Limits to Growth*, rely on a physical measure, reserves, or the ratio of reserves to annual consumption. The difficulty in using such a measure to infer anything about ultimate or Malthusian limits is that reserves are defined as the known amounts of a mineral profitably recoverable at current prices, using current technology (Brobst and Pratt, 1973). New discoveries, technical breakthroughs, rising resource prices—all result in increases in reserves. Thus, though consumption of most resources has increased over time, reserves-to-consumption ratios have tended to be fairly constant (Fischman and Landsberg, 1972). This probably tells us more about the inventory policies of firms and governments than it does about ultimate availability of the resource in question.

Perhaps a more inclusive physical measure would be better, but the problem is knowing where to draw the line. Crustal abundance, the material that exists in minute concentration in the "average rock" of the earth's crust, is typically millions of times greater than reserves. But crustal abundance, like reserves, is a misleading indicator of availability. As Jevons (1865) pointed out a long time ago in a study of Britain's coal prospects, cost barriers will in most cases prevent the mining of very low grade sources. Jevons's argument is based on Ricardo's (1817) still earlier distinction of different grades of a resource corresponding to different costs of production. As an economy grew, and demand for a resource increased, poorer quality, higher cost sources would be drawn into production. The higher costs would in turn exert a drag on growth and incidentally signal increasing scarcity.

Barnett and Morse (1963) have applied this interpretation of Ricardo to extractive resources in the United States. Their influential study examines the behavior of the real unit cost of extractive output over nearly a century. Somewhat surprisingly, it turns out that cost has been falling, not rising. Moreover, the fall is greater for the *exhaustible* resources, such as metals and fuels.

The unit cost measure is not without drawbacks, however (Brown and Field, 1978). The basic problem is that cost is not a "leading indicator." For instance, technical advances can cause extraction costs to drop even as a resource nears exhaustion (this is one explanation for Barnett and Morse's results). More generally, a unit of an exhaustible resource extracted and consumed today is not available for consumption in the future, and the resulting loss is not captured by the cost of today's extraction. The loss is literally the shadow price of the unit, the change in the (optimal) value of the resource stock with respect to a unit change in the stock. If one is interested in scarcity of the "pure" resource, unmixed with human labor or other productive factors, the shadow price or rent is an appropriate measure.

The resource product price is also a measure of scarcity and, depending on the purpose of the inquiry, conceivably a better one. A result widely established in the literature, and again in section 3, is that, along a socially efficient extraction path, the resource price is equal to the sum of marginal extraction cost and rent. If one is interested in the sum of sacrifices made to obtain a unit of the resource, then both cost and rent are relevant. The argument for rent alone is that cost reflects a number of things besides resource scarcity, such as supply conditions for other factors and the level of technology. Rent abstracts from these, and focuses exclusively on the resource.

Our position here is that each of the measures of scarcity discussed thus far is capable of providing useful information. Just how useful depends on the purpose for which the measure is designed. However, rent is appealing, and deserves further study, for two reasons. One is that it perhaps comes closest to reflecting what the economist understands by "resource scarcity." The other is that it is less intuitive and has been studied and used less than the alternative measures.

Certainly one explanation for the fact that rent has not been used to measure scarcity is that it ordinarily is not observable. Nevertheless, the result mentioned just above suggests a way in which rent could be estimated: as the difference between product price and marginal extraction cost. One possible objection to any inferences about scarcity that might be made, though, is that the product price reflects various market imperfections or government-induced distortions. In the next section we consider another method of inferring rent, based on its relation to discovery cost.

## 2. Rent, Discovery Cost, and Uncertainty

Why, and how, is rent related to discovery cost? The model of section 3 answers this question in a formal way, along somewhat different lines than those taken in the recent literature. But there is a clear intuitive answer as well. Rent is, by definition, the value of having an additional unit in the stock; the benefit, therefore, of discovering it. It is this benefit that is equated with the marginal cost of discovery. Brown and Field (1978) derive this result in their simple model of exploration and extraction. Fisher (1977) and Pindyck (1978) derive a slightly more complicated condition: rent equals "adjusted" marginal discovery cost, with the adjustment the shadow price of discovery.

The relationship between rent and discovery cost is not only intuitive, it offers the promise of avoiding dependence on an unreliable price measure. Unfortunately, the independence may only be temporary. The value of a unit in the stock does depend on the expected *future* price of the resource, as shown in the next section's model. Nevertheless, there are a number of reasons why one might want to study discovery cost.

First, it provides a check on the price-minus-extraction cost method of inferring rent. Second, a plausible argument might be made that estimates of (distant) future prices are less likely to be affected by resource market aberrations. Various combinations of monopoly and price controls characterize today's energy market, for example, but these might be considered transitory phenomena by resource owners who estimate values—and trade stocks—based on projections of underlying demand. Third, if discovery exhibits constant returns over the relevant range, rent will be cost-determined.

If it is accepted that rent can be inferred from discovery cost, an interesting area of econometric research is opened up: to learn how discovery costs for major minerals have behaved in recent years. This may not be a straightforward problem. For example, it may be difficult to determine what part of the costs of drilling an oil well are due to exploration and what part to the development of a field.

Our concern here is with another difficulty: observed discovery costs reflect not just conventional factor costs but also adjustments to uncertainty. To deal with this possibility, we have considered several ways in which uncertainty might affect discovery costs. This is the subject of the remainder of this section. In the next, we develop a model to look in more detail at one particular way that seems central to the discovery process.

In essence, there are two kinds of uncertainty: demand, and supply. Consider the situation of a firm deciding how much to invest in exploration equipment. A sudden increase in the expected future price of the resource would (other things being equal) lead the firm to devote more effort to exploration. But might it not be better off if it anticipates this possibility and opts for flexibility in choosing equipment? If the firm does behave in this way, the average cost curve for exploration under demand uncertainty would be higher but flatter than if there were no uncertainty. Such an effect was first suggested by Stigler (1939), though not in the context of mineral exploration.[1]

More generally, suppose some of the firm's inputs are chosen *ex ante*, that is, before the firm knows output price, and others *ex post*. Under these cir-

---

[1] Lewis (1977) has looked at the effect of price uncertainty on the optimal exploitation of an exhaustible resource. Not surprisingly, the results depend crucially on the resource owner's attitude toward risk.

cumstances one might imagine a number of things that could cause the choice of inputs to deviate from the cost-minimizing one: attitudes toward risk, the degree of substitutability between inputs, the cost of adjusting a previously determined investment, and so on. A small literature on choice of inputs under uncertainty has begun to deal with these possibilities (see Batra and Ullah, 1974; Hartman, 1976; and Stewart, 1978).

Thus far we have been talking about output price, or demand uncertainty, though Stewart considers input price uncertainty as well. More important, the uncertainty is not special to the natural resource sector. There is, however, one kind of uncertainty that is. It is supply uncertainty, arising from the relation between discovery inputs and outputs. The work that has established a connection between rent and discovery cost is not fully satisfactory in that it models discovery as a deterministic process. A kind of production function relates input of effort to output of mineral finds. Of course the process is stochastic; the firm does not know for sure what it will find. Does explicitly allowing for this uncertainty affect the firm's optimal exploration and extraction behavior? And is discovery cost still equated with rent? In the next section we describe a model that deals with these questions. We think this is worth doing for two reasons. First, as noted, the uncertainty is special to the discovery process. Second, it is probably empirically important. Nothing in this world is certain, but the search for minerals is probably less certain than most economic activities.

## 3. Exploration and Extraction Under Uncertainty

In order to analyze explicitly the rent-discovery cost relationship, we develop in this section a simple two-period model of optimal exploration and extraction under uncertainty.

Our model differs from others in this literature in its treatment of exploration. Gilbert (1976) and Loury (1976), among others, consider the extraction path of an unknown stock, with no exploratory activity and indeed, no learning about the stock as extraction proceeds. Hoel (1978) has recently extended their work to include learning, but this learning takes place only by depleting a known stock, which provides information about the size of a second, unknown stock. Moreover, all of these models assume that the unknown reserve is of uniform quality. By contrast, our model assumes that the quality of a reserve worsens as more of it is depleted. This is reflected in the extraction production function $F$ which contains the stock $X$ as well as extractive effort $L$ as arguments. The larger the stock, the easier it is to extract an additional unit, so that $dF(L,X)/dL$ is an increasing function of $X$. Also, in our model, firms undertake exploration alongside their extractive activity. However, the motivation for exploring is not to gain information about the reserve base, but to add to the stock of reserves. Since we assume marginal extraction costs fall as the stock increases, successful discoveries·by the exploring firm also help to reduce future extraction costs.[2]

Exploration in our model, therefore, can be viewed in more general terms as any research and development activity by the firm aimed at shifting the production function. In this sense, our work is close in spirit to the literature on R&D activities by profit-maximizing firms (see, for example, Kamien and Schwartz, 1976). However, the questions addressed in this literature are different.

A recent paper by Arrow (1977) incorporates the two motivations for exploration—expanding reserves and learning—into the same model. Results show some similiarity to those in the deterministic models of exploration, as well as to ours. However, this model is different from ours in a number of ways. First, it has zero extraction costs (expanding reserves simply increases their availability). As we show, the nature of extraction costs can be crucial in determining the effects of uncertainty. Second, it is framed in continuous time, over an infinite horizon, whereas ours is a simpler and (we believe) more transparent discrete-time, two-period exercise. Finally, Arrow does not address a major concern of our study: the estimation of resource rent from discovery costs.


## A Model with No Uncertainty

We first establish the result that, in the certain case, rent equals marginal discovery cost. We then proceed to investigate how firm·behavior, and hence this equality, are affected by uncertainty in exploration.

Our intention is to present the simplest possible model which captures all the features necessary for our analysis. Relaxing many of our assumptions, while more realistic, will only complicate the analysis—and not qualitatively alter our results.

In this spirit, the firm in our model makes its decisions over a two-period horizon. The two periods can be roughly interpreted as "present" and "future." Although this is a crude approximation to other models in the literature (not to mention the real world), it is interesting to note that the major results of the optimal control models of Fisher (1977), Pindyck (1978), and others can be produced by our model.

Consider, then, the following two-period model of a competitive firm that engages in exploration and extraction activities in the first period, and only extraction in the second. The firm's problem is to maximize the present value

---

[2] In a certain world, there would be no need to explore to learn more about the resource base. However, if expanding reserves (by exploration) lowers extraction costs, then it does pay for the firms to put more effort into discovery. Exploratory activity in this case may be considered as a kind of development of low-cost deposits for production: an oil field must be drilled, overburden removed from a surface mine, and so on.

of its revenue from sales less its costs of exploration and extraction. In symbols, the firm's problem is

$$\max_{L_1,L_2,R} W = p_1 F(L_1,X_1) - wL_1 - wR + \beta\{p_2 F[L_2,X_1$$

$$+ G(R) - F(L_1,X_1)] - wL_2\} \tag{1}$$

where $p_i$ is the price of the resource in period $i$ ($i = 1,2$)

$L_i$ is effort devoted to extraction in period $i$ ($i = 1,2$)

$X_1$ is resource stock at start of first period

$F(L,X)$ is the extraction production function, with $F_L > 0$, $F_X > 0$, $F_{LL} < 0$ and $F_{LX} > 0$

$w$ is the wage of effort

$R$ is effort devoted to exploration

$G(r)$ is exploration production function[3]

$\beta$ is discount factor

Note that there is no constraint because the expression for the resource stock at the start of the second period, $X_2 = X_1 + G(R) - F(L_1,X_1)$, has been substituted directly into the objective function. This will lead to an illuminating expression for rent. Ordinarily, rent is the interpretation given the auxiliary variable attached to an explicit resource constraint. Here, we shall derive an expression in terms of expected future resource price.

Before going any further, we must say a few words about the presence of the stock variable $X$ in our extraction production function $F(L,X)$. First, $X$ is measured in the same units as extractive and exploratory output. For example, with minerals, $X$ is in units of pure metal rather than ore. Second, given $F_{LX} > 0$, the fact that extraction lowers $X$ means that the best available quality of the resource is extracted first. Similarly, since exploration increases $X$, only discovery of ores at the currently best concentration is considered. Thus, discovery of inferior ores is not included in the figures for exploration output. (This view of exploration is echoed by Harris and Skinner, 1979.) If extraction far exceeds exploration in some period, $X$ is reduced, and so is the "best" quality level; from now on, extraction and exploration take place at the new, lower ore quality.

Our task, then, is to derive an expression for rent and show that it is equated to marginal discovery cost. Rent is, by definition, the shadow price of the resource, the change in the optimal value of the objective function with respect to a change in the stock. The optimal value of the objective function is

---

[3] The output of exploratory activity will, in general, depend not just on $R$ but also on the stock of cumulative discoveries over time. Since we are concerned with comparing the relationship between marginal discovery cost and rent under certainty and uncertainty, however, introducing this cumulative stock as an additional argument of $G$ would not add much to our analysis. It would complicate the expressions we derive for both the certainty and uncertainty cases, without shedding any more light on the comparison between the two.

$$V = \max W = p_1 F(L_1^*, X_1) - wL_1^* - wR^*$$
$$+ \beta\{p_2 F[L_2^*, X_1 + G(R^*) - F(L_1^*, X_1)] - wL_2^*\} \tag{2}$$

where asterisks denote solutions to the problem (1). We are interested in the effect on $V$ of a change in $X_2$, the stock at the start of the second period as influenced by exploration and extraction during the first period. To determine this, we differentiate $V$ with respect to $X_2$, and obtain

$$\frac{\partial V}{\partial X_2} = \beta p_2 F_x(L_2^*, X_2) \tag{3}$$

The right-hand side of equation (3) is, reading from the right, the change in output associated with one more—or one less—unit in the stock $[(F_x(L_2^*, X_2)])$, multiplied by the price of output ($p_2$) and the discount factor ($\beta$).

This expression for rent is also obtained as the difference between the price and the marginal cost of extraction along an optimal path. To see this, differentiate equation (1) with respect to $L_1$:

$$\frac{\partial W}{\partial L_1} = p_1 F_L(L_1, X_1) - w - \beta p_2 F_x F_L(L_1, X_1) \tag{4}$$

Setting the result equal to zero and rearranging terms gives

$$p_1 - \frac{w}{F_L} = \beta p_2 F_x \tag{5}$$

where $w/F_L$ is the marginal cost of extraction.

Now, how is rent related to marginal discovery cost? Here we are interested in the effect of a change in units discovered, which results in turn from a change in discovery effort in our simple model with no uncertainty. Differentiating the profit function (1) with respect to discovery effort $R$ and setting the result equal to zero, we obtain

$$-w + \beta p_2 F_x G'(R) = 0 \tag{6}$$

or

$$\frac{w}{G'(R)} = \beta p_2 F_x$$

The expression on the right-hand side is the rent, and the expression on the left $w/G'(R)$ is the marginal cost of discovery.[4]

As we noted earlier, Fisher (1977) and Pindyck (1978) derive a more complicated condition, namely that rent equals an adjusted marginal cost

---

[4] This certainty model is similar to Barnett and Morse's (1963) formalization of the Ricardian scarcity model. Their production function, which converts "unhomogeneous resources" $R_u$ into "standard resources" $R$, is akin to our exploration production function $G(R)$. Not surprisingly, they derive the result that marginal conversion cost equals resource rent.

of discovery, adjusted by the shadow price of discovery. This result depends on the presence of another argument, for cumulative discoveries, in the "production function." This affects firm behavior only when discovery occurs in more than one period—that is, in a multiperiod setting. This cumulative discovery effect is one result of the multiperiod model which is not captured by our two-period formulation. But we feel this difference is not germane to our concern, which is with the relationship between discovery cost and rent in a deterministic and in a stochastic world.

## A Model with Uncertain Exploration

We now extend this analysis to the case where the relationship between the inputs and outputs of exploration is uncertain. This uncertainty can be expressed by a stochastic exploration production function $\tilde{G}(R)$. Let the expected value of $\tilde{G}(R)$ be $G(R)$. Denoting the expectation operator as $E$, we can model the uncertainty as either additive:

$$\tilde{G}(R) = G(R) + \phi, \quad E\phi = 0 \tag{7}$$

or multiplicative:

$$\tilde{G}(R) = \theta G(R), \quad E\theta = 1 \tag{8}$$

We choose the latter because it seems more reasonable that the variance of the distribution of $\tilde{G}(R)$ would increase with $R$, rather than stay constant. Furthermore, if $G(\phi) = 0$, additive uncertainty implies the possibility of "negative" exploratory output—which has no realistic interpretation.[5]

In order to analyze the competitive firm's decision under this exploration uncertainty, we have to make two more changes to the two-period model of the previous section. First, whereas the firm in the certainty case maximized the present value of profits, we model the uncertain firm as maximizing the expected utility of profits. This is to allow for different attitudes toward risk on the part of the firm. The special case when the firm is risk neutral is equivalent to maximizing the expected (present) value of profits.

Second, in the certainty case, the firm makes all its input decisions at the beginning of the initial period. Hence in the specification (1), $L_1, L_2$ and $R$ are all control variables in the maximization of $W$. Under uncertainty,

---

[5] This approach is also consonant with the various stochastic models of exploration developed by geologists (Crabbé, 1977; Harris and Skinner, 1979). These models postulate as random variables: $N$, the number of deposits of a particular type of mineralized rock; $T$, the deposit tonnage; $\overline{Q}$, the deposit average grade; and $Q$, the actual grade. The output of our production function, $\tilde{G}(R)$, is the product of $Q$ and $T$ (for each of the $N$ deposits discovered). As a special case, suppose $N$, $T$, and $\overline{Q}$ were known with certainty, and $Q$ was the only random variable. Without loss of generality, we can set $N = 1$. Then for every $t$ tons of ore dug out, we get $Q \cdot t$ tons of pure metal, which is our exploratory output. In terms of our model, if effort $R$ yields $t(R)$ tons of ore, we define $G(R) = \overline{Q}t(R)$ and the random element would then be $\theta = Q/\overline{Q}$.

however, a more appropriate scenario would be for the firm to choose the first period inputs $(L_1, R)$ initially, but to decide on $L_2$ at the beginning of the second period, when the uncertainty has been resolved. Clearly, it would be better for the firm to wait and see the result of its exploratory activities before determining second-period output, than to commit itself to a certain level of output in that period *ex ante*.

This discussion suggests a dynamic programming framework for modeling these decisions. The firm chooses $(L_1, R)$ in period 1 to maximize the expected utility of profit, with the knowledge that its choice of $L_2$ will always maximize the (certain) utility of second period profit for whatever value of $\theta$ obtains.

In symbols, the firm's problem is

$$\max_{L_1, R} W' = U_1[p_1 F(L_1, X_1) - wL_1 - wR]$$
$$+ EU_2\{p_2 F[L_2^*, X_1 + \theta G(R) - F(L_1, X_1)] - wL_2^*\} \tag{9}$$

where $L_2^*$ is the solution to

$$\max_{L_2} U_2\{p_2 F[L_2, X_1 + \theta G(R) - F(L_1, X_1)] - wL_2\} \tag{10}$$

where $U_1(\cdot)$ is the first-period utility function, and
$U_2(\cdot)$ is the second-period utility function[6]
If we define

$$V' = \max_{L_1, R} W' = U_1[p_1 F(L_1^*, X_1) - wL_1^* - wR^*]$$
$$+ EU_2\{p_2 F[(L_2^*, X_1 + \theta G(R^*) - F(L_1^*, X_1)] - wL_2^*\} \tag{11}$$

[6] This specification constrains the firm owner to consume each period's profit in that period. No intertemporal adjustments—borrowing from or saving for the future—are allowed.

On the other hand, in a regime with perfect and complete capital markets, the firm would be indifferent among profit streams with the same expected present value. A single utility function over the discounted profit stream would be the appropriate formulation. Of course, it is the absence of these complete markets that we are trying to capture here.

The truth must be somewhere in the middle. The resource manager is able to transfer profits across time periods subject to a no-bankruptcy constraint. In other words, he can borrow up to his lowest possible profit in period 2, or when $\theta = 0$. Calling $C_1$ the manager's first-period consumption (a decision variable), his problem becomes

$$\max_{C_1, L_1, R} E\left[U_1(C_1) + U_2\left(\tilde{\pi}_2 + \frac{\pi_1 - C_1}{\beta}\right)\right]$$

s.t. $C_1 \leq \pi_1 + \beta \bar{\pi}_2$

where $\pi_1 = p_1 F(L_1, X_1) - wL_1 - wR$

$$\bar{\pi}_2 = \max_{L_2} p_2 F[(L_2, X_1 - F(L_1, X_1)] - wL_2$$

$$\tilde{\pi}_3 = \max_{L_2} p_2 F[(L_2, X_1 + \theta G(R) - F(L_1, X_1)] - wL_2$$

[with $L_2^*$ given by (10)], then the resource rent is once again the change in $V'$ from a change in the size of $X_2$, the second-period stock. Now, from equation (11),

$$\frac{\partial V'}{\partial X_2} = E p_2 F_x(L_2^*, X_2^*) U_2'[p_2 F(L_2^*, X_2^*) - w L_2^*] \tag{12}$$

Since the original problem is one of maximizing expected utility, the effect on the optimand of a change in $X_2$ is the expectation of the value of the increased output $[p_2 F_X(L_2^*, X_2^*)]$ weighted by the marginal utility of this increased revenue.

In the preceding section, it was shown that the expression for rent was exactly equal to the difference between first-period price and marginal extraction cost. Taking first-order conditions for the uncertainty case (9) yields a similar result:

$$\frac{\partial W'}{\partial L_1} = 0 \Rightarrow [p_1 F_L(L_1^*, X_1) - w] U_1'(\pi_1^*)$$

$$= F_L(L_1^*, X_1) E[p_2 F_X(L_2^*, X_2^*) U_2'(\pi_2^*) \tag{13}$$

where $\pi_1^*$ is $p_1 F(L_1^*, X_1) - w L_1^* - w R^*$
     $\pi_2^*$ is $p_2 F(L_2^*, X_2^*) - w L_2^*$
     $X_2^*$ is $X_1 + \theta G(R^*) - F(L_1^*, X_1)$

Rearranging equation (13), we get

$$p_1 - \frac{w}{F_L(L_1^*, X_1)} = \frac{E p_2 F_X(L_2^*, X_2^*) U_2'(\pi_2^*)}{U_1'(\pi_1^*)} \tag{14}$$

The only difference between this expression and that derived for rent is the $U_1'(\pi_1^*)$ in the denominator of equation (14). However, since utility functions are invariant to linear transformations (see Samuelson, 1947), we can set $U_1'(\pi_1^*) = 1$ without loss of generality, so that equation (14) coincides exactly with the original expression for rent. Note further that if $U_2$ differed from $U_1$ only by a discount factor $\delta$, so that $U_2 = \delta U_1$, and if the firm were risk-neutral, so that $U_1'$ is a constant, then (14) reduces to

$$P_1 - \frac{w}{F_L(L_1^*, X_1)} = E p_2 F_X(L_2^*, X_2^*) \delta \tag{15}$$

This is exactly the equality derived for rent in the certainty case, except that here the expectation operator governs the right-hand side.

Now, how is the measure of rent in equations (12) or (14) related to marginal cost? In the preceding section, it was observed that, with a deterministic exploration function, marginal discovery cost equals rent when there is no cumulative discovery effect. For the case of the stochastic exploration production function, we take "marginal discovery costs" to represent the expected marginal cost, that is $E[w/\theta G'(R)]$. We are interested in the relationship between $E[w/\theta G'(R^*)]$ and rent as derived in equations (12) or (14). Now, the first-order condition for optimizing $W'$ with respect to $R$ yields:

$$wU_1'(\pi_1^*) = G'(R^*)E[\theta p_2 F_X(L_2^*,X_2^*)U_2'(\pi_2^*)] \tag{16}$$

In the certainty case, we are able to equate marginal discovery cost to rent from the analogous first-order condition. *However, it is not at all clear that the same equality can be derived from equation (16)*. Indeed, we will derive conditions for which expected marginal costs, under uncertainty, will overstate the rent.

First, if we observe that $w/\theta G'(R)$ is a convex function of $\theta$, by Jensen's inequality,[7]

$$E\frac{w}{\theta G'(R^*)} > \frac{w}{G'(R^*)} \tag{17}$$

since $E\theta = 1$.

Substituting the expression in equation (16) for $w/G'(R^*)$,

$$E\frac{w}{\theta G'(R^*)} > \frac{E\theta p_2 F_X(L_2^*,X_2^*)U_2'(\pi_2^*)}{U_1'(\pi_1^*)} \tag{18}$$

If we set $U_1'(\pi_1^*) = 1$ again, since $E\theta = 1$, equation (18) can be rewritten as

$$E\frac{w}{\theta G'(R^*)} > Ep_2 F_X(L_2^*,X_2^*)U_2'(\pi_2^*) + cov[\theta,p_2 F_X(L_2^*,X_2^*)U_2'(\pi_2^*)] \tag{19}$$

The first term on the right-hand side is the previously derived expression for rent. If the covariance term in equation (19) were nonnegative, we could say unambiguously that expected marginal exploration costs would *overstate* rent. On the other hand, if it were negative, the relationship between marginal costs and rent would be ambiguous.

In what follows, therefore, we try to identify conditions under which the covariance term is positive, since that is the case when the direction of the bias caused by uncertainty can be determined.

## The Case of the Risk-Neutral Firm

Although we are ultimately concerned with behavior in the more general case in which risk aversion is possible, we can begin to understand what is happening by looking first at the simpler case of the risk-neutral firm. In this

---

[7] We are assuming $w$ is fixed and therefore independent of $\theta$. If this were not the case, and if the supply schedule of exploratory effort were sufficiently inelastic (i.e., $dw/d\theta > 0$), the inequality in equation (17) might be reversed.

case, $U_2'$ is a constant, so the sign of the covariance term depends on the sign of $[\partial F_x(L_2^*,X_2^*)]/\partial\theta$. To establish this sign, first note that the first-order condition in (10) is

$$p_2 F_L(L_2^*,X_2^*) = w \tag{20}$$

Differentiating both sides with respect to $\theta$,

$$p_2\left[F_{LL}(L_2^*,X_2^*)\frac{\partial L_2^*}{\partial\theta} + F_{LX}\frac{\partial X_2^*}{\partial\theta}\right] = 0 \tag{21}$$

Since $\partial X_2^*/\partial\theta = G(R^*)$,

$$\frac{\partial L_2^*}{\partial\theta} = \frac{-F_{LX}}{F_{LL}}G(R^*) \tag{22}$$

Now,

$$\frac{\partial F_X(L_2^*,X_2^*)}{\partial\theta} = F_{XL}\frac{\partial L_2^*}{\partial\theta} + F_{XX}G(R^*) \tag{23}$$

The sign of the partial derivative (23) therefore depends on the sign of $[(F_{LX})^2 - F_{LL}F_{XX}]$. Since $F_{LL} < 0$, if $F_{XX} > 0$ this sign is unambiguously positive. Loosely speaking, the sign of the covariance term in equation (19) can be interpreted as the effect of fluctuations in $\theta$ on resource rent. It is not surprising therefore that, with $F_{XX} > 0$, increases in $\theta$ increase rent. Whereas under certainty the firm explores to the point where marginal discovery cost equals rent, with uncertainty, it may (on average) be induced to explore beyond this point because of increasing returns to scale from "successful finds."

### The Case of the Risk-Averse Firm

The above result depends also on the assumption of risk neutrality. However, even if the resource owner were risk averse ($U_2'' < 0$), it is possible that his marginal discovery costs would exceed rent. To sign the covariance term in (19), we would be interested in the sign of $\partial(F_X U_2')/\partial\theta$:

$$\frac{\partial F_X}{\partial\theta}[(L_2^*,X_2^*)U_2'(\pi_2^*)]$$

$$= F_X U_2''(\pi_2^*)\frac{\partial\pi_2^*}{\partial\theta} + U_2'(\pi_2^*)\frac{\partial F_X}{\partial\theta}$$

$$= F_X^2 G(R^*)U_2''(\pi_2^*) + U_2'(\pi_2^*)G(R^*)\left[\frac{-F_{LX}^2}{F_{LL}} + F_{XX}\right] \tag{24}$$

Although the first term on the right-hand side is negative, if $F_{XX} > 0$, the second term is positive. In this case, the sign of the covariance term depends on the relative magnitudes of these two components. The intuition here is that even though risk aversion "dampens" the benefits from successful finds, the increasing returns act as an incentive to explore more, and the net result depends on how these forces stack up against each other.

Notice further that even a combination of risk aversion and diminishing returns to the stock variable ($F_{XX} < 0$) does not guarantee a negative covariance term. Substituting $\partial L_2^*/\partial\theta$ for

$$\left[ -\frac{F_{LX}}{F_{LL}} G(R) \right]$$

the second term on the right-hand side of equation (24) can be rewritten as

$$U_2'(\pi_2^*)\left[ F_{LX}\frac{\partial L_2^*}{\partial\theta} + F_{XX}G(R) \right]$$

Since $\partial L_2^*/\partial\theta$ is positive, even with $F_{XX}$ negative, the expression in brackets, and therefore the entire right-hand side of (24), could be positive.

The explanation for this result lies in the two-stage decision process. Even with diminishing returns, the firm can (and will) react to a successful search by increasing second-period output ($\partial L_2^*/\partial\theta > 0$). This preserves some incentive to explore more. Had we not specified the two-stage decision process, that is, if $L_2^*$ were picked before $\theta$ is realized, then $F_{XX} < 0$ would be sufficient to guarantee that the covariance term be negative.[8]

In the preceding discussion, we have been able to identify conditions under which expected marginal discovery costs overstate resource rent. Another way of interpreting this result is that we can let marginal exploration costs serve as an upper bound for rent. We have no lower bound because of the Jensen inequality bias in the marginal cost measure, as shown in equation (16). Although the covariance term in (17) captures the firm's response to risk, a negative sign associated with it does not make marginal exploration cost a lower bound on rent.

However, it is possible to use discovery cost data to obtain consistent although biased estimates of $w/G'(R^*)$—rather than of $E[w/\theta G'(R^*)]$—so

---

[8] Unlike the literature dealing with the firm under uncertainty, we cannot derive unambiguous results by imposing restrictions (such as decreasing absolute risk aversion) on the utility functions. Such restrictions are used in comparing a firm's resource allocation decisions under certainty and uncertainty; for example, with decreasing absolute risk aversion, the competitive firm produces less when facing uncertain prices than when faced with the expected value of the random price. We are comparing a particular equilibrium condition under certainty and uncertainty. We are not making any statements about whether a firm explores more or less between the two regimes, but rather that a firm may not explore to the point where marginal discovery cost equals rent under uncertain exploration.

that we obtain a lower *or* an upper bound on rent, depending solely on the sign of the covariance term in equation (17).

To do this, we look at the reciprocal of marginal discovery cost, $\lambda = \theta G'(R^*)/w$. If the $n$ observations $\theta_1, \ldots, \theta_n$ are independent, the sample average

$$\bar{\lambda} = \frac{1}{n} \sum_{i=1}^{n} \frac{\theta_i G'(R^*)}{w}$$

is a consistent estimate of $E(\lambda) = G'(R^*)/w$. Then, if we only consider observations where $\theta > 0$, $1/\bar{\lambda}$ is a consistent (although biased) estimate of $w/G'(R^*)$. Applying equation (16),

$$\frac{w}{G'(R^*)} = E p_2 F_X U_2'(\pi_2^*) + cov(\theta, p_2 F_X U_2')$$

so that our data can be used to bound rent, depending on the sign of the covariance term.[9]

Furthermore, if the distribution of $\theta$ were known in advance (or assumed), then an unbiased estimate of $w/G'(R^*)$ can be obtained by applying the Jacobian transformation formula for deriving the distribution of a function of a random variable.[10]

It should be noted that knowledge of the distribution of $\theta$ is not an unreasonable requirement. As we said in the discussion on the stochastic exploration function (see especially footnote 5), the distribution of $\theta$ is closely linked to the tonnage-grade distributions estimated by geologists. Since data on the

---

[9] We are indebted to Kenneth Arrow for pointing this out to us.

[10] As a concrete example, suppose $\theta$ has a gamma distribution with parameter $\nu$:

$$f(\theta) = \frac{\eta^\nu e^{-\eta\theta} \theta^{\nu-1}}{\Gamma(\nu)}$$

where

$$\Gamma(\nu) = \int_0^\infty e^{-x} x^{\nu-1} dx$$

Note that

$$E(\theta) = \frac{\Gamma(\nu + 1)}{\eta \Gamma(\nu)} = \nu/\eta$$

Now the distribution of $\lambda = 1/\theta$ is given by

$$h(\lambda) = \theta^2 f\left(\frac{1}{\theta}\right) = \frac{\eta^\nu e^{-\eta/\theta} \theta^{3-\nu}}{\Gamma(\nu)}$$

Then,

$$E(\lambda) = \frac{\eta}{\nu - 1}$$

so that an unbiased estimate of $1/E(\lambda)$ is given by $(\nu/\nu - 1) E(\theta)$.

latter distributions already exist for many major mining areas in the United States, it is simply a matter of transforming them to fit our production function approach.

## 4. Concluding Remarks

Summary

The main body of this chapter, section 3, has addressed in a preliminary way two questions: (1) how might uncertainty about the yield from discovery effort affect a firm's decision about the level of that effort, as well as the effort devoted to extraction and (2) how might marginal discovery cost (the cost of finding another unit of a resource) correspondingly deviate from rent? The latter question is of interest because, as we argue in the early sections (1–2), rent is an appealing measure of resource scarcity, and is in turn equated, in a deterministic competitive equilibrium, to (adjusted) marginal discovery cost, from which it might be estimated.

A simple two-period model of exploration and extraction is developed to shed some light on both questions. Not surprisingly, we find that uncertainty does affect the behavior of a risk-averse firm that maximizes the expected utility of profits. Surprisingly, perhaps, the direction of the effect is ambiguous. Typically, uncertainty leads to a reduction in the level of an activity, such that marginal benefit exceeds marginal cost, with the difference equivalent to a risk premium. We find, instead, that the uncertain firm may explore to a point where expected marginal cost *exceeds* rent, the marginal benefit. Whether it does in fact depends on some key parameters in the exploration and extraction production functions, and the two-stage decision process, as well as the strength of the firm's aversion to risk. But the main point is that, in general, expected marginal discovery cost will not be equated to rent.

These results do *not* speak to the question of whether the firm will explore more or less under uncertainty than under certainty, even when we can sign the difference between marginal costs and benefits. The difficulty is that rent is not the same in the two cases. The response of the optimal value of the objective function to a change in the stock will be different, because the optimal values are different. Suppose, for example, we know that marginal discovery cost exceeds rent under uncertainty. We still do not know that the firm explores more than in the certain case, where marginal discovery cost equals (a different) rent. The analysis of section 3 might be extended to deal with comparisons of exploration (and extraction) in the two cases. This seems to us a promising area for further study.

### Qualifications and Suggestions for Further Study

Our results need to be qualified in a number of other ways as well—though in the academic tradition, we view the deficiencies as future research opportunities. The deficiencies, or opportunities, might include some of the following.

We have implicitly assumed that the motive for exploring is to add to the resource stock. The benefit from discovery is then just the value of the unit discovered and added to the stock, or the rent. But a firm might explore for other reasons as well. As noted first by Allais (1957) and more recently by Gilbert (1978), the firm might explore to gain information about the size and grade of the stock. Such information would be of value because it would allow the firm to do a better job of optimizing the rate of extraction. The important point here is that this value is not tied to the physical addition of units to the stock. A dry hole also has value. If the marginal cost of exploration continues to be closely related to the marginal benefit, then it need not be closely related to rent, the value of a unit added to the stock.

Another possible motive for exploring that could drive a wedge between rent and exploration cost is to diversify an investment portfolio. If returns to one type of exploration are not positively correlated with returns to other types, or indeed other investments made by the firm, some exploration might be undertaken to lower the variance of the firm's portfolio. On the other hand, some exploration might be joint, a search for two or more minerals commonly found together. Again, the relation between rent and exploration cost could be affected. We cannot say how important these additional motives for exploration are, or how seriously they affect the rent-exploration cost relation. These are questions for further study which we just raise here.

Still another difficulty is posed by institutional constraints on exploration. For example, many mineral leases contain "diligence" clauses that require the winning bidder to explore at a certain rate. Conceivably this raises the cost of exploring above what it would be if the firm could freely optimize. Or a firm could explore too quickly to get information on whether to exercise an option on a neighboring tract, again raising the cost. Here again we cannot say how important these effects are, and simply note them for further study.

One more shortcoming of this chapter is its lack of empirical content. Given that uncertainty in exploration can cause (expected) marginal discovery costs to deviate from rent, which parameters should be estimated to determine the sign and magnitude of the deviation? More generally, what type of empirical analysis can shed some light on the uncertain firm's exploratory and extractive behavior? It should be apparent from our earlier discussion that knowledge of the *extraction production function* can make a major contribution. For instance, we showed in section 3 that the magnitudes of the second partial derivatives of $F(L,X)$ can determine whether marginal discovery costs over- or understate resource rent.

Second, it is important to determine if the uncertainty surrounding the exploration production function is multiplicative or additive. Our results depend crucially on its being multiplicative. Although we find this type of uncertainty to be intuitively plausible, we would prefer to base our conclusions on solid, empirical evidence.

Third, much effort has recently been devoted to estimating the distribution of the random variable, $\theta$, in the exploration function (see, for example, Harris, 1977). While knowledge of these distributions has significantly increased our understanding of resource issues, it is interesting to note that the qualitative nature of our results is unaffected by the assumed distribution of $\theta$. Of course, for any empirical application, a specific distribution function is necessary.

## References

Allais, Maurice. 1957. "Method of Appraising Economic Prospects of Mining Exploration over Large Territories," *Management Science* vol. 3, no. 4 (July) pp. 285–347.

Arrow, Kenneth J. 1977. "Optimal Pricing, Use and Exploration of Uncertain Natural Resource Stocks," Paper presented at Conference on Natural Resources Pricing, Trail Lake, Wyoming, August.

Barnett, Harold J., and Chandler Morse. 1963. *Scarcity and Growth* (Baltimore, Md., Johns Hopkins University Press for Resources for the Future).

Batra, R. N., and A. Ullah. 1974. "Competitive Firm and the Theory of Input Demand under Price Uncertainty," *Journal of Political Economy* vol. 82, no. 3 (May/June) pp. 537–548.

Brobst, Donald, and W. Pratt, eds. 1973. "United States Mineral Resources," U.S. Geological Survey Professional Paper 820 (Washington, D.C., Government Printing Office).

Brown, Gardner M., and Barry C. Field. 1978. "Implications of Alternative Measures of Natural Resource Scarcity," *Journal of Political Economy* vol. 86, no. 2 Part I (April) pp. 229–243.

Crabbe, Philippe. 1977. "L'exploration des Ressources Extractives Nonrenouvelables: Theorie Economique, Processus Stochastique et Verification," *L'Actualite Economique* (October/November).

Fischman, Leonard L., and Hans H. Landsberg. 1972. "Adequacy of Nonfuel Minerals and Forest Resources," in Ronald G. Ridker, ed., *Population, Resources and the Environment* (Washington, D.C., Government Printing Office).

Fisher, Anthony C. 1977. "On Measures of Natural Resource Scarcity," International Institute for Applied Systems Analysis, Laxenburg, Austria, Research Report 77-19.

Gilbert, Richard J. 1976. "Optimal Depletion of an Uncertain Stock," Institute for Mathematical Studies in the Social Sciences, Stanford University.

———. 1978. "The Social and Private Value of Exploration Information," Department of Economics, University of California, Berkeley, Working Paper No. 91.

Harris, DeVerle P. 1977. "Mineral Endowments, Resources and Potential Supply: Theory, Methods for Appraisal and Case Studies," Tucson, Arizona, Minresco, 333 N. Jackson Ave.

Hartmann, Richard. 1976. "Factor Demand with Output Price Uncertainty," *American Economic Review* vol. 66, no. 4 (September) pp. 675–681.

Hoel, Michael. 1978. "Resource Extraction, Uncertainty and Learning," *Bell Journal of Economics* vol. 9 (Autumn) pp. 642–645.

Jevons, W. S. 1865. *The Coal Question* (London, Macmillan).

Kamien, Morton I., and Nancy L. Schwartz. 1978. "Self-financing of an R and D Project," *American Economic Review* vol. 68, no. 3 (June) pp. 252–261.

Lewis, Tracey. 1977. "Attitudes Towards Risk and the Optimal Exploitation of an Exhaustible Resource," *Journal of Environmental Economics and Management* vol. 4, pp. 111–119.

Loury, Glenn. 1976. "The Optimal Exploitation of an Unknown Reserve," Discussion Paper No. 225, Center for Mathematical Studies in Economics and Management Science, Northwestern University.

Marglin, Stephen. 1963. "The Social Rate of Discount and the Optimal Rate of Investment," *Quarterly Journal of Economics* vol. 77, no. 1 (February) pp. 95–111.

Meadows, Dennis H., Donella Meadows, Jørgen Randers, and William Behrens III. 1972. *The Limits to Growth* (New York, Universe Books).

Pindyck, Robert S. 1978. "Optimal Exploration and Production of a Non-renewable Resource," *Journal of Political Economy* vol. 86, no. 5 (October) pp. 841–861.

Ricardo, David. 1817. *The Principles of Political Economy and Taxation* (London).

Samuelson, Paul. 1947. *Foundations of Economic Analysis* (Cambridge, Mass., Harvard University Press).

Stewart, Marion. 1978. "Factor Price Uncertainty with Variable Proportions," *American Economic Review* vol. 68, no. 3 (June) pp. 468–493.

Stigler, George J. 1939. "Production and Distribution in the Short Run," *Journal of Political Economy* vol. 47, no. 3 (June) pp. 305–327.

Stiglitz, Joseph. 1979. "A Neoclassical Analysis of the Economics of Natural Resources," in V. Kerry Smith, ed., *Scarcity and Growth Reconsidered* (Baltimore, Md., Johns Hopkins University Press for Resources for the Future).

# Index

Aggregates, 12–17, 168
  across end use, 190–196
  economy as a whole, 196–198, 199
  factor input, 206–209, 218, 237–241
  price index, 219–221, 229, 231, 232, 236
  same end use, 169, 174–175; across plants, 186–190; in joint production, 184–186; at plant level, 176–182
  substitution, 206–209, 229–223
  unit cost index, 220
Air pollution. *See* Pollution
Allen, R. G. D., 214, 216, 223, 225, 233
Allocation of resources. *See* Resource allocation
Arrow, Kenneth J., 80, 115, 122*n*, 333
Ayres, Robert U., 14, 15, 34, 52

Bailly, P. A., 274, 280, 282, 283
Barnett, Harold J., 29, 201*n*, 202, 329, 335n
Baumol, William J., 84
Benefit-cost analysis
  common property resources, 75–78
  pollution control with uncertainty, 112–114, 123
Berndt, Ernst R., 15, 35, 204*n*, 207*n*, 221*n*, 241
Bever, R. C., 214*n*
Binswanger, H. P. 215*n*, 221*n*
Blackorby, Charles, 14, 218*n*
Bohm, Peter, 27
Bower, Blair T., 35, 209*n*

Bradford, David F., 25, 28
Brobst, D. A., 256, 285, 329
Brown, Gardner M., 29, 36, 327, 330
Burmeister, Edwin, 9, 49
By-products
  discharge treatment, 236
  metals produced as, 269–270
  pollution as, 7, 9, 57

Canada, 275, 276, 281–283
Capital
  depreciation, 48, 57
  exploration, 35, 331
  inputs, 182, 184, 203*n*; and exhaustible resources, 51–53, 56; pollution-control, 55, 212; steady-state, 55; substitution, 5, 11–12, 49, 52, 188–189, 212
  stock, 65, 188–189
Charles River Associates (CRA), 276, 278, 320
Chemicals, minerals mined for, 254–255
Cicchetti, Charles, 9, 27, 103*n*
Clark, Colin W., 49, 97
Clarke, Edward, 121
Coal, 212, 258
Coase theorem, 80, 104
Commission on Mineral Resources and the Environment (COMRATE), 262, 271, 280
Common property resources, 11, 72
  back-to-the-market approach to, 78–80, 83

347

benefit-costs, 75–78
firm entry and departure, 92
legal rights to, 80–81, 83, 104
licenses for, 81–82, 83, 84–85
own rate of return on, 88–89
pollution absorption by, 90
quotas on, 81, 84
taxes on inputs, 82–83, 84
use: competitive level of, 73–75; free, 85–88; impact of human, 91–94; to maximize profits, 96–98; over-, 73, 76–77, 104
*see also* Exhaustible resources; Extraction, resource; Resource allocation; Scarcity, resource
Complementarity, 25, 26, 27, 203–204, 239
COMRATE. *See* Commission on Mineral Resources and the Environment
Conservation of resources, 49, 328
Consumption, 5
hedonic models for, 13, 14, 34, 35, 179, 183, 185
immediate utility from, 48
maintainable level of, 52
output divided between investment and, 99
pollution and, 9, 50, 55, 65, 98–99
Continental crust, 257, 258
Conversion function, 12–13, 14, 17, 32, 180–181
Cost-benefit analysis. *See* Benefit-cost analysis
Cost function
conversion function, 14, 180–181
materials aggregation from, 15, 183, 186–188
neoclassical model, 12, 218–229, 239
Costs
discovery, 281–284, 327, 328, 330–331, 334–336, 338–339
exploration, 281–284, 323
extraction, 53, 329
health effects, 157–158
metals transportation, 254–255
pollution control, 111
waste disposal, 95
CRA. *See* Charles River Associates
Crocker, Thomas D., 19, 22, 24, 147n, 151n, 154
Cropper, Maureen L., 7–8, 9, 50, 104
Crustal abundance, 257–259, 260–261, 329
Cummings, Ronald G., 11n, 52, 203n
Cyclic behavior, 8, 9, 55

Dales, J. H., 84, 133
Daly, Herman E., 47
d'Arge, Ralph, 52, 53
Dasgupta, Partha, 11, 27–28, 51–52, 53, 61, 65, 81, 109, 110n, 112, 119, 121, 122n, 203, 205
Depletion. *See* Exhaustible resources; Extraction, resource
Depreciation, capital, 48, 57
Devarajan, Shantayanam, 31–32, 35–36, 327
Diewert, W. E., 192n, 206, 220

Discounting, 8
capital, 48, 61
utility, 49, 51, 99
Discovery
costs, 281–284, 327, 338–339; rent and, 328, 330–331, 334–336
depth of deposit and, 276–279, 284
distribution, 275–276
exponential curve for oil, 289–291
phases of, 323
uncertainty in, 327
Dobell, A. Rodney, 9, 49
DOE. *See* Energy, Department of
Dorfman, Robert, 75
Drew, M. W., 301
Drilling, 280–281, 331
Duality theory, 12, 16, 204, 206n, 209

Economic growth, 4
optimal aggregate planning models for, 5–17, 37, 47ff
Economic resources, 249, 250–251
Efficiency
government intervention to improve, 141
incremental production, 61–62
Pareto allocation, 82
Pareto social welfare, 117–118
Elasticity, substitition, 52, 202, 206, 213–215, 223, 225, 239
Energy
inputs, 180, 182, 184, 212; for mining, 261; for production, 178, 204; substitution, 223, 225
minerals used as sources of, 255
for smelting and refining metals, 261–263
Energy, Department of (DOE), 287, 307
Environment
degradation, 61, 62, 65
economic planning and, 55, 56
free-rider problem in improving, 111–119, 121
impact function, 61
industrialization and, 103
management, 111; cost-benefit analysis of, 24–28, 112–114; investment options, 114–116
pollutants caused by, 152–153
pollution control and, 26, 54, 109, 111, 112
risks from, 110, 112
Equilibrium relationships
Nash, 74, 119, 120–121
strategies for, 118
Evaporite resources, 256
Exhaustible resources, 4–5, 47, 49–50
capital and, 11–12, 51–53, 56
cost of extracting, 329
elasticity of substitution, 202–203
pollution and, 53–55, 56
technology to offset, 52, 54

Exponential curve, for oil discovery rate, 289–291
Exploration
  costs, 281–284, 323
  effectiveness, 282, 323
  factors influencing, 276–279
  models, 31–32, 252, 305, 328, 332–339, 343
  motives for, 344
  optimum amount of, 252
  problems relating to, 274
  technology, 275, 276
  uncertainty in, 35, 328, 331, 332–333, 345
Externalities analysis, 75, 80
Extraction, resource, 49
  costs, 53, 329
  cumulative, 57, 59, 60
  model, 328, 332–339, 343
  pollution and, 57–58
  rate, 52–53, 54, 56
  uncertainty effect on, 328, 332

Factor inputs, 51
  aggregates, 206–209, 218
  complementarity between, 203–204, 239
  quantity index, 206
  substitution, 5, 11–12, 15, 49, 201, 203–205;
    elasticity, 52, 202, 206, 213–215, 221, 223,
    225, 239–240
  uncertainty and choice of, 332
Ferejohn, John A., 27
Fertilizers, 254–255
Field, Barry, 29, 36, 327, 329
Fischman, Leonard L., 329
Fisher, Anthony C., 4, 6, 9, 19, 30, 31, 33, 35–36, 50,
  103n, 115, 140, 202n, 204n, 208n, 213n, 327,
  333, 335
Fisher, Franklin M., 17, 35
Fisheries, 72
  free entry to, 91–94
  population size, 85–88, 92
Forecasting, resource scarcity, 328–329
Forrester, J. W., 90
Forster, B. A., 50, 54, 55
Freeman, A. Myrick, III, 13, 18–24, 26, 140, 150,
  158n
Free-rider problem, 111, 119–121
Fuss, Melvin, 14, 35, 206n, 220, 240n

Geochemistry, 31, 276
Geological analyses, 287, 307, 308
Georgescu-Roegen, Nicholas, 47
Gorman, W. M., 213n
Government
  conservation and, 328
  information gap between polluting firms and, 117,
    121
  regulation of environment, 110–111
  regulation of resources, 81–83, 84–85, 104

Green, H. A. J., 19
Gregory, P. R., 221n
Griffin, J. M., 217, 221n
Griliches, Zvi, 175
Groves, Theodore, 27, 111n, 119, 121

Halvorsen, Robert, 221n
Hammond, Peter J., 119, 120, 121
Hardin, Garrett, 76
Harris, D. P., 29–37, 247, 286, 296, 300, 304, 317,
  336n, 345
Hazilla, Michael, 215n
Heal, Geoffrey M., 7–8, 10, 51–52, 53, 55, 61, 65, 72,
  79, 100, 102–103, 104, 110n, 122n, 203, 205
Health, Education, and Welfare, Department of,
  141n, 147
Hedonic models, 13, 14, 34, 35, 179, 183, 185
Henry, Claude, 77, 115
Hicks, J. R., 212n
Hildebrandt, George C., 25, 28
Hoch, Irving, 151n
Hoel, Michael, 50, 54–55, 332
Hotelling, Harold, 6, 29, 49
Houthakker, H. S., 206, 207
Hubbert, M. K., 288–292
Humphrey, David B., 37, 215n, 221n, 241

Income, utility function with, 119–120
Information, resource use
  difficulty in obtaining, 84
  for environmental R&D, 113–114
  gap in pollution, 117, 121
Inputs. See Capital, inputs; Energy, inputs; Labor
  input; Raw materials inputs; Substitution,
  input
Institutional influences, over resource use, 78–81,
  104
Intriligator, Michael D., 49
Investment, 9, 48
  environmental R&D, 114–116
  output divided between consumption and, 99
  over-, 116

Jevons, W. S., 47, 329
Jones-Lee, Michael W., 157, 159

Kamien, Morton I., 4–7, 8, 30, 47, 53, 333
Kearl, James M., 17, 204n, 208n, 213n
Keeler, Emmett, 55, 98n
Kemp, Murray C., 49, 50
Kneese, A. V., 84
Kogiku, K. C., 53
Koopmans, Tjalling C., 52
Kopp, Raymond J., 14, 15–17, 35, 37, 201
Krutilla, John V., 9, 11n, 103n
Kurz, Mordecai M., 7, 8, 63

Labor input, 48, 51, 52, 203n, 180, 182, 184, 212
Landsberg, Hans L., 329
Lau, Lawrence J., 12–17, 27, 32, 34, 35, 37, 167, 188, 192n
Lave, Lester B., 19, 22, 141, 143n, 144, 146n, 147n, 153
Ledyard, John, 27, 111n, 119
Leone, Robert A., 151n
Leontieff, Wassily, 212n, 213n
Levhari, David, 206n
Lewis, Tracy R., 49, 331n
Licenses, for resource use, 81–82, 83, 84–85, 133–134
Lieberman, M. A., 288, 289, 293, 294
Life tables, 145
Liviatan, Nissan, 9, 10
Lusky, Rafael, 50, 54

McFadden, D. L., 209
McKelvey, Vincent E., 250, 253, 295
Mäler, Karl-Göran, 25, 26, 28, 51, 52, 56
Malthus, Thomas Robert, 47, 329
Marginal costs
    for discovery, 330, 334–336, 338–339
    for environmental services, 24–25, 36
Market system, resource scarcity and failure of, 140, 141, 330
Marsden, James R., 14, 215n
Martin, H. L., 281–282, 283
Maskin, Eric, 119, 120, 121
Materials balance constraint, 52
Meadows, Dennis, 47, 90, 102
Metals
    crustal abundance, 259, 260–261, 266–267
    geochemically scarce, 267–269
    number, 258
    produced as by-products, 269–270
Michigan University Survey Research Center, 151n
Migration, pollution exposure mortality and, 151
Mineral endowment
    defined, 247
    estimates: by intradeposit grade variance, 317, 320–321; models for, 305–307, 309–310; probabilistic appraisal for, 311; by tonnage-grade relation, 32, 35, 312–317
    measurable characteristics, 248–249
Mineraloids, 31, 248
Minerals
    appraisal, 284–285; by crustal abundance, 294–304; by discovery-rate method, 289–294; by geological analogy, 285–287, 307, 308; by life-cycle method, 288–289, 294
    defined, 31, 247–248
    deposits: defined, 248; distribution, 273; exploration for, 274–281; grade, 271, 273; size, 270–271, 273

number, 258, 259
potential for new, 259, 260, 265–266
substitution, 31, 255, 256–260
supplies, 255–256, 264–265
use, 33–34, 254–256
Mishan, Erza, 102, 157
Models, optimal planning, 4–5, 37
    exhaustible resources, 47–56
    exploration, 31–32, 252, 305, 328, 332–339
    extraction, 328, 332–339, 343
    free access of common property resources, 73–78
    interaction production technology, 12–17, 174ff
    mineral endowment, 305–307, 309–310
    mortality-air pollution, 18–24, 153–156
    neoclassical production, 203–204, 207–209; benchmark samples, 221–229; cost-minimizing, 209, 215, 216–221, 233–236, 237; indexes of substitution, 213–214; input aggregation, 229–233
    pollution management, 98–103
    recoverable resources: abundance reserve, 295–296; Brinck's crustal abundance, 296–300; discovery-rate, 289–294; evaluation, 307, 323; life-cycle, 288–289, 294; PAU crustal abundance, 296, 300–304
Moroney, John R., 37, 215n, 221n, 241
Morbidity, 21
    determining value of, 156–157, 161
    factors influencing, 152–153
    measure of, 146–148
    medical insurance for, 161
    willingness to pay to avoid, 158, 160, 161
Morse, Chandler, 29, 201n, 202, 329, 335n
Mortality, 18–24
    determining value of, 156–157
    factors influencing, 152–153
    measure of, 145–146, 148
    willingness to pay for change in probability, 157–158, 160

National Academy of Sciences, 141n, 154n
Natural gas, 212, 223, 225, 258
Natural resources. See Common property resources; Exhaustible resources; Exploration; Extraction, resource; Resource allocation
Neoclassical theory. See Models, neoclassical production
Netschert, Bruce C., 250, 257

Oates, W. E., 84
Ohta, M., 13, 175
Oil, 212, 223, 225, 258, 287
    life cycle model, 288–294
Optimal planning. See Models, optimal planning

Pareto efficiency, 82, 117–118
PAU. See Programmes Analysis Unit

Peterson, Frederick M., 30, 49, 50, 202*n*
Pielou, E. C., 49
Pindyck, Robert S., 4, 32, 35, 36, 49, 206*n*, 215*n*, 220, 221*n*, 240*n*, 327, 329, 333, 335
Pingry, David, 14, 215*n*
Plourde, C. G., 50
Pollution
  abatement, 26, 54, 112
  alternative sources of, 64
  as by-product, 7, 9, 57
  capital and, 55
  consumption and, 50, 55, 65, 98–99
  control, 109, 111
  exhaustible resources and, 50, 53–55
  health effects, 18–19; biological, 143–144; determining value of, 156–161; individual differences in, 143; measurement of, 19–21, 142–143, 145–149, 156; model structure for, 143–145, 153–156; mortality and, 18–24, 145–146; nonlethal unconventional, 145, 148; recommended research on, 141–142, 162; time between exposure and, 153
  measuring dose of, 144, 149–151, 154, 155
  production and, 5–6, 56–59
  social damage from, 123, 124–127
  threshold effects, 110, 122, 123
  and utility function, 7, 9, 10, 58, 63
Pratt, W. P., 256, 285, 329
President's Commission on Critical Supplies and Shortages, 202*n*
Price function, 180, 181
  hedonic, 32, 179, 185, 187, 199
Prices
  factor aggregates, 219–220
  marginal cost, 79
  metal, 284
  resource product, 330
  shadow, 60, 327, 329–330, 334
Production
  exhaustible resources role in, 4, 51–53
  pollution effect on, 5–6, 56–59
  *See also* Technology, production
Production function, 11–12
  Cobb–Douglas, 6, 52, 54, 59, 203*n*, 206
  exploration, 336, 345
  extraction, 344
  joint production, 184–186
  neoclassical model, 205–206
  single plant, 176–177, 179
Productivity, 157
Profit function, restricted, 189–190
Profit maximization
  exploration and, 336–337
  licensing and, 83
  raw materials inputs and, 189
  R&D and, 333
  from resource use, 95–98

Programmes Analysis Unit (PAU), 296, 300–304

Quality Adjusted Life Years index, 148–149
Quotas, on resource use, 81, 84, 133

Ramsey, Frank P., 48, 49
Raw materials inputs, 12–17
  availability, 3–5, 29–37, 169, 329
  characteristics, 170–171
  classification, 170–174
  function: conversion, 177, 180, 181, 190; cost, 180–181, 186–188, 191–196, 199; price, 179, 180, 181, 185, 187, 199; production, 11–12, 176, 179, 182; requirement, 178–179
  importance, 169, 197–198
  interaction with other inputs, 182–184
  quantity index, 197
  substitution, 169
  sufficiency, 167–168, 198
  supply, 196–197
Recycling
  capital for, 53
  technology, 173–174
  waste, 50, 54–55
Regulation
  common property resource use, 81–83, 84–85, 104
  environmental, 110–111
  information gap and, 117, 121
  taxation versus, 122–124
  under uncertainty, 122, 125–132
Rents, 36, 327, 328, 330–331, 334–336
Research, 48, 141–142
Research and development, 53, 112–114
Reserves, resource, 329, 333
Residuals discharge, 35
  constraints on, 212, 217, 233–237
  health status and changes in, 144
Resource allocation, 4–7, 18, 24–28, 49, 77–78, 328
Resource base, 30, 257
Ricardo, David, 329, 335*n*
Risk, 110, 112, 332, 339–342
Rocks, 31, 248, 255, 260
Rosen, Sherwin, 13, 34, 158*n*, 159
Russell, C. S., 209, 211*n*, 233
Russell, R. Robert, 14, 218*n*
Ryder, Hal E., Jr., 7, 100, 102–103

Samuelson, Paul A., 9, 10, 120, 121, 338
Scarcity, resource
  forecasting, 328–329
  geochemical approach to, 267–269
  indexes, 202
  measures of, 140–141, 328–330
  rents as indicators of, 36, 327, 328, 330
Schanz, J. J., 250

Schelling, Thomas C., 157
Schulze, William D., 11n, 27, 49, 50, 52, 54, 203n
Schurr, S. H., 250
Schwartz, Nancy L., 4–7, 8, 30, 47, 53, 333
Scott, Anthony, 34
Seskin, Eugene P., 19, 22, 141, 143n, 144, 153
Shell, K., 35, 49
Shephard, R. W., 209
Skinnner, B. J., 29–37, 171, 247, 273, 300, 336n
Smelting, 261–263
Smith, V. Kerry, 3, 11n, 14, 15–17, 24, 27, 35, 37, 201, 211n, 215n
Smith, Vernon L., 9, 50
Social choice rule, 117–118, 119, 120–121
Solow, Robert M., 17, 47, 52, 202, 203, 204n, 205, 208n, 213n
Spence, Michael, 55, 98n
Stanford Research Institute, 311
Steady-state economy, 7, 8, 47, 55
Steelmaking, technology for, 209–211, 217–221, 221–233, 239–241
Stevens, Joe B., 26
Stiglitz, Joseph E., 47, 52, 112, 328
Substitution
  input, 5, 11–12, 15, 49, 201, 203–205; aggregation and, 206–209; constraints on residual discharges and, 233–237; elasticity, 52, 202, 206, 213–215, 223, 225, 239; errors, 214–216, 227, 230–233, 236
  mineral, 31, 255, 256–260
  processed and raw materials, 169

Taxation
  on common property resources inputs, 82–83, 84
  regulation versus, 12
  under uncertainty, 122, 127–132
Tax subsidy, for recycling, 54
Technology
  engineering, 201, 204, 205; for steelmaking, 209–211, 217–233, 239–241
  environmental cleanup, 119
  expansion of mineral resources through, 313
  exploration, 252, 275, 280–281
  to offset resource exhaustibility, 52, 54
  pollution abatement, 112
  production, 12–13, 203; aggregating inputs for,

206, residual discharge constraints on, 204–205, 212, 217, 233–237
  and raw material sufficiency, 167–168
  recycling, 173–174
Theil, Henry, 22–23
Threshold effects, 110, 122, 123
Tiebout, Charles, 26
Toers, Alden, 37, 215n, 221n, 241
Transportation of metals, costs, 254–255

Uncertainty
  chice of inputs under, 332
  in discovery process, 327, 332
  in environmental management, 109, 111–116
  exploration under, 35, 328, 331, 332–333, 345
  regulation under, 122
  taxation under, 122
United Nations, 152n
Uranium resources, 287
  models, 288, 298–300, 309–311, 314
U.S. Geological Survey, 256, 285
  evaluation of uranium supply, 309
  geological analyses, 287, 307
  tonnage-grade investigations, 314, 317
U.S. Public Health Service, 146
U.S.S.R., mineral self-sufficiency, 273
University of Arizona, 311
Utility function, 7, 8, 101
  capital in, 63
  consumption in, 7, 8, 57, 64, 65
  discounting, 49, 99
  income and, 119–120
  pollution and, 7, 9, 10, 58, 63
  profit, 337, 338
Uzawa, Hirofumi, 209

Vaughan, William J., 35, 209, 211n, 233, 241n

Wastes, 50, 53, 54, 95
Welfare
  economic, 202
  social, 117–118
Whinston, Andrew, 14, 215n
Willingness to pay, 157–159, 161
Wood, D. O., 15, 221n, 241

Zeckhauser, Richard, 19, 55, 98n, 148
Zimmerman, E. W., 29, 249